THE CHINA FIRM

A NANCY BERNKOPF TUCKER AND WARREN I. COHEN
BOOK ON AMERICAN-EAST ASIAN RELATIONS

NANCY BERNKOPF TUCKER
and WARREN I. COHEN
Books on American–East Asian Relations

Edited by
Thomas J. Christensen
Mark Philip Bradley
Rosemary Foot

John T. Downey, Thomas J. Christensen, and Jack Lee Downey, *Lost in the Cold War: The Story of Jack Downey, America's Longest-Held POW*

Anne F. Thurston, ed., *Engaging China: Fifty Years of Sino-American Relations*

Andrew B. Kennedy, *The Conflicted Superpower: America's Collaboration with China and India in Global Innovation*

Jeanne Guillemin, *Hidden Atrocities: Japanese Germ Warfare and American Obstruction of Justice at the Tokyo Trial*

Michael J. Green, *By More Than Providence: Grand Strategy and American Power in the Asia Pacific Since 1783*

Nancy Bernkopf Tucker was a historian of American diplomacy whose work focused on American-East Asian relations. She published seven books, including the prize-winning *Uncertain Friendships: Taiwan, Hong Kong, and the United States, 1945-1992*. Her articles and essays appeared in countless journals and anthologies, including the *American Historical Review*, *Diplomatic History*, *Foreign Affairs*, and the *Journal of American History*. In addition to teaching at Colgate and Georgetown (where she was the first woman to be awarded tenure in the School of Foreign Service), she served on the China desk of the Department of State and in the American embassy in Beijing. When the Office of the Director of National Intelligence was created, she was chosen to serve as the first Assistant Deputy Director of National Intelligence for Analytic Integrity and Standards and Ombudsman, and she was awarded the National Intelligence Medal of Achievement in 2007. To honor her, in 2012 the Woodrow Wilson International Center for Scholars established an annual Nancy Bernkopf Tucker Memorial Lecture on U.S.-East Asian Relations.

Warren I. Cohen is University Distinguished Professor Emeritus at Michigan State University and the University of Maryland, Baltimore County, and a senior scholar in the Asia Program of the Woodrow Wilson Center. He has written thirteen books and edited eight others. He served as a line officer in the U.S. Pacific Fleet, editor of *Diplomatic History*, president of the Society for Historians of American Foreign Relations, and chairman of the Department of State Advisory Committee on Historical Diplomatic Documentation. In addition to scholarly publications, he has written for the *Atlantic*, the *Baltimore Sun*, the *Christian Science Monitor*, *Dissent*, *Foreign Affairs*, the *International Herald Tribune*, the *Los Angeles Times*, *The Nation*, the *New York Times*, the *Times Literary Supplement*, and the *Washington Post*. He has also been a consultant on Chinese affairs to various government organizations.

The China Firm

AMERICAN ELITES AND THE MAKING
OF BRITISH COLONIAL SOCIETY

Thomas M. Larkin

Columbia University Press
New York

Columbia University Press
Publishers Since 1893
New York   Chichester, West Sussex
cup.columbia.edu
Copyright © 2024 Columbia University Press
All rights reserved

Library of Congress Cataloging-in-Publication Data
Names: Larkin, Thomas, author.
Title: The China firm : American elites and the making of
British colonial society / Thomas Larkin.
Description: New York : Columbia University Press, [2024] | Series: A Nancy Bernkopf
Tucker and Warren I. Cohen book on American-East Asian relations |
Includes bibliographical references and index.
Identifiers: LCCN 2023030921 (print) | LCCN 2023030922 (ebook) | ISBN 9780231210669
(hardback) | ISBN 9780231210676 (trade paperback) | ISBN 9780231558532 (ebook)
Subjects: LCSH: Augustine Heard & Company—History. | United States—Commerce—China. |
China—Commerce—United States. | United States—Politics and government—19th century. |
United States—Relations—Great Britain. | Great Britain—Relations—United States.
Classification: LCC HF3128 .L37 2024 (print) | LCC HF3128 (ebook) |
DDC 382.0951—dc23/eng/20231024
LC record available at https://lccn.loc.gov/2023030921
LC ebook record available at https://lccn.loc.gov/2023030922

Cover design: Noah Arlow
Cover image: Artist unknown, Residence of Augustine Heard and Company, Hong Kong,
c. 1860. The Picture Art Collection/Alamy Stock Photo.

For Ruth & Tom, Monty, Mom

CONTENTS

ACKNOWLEDGMENTS xi

NOTE ON TRANSLATION AND CURRENCIES xiii

ABBREVIATIONS xv

GLOSSARY OF PEOPLE xvii

GLOSSARY OF TERMS xxi

Introduction:
An American Firm, a British Colony, and a Global Microhistory 1

Chapter One
A Very Profitable Crisis: Canton's American
Merchants on the Eve of the First Opium War 21

Chapter Two
A House Is Not a Home:
The American Merchant House in Hong Kong 52

CONTENTS

Chapter Three
Lives Lived in Public:
American Encounters with British Colonial Society 84

Chapter Four
Missed Opportunities:
Balancing Metropolitan Politics and Private Interests in China 120

Chapter Five
Friends Near and Far:
Creating and Maintaining Global Networks Through Hong Kong 149

Chapter Six
Wealth or Expertise: The Social and Professional
Paths of Returned American Merchants 186

Conclusion: Lives of Consequence 217

NOTES 225

BIBLIOGRAPHY 275

INDEX 297

ACKNOWLEDGMENTS

In writing this book, I've come to owe much to many.

George Cautherley set it properly on its path, and it is no exaggeration to write that without him it could not have been done. So did Robert Bickers and Grace Huxford, whose advice and guidance helped to shape the project and have always been welcomed as this book underwent revision and evolution. I am grateful to Joan Judge for her mentorship; John Carroll and Stephen Tuffnell for their comments and suggestions, which have made the work undoubtedly stronger; and the faculty at the University of Bristol's history department, generally, for providing a congenial place to work and numerous opportunities to share.

I would like to thank Catherine Chan, Gemma O'Neill, Jiayi Tao, Shawn Liu, Katon Lee, and Vivian Kong; Su Lin Lewis and Josie McLellan for reading proposals; Cécile Armand, Christian Henriot, and their team at Aix for the inspiration to try new things; and friends and colleagues in the American Studies Research Group and the Hong Kong History Centre for providing community.

Thanks are due to the revolving group of peers occupying the basement of 13 Woodland Road: Lorenzo Costaguta for the push to just write the thing; Katie Carpenter, although her stay was short-lived; Beth Rebisz for working through pedantries; James Watts for ceding his whiteboard; and Darius Wainwright for being generous with his time.

I owe a particular debt to archivists, editors, and reviewers. Heather Oswald and the Baker Library archivists helped make winter treks across the Charles River bearable and provided creative and appreciated assistance during the pandemic. Staff at the Massachusetts Historical Society, Hong Kong Baptist University and Cambridge Special Collections, British National Archives, and Academia Sinica helped in their own way. Stephen Wesley, Christian Winting, and Marisa Lastres at Columbia University Press, as well, for making the process of publishing this book feel seamless. Thanks to Gregory McNamee for his editing, and thanks as well to my anonymous reviewers, who were insightful in their comments and generous with their encouragement.

A special thank you to those who kindly made available new materials; Shirl Buss for permission to use the Hooper diaries; Penny West for sharing her work and enthusiasm; and George Cautherely once more for putting to rest one or two outstanding mysteries.

My final thanks are reserved for my father, Michael, and for Joan; for Judy; for my grandmother Janet and for Christine; and for Ted and Diane, who helped break up the solitude of long research trips. But most of all I would like to thank my wife, Nicole, who has graciously learned far more about this topic than she had ever intended.

NOTE ON TRANSLATION AND CURRENCIES

As a rule, I have used the standard Pinyin system of transliteration when recording Chinese words and names, and even in cases where the Cantonese pronunciation is common, I have supplied the Mandarin as well for reference. Still, many of the Chinese names recorded in the archive, and resultant English attempts to record them phonetically, reflect the Cantonese pronunciation. In these cases, I have used the Jyutping system to illustrate the phonetic similarities.

Place names are recorded, in the first instance, alongside their current usage as such: Canton (Guangzhou 廣州). For the sake of consistency, every subsequent usage employs the name as it was known to contemporary foreign residents. I have included these names and their current iterations in the glossary for those that wish to follow the Heards' travels using present-day maps. Where a location is given based on Chinese sources, I have translated it verbatim (e.g., the governor general of Liangguang 兩廣).

In the rare instance where a contemporary English translation of Chinese texts exists but is approximated or simplified, I have included the original English translation, the actual translation, and the Chinese Pinyin.

I have tried, sometimes in vain, to trace all transliterations to their original Chinese source, both to ensure historical accuracy and out of respect to those individuals whose names have been occluded in the records. Occasionally the transliteration is obvious, as with Augustine Heard Jr.'s daughter "Anui," from the Cantonese *aa neoi* (*a nü* 阿女), whose recorded name literally meant "daughter." Other times it is less so, as with his protected woman, Apook.

Whether dollar ($) refers to Spanish or American dollars in archival materials is usually unclear. Prior to the U.S. Coinage Act of 1857, both Spanish and American dollars were accepted as legal tender in America. Spanish dollars were commonly found in the United States before the act and continued to be circulated as currency in China. It can be reasonably assumed that amounts listed with the symbol $ were in Spanish dollars when the bill or receipt was drafted in China or Hong Kong. Trade dollars were also commonly used by Western nations, minted to the same specifications as Spanish dollars, but the American trade dollars did not come into circulation until the 1860s.

When an amount is given in British pounds (£) it has been noted as such, and the conversion has been cited if applicable.

Taels (tls), a weighted coin, and sycee, an unregulated silver ingot whose value was determined by weight, were both common forms of currency in the Qing Empire, but American merchants tended to refer to them only in connection with trade.

ABBREVIATIONS

GT   Gustavus Tuckerman Papers, Baker Library, Harvard Business School, Cambridge, MA
HBS   Heard Family Business Records, Baker Library, Harvard Business School, Cambridge, MA
JMA   Jardine Matheson Archives, Cambridge University Library, Cambridge, UK
MHS   Massachusetts Historical Society, Boston, MA
NARA   Despatches from the U.S. Consuls in Hong Kong, 1844–1906, RG: 59, General Records of the Department of State, U.S. National Archives
PEM   Phillips Library, Peabody Essex Museum, Salem, MA
TNA   The National Archives, Kew, UK

GLOSSARY OF PEOPLE

THE HEARD FAMILY

Anui (fl. 1872–1873) Daughter of Augustine Heard Jr and "Apook." It is safe to assume *Aa neoi* (*a nü* 阿女), or "daughter," is not her actual name.

Apook (fl. 1872–1873) Augustine Heard Jr.'s protected woman in China.

Eunice Farley (1855–1932) A cousin of the Heards. She traveled to China briefly to live with Albert and Mary Heard. Her brother Gustavus Farley worked for the company in Japan.

Albert Farley Heard (1833–1890) The third eldest of the Heard brothers. Joined Augustine Heard & Co. following his graduation from Yale. He headed the firm from its peak to its bankruptcy in 1875.

Alice Heard, née Leeds (1846–1917) Wife of John Heard. Lived with John and their children in Boston following his return from China.

Augustine Heard Sr. (1785–1868) Ship captain and China trade merchant from Ipswich, Massachusetts. Uncle to the four Heard brothers and the namesake of Augustine Heard & Co.

Augustine Heard Jr. (1827–1905) The second eldest Heard brother. Followed John to China, became partner in Augustine Heard & Co., and oversaw the firm's migration to Hong Kong.

Elizabeth Ann Heard, née Farley (1802–1865) Wife of George Washington Heard and mother to the four Heard brothers. Lived in Ipswich, Massachusetts.

George Farley Heard (1837–1875) The youngest Heard brother and the last to reach China. Besides business, he participated widely in American diplomacy and Hong Kong civic life. Died sailing home to America.

GLOSSARY OF PEOPLE

George Washington Heard (1793–1863) Father to the four Heard brothers and brother of Augustine Heard Sr. Lived in Ipswich, Massachusetts.

Jane Heard, née deConinck (1832–1899) Wife of Augustine Heard Jr. and daughter of a Belgian diplomat.

John Heard (1824–1894) The eldest of the four Heard brothers and the first among them to go to China. Became a leading partner of Augustine Heard & Co.

Mary Heard, née Livingston (fl. 1868–1881) Wife of Albert F. Heard. Lived with Albert in Hong Kong and traveled with him in Europe. The two had no children and separated shortly after the company's bankruptcy.

Richard Howard Heard (fl. 1862–1913) Son of John Heard and "Sai Louey," born in Macao.

"Sai Louey" (fl. 1844–1862) John Heard's protected woman in Macao. Sai Louey is a pseudonym, likely from the Cantonese *siu-neoi ji* (*xiao nü er* 小女兒) or "little daughter."

AUGUSTINE HEARD & CO., PERSONS OF INTEREST

Ellen W. Coolidge, née Randolph (1796–1876) Granddaughter of Thomas Jefferson and wife of Joseph Coolidge. Spent two years living in Macao while Joseph traded in Canton.

Joseph Coolidge Jr. (1798–1879) China trader from Boston. Following his departure from Russell & Co., he founded Augustine Heard & Co. in Augustine Sr.'s name.

Ira Crowell (fl. 1863–1872) Ship captain and husband of Ruth Bradford. From Cape Cod. Returned with Ruth to China to work for Augustine Heard & Co.

Ruth Crowell, née Bradford (1841–1928) Daughter of the first U.S. consul to Amoy, from Darlington, Pennsylvania. She traveled to China first with her father and brother and later lived in Hong Kong and Shanghai with her husband, Ira Crowell.

Charles Dixwell (fl. 1868–1930) Son of George B. Dixwell and his protected woman. Born in Shanghai in 1868, and later migrated to Boston.

George Basil Dixwell (1814–1885) With Joseph Coolidge and Augustine Heard Sr., one of the original partners of Augustine Heard & Co. Managed business in Hong Kong and Shanghai.

GLOSSARY OF PEOPLE

John James Dixwell (1806–1876) Financier from Boston, Massachusetts. Brother of George B. Dixwell.

Percival Lowell Everett (1833–1908) Agent of Augustine Heard & Co. in Boston. Managed company finances. Widely blamed for the firm's bankruptcy.

Mok Sze Yeung (Mo Shiyang 莫仕揚) (1820–1879) Comprador of Augustine Heard & Co. Native of Xiangshan County (*Xiangshan xian* 香山縣).

Mok Tso Chun (Mo Zauquan 莫藻泉) (c. 1857–1917) Second son of Mok Sze Yeung. Became a comprador for Butterfield & Swire.

C. D. Williams (fl. 1861–1866) Agent of Augustine Heard & Co. Sent to Hankou to establish the firm there. Served as first U.S. consul to the port.

THE FORBES FAMILY

Francis (Frank) Blackwell Forbes (1839–1908) New England merchant and botanist. Went to China to become a partner in Russell & Co. Cousin of John Murray and Robert Bennet Forbes.

James Murray Forbes (1845–1937) Son of Robert Bennet Forbes. Traveled to China in 1863 and worked his way up through Russell & Co.

John Murray Forbes (1813–1898) Brother of Robert Bennet Forbes. Spent a brief period working for Russell & Co. in China but preferred to invest in American enterprises.

Paul Siemen Forbes (1808–1886) China trader and cousin of John Murray and Robert Bennet Forbes. Partner in Russell & Co. and first U.S. consul at Canton.

Robert Bennet Forbes (1804–1889) Boston merchant, captain, and partner of Russell & Co. in China. His admission to the firm sparked the fallout between Joseph Coolidge and the rest of firm's partners.

William Howell Forbes (1837–1896) Son of Paul Siemen Forbes and partner in Russell & Co. Lived at Rose Hill in Hong Kong with his wife "Dora" Delano. Uncle of Franklin Delano Roosevelt.

OTHER CORE ACTORS

Helen Beal (fl. 1828–1860) New Englander. Socialite. Accompanied husband Dr. George Rogers Hall to Shanghai in 1850.

GLOSSARY OF PEOPLE

Houqua (Wu Bingjian 伍秉鑑) (1769–1843) Founder of the Ewo (Yihe 怡和) Hong and the richest Chinese merchant in Canton. Joseph Coolidge's mismanagement of his funds in London contributed to Coolidge's fallout with Russell & Co.

Nathaniel Kinsman (1789–1847) American trader in Canton. Joseph Coolidge's first pick for Augustine Heard & Co.'s third partner. Nathaniel declined the offer, and George Dixwell took the spot.

Rebecca Kinsman, née Chase (1810–1882) Nathaniel Kinsman's wife. Remained in Macao, where she advised him on business and managed affairs on his behalf.

Russell Sturgis (1805–1887) Boston merchant and onetime partner of Russell, Sturgis & Co. in Canton. Became head of the Baring Brothers bank in London.

Gustavus Tuckerman (1824–1897) American merchant based in Calcutta and business associate of Augustine Heard & Co.

Elizabeth Warden, née Beal (fl. 1827–1873) New Englander and sister of Helen Beal. Married Henry H. Warden of Russell & Co. and lived in Shanghai.

Henry H. Warden (1817–1899) New Englander and partner of Russell & Co. based in Shanghai. Husband of Elizabeth Warden, née Beal.

The Boston Brahmins An insular community of elite families in New England. Brahmins headed most of the major American firms active in the China trade. Families include Forbes, Coolidge, Russell, Sturgis, Peabody, Cushing, Perkins, Low, Endicott, Nye, Crowninshield, and Saltonstall, among others.

A NOTE ON NAMING

Although at times awkward, many individuals are referred to throughout the text using their full name. I have made the decision to do so in order to ensure clarity, since many of the core actors in this history are from the same families (e.g., The Heards and the Forbeses), share similar initials (John Murray Forbes and James Murray Forbes; Augustine Heard Sr., Augustine Heard Jr., and Albert Heard), and are discussed in reference to each other.

GLOSSARY OF TERMS

Amoy Xiamen 廈門. City in southeastern Fujian Province. One of the original five treaty ports.
Back Bay From 1859, an affluent neighborhood in Boston built on land reclaimed from the Charles River basin.
Beacon Hill Located near the Massachusetts State House and Boston Common, the affluent south slope of Beacon Hill was home to many Boston Brahmins.
Boston Brahmin A term coined by Oliver Wendell Holmes Sr. in the nineteenth century to refer to the traditional elite class in Boston. The insular class was made up of a core cluster of wealthy and influential families.
Boston Concern The self-referential name for the New England community at Canton, most notably associated with Russell & Co., as well as the Forbes, the Perkins, and the Sturgis families.
Brother Jonathan A nineteenth-century pseudonym for New Englanders, functioning parallel to Britain's personification as "John Bull."
Canton Guangzhou 廣州. City on the Pearl River in Guangdong Province. The official site of Sino-foreign commerce prior to the First Opium War.
comprador A Chinese agent employed by foreign firms to assist in trade and investment, and in some cases to oversee Chinese staff.
Consoo House English transliteration of *gongsuo* 公所, customshouse.

GLOSSARY OF TERMS

demurrage A fee paid to a ship owner for failure to load/unload cargo in the agreed upon time. In the case of the opium trade, this fee was levied by hulk owners for storing the product owners' chests awaiting sale.

Fah Kee Transliteration of *fakei* (*huaqi* 花旗). Literally "flower flag," the Chinese at Canton used the term as a name for the United States. The Americans quickly adopted the term themselves for their clubs and organizations in China.

Fast Crab *Kuai xie* 快蟹. A narrow, oared vessel suited for navigating the waterways of the Pearl River Delta and used for smuggling opium.

Fuzhou 福州. Alternatively romanized as Foochow. A port city in Fujian Province on the Min River. One of the original five treaty ports.

Godown Warehouses for storing goods.

Hankou 漢口. Alternatively romanized as Hankou. Treaty port on the Yangzi opened following the Second Opium War. One of three cities that make up present-day Wuhan.

John Bull A caricatured personification of England and by extension the British. Used often in political cartoons as an archetype for the country and its people.

joss A pidgin word for the superstitious power of luck.

junk A type of Chinese sailing vessel with fully battened sails.

Keechong Russell & Co.'s Chinese name, transliterated by the American partners from the firm's Cantonese name, *kei cheung* (*qi chang* 旗昌).

Kiukiang Jiujiang 九江. City on the Yangzi River. Briefly occupied by the Taiping, and later an important treaty port.

Knickerbocker A term referring to people from Manhattan, comparable in the nineteenth century to "Boston Brahmin."

lascar Sailors or militiamen, typically from South or Southeast Asia, employed aboard European vessels.

Lintin Nei lingding 内伶仃. An island roughly 24 miles (38 km) from Hong Kong in the mouth of the Pearl River Delta.

lorcha A sailing vessel in which a junk rig was affixed to a Portuguese- or European-style hull.

memsahib A term of address for white or upper-class women.

Peiho The White River, or Hai River (*haihe* 海河), connecting the Bohai Sea to Tianjin and Beijing.

pidgin In the case of China, a grammatically simplified Chinese-English patois used to communicate between foreigners and Chinese.

GLOSSARY OF TERMS

protected woman One of a class Chinese or Macanese women who entered into relationships with European and American men. Although interracial marriage was frowned upon, protected women were often provided housing and stipends.

punkah A large cloth fan suspended from the ceiling and operated by a pull cord.

Qin Chai 欽差 Title meaning "Imperial Envoy."

sahib A term meaning "owner" in Arabic. A term of address used often during British rule in India, sometimes as a legitimate reference to the addressee's status, but usually just as a replacement for "mister."

Scrambling Dragon *Pa long* 爬龍. See 'Fast Crab.'

shroff An agent employed by Western firms to test and evaluate silver coins used in trade.

shroffage A fee levied for shroffing duties, namely testing, guaranteeing, and tallying coins paid for goods.

supercargo An agent employed by the owner of the cargo on a ship to accompany the cargo, manage the owner's trade, and buy and sell merchandise at the port of destination.

sycee A gold or silver ingot used as currency in imperial China.

Taku Forts Also referred to as the Dagu Forts. These forts protected the entrance to the Peiho.

tael A monetary unit based on the value of a tael (50 grams) of silver.

Taipingshan Throughout the nineteenth century, Taipingshan was a neighborhood on the western edge of the settlement of Victoria. It was home to a mostly Chinese population.

The Thirteen Factories Also referred to as *shi san hang* 十三行. The designated compound for foreign merchants at Canton.

Tientsin Tianjin 天津. City in China on the Bohai Sea. The site of the Treaty of Tientsin (1858), and one of the subsequent treaty ports opened by it.

Tsarskoye Selo A town south of Saint Petersburg containing the residence of the Russian imperial family.

Whampoa Huangpu 黃埔 Island, now known as Pazhou 琶洲 Island, which provided anchorage for foreign ships participating in the China trade. Roughly 12 miles (19 km) from the Thirteen Factories.

Zongli Yamen The Qing government body overseeing foreign policy from 1861 to 1901.

THE CHINA FIRM

INTRODUCTION

An American Firm, a British Colony, and a Global Microhistory

> Changes on changes have occurred since I last took pen in hand to note the momentary sensations of daily life. More than a year has past [sic]. I was then nearing England now I am thousands of miles away. Then a boy with anxious and aspiring hopes now as it were a man, doing a man's part and a serious sober part, responsible too; then looking forward to unknown duties and strange scenes, now those duties are familiar and the scenes old and changed again. Then not even a clerk now a merchant and a head man of a firm.
>
> Truly I am changed.
>
> —ALBERT F. HEARD (1855)

Few words describe China's influence on American merchants better than the businessman Albert Heard's sentiment, written in Shanghai in 1855: "truly I am changed." These words could have been written by any number of the Americans who had traveled to China to make their fortunes in the nineteenth century. In February 1784, little more than a month following the end of the War of Independence, the American ship *Empress of China* departed New York for Canton (Guangzhou 廣州).[1] This voyage anticipated a century-long wave of American mercantile interest in China. In the following years, American firms established themselves in Canton's Thirteen Factories (*shi san hang* 十三行) before spreading their enterprises along the China coast and throughout the East Asian littoral.[2] By the 1850s these companies became prominent fixtures in the young British colony of Hong Kong, taken from the Qing in 1841.[3] They continued to enjoy great success well into the 1860s, but as the China trade grew it evolved, and the old firms practicing traditional business models struggled to adapt. Throughout the 1870s and 1880s each of the major firms, relics of the old China trade and this first wave of Sino-American commerce, failed.

Albert Heard was a partner in one such company, Augustine Heard & Co., known in Cantonese as King Gei 瓊記, and while not present at its founding, he played no small part its bankruptcy.[4] As the second youngest of the four Heard brothers, familial ties secured Albert his position in the firm, as they had his elder brothers John and Augustine Jr. before him and his younger brother George afterward (figures 0.1–0.5). The firm had been founded in 1840, when the brothers' uncle, Augustine Heard Sr., implicitly granted his colleague Joseph Coolidge permission to establish an independent consignment business bearing Augustine Heard Sr.'s name. Like the other American firms, Augustine Heard & Co.'s history began in the

FIGURE 0.1. Augustine Heard Sr. (1785-1868). *Source*: Photograph, Undated, Box 9, Mss:1414, HBS.

INTRODUCTION

FIGURE 0.2. John Heard (1824–1894). *Source:* Sketch, Undated, Box 7, Mss:1414, HBS.

Canton factories, but it quickly spread throughout China's treaty ports and Japan, all overseen from the company's Hong Kong headquarters.

The British colony served as each of the brothers' home at some point during their tenures. From Hong Kong the Heards managed the firm, and with their American peers they contributed to the developing port's vibrant society and culture. The brothers integrated into a white foreign community whose sociocultural norms were largely determined by the British. They attended races and regattas, joined clubs, and served on committees and as consuls. They rubbed shoulders with the British when expedient and grumbled about Anglo-American political contests when prompted by the news cycle. They worried about business, the stability of China's interior, coastal piracy, and Sino-British conflicts. They formed strong and racialized views about their Chinese neighbors, refined ideas of Anglo-Saxon

FIGURE 0.3. Augustine Heard Jr. (1827-1905). *Source*: Photograph, Undated, Box 7, Mss:1414, HBS.

brotherhood, and discovered that class meant something more than generational wealth in the British colonial context. Through Hong Kong, the brothers encountered colonial sociocultural systems that forced them to rethink their core values, what it meant to be American, and what it meant to be white. Their overall success confirmed their ability to adapt to and exploit the hierarchies that defined colonial society. In these respects the Heard brothers were not exceptional. Their experiences paralleled those of the other American merchants who navigated Hong Kong's mercantile community.

But while Hong Kong was unique in its status as a British colony, it was also part of a wider treaty-port network through which Augustine Heard & Co. expanded during the 1850s and 1860s (figure 0.6). From their base in Canton, the partners leaped at the opening of China following the First Opium War (1839–1842), establishing branches in Shanghai (c. 1846) and Fuzhou (c. 1854). In 1857 the firm shifted its headquarters to Hong Kong. From the colony, the lead partners oversaw the rapid growth and nearly as

INTRODUCTION

FIGURE 0.4. Albert Farley Heard (1833–1890). *Source*: Photograph, Notman Photographic Co., Undated, Box 3, Mss:1414, HBS.

rapid decline of their company as the Heards attempted to adapt its initial capacity as a consignment house trading mainly in tea and opium to the evolving commercial systems along the China coast. With the opening of new treaty ports following the Second Opium War (1856–1860), the Heards established branches and agents in Amoy (Xiamen 廈門), Kiukiang (Jiujiang 九江), Tientsin (Tianjin 天津), and Hankow (Hankou 漢口). Agents were recorded generally in Japan's Kanagawa prefecture (c. 1861–1862), and from 1865 the company branch was a permanent fixture in the prefecture's capital, Yokohama. An additional branch was established in Japan in "Hiogo" (Kobe) in the early 1870s. To augment dealings in teas, opium, and other products, the Heards ordered steamships and established lines on the Yangzi and the Pearl River, and in some ports the partners even functioned as

FIGURE 0.5. George Farley Heard (1837-1875). *Source*: Photograph, the London Stereoscopic & Photographic Company, London, Undated, Box 3, HBS.

insurance brokers. This period of expansion and diversification was short-lived, and those branches that lasted more than a couple of years employed fewer and fewer agents into the 1870s. By the firm's 1875 collapse the remaining six branches operated on skeleton rosters of two or three men. Augustine Heard Jr. and John Heard briefly resurrected the firm in 1876 under the shortened name Heard & Co., but abandoned the attempt within the year.

In the course of building and maintaining their company, the Heards brought more than one hundred men to China who invariably became

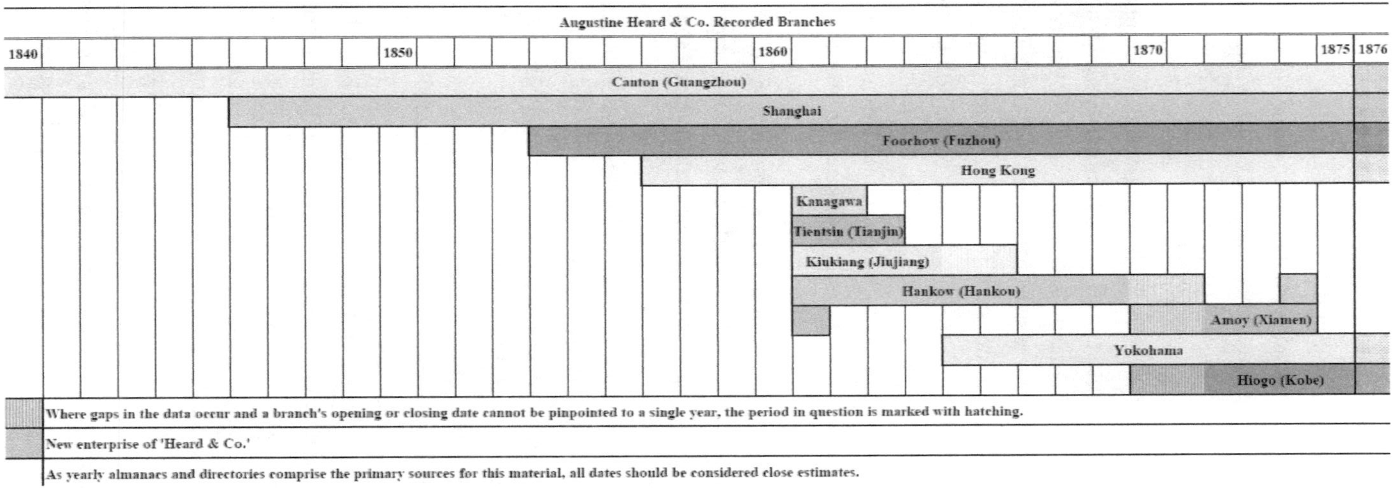

FIGURE 0.6. Augustine Heard & Co. branches from its founding to its bankruptcy. Courtesy of the Baker Library, Harvard Business School.

members of treaty port networks linking Hong Kong to the China coast, the interior via the Yangzi, and Japan. Their occupations ranged from clerks and partners to tea-tasters and captains. Some came alone; others brought their families. Men of talent were poached from competing firms, and positions were found for cousins and distant relatives. While the history that follows is concerned largely with the Heards themselves and with a handful of the contacts they maintained, it is important to emphasize that by providing these opportunities, they and the other American firms helped establish the same American community of which they were a part of, and that would grow throughout nineteenth-century China's treaty ports.

This mostly New Englander community of Americans was modest in size compared to the larger British and much larger still Chinese communities that populated Hong Kong. In 1841, *The Chinese Repository* counted only forty-six Americans in China compared to the roughly 250 Britons.[5] By 1845, Hong Kong's total population was 24,157, and the non-Chinese community numbered 1,043, but there were only around eighty-four Americans registered throughout China.[6] This imbalance continued to grow throughout the nineteenth century.[7] Still, Americans comprised the colony's second largest group of white foreigners, and one that shared much culturally and historically with their British neighbors. Not colonizers themselves, but still privileged within colonial space, the American merchants capitalized on their race and their culture to cement their status among elite society. In the process they developed new interests and aspirations that deviated from those of the American metropole, mirroring instead those of the wider British community. The experiences of these Americans clarify the ways extraimperial communities navigated, adapted to, and exploited British empire.

Both the American community's relative size and their affinity for British culture inflected how they engaged with Hong Kong's British and Chinese communities. As a minority within the colony's foreign society, they naturally sought acceptance among their British peers, fashioning their lives in Hong Kong after the colonial style to secure it. As a greater minority still compared to the Chinese, the Americans came face-to-face with the racial and ethnic differences that cut across Hong Kong. These differences often seemed insurmountable, magnifying the American desire to carve out a space within the more familiar British society. Their efforts to adapt to one community and distance themselves from the other lay in tension with their desire to preserve their unique "Americanness."

Albert Heard's declaration "truly I am changed" encapsulates the transformative experience of living within a British colony on the edge of the Qing Empire. American merchants arriving in China carried a sense that, despite a shared claim to an English-speaking Anglo-Saxon heritage, Americans were notably distinct from their British cousins; that there were inherent American traits such as frugality, modesty, and the Protestant work ethic that set them apart from other foreigners, the British in particular.[8] They championed their religious and political beliefs as more equitable than the British and juxtaposed their republican values, their respect for Chinese sovereignty, and their morality against the British Empire and its bellicose approach toward the Qing. At various levels the experiences of American merchants in China produced new understandings of Sino-American and Anglo-American relationships and destabilized their sense of what it meant to be American.

Yet they were not passive agents waiting for colonial space to remodel them. At their height, members of the large American firms played a prominent role within these foreign enclaves. They brought to China their own culture, politics, and agendas. Tracing the rise and decline of one such firm and the lives of its partners, the following chapters explore the extent to which American merchants made, and were made by, British colonial society. I argue that the British colony in the mid-nineteenth century provided a space in which non-British communities such as the Americans were forced to reconcile their national identity with local colonial society and culture; that in doing so they reinforced colonial social and racial hierarchies, secured the means to expand their enterprises throughout China, and were drawn into the British imperial world.

The history that follows uses the case study of Augustine Heard & Co. to establish a more complete understanding of how Americans abroad interacted with nineteenth-century British colonialism and shaped Sino-foreign contact. While each chapter roughly proceeds chronologically, mapping the firm's rise and decline, they are also organized along a scalar progression, extending from the microhistorical to domestic, societal, regional, and finally transnational contexts to fully explore the varied forces shaping American understandings of, and interactions with, colonial society. At its core, this book is centered on a family, a firm, and a colony. The histories of each, however, were invariably integrated into global and imperial networks of people, things, and ideas. From the perspective of the Heards and the wider American community in Hong Kong, this case study demonstrates how the experiences of a small community in this distant British colony on the margins of the Qing Empire were at once the products and drivers of transnational networks linking people, entrepôts, and trade routes across China, America, and Europe.

The Augustine Heard & Co. case study expands upon a well-established body of research concerning early American encounters with China. Historians have paid close attention to America's contact with the Qing Empire during the late eighteenth and early nineteenth centuries, detailing especially the ways American merchants navigated the "Canton system" in the 1830s and 1840s, and how Sino-American trade shaped U.S. capitalism.[9] Others still have looked beyond commerce to examine sociocultural aspects of American involvement in the old China trade, or woven Americans into well-trodden narratives of the First Opium War.[10] The narrative seldom extends beyond the First Opium War's end in 1842, perpetuating a logical if somewhat arbitrary division between the first and second halves of the nineteenth century. But those Americans that thrived in the "Canton days" continued to do so following 1842.[11] As business interests expanded Americans participated in colonial and regional life and commerce, founding coastal shipping enterprises, dominating the steamship trade in the 1860s, making important inroads into China's interior, and even helping open Japan to foreign merchants.[12]

The American presence beyond 1842 has been largely framed through Sino-American politics and diplomacy or taken the form of valuable but targeted studies of specific communities and historical moments. Much is known, for example, about the developing formal relations between the Qing and the United States in the nineteenth century.[13] Missionary encounters, gendered interactions between American men and Chinese women, and between American women and the wider Chinese and foreign communities have likewise proved crucial to historical understanding Sino-American contact.[14] With minor exceptions, this collection of work provides impressions rather than a thorough history of nineteenth-century China's American community. Sensitive to their underrepresentation within studies of mid- to late nineteenth-century China, this book restores Americans to their active place in the history of Hong Kong and the treaty ports.

Reinserting Americans into the history of British empire in China further emphasizes the transimperial dimension of white colonial spaces. These were complex sites, riven by internal divisions and the subjective interests of their inhabitants.[15] Yet, while their unique racial, class, and gendered compositions have been increasingly recognized, questions concerning colonial space's national diversity, how such diversity eroded or sharpened internal divisions, and how such spaces in turn influenced the lives of those varied communities that lived and worked within them are only starting to be asked.[16] For various communities, foreign or otherwise, British colonies provided opportunities to work and network, but these communities also bore uneasy relationships with the British Empire and the implications of colonialism. The reasons for their ambivalence varied, ranging from cultural dissonance to historical rivalries, ongoing transnational conflicts, and diplomatic crises. Yet colonial spaces, miles and months distant from the metropole, also had an insulating effect on those living within them, and the local society proved surprisingly resilient to external tensions.

The ways these extraimperial groups, such as Hong Kong's Americans, integrated themselves into colonial spaces demonstrate the complex relationships between race, society, and culture. Exploring the nuances in these relationships provides a more complete understanding of how colonial hierarchies were formed and maintained. Through their whiteness, their claims to Anglo-Saxon ancestry, and their shared language, Americans accessed elite colonial society, and in doing so cemented the importance of these qualifiers.

As a formal British colony, but also as a global entrepôt, Hong Kong provides a microcosm for observing the ways non-British and British communities interacted within empire's liminal spaces. Americans were disproportionately present in the colony's elite society, successful in trade, and witnessed firsthand the opening of China. As each of the following chapters demonstrates, their successes, failures, and experiences there were intimately tied to foreign aggression, colonialism, and imperial expansion. American encounters with Hong Kong society, understood within the broader context of Anglo-European empire in China, lay bare the tensions underpinning how non-British communities encountered, adapted, and contributed to British colonialism.

Studies of British and non-British experiences in Hong Kong and the treaty ports provide a roadmap to understanding China's American community. Historians have variously problematized insider/outsider binaries and stark distinctions between migrant, colonizer, and colonized, as diverse groups navigated imperial networks and converged in contact zones along China's coast.[17] Efforts to nuance the narrative have helped extend the focus beyond high politics to produce granular understandings of how varied groups experienced empire, migration, and cross-cultural contact and how colonial or semicolonial societies developed and functioned.

Studying Hong Kong itself allows us to better engage with the complexity of such colonial encounters. Where disconnected Chinese and British narratives once dominated the field, punctuated by the odd account of alternative nationalities, new research has been dedicated to promoting the complexity of the colony's sociocultural development.[18] Macanese and Eurasians communities have attracted renewed attention, as has the economic and political "dialogue" that developed between Chinese and foreign communities despite systems of "social segregation."[19] Differences and hierarchies remain essential themes permeating the field, but researchers are increasingly sensitive to the porosity of demarcations once thought rigid.[20] Such efforts have not only contributed to understanding Hong Kong's history but have also provided new frameworks for understanding the sociocultural complexity of colonial spaces, and articulating the individual agencies of those navigating them.[21] These efforts have, in turn, made apparent the space for histories of Americans in China to address the sociocultural aspects of their lives in colonial and semicolonial spaces.

As the hub of American commerce in East Asia, home to China's largest foreign community, and as a formal colony of Britain, Hong Kong anchored the American experience in China. The colony's global and regional significance was a product of its development as an "in-between" space shaped by the movement of people and goods.[22] But while this was a transitory society, it was also a "meeting place" where complex interactions between mobile communities contributed to its unique development.[23] The colony was at once woven into imperial networks and functioned as "its own cultural-historical place."[24] In this place contact with non-British communities redefined British perspectives of empire, race, and class, and British and non-British alike contributed to the port's developing local identity. Understanding American lives in the port, better still their lives within a wider global framework, is thus an integral step toward understanding the wider interests that bound Americans to nineteenth-century China.

Although their commentaries often criticized Britain and its empire, American success in China was welded to the British and their imperial and colonial interests. In some regards this relationship was "parasitic." Even as Americans denounced Britain's aggressive actions in China, they reaped "great benefits from those very same actions."[25] But it was also often symbiotic, as British merchants likewise capitalized on American initiatives. The presence of American traders in Canton in the 1820s and 1830s, for instance, helped the British firms Jardine Matheson & Co. and Dent & Co. justify dismantling the East India Company's monopoly.[26] In the trading system that followed British and American merchants worked in concert, Americans even carrying trade for embargoed British merchants while Britain fought the Qing during the First Opium War.[27] Americans in turn exploited British military victories to sign their own treaties with the Qing, all under a neutral mantle.[28]

The system retained parasitic qualities, however, and for Americans at odds with British bellicosity, the Anglo-American symbiosis was generally unstable. National politics often contradicted local interests, and while such incongruities might be reconciled to lubricate trade, they complicated the relationships between American and British merchants on a social level. Although the distant tensions that filtered into Hong Kong through mail and the news cycle were met with a degree of local ambivalence, they still strained the Anglo-American relationship.[29] But for business to succeed Americans had to play the system, and so they reconciled their new colonial interests with those of the metropole.

For all their preexisting rivalries, the Americans and British were outsiders in a predominantly Chinese space, and so sought to foster a sense of Anglo-American unity. Race became a means of doing so. Historians of empire and colonialism have noted how the racial hierarchies that solidified in colonies influenced the "British" identity that developed abroad.[30] Ideals of "white virtues," popularized through a developing colonial discourse of race, crystallized "whiteness" as a prerequisite to elite status.[31] For white Americans in Hong Kong, this same process of racial hierarchical posturing imparted if not a "colonial identity" at least a sense of status relative to the wider community. Possessing a precoded sense of Anglo-Saxon superiority, American merchants fit in comfortably with their British neighbors, measured their own civilization and culture against the Qing Empire, and repeated common racist tropes about the Chinese in their letters home.[32] Race functioned as a marker of belonging, and through such rhetorical acts the Americans articulated their shared claim to elite colonial society's requisite "whiteness" and culture.[33] At the same time, these acts helped distance Americans from what they described as culturally and racially inferior Chinese others.[34]

As the following chapters show, however, race was just one marker of belonging, working in concert with class and culture to influence American willingness to integrate into British colonial society. Outward appearance of conformity did not, after all, prevent Americans from inserting acidic critiques of British society and class into their private records. When it was opportune to be so, Americans were committed participants in upper-class society. Firms failed, however, and the veneer of affluence and respectability wore thin. As struggling Americans grew anxious about their social status, their awareness of Anglo-American social and cultural differences sharpened.[35] The history of Augustine Heard & Co. provides an opportunity to observe the ways Americans engaged with British colonial society, and how race, class, and national identity functioned in the colonial context.

SOURCES, STRUCTURE, AND FRAMING

At its core, this book follows transnational agents working and interacting between distant but interconnected spaces. The main setting, however, remains local Hong Kong society and culture, as observed through the lens of a single firm. The book brings the transnational and the local into dialogue and offers a framework for using micro-level accounts of individuals or localities as starting points from which to build transnational histories sensitive not only to global connections but also to disconnections; in effect, to nuance the ways historians identify and superimpose global links between distant people, locales, and events.

INTRODUCTION

Throughout this book, I use local histories of "small spaces" such as a bounded community (the Americans) or locality (Hong Kong) to guide the overarching global historical narrative.[36] Too narrow a focus could elide the complex ways metropolitan events influenced life in Hong Kong. Conversely, too broad a focus would risk giving undue weight to these same events, as colonial space was often shielded from metropolitan concerns. My focused history of the colony, then, sensitive to metropolitan contexts, helps delimitate the case study's "constraints and possibilities," revealing the extent to which global circumstances affected local sociocultural systems. Such a sensitivity likewise informs how the case study incorporates the mobilities of its core actors who, in traveling to and from China, crossed "boundaries between different colonial spheres as well as between different empires."[37] Their micro-level experiences reveal an interconnected nineteenth-century world of permeable and often overlapping colonial and imperial spheres.

I rely upon a diverse range of source material to tie the core narrative of Augustine Heard & Co. and the Heard brothers to the experiences of the wider American community in China. The central materials are drawn from the Heard Family Business Records, rich in personal correspondence, business papers, and the ephemera of roughly forty years operating in China. Reading against the commercial narrative that threads these records, I have used the discursive letters between the Heard brothers to reconstruct their impressions of living and trading between China and the United States. To avoid producing a circumscribed view of American society in China, I have supplemented this reading with firsthand and published accounts by elite men and women from the wider American community in Hong Kong and the treaty ports who were contemporary to the Heards.

To contextualize the Heards within both the local and global historical moment, I have consulted major newspapers from the China coast, Hong Kong, Britain, and the United States—both serious and satirical periodicals—as well as guidebooks and directories published for China's foreign community. The latter materials, especially, have been instrumental in providing the data to the quantify the networks the Heards established and maintained through the China trade. My reading of periodicals and published primary materials has required a bottom-up approach. Issues discussed in private correspondence have been used to identify those topics worth following up in the newspapers to understand which transnational events had tangible impacts in China. In this manner, the global has been reframed through the lens of the local.

The one major shortcoming with this corpus, however, is the absence of Chinese—and indeed "other"—voices in the company and colonial archive. While limited official Chinese records, company contracts, and materials that Augustine Heard & Co. compradors produced hint at the entanglement between the American and Chinese communities, the Chinese employees and public that Americans interacted with daily cannot be adequately quantified. Chinese laborers appear in asides about amahs and "houseboys," company staff are tallied in pay ledgers and inventories, the Chinese public is spoken of through generics and tropes. I have accordingly tried to read both along and against the archival grain to reconstruct a sense of the quotidian encounters between Americans and the wider Chinese public in Hong Kong and the treaty ports, and much of this work has focused on sentiment and making the most of archival scraps. Far from circumventing the Chinese community central to this narrative, I have worked with, against, and through elite white perspectives to articulate the multiple forms Sino-American contact took.

Drawing upon these materials, the following chapters explore the complex ways colonial and metropolitan social, cultural, and political concerns intersected, emphasizing the thematic threads that bound the local and the transnational. A scalar approach incorporating micro and macrohistorical contexts has been adopted to test the relationship between local and transnational influences and to show the negotiated processes through which groups such as the Americans reconciled these influences within colonial peripheries such as Hong Kong. Inescapably, much of the research extends beyond the colony's boundaries, which indicates the channels through which the port was interwoven with transnational and intraregional histories. Through this approach, I have used individual and subjective experiences to assess the relationships between metropolitan and peripheral settings, to explain how extraimperial communities encountered and interacted with British imperial and colonial spaces, and to draw Hong Kong into global histories.

The first chapter frames Augustine Heard & Co.'s origins through two of the firm's original partners, Joseph Coolidge and George B. Dixwell, during the period between the firm's 1840 founding and the Second Opium

War's outbreak in 1856. Through their activities in Canton, Coolidge and Dixwell represent the two sides of the Anglo-American relationship in China. Coolidge established Augustine Heard & Co. during the First Opium War, a period which forced American merchants to recalibrate their relationships with the British and Chinese. The warmongering spirit of the British and the conflict's injustices shocked American observers, who denounced British bellicosity and declared their respect for Chinese sovereignty. Yet the instability the hostilities caused benefited American merchants. In some cases, such as Coolidge's, Americans exploited the situation, relying on the British to secure indemnities for both legitimate and exaggerated losses sustained during the conflict. In others they collaborated, helping embargoed British firms carry on a clandestine trade, and learning, as Dixwell did, how to sell opium in the process. In each instance, the Americans risked alienating the British, the Chinese, or both, while attempting to reconcile their sense of benevolent national identity with their interests in the China trade. The story of these two traders in Canton pulls competing themes of national rivalry and Anglo-American solidarity into focus while laying the historical foundation for the proceeding discussion of how Americans fit into Hong Kong society.

Beginning with the Second Opium War, the second chapter expands the scope to consider the composition of the Heards' Hong Kong household between 1856 and the 1870s. The 1857 destruction of the Canton factories forced most American firms to relocate to the British colony, acquired fifteen years earlier. Augustine Heard Jr., foreseeing the shift, purchased and prepared a property at Hong Kong for just such an eventuality. Everything about the household, from its architecture to its location and the lives lived within signals the degree to which Americans integrated with or remained aloof from Hong Kong culture and society. In theory the household provided a private refuge removed from the colony's social pageantry. But it was also a space open to outsiders who penetrated its privacy through social visiting conventions, balls, business, or official receptions. In doing so they broke down private barriers and forced Americans to perform colonial sociocultural mores within their homes. Nor was American life actually private anyway. Their household functioned through the labor of Chinese employees, invisible in the record but ever-present and ever observant. Still, the Heards took measures to fortify the space against the perceived external threat of Chinese violence—a product of their growing unease about the Sino-foreign relationship that had been lauded as amicable during the Canton days. The American household thus developed as an unstable space that exemplified how racial, social, and cultural tensions were sharpened in Hong Kong.

Although the house was effectively a public space, most encounters with Hong Kong's foreign community occurred in the port's common areas and social institutions. On the parade ground fronting the Heard house, in race-day booths, at parties and balls, and through clubs and committees, American merchants such as the Heards found opportunities to participate and stake their claim to a place within elite society. The process of doing so was straightforward: one needed to be wealthy, to be white, and to adhere to the colony's sociocultural rituals. In practice, however, American efforts to secure status brought underlying tensions to the surface, and a nagging sense of difference affected Anglo-American relationships. Although Hong Kong's elite society and culture was imported from Britain, it was refracted through long-standing colonial traditions. So, while in some respects Anglophilic American merchants found social decorum familiar, other practices were peculiar to societies developing on the margins of British empire. In an imperial-colonial space such as Hong Kong, where the foreign elite comprised a clear minority, class and race were imbued with greater meaning, and careful gatekeeping upheld fabricated barriers between the colony's white elite and Chinese, Indian, Filipino, and Macanese communities. American efforts to navigate and adapt to Hong Kong society were often successful, and American merchants were conspicuous among the colony's upper class, but as businesses failed the instability of their status was made apparent. The third chapter engages with these efforts to assimilate, following the same chronology as chapter 2 but stepping beyond the household to explore the position American merchants occupied within a racially and socially hierarchical colonial society.

So much of the American experience of Hong Kong and their capacity to contribute to its foreign society was tied to their mercantile ventures. As transnationally oriented businesses, the successes of American firms were accordingly subject not only to Hong Kong's or China's political and economic circumstances but to the metropole's as well. The fourth chapter departs from Hong Kong to measure the impact wider intraregional and transnational instability had on China's American merchants. As Sino-American commerce increased, American mercantile interests diverged from the amicable and neutral posturing of U.S. diplomats, their understanding of national interests clashing with their desire to participate in and benefit from the foreign carving of China. By the 1860s the simultaneous American and Taiping civil wars would both produce new opportunities and undermine American merchants looking to expand their trade in China. Politically, commercially, and socially, these conflicts tested the binds of China's foreigners. Even if the Anglo-American community weathered the transnational and intraregional tensions these wars ignited, American businesses faltered, setting in motion the bankruptcies of the 1870s and 1880s.

Looking back from Augustine Heard & Co.'s decline in the 1870s, the fifth chapter considers the shape and legacy of the global social, political, and commercial networks the Heard brothers anchored to Hong Kong. Networking was integral to American trade in China and remained so throughout the nineteenth century. Kinship ties and friendships secured employment for young clerks headed to China and ensured their entry into the tightly knit American mercantile community. Americans thus reproduced metropolitan networks in the colony, but they also capitalized on the colony's diverse society to foster ties to key individuals from around the world. The chapter uses digital methods to sketch the contours of this global network before engaging in detail with the specific types of relationships that developed through contact in transient and syncretic spaces such as Hong Kong. The resulting networks shaped the global character of the colony—and China's port cities generally—and continued to "make" colonial society long after the old China firms retreated to the United States.

Although American firms failed, the networks of contacts and experiences acquired during sojourns in China and on voyages to and from the United States remained an asset as American merchants returned to the metropole. Serving as an epilogue to the Heard narrative, the final chapter considers how their time in China influenced the Heard brothers' lives following Augustine Heard & Co.'s bankruptcy. While in some respects marginalized from elite society due to their insolvency, the Heards' post-China aspirations still reflected the ideal life of the returned merchant and the ways this life remained entangled with China. Their varied schemes after they left Hong Kong, the societies they reintegrated into, and the diplomatic posts they pursued each owed something to the experiences and contacts that they acquired in the colony. In this respect, the history of the port and its influence extends well beyond its shores, Hong Kong remaining, for those who had come up in it, a transformative part of their lives long after they departed.

Tracing Augustine Heard & Co.'s rise and decline, the present book asserts the significance of Americans in colonial and semicolonial spaces during the twilight years of nineteenth-century Sino-American trade. Whether through the firm's founding partners' individual actions, the private and public lives of Hong Kong's American community, the transnational and intraregional contexts influencing their success and the port's social cohesion, or the globe-spanning networks Americans built in and through Hong Kong, the American case recalibrates understandings of both how colonial society was composed and of Hong Kong's centrality within transnational histories of colonialism and empire. Augustine Heard & Co. is crucial to this discussion. Using the Heards as an access point, this book provides a framework for global-microhistorical inquiry that recognizes the overlapping sociocultural, political, and commercial contexts through which British colonies "made" and were in turn "made by" an American mercantile elite.

Chapter One

A VERY PROFITABLE CRISIS

Canton's American Merchants on the Eve of the First Opium War

Captain Charles Elliot's orders the evening of May 21, 1841, had been clear: the British and other foreigners of Canton's Thirteen Factories, or "Hongs" (*hang* 行), must evacuate "before sunset" the following day.[1] This was not the first time Elliot had issued such orders, and two years earlier a similar incident had forced British merchants to quit the factories. The new Qin Chai 欽差 (imperial envoy) in 1839, Lin Zexu 林則徐, had been serious about stamping out the illegal opium trade in which almost every foreign merchant in Canton participated. Lin first threatened to decapitate the leading Chinese merchants, Houqua (Wu Bingjian 伍秉鑑) and Mouqua (Lu Wenjin 盧文錦), should the trade persist. When this failed to secure the desired response, Lin placed the foreign community under house arrest, prohibiting them from leaving the Thirteen Factories compound.[2] Their captors treated them with civility, but the foreign community's freedom hinged on their acceptance of Lin's demands for the surrender of some twenty thousand chests of opium.[3]

As soon as the merchants had surrendered the opium, Elliot urged all British subjects to vacate the factories and retire to the safety of Macao.[4] Twenty-five Americans, however, had chosen to remain in 1839 and continue trading for teas and silk. By the end of May that year they were the only foreigners left in Canton.[5] Recognizing the opportunity this position afforded, they used their country's mantle of neutrality to profit from the hostilities between China and Britain. Throughout the coming conflict they would serve as middlemen, shipping a range of cargo to and from Canton for their British peers anchored safely at Hong Kong, Macao, Whampoa (Huangpu 黃埔), and Lintin (Nei Lingding 內伶仃).

Yet May 1841 felt different from the proceedings two years earlier. The *Canton Press* noted the tense atmosphere that seemed to pervade the compound and surrounding suburb.[6] Chinese forces had established batteries at the French and Dutch Follies guarding the route in and out of Canton and erected a makeshift fort at Shamian 沙面 just upriver. Soldiers were suddenly conspicuous, hoisting pennons at the ends of the streets leading from the factories. The foreign merchants took the hint, and by seven in the evening of 21 May the last schooner, *Aurora*, departed for safer moorings downriver. All the foreigners had left. All, that is, save two Americans: Joseph Coolidge of Augustine Heard & Co. and William Howard Morss of Olyphant & Company. That same evening Chinese soldiers stormed the factories. They took Coolidge into custody, while Morss escaped to Whampoa with a Chinese official's aid. The American vice consul, Warren Delano, secured Coolidge's release, and Coolidge was dropped defenseless in the square fronting the factories. Coolidge took refuge in the customshouse (*gongsuo* 公所), transliterated in English as "consoo house," remaining there "several days, without food, apparently forgotten," until Elliot and a contingent of British soldiers finally extracted him.

While unique, Coolidge's experience is worth remembering, for through his brief captivity the sociopolitical worlds of the Chinese, British, and Americans at Canton converged. Throughout the First Opium War and long after, Americans in China had purported neutrality. American merchants used this status and their shared interests with the British in China to profit from the latter's aggressive posturing. At the same time, they presented themselves as ambassadors of peace and amity to the Chinese. Protected by their neutrality, the Americans formed what has been described as a "parasitic relationship" with "their British rivals." The relationship provided the means to increase their own profits at the expense of British efforts, all the while presenting themselves "as a friendly and peaceful Western power" to the Chinese "in hopes of undermining the British through diplomacy."[7]

A VERY PROFITABLE CRISIS

The process through which U.S. merchants carved a space for themselves in nineteenth-century China is a central thread throughout this book, but one that necessitates a more nuanced approach to the simultaneously competitive and collaborative relationship between American and British traders in China. The ways Americans navigated Sino-British relations were complex, often more symbiotic than parasitic. While true that Americans leveraged their neutral position for gain, American and British interactions often bore mutual benefits. The relationships between the United States, British, and Chinese communities shifted relative to pressing political, social, and commercial circumstances.

The activities of two Augustine Heard & Co. partners, Joseph Coolidge Jr. and George Basil Dixwell, during and immediately following the First Opium War demonstrate how the complex and ambiguous ties between the U.S., British, and Chinese actors at Canton developed on an interpersonal level that anticipated the wider American community's experiences in Hong Kong and China throughout the remainder of the nineteenth century. Whether collaborating with, exploiting, or condemning the British, both men tried to reconcile local circumstances and personal ambitions with the official American position in China, and with American ambivalence toward the First Opium War and the drug trade. In the process, they built a solid foundation for Augustine Heard & Co. to expand in China, but not without inciting the ire of others. Although Coolidge, Dixwell, and the other American merchants leveraged their position in Canton for personal gain, their British and Chinese peers and rivals recognized the discord between American mercantile and diplomatic interests and responded in their own ways.[8] Competition between Americans and British, and between both and the Chinese, thus occurred in a unique space in which individuals negotiated and reconciled national, local, and personal interests.

Coolidge and Dixwell are perfect candidates to explore this shifting relationship because, while members of the same firm, they represent opposite faces of the Anglo-American relationship. Following the events of May 1841, Coolidge became the subject of general derision among the British community.[9] Investigating why there were such visceral reactions among the British toward Coolidge's "parasitic" conduct explains much about the underlying tensions extant between the British and U.S. traders in China. In contrast, Augustine Heard & Co.'s partners sent Dixwell to Macao during the First Opium War to learn everything from the British firm Jardine Matheson & Co. about the drug trade. Augustine Heard & Co. was among the first firms to resume trading opium openly following the war, and Dixwell headed the initiative as its preeminent "opium man."[10] His path during this episode represents the ways Americans and the British cooperated in China and prompts the question of what encouraged such cooperation. Were both parties strictly driven by profit, or were there other elements connecting the two communities?

To answer these questions, this chapter adopts a microhistorical approach, demonstrating how Coolidge's and Dixwell's parallel narratives presented a microcosm of the American community's developing relationship with the British in China. When linked to wider American, British, and Chinese perspectives, their activities during the First Opium War and the proceeding interwar period (1842–56) signpost how broader forces of transnational and transimperial competition, Anglo-American rivalry, and Sino-American trade in the mid-nineteenth century were reconciled on a local scale. They serve as a means to test the "models and theories" populating global history and interrogate metanarratives that have influenced understandings of the past—in this case Sino-American amity, Sino-British conflict, and Anglo-American competition. Their actions, indeed their individual agency, helped shape a dynamic society that, while subject to global influences, was also the product of complex interactions between a handful of individuals. Their conflicting paths thus form two sides of a single narrative of Anglo-American interactions in China, illustrating which interests unified or divided British and American communities, and how encounters in Canton contributed to the later shaping of Hong Kong's distinct colonial community.

THE CANTON SYSTEM

Preoccupation with the First Opium War often overshadows histories of the Canton system, which has been cast as little more than a "prelude" to the Sino-British relations that followed. Prior to 1839 the Canton trade developed in ways unmarred by the violence and tensions associated with the later conflict.[11] Still, the lens of the First Opium War remains useful as it captures Canton at one of its most dynamic—and volatile—phases. The conflict unearthed anxieties that had been growing among the different communities residing at Canton's Thirteen Hongs by upsetting the relatively stable and unremarkable rhythm of their trade. Changes within the system in turn affected how American and British merchants responded to the conflict and to each other's actions and laid the groundwork for foreign colonial society at Hong Kong.

American merchants came to China, almost without exception, from New England, New York, and Philadelphia. These merchants were the relations of established families in cities such as Philadelphia, New York, and Boston who were already engaged in long-distance trading.[12] The first Americans had come as supercargoes, making a profit on commissions placed by contacts back home, and eventually settling semipermanently in Canton's Thirteen Factories as business picked up. In many cases a family precedent was set, and several members of the same family would engage in similar enterprises related to the China trade. Augustine Heard Sr. was one such case, following in the footsteps of his brother Daniel Heard, also a supercargo, who was among the first Americans to die in China, buried at Whampoa on December 13, 1801.[13] The next generation of men, including Coolidge, Dixwell, and John Heard, learned the trade in Boston and New York firms before sailing for Canton. These men came from well-connected families in New England and New York society, and in both the United States and China their commercial bonds were built upon these close-knit social networks of kinship and friendship.[14] Based on these networks, it could be assumed that once in Canton they would form an insular, homogenous, community based on shared domestic culture. The constrained living quarters the Qing afforded to the foreign merchants, however, made intermixing with other foreigners inevitable.

New arrivals first anchored at Macao, where they would chart a boat upriver to Canton to begin their careers as clerks in a trading company. Harriet Low, one of the few American women ever to visit the place, described the journey first past the island of Lintin, with its "outlaws" and "smugglers" of opium, through the Bocca Tigris (the Tiger's Mouth), a strait flanked by Chinese forts, and onto Whampoa, where the foreign ships anchored, waiting to load and offload cargo.[15] From Whampoa it was a short trip up to the Thirteen Hongs in Canton, where a small foreign community of merchants resided in narrow apartments called "factories," built on a strip of land fronting the river (figure 1.1). The initial thirteen factories bore the names of the nationalities they had housed, but by 1841 the

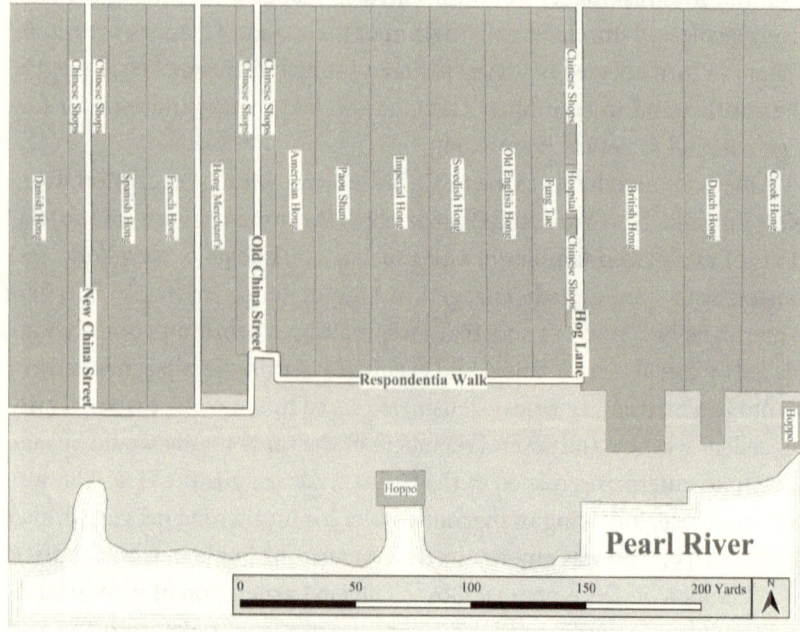

FIGURE 1.1. Thirteen Factories Compound, based on William Bramston and James Wyld, *A Plan of the City of Canton and Its Suburbs*, London, 1840, FO 925/2288, TNA. Image by author.

names were arbitrary as the population was "principally English and Americans."[16] Three streets lined with Chinese shops ran perpendicular to the river, punctuating the factory rows, and a flat open ground that would become a garden following the Opium War separated the factory facades and the river. During the trading season, these three streets, thirteen factories, and the immediate surrounding neighborhood constituted the entire world of the foreign merchants. The men might row upon the river, walk the streets between the factories and the city walls, visit a nearby garden once a month, or make brief excursions into the surrounding countryside (although it was ill advised), but otherwise their day-to-day life lacked variety.[17] When the season ended, they would return to their ships at Whampoa or to Macao.[18]

While in Canton, the American merchants lived in close proximity to the British, and for the sake of society and commerce it was necessary that the two communities remain on good terms. Anglo-American relationships were fairly relaxed, and American merchants often recalled the amicable feelings that existed between all members of the community.[19] Yet, despite the good feelings their shared experiences elicited, some cultural differences between the British and Americans were difficult to reconcile. Class and culture were conspicuous, and, at least in the days of the East India Company monopoly, Americans were conscious of their social position relative to the British merchants at Canton.[20] In theory, divergent values and ideas set them apart from the British, stemming in part from the different roles wealth played within both countries' class systems. American money could not secure rank or peerage, so capital itself became a marker of status to be displayed through urban property and business. But while such cultures defined class within their respective metropoles, the ways in which British and American merchants in China secured rank were not prohibitively different, and capital increasingly conferred elite status in the Canton system.[21]

From the early days of the trade, Americans and British in Canton had enjoyed similarities—the British missionary Robert Morrison had even passed as an American when first arriving at the Thirteen Factories in 1807—and by the 1840s the American and British merchant elite appeared increasingly alike. Both communities maintained lavish lifestyles at the Thirteen Factories. Communal meals where company partners and clerks sat down together to eat were standard. Visits were commonplace, and dinner parties were the most notable form of entertainment at the merchants' disposal. Factories were bare, lacking the comforts of more settled spaces, but well-staffed with a retinue of Chinese laborers. Newly arrived American merchants adjusted well to being waited on by their own personal "boy." Life was such in the factories that irrespective of national predispositions, British and American merchants began to fall into the same daily rhythms. Tensions existed between the two communities, and Americans frequently complained of the stuffiness of the British, but in the end both displayed similar aspirations for their lives in and after China.[22]

British merchants used their wealth to refashion themselves in the metropole as aspirants to the upper class. William Jardine, for example, maintained a residence at London's Upper Belgrave Street and became involved in the company Magniac Smith before entering politics.[23] As will be seen in chapter 6, the Heard brothers would similarly follow in the footsteps of other American China traders, acquiring property in fashionable Boston neighborhoods and using China and metropolitan networks to pursue further business opportunities and diplomatic offices. There may have been cultural and political differences between the two communities, but these differences could be overlooked in the short term to benefit social cohesion and mercantile collaboration. As Coolidge's and Dixwell's activities demonstrate, both communities stood to gain from exploiting the Canton system's instability during the First Opium War.

COOLIDGE MAKES A CLAIM

Joseph Coolidge Jr. arrived at Canton as a clerk in the prominent American firm Russell & Company. Like many of his American contemporaries in China, he came from a respectable family in Boston, Massachusetts. Harvard-educated and trained in the countinghouse of the Boston-China merchant Robert Gould Shaw, Coolidge was an ideal fit for life in the China trade. He was capable, well-connected, and married to Thomas Jefferson's granddaughter Ellen Wayles Randolph.[24] By all accounts, Coolidge was representative of the old cohort of China traders. Years later, John Heard would recall Coolidge as an "agreeable," "well read and intelligent" man, if rather stiff in manner.[25] Coolidge's contemporaries felt differently, however, and it appears that the man possessed a special talent for drawing the ire of his peers.

Upon arriving in Canton, Coolidge became part of what was known as the "Boston Concern." This was an elite community that comprised the New England Perkins, Sturgis, and Forbes families and their extended relations. Considering the degree to which their kinship networks were intertwined, it is apparent that a few key families dominated the American community, with the largest group forming around Thomas Perkins and his extended relatives (figure 1.2).[26] While a member of the Boston Concern and Russell Co. respectively, Coolidge remained, in many ways, an outsider to the insular family circles that bound the community's most prominent members. His future partner, Augustine Heard Sr., was in much the same position. Their ability to sustain positive relations with members of the community was accordingly critical, as it was far easier for ties to break down—as Coolidge's experiences demonstrate—when the attribute of kinship was absent.

Nepotism was a cornerstone of the U.S. firms active in Canton. The trust afforded through familial and social ties to the metropole was a crucial

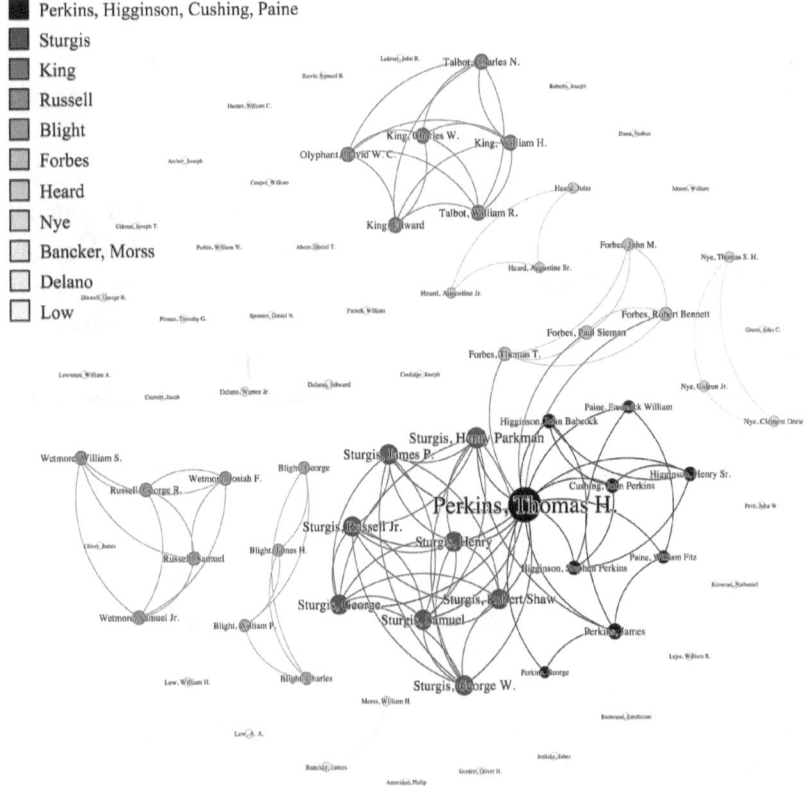

FIGURE 1.2. "Boston Concern" kinship networks. Image by author.

aspect of these transnational businesses, and as a result also influenced one's personal advancement in Canton. With their strong social connections in Boston and New York, the members of the Boston Concern aided each other's businesses, employed each other's kin, married into each other's families, and entered partnerships on the strength of their longstanding bonds. To Joseph Coolidge, already thirty-five in 1833, Canton was a disagreeable place, with "little or no society," "no connection with the English," and dampened by "a great jealousy of each other among the few Americans" there.[27] Misgivings aside, Coolidge secured a promotion to partner with the leading American firm, Russell & Co., in January 1834 through the recommendation of Augustine Heard Sr., who had himself been accepted as a partner in 1830.[28]

A VERY PROFITABLE CRISIS

It was during his tenure as a partner of Russell & Co. that Coolidge first began to stir up trouble, alienating both his partners and the leading Chinese Hong merchant Houqua. The wedge Coolidge drove between himself and his partners at Russell & Co. testifies to the insular character of Canton's American community, and the importance Sino-American relations held for the merchants. Exhibiting what was, according to contemporaries, characteristic behavior, Coolidge began by splitting hairs over the amount of interest he was due in the company.[29] He then lost a considerable sum, invested on Houqua's behalf, while trading in London. Making matters worse, he showed the firm's private correspondence to his clients in an attempt to justify his actions. Coolidge claimed the whole business turned out well, but he acknowledged that much of the animosity between himself and his employers stemmed from the Houqua affair.[30] Already condemned by Houqua, and at odds with his employers, Coolidge then wrote a letter from London opposing Robert Bennet Forbes's 1839 admission as partner to Russell & Company.[31]

Each of the final two offenses was damning within the context of Sino-American trade given the value that both Houqua and the Forbeses placed in their relationship. For the Chinese merchant, Russell & Co., and the Forbes family in particular, provided "leverage to break free from the British hegemon." Through the American firm, Houqua could cultivate networks of economic interests in a "worldwide flow of goods and capital." It has even been argued that Houqua engineered these networks to the "detriment of British commercial profitability." Russell & Co. represented an opportunity, then, to reconfigure the balance of commerce in Canton. For the American merchants as well, this symbiosis was extremely profitable and desirable. Houqua's patronage afforded the firm prestige and a stable flow of goods and funds. The Forbeses, sensitive to the stock the Chinese placed in familial ties, in turn used their special relationship with Houqua to justify bringing other family members into the fold of Russell & Company. Robert Bennet Forbes and then Paul Siemen Forbes were each introduced to Houqua through the influence of the family name. They both became chief intermediaries between the firm and the Chinese merchant.[32] Robert Bennet Forbes traced this close relationship back to Perkins and Co., and Thomas T. Forbes. While the decorum with which the Forbeses maintained such relationships may have been part of a calculated American effort to diffuse rising tensions on the eve of the Opium War, the reverence with which Robert Bennet Forbes described Houqua in his *Reminiscences* underscored the importance of the Chinese merchant's patronage to the firm and its interests.[33]

Coolidge's actions were thus both presumptuous and miscalculated, taking the Houqua-Forbes relationship for granted. By mismanaging Houqua's business in London, Coolidge jeopardized the prized contact Russell & Co. had cultivated in Canton. Then, by opposing Robert Bennet Forbes's admission to the firm, Coolidge offended the Russell & Co. partners and Houqua further, each possessing a special relationship with the Forbes family. Aware that things in Canton were not going in his favor, Coolidge wrote to Augustine Heard Sr., recuperating in Boston, and made plans with the latter's consent to start a new firm should Coolidge find, upon arrival in Canton, that his agreement with Russell & Co. had been terminated.[34] The 1839 decision at Canton to drop Coolidge from the firm was unanimous, and when Coolidge reached the Thirteen Factories that winter, Robert Bennet Forbes met him to outline the conditions of his departure.[35] Indignant, Coolidge was initially of a mind to start his new enterprise under the name of Russell & Co., but cooler heads prevailed, and at the urging of Robert Bennet Forbes and Houqua he dropped the issue.[36] Instead, Coolidge formed the new firm under the unsullied name of Augustine Heard & Co., with Augustine Heard Sr. and George Dixwell as partners, neither of whom were in Canton at the time.[37]

A little over a year later Coolidge found himself at the center of more scandal, this time inviting the entire foreign community's derision. When John Heard arrived in Canton in 1841 to enter the new firm as a clerk, he found a "perfect war ... raging against" Coolidge.[38] The cause had to do with the aftermath of the incident involving Coolidge's detainment at Canton in May. The very night the foreign merchants quit the factories, Chinese soldiers launched an attack and in the disorder the factories were ransacked.[39] Elliot called upon those who lost possessions in the rioting to submit claims for indemnification. Many of the requests were reasonable, with the largest belonging, as expected, to the British firms Jardine Matheson & Co. ($66,450) and Gemmel & Co. ($140,428). There were very few individual claims submitted, and David Jardine's only came to $1,000. The Americans, in total, claimed $41,243. Coolidge personally accounted for a staggering $33,710 of this.[40] The *Canton Register*, rounding off the sums, published an even higher total of $36,000.[41] The *Canton Register* and the

TABLE 1.1
Coolidge's claim for indemnification, based on an 1841 editorial in the *Canton Press*

Office furniture	$1,640
House furniture	$4,570
Wardrobe	$1,800
Comprador's and servant's effects	$1,300
Books	$400
Cow and dog	$250
"Some item not remembered by us"	$300
Sum: $10,260	
Add 100% for inconvenience	$10,260
Loss of office books	$5,000
Loss of private books	$1,000
Repairs to the Factory	$2,000
Cash taken from treasury	$5,100
Total sum: $33,710.44	

Note: The final number given is the exact total of the claim, with the preceding sums being rounded off in the publication.

Canton Press, both British-run papers, printed incendiary editorials, becoming forums for a debate between Coolidge and his critics that lasted for three weeks. But why, besides its immense total, did Coolidge's claim encourage such emotive and outraged responses?

The anger was initially directed at the absurd sum to which Coolidge felt himself entitled. The *Canton Press* gave the most precise list of the claim (table 1.1), but the numbers did not vary significantly across sources. John Heard recalled a rounded sum (personal inconvenience included) of $30,000, and the *Canton Register* published nearly identical numbers, slightly inflating the amount claimed for personal inconvenience.[42] Most offensive to the wider community were the values placed on furniture, wardrobe, servants' effects, and Coolidge's cow and dog. On publishing the initial claim, the editor of The *Canton Press* expressed astonishment that anyone should be "bold enough to ask" for such a sum, and moreover that it had been granted.[43] The editor of the *Canton Register*, wryer in tone, questioned that "a thrifty U.S.'s [sic] merchant" should have so much in Canton to justify such a request.[44]

In subsequent issues of both papers, critics took up the mantle, and lengthy submissions scrutinized the claim's every detail. "An Englishman" noted that of the thirty-one claimants, only six had totals equaling Coolidge's "household furniture alone." It was also public knowledge that Coolidge kept a sparse office, fitted for only two people. Of the wardrobe value, the "Englishman" balked—"no man can dispute [it]; any man may doubt it." The sum for books invited disbelief, and the estimated $100 requested for the dog—everyone knew it was given to Coolidge as a gift—was "too shameless for comment." As for the servant's effects, even the greatest houses in Canton could not say their servants possessed more than $300 in personal property.⁴⁵ An anonymous commenter in the *Canton Register* launched a similar interrogation, claiming that the "family mansion" of the richest Portuguese in Macao had no more than $4,000 in furniture, and the leading British merchants in Canton could not claim more than $2,000. Besides, in anticipation of hostilities, Coolidge's house had been "so totally emptied of furniture that he had not a chair to offer his visitor." The commenter stated acerbically that while "Coolidge had lost what no sum of money could replace or atone for" (personal letters from family), he seemed content to "sell the expressions of maternal affection for a price." The critique concluded that to entertain such a claim would render English honor in China a "standing jest."⁴⁶

In a statement reprinted in the *Canton Register*, Coolidge defended himself to the *Canton Press*. He had not wished to impose upon the British; rather, he had intended to take all from the Chinese authorities that he "could rightly claim." Besides, he had highballed his claim as he was under the impression a committee would "pass on every item sent in." Instead, Coolidge argued, it had been Captain Elliot who, completely unsanctioned and without the intention to sustain said claims by force, had presented those "of all persons not British subjects."⁴⁷ There had been, after all, murmurs in the community that Coolidge had used his "private friendship" with Elliot to secure the reparations, giving Elliot a percentage and thereby taking advantage of the British.⁴⁸

Deeper underlying tensions affected the commentaries surrounding the claim. Conflicting national policies toward the Opium War had placed stress on Canton's Anglo-American community, and the incident involving Coolidge provided the final push needed to snap already fraying tempers. The British community considered Coolidge to have "knowingly and willingly" placed himself in danger. He had been "frequently warned" to vacate the Thirteen Factories, and "all his countrymen, with a single exception" had left.⁴⁹ Ignoring these warnings, he had been rescued through personal risk to British soldiers, and to observers he possessed great audacity in submitting a claim to the British for compensation.[50] The *Canton Register* extended the issue beyond Coolidge, highlighting the indignity the Americans were believed to have inflicted upon the British: "To think of a claim for losses from those who have been and are now riding roughshod over the ruined English pedestrians in Macao, through the rich fruits of their two years neutral agency—whilst British blood has flowed like water, and British treasure has been scattered by the hand, that will never regather it, to the winds."[51]

More than wary of the Americans' performative neutrality and their parasitic relationship with the British war effort, the British community was incensed. In some ways American merchants were the Opium War's greatest beneficiaries, but their gain was achieved to the detriment of their relationship with the British.[52] The 1844 Treaty of Wanghia (Wangxia 望廈), also known as the "Treaty of Peace, Amity, and Commerce," that American envoy Caleb Cushing signed with the Chinese Governor General Qiying 耆英, highlighted Britain's bellicosity during the previous years, emphasizing instead American neutrality and the desire for "perfect, permanent, universal peace" with China.[53] Yet, despite pretentions of neutrality, American merchants like Coolidge seized upon the opportunity to profit from Sino-British conflicts. In just the second article of the Treaty of Wanghia, the United States laid out the provisions of its own "most favored nation" status, whereby it would receive the same future advantages and privileges granted "by China to any other nation."[54]

In such a manner, escalating hostilities between the Qing and the British provided space for American merchants to operate while destabilizing relations between the United States and the two empires. If U.S. neutrality permitted the nation to promote its republican, anti-imperial political identity on a world stage, the activities of its merchants in China, and even of U.S. consular officials, diverged from the official diplomatic program. Emboldened by the opportunities secured through their own treaty, American merchants increasingly aligned themselves with the British imperial project even while rhetorically denouncing the exploitation of the Qing. Diplomatic language lauding amicable ties with both the Qing and the British thus masked a far more nuanced environment where political ambiguities created economic opportunities for American merchants such as Coolidge.

Such inconsistencies were clear to Chinese officials and the British community, both remaining wary of American designs. Acknowledging the underlying rivalry between the United States and its former ruler, Qing officials advocated divisive tactics, treating Americans preferentially to drive a wedge between the encroaching foreign powers.[55] They engaged, effectively, in a "pedagogical project" that employed "coercion and enticement" to inculcate Americans with reverence for China's diplomatic systems.[56] In one sense it worked. Such brazen exploitations of Sino-British rivalries as Coolidge's audacity to submit a claim while the Qing permitted Sino-American trade to continue frustrated the British community. Qing methods failed, however, to inspire respect for their sovereignty among American merchants, who would increasingly support Britain's bellicosity.

As congress between the United States and the Qing empire increased, Chinese officials became familiar with the facade of U.S. neutrality and the tensions that underlay Anglo-American relations during the mid-nineteenth century. The Qing had once maintained extensive projects expanding the western limits of the empire, mapping these frontiers, and collecting knowledge of foreign lands, but internal concerns in the eighteenth century had diverted attention from the littoral and inland borderlands, resulting in a generation of scholars "ill-prepared to understand and deal with changing power relations" along the coast.[57] Chinese merchants in Canton and the southern coastal region had long been acquainted with the various foreigners who came to trade at the Thirteen Factories, but officials felt ill informed about the West prior to 1840.

The sudden defeats during of the Opium Wars prompted these officials and Qing scholars to promote nuanced studies of the characteristics, culture, and politics of the foreign belligerents.[58] The first war provided the push necessary for Qing officials and scholars to develop a practical interest in the "West" and the workings of the British Empire.[59] Although they would not immediately shift court policy, the resulting Chinese studies provided astute interpretations of the global geopolitical environment.[60] Following the First Opium War, Qing policymakers such as Lin Zexu and his rival Qishan 琦善 launched information gathering drives to bolster the country against future foreign aggression. Observing foreign rivalries, these officials promoted divisive tactics to manage the various foreigners. Reports identified America and France as "the strongest, largest, and most-feared-by-the-English" countries.[61] Officials considered "Americans somehow special, more trustworthy and less predatory than the British," granting American merchants preferential rights to hedge the threat of foreign aggression and enflame Anglo-American rivalries.[62]

Scholars such as Xu Jiyu 徐繼畬 and Wei Yuan 魏源 contributed to this postwar interest in Europe and the Americas, publishing broad geographies that described the world, its history, and its politics, and "greatly influenced the attitudes of their countrymen."[63] Although ambitious in scope, these works situated foreign political relationships within China's cosmological traditions, producing an occidentalist outlook that "responded more to the culture that produced it than to its putative object."[64] Their analyses of foreign relations additionally drew heavily upon translated English accounts published by members of the Society for the Diffusion of Useful Knowledge in China. The self-flattering narratives found in the American missionary Elijah Coleman Bridgman's 1838 *Concise Account of the United States of America* (produced in Chinese specifically for Chinese readers) and British missionary Robert Morrison's translation of *A Brief Account of the English Character*, as well as translated works by the British geographer Hugh Murray, thus influenced the tone of Xu's and Wei's texts.[65]

Wei and Xu were nonetheless sensitive to differences within foreign politics and culture and speculated that the divergent histories of Britain and the United States might be exploited to China's advantage.[66] Xu's *Ying huan zhi lüe* 瀛環志略 (A Short Account of the Maritime Circuit) went into great detail about the American Revolution and the anti-imperial sentiments it inspired. Xu described the distinct characters of Britain, the United States, and their people, underscored the prominence of American merchants at Canton, and clarified how his countrymen might identify their ships.[67] He paid particular attention to the economic and technological advancements of Americans, producing an image of a developed country that, properly courted, had the power to check Britain.[68]

Such insecurities about the triangular relationship between China, the United States, and Britain appeared frequently in official correspondence between the three nations. In December 1842 Qiying guessed that "British and Americans were colluding" to squeeze more favorable treaty rights from the Chinese.[69] Should the conspiracy be true, it was troubling, as "on the eve of the Opium War" Chinese authorities had "unsuccessfully tried to set American merchants against their British cousins."[70] While Americans and British in China squabbled over policy, they often "swallowed their differences in contests with the Chinese."[71] Such was clear to Qing administrators, and an 1842 imperial edict cautioned that all foreigners were treacherous and that foreign representatives used overt respect and submissive language as a "pretext for spying on [the Qing's] internal weak points." The edict, aimed at provincial officials, warned that although Americans were permitted to continue trading, they too should be treated with suspicion, respectfully repelled in their requests for official audiences, and instructed by no means to assist the British.[72]

But if not strictly rivals, the Americans and the British were hardly steadfast allies. The indignation the British community voiced over Coolidge's 1841 claim was a natural extension of the fear that Americans were attempting to take over the "whole trade of China" to the "exclusion" of British merchants, as Hugh Hamilton Lindsay, onetime chairman of the Canton Chamber of Commerce, recorded in 1840.[73] In a tone reminiscent of Chinese concerns about Anglo-American cooperation, Lindsay suggested that the Americans were colluding with Houqua to achieve this. Officially each nation championed cooperation, but private concerns circulated of exploitation, collusion, and prejudice, which circumstances such as Coolidge's antagonized.

The *Canton Press* and the *Canton Register* debates implied that Coolidge received the full amount of his claim, but it is unclear what came of the debacle, and the animosity it inspired eventually passed. Still, the man continued to make himself unwanted in the following years. By 1844 Augustine Heard & Co.'s partners edged Coolidge out as well. Although John Heard had initially been sympathetic and wrote well of Coolidge in retrospect, he and George Dixwell grew cold toward the founding partner. With prospects exhausted, Coolidge departed from China and in the summer of 1844 his shares were divided among his two other partners, John Heard, and Joseph Roberts.[74] With or without Coolidge, there remained plenty of opportunities for tensions to arise between the various communities in Canton, but Coolidge's case study exemplifies the range of anxieties affecting Sino-American, Sino-British, and Anglo-American relations. Issues surrounding cooperation, competition, and questionable neutrality would continue in Canton for the next decade, resulting in a general sentiment where the British believed they were being unfairly singled out by the Chinese, while preferential treatment was being afforded to the American community.[75]

Such issues filled consular letters, the time devoted to debating them pointing to the undercurrent of tension that developed between the Chinese, British, and American communities in Canton. The animosity directed toward Coolidge suggests that despite a general sense of foreign unity, the political differences and divisions drawn along national boundaries during the tense Opium War period effected ill will between the British and Americans. Qing officials' efforts to appease American interests and exacerbate Anglo-American relations contributed to this ill will, even as they kept a wary eye on American activities. The behavior of Americans was, after all, hardly pristine, but their country's diplomatic stance, Britain's violent reputation during and after the Opium War, and the Qing's vested interest in mitigating foreign threats worked together to keep them on a pedestal. From their perch, they could pass judgment on their British contemporaries while benefiting from the various opportunities that British belligerence and Chinese instability produced. Such opportunities were not subtly pursued, however, and both the Chinese and British understood the contradictions inherent in America's "neutral" stance. Therein lay the problem. The duplicity of America's presence in Canton was both explicit and reviled. It built animosity within the foreign community, and in instances when it was particularly obvious it became the subject of heated critique.

DIXWELL LEARNS THE BUSINESS

Months before Coolidge arrived in China to establish Augustine Heard & Co., the escalating violence of the Opium War forced the British to temporarily retire from the compound at Canton to Macao, leading to the most obvious (and mutually beneficial) system whereby Americans profited from Britain's war with the Qing. As tensions escalated in August 1839, Lin Zexu leaned heavily on Macao's Portuguese governor, threatening to cut off supplies to the city if the Portuguese and American communities continued to aid the British.[76] Rather than imperil their neighbors, the British withdrew, women and children included, to a flotilla sixty or seventy ships strong anchored at Hong Kong Bay.[77] Bearing witness to both withdrawals, Robert Bennet Forbes noted the bad feeling that pervaded the situation. Prior to the exodus, Americans endeavored to remain aloof from the affair, compradors for American firms going so far as to paint the "names and country" of their employers in Chinese above American doors.

Chinese authorities responded to any remaining American contact with the British with strict reproach. Tightening his squeeze on the British, Lin threatened to remove the servants of the American community, as he had done with the British, since the Americans were "said to entertain the English" at Macao. Forbes related how the British, "very annoyed" because the Americans had remained at Canton, left Macao "with very bad grace," "evidently much annoyed to think the Yankees" quietly remained transacting business.[78] American merchants used this instability between 1839 and 1842 to carry a brisk and unimpeded trade in both legitimate goods and opium. So long as they kept quiet, the Americans stood to profit from the situation, but their position was precarious, balanced between social ties to the British, private commercial interests, and official national policy. A single misstep could jeopardize their relations with both the Chinese officials and British community.

By remaining and unobtrusively going about their affairs, the Americans nurtured new opportunities for themselves and their British peers. Gauging that the Chinese were "very friendly" toward the Americans, Forbes emphasized the need to remain on "good terms with them." Positive relationships would preserve American access to Canton, and Forbes recognized an opportunity to work as middlemen, transshipping goods on behalf of embargoed British firms operating out of the ships in Hong Kong Bay. His hunch was accurate, and on August 29, 1839, Alexander Matheson of Jardine Matheson & Co., the largest British firm in China, engaged Forbes to carry their goods to Canton on consignment.[79] The volume of this business was staggering, and Americans in general drew in "a rich harvest out of the English." The opportunity proved so profitable that it surpassed traditional practices, and a short round trip from Lintin to Whampoa could net $36,000 freight.[80] The trade provided a safer, quicker, and more lucrative opportunity than shipping goods between America and China. Forbes wished English ships "be kept out of port a good while," and as the situation normalized he expressed his regret that the Americans would not retain the "great advantages" they had gained during the period of instability.[81]

The quantity of trade Jardine Matheson & Co. consigned to Russell & Co. was too great for the firm, and although it pained him, Robert Bennet

Forbes was forced to recommend his rival Coolidge to Matheson as a viable alternative.[82] Having just founded Augustine Heard & Co. in 1839, Coolidge cheered that Dent, Jardine, Grey, and other British firms had placed all trade "into the hands of Americans." American firms carried "teas for the English markets" from Canton to Hong Kong harbor to be offloaded and sent "in English [vessels] to Great Britain."[83] This symbiosis resulted in immediate gain for both parties, helping cement contracts between firms such as Jardine and Heard that would outlive the conflict.[84] Still, while such cooperation might suggest the "bitter rivalries and antagonisms" extant between the two countries elsewhere were absent in China, the conduct of American merchants frustrated the British, who resented the lost business and the beneficial treatment Americans received from Qing officials.[85]

It is thanks in part to Robert Bennet Forbes's contacts that George Basil Dixwell fell into his initial role within Augustine Heard & Co., transacting business for the British. Coolidge had intended to bring Nathanial Kinsman in as the third partner of Augustine Heard & Co., and although Kinsman entertained the idea, he passed on it in favor of a partnership with Wetmore & Company. When this plan fell through, Augustine Heard Sr. suggested Dixwell, whose brother John James Dixwell was already lined up as the company's American agent. Dixwell came out to China from New York in 1841, taking a third share as partner in the new firm.[86] Owing to a second stoppage in trade, the British were again conducting their business from Macao, where Dixwell was put to work transshipping goods to Canton for Jardine Matheson & Company.

This consignment trade encompassed more than the general stock of teas, silks, and sundry goods. Opium was the clearest way to increase profits, but before their ships would be permitted upriver to Canton Lin compelled the Americans to sign bonds at Whampoa declaring they would not engage in trafficking the drug.[87] These bonds were signed December 1839, thus technically not applying to Augustine Heard & Co., formed a month later in the new year.[88] The partners, at least, held it in little regard, and by the spring of 1841 Augustine Heard & Co. was carrying great quantities of opium for Jardine Matheson & Co. and their Bombay contacts.[89] It was decided around this time that Dixwell would become the firm's preeminent "opium man." From his station at Macao, he would be able to watch "the coast trade of the drug" while learning from Mr. Sturgis, who was "very shrewd in the illicit traffic."[90]

A VERY PROFITABLE CRISIS

Dixwell's activities represent a paradox of Anglo-American collaboration which merchants in Canton and commenters in the metropole struggled to navigate. For these subjects of the newly independent United States, respect for republicanism, (white) self-determination, and sovereign rights was woven into the fabric of an American founding mythology that celebrated the United States' declaring independence from the British Empire in 1776.[91] Americans in China and the metropole championed these political tenets alongside their cultural and religious values to contrast their presence in China with the British, their commentaries in turn shaping the American public's understanding of the First Opium War. According to American traders such as William Low, by taking military action against the Chinese, their former overlord and current rival in westward continental expansion, the British, or "John Bull," played a familiar antagonistic role in the American imagination.[92] Numerous stateside pamphlets drew parallels between the evils of opium and slavery, condemning the British for proclaiming moral superiority over the latter issue while peddling the drug.[93]

But when discussing the drug trade, American firms were conspicuously absent from the condemnations filling such letters and pamphlets. The fact that America imported a small percentage of the drug compared to the British—an estimated 4 percent in 1833—obscured the extent of their entanglement with the British trade through shipping, storing, and brokering sales of the Indian opium.[94] Even following the war, American merchants were credited with carrying no more than three percent of the trade, and the pious firm Olyphant & Co., which abstained from the trade entirely, was held up as a paragon of correct practice.[95] Olyphant & Co. was in fact the only American company in the Pearl River Delta not selling opium. Still, critics in the metropole, blind to the irony, satirized British distribution of the drug. Newspapers argued that by carrying on the trade through force of arms, the British "forfeited all right to pass judgment" on the United States for its moral indiscretions.[96] John Heard remembered the Opium War as "unjust," even by British standards; the American William Hunter of Russell & Co. called it the "most unjust war ever waged."[97]

By act of omission, John Heard, Hunter, and the partners in American firms such as Augustine Heard & Co. and Russell & Co. sustained the fiction of their abstention, downplaying the illicit side of their business to politicians and the American public even while demanding military protection in the coming war.[98] While the merchants passed the odd judgment on the British community's warmongering and conduct in Canton, opium itself rarely figured in their letters and memoirs. British disregard for Chinese sovereignty may have been contemptible to the republican-minded Yankees, but it would not do to denounce a trade, or a system for that matter, that could so easily generate a profit. It was simpler to skirt the topic entirely. As a result, the drug's trade belonged, in the American imagination, to the British, a fiction made easier to uphold due to the far greater proportion of the trade the British controlled.[99] This denial proved to be the merchants' "greatest contribution to government policy," allowing the American government to "plausibly claim that Americans had respected Chinese laws and that the British had not." As Dael Norwood argues, "The fantasy of American innocence at Canton—the founding myth of the 'special' relationship between China, Britain's latest victim, and the United States, one of its first—was a key part of American policy in China for many years, in large part because the special political situation surrounding its creation made the lie so useful."[100] It should be emphasized, however, that this fantasy of innocence was almost entirely rhetorical, and although they may have denounced the British to those back home, American merchants in China held few pretensions that theirs and the British merchants' intentions differed. In their desire to see China opened by any means to foreign commerce, the two communities were largely of one mind.

This unity of vision was formally realized in 1844 when U.S. diplomats secured the Treaty of Wanghia, which, in addition to commercial benefits, laid out the infamous most-favored-nation clause ensuring the same concessions as Britain's Treaty of Nanking. The treaty banned Americans from trading opium, appearing "at first glance . . . to be more fair to China."[101] Politically empowered by the most-favored-nation clause and disregarding the opium ban entirely, Dixwell expanded Augustine Heard & Co.'s operations, and by 1844 four-fifths of its opium business had spread along the coast.[102] Between 1849 and 1851 Augustine Heard & Co. imported 62,595 chests of the drug to its Wusong station outside Shanghai alone.[103]

Dixwell's assignment brought him into direct collaboration with the British as he learned through Jardine, Matheson & Co. how to deal in opium. The drug in turn became a vital source of revenue for the firm, influencing Dixwell's decision making as senior partner in the following years. The practices Dixwell implemented reflected the gray areas of

FIGURE 1.3. Pearl River Delta, based on Hosea Ballou Morse, *The International Relations of the Chinese Empire* (New York: Longmans, Green, and Company, 1910), 1:1.

Anglo-American cooperation as the company at once aided, profited from, and sought to undercut its British competitors. But to understand how the trade affected business practices and relationships, it is first necessary to sketch the system of opium smuggling that existed in the Pearl River Delta (figure 1.3) and along the China Coast.

Early resistance to Opium smuggling had caused the trade's epicenter to migrate south from the traditional waiting station at Whampoa to Lintin in the 1820s.[104] The compradors of foreign firms selected Lintin as a suitable mooring to restock ships for it had the added benefit of remoteness and came under ambiguous jurisdiction. Here it was more difficult for

Chinese patrols hunting smugglers to exercise their authority than at either Macao or Whampoa. Anchored off the island, the foreign community operated a small fleet of "untouchable" hulks: large vessels at perpetual rest whose masts had been removed and whose decks were covered by a permanent canopy (figure 1.4). These vessels served as warehouses, offices, and accommodation for those engaged in the sale of opium. Clippers inbound from India would offload opium chests onto the hulks to await transfer under armed guard to buyers. The clippers would then fill their now empty holds with rice and proceed upriver to Canton. The Chinese customs superintendent at Whampoa encouraged this trade, granting vessels a break from high port fees as he received imperial favor by logging high imports of the staple grain. Once in Canton, a ship's supercargo would sell their rice and secure a buyer for their opium stock at Lintin, for which the supercargo issued a receipt. The ship would then load up with tea or specie and return home.[105]

Once buyers had secured the cargo, they arranged to transfer the opium chests stored off Lintin up the coast to other receiving stations or into the

FIGURE 1.4. Opium hulk stationed outside Shanghai, c. 1860. Roofed and stripped of sails and masts. *Source*: Virtual Shanghai, https://www.virtualshanghai.net/Photos/Images?ID=1774.

smuggling networks permeating the mazelike Pearl River Delta. Narrow, heavily manned, many-oared vessels called "Fast Crabs" (*kuai xie* 快蟹) or "Scrambling Dragons" (*pa long* 爬龍) brought receipts from the sales upriver where they picked up their cargo and disappeared into one of the many inland waterways separating Lintin and Canton.[106] These ships could easily outstrip the heavier junks that might give chase, and their bow-mounted swivel cannon served as a powerful deterrent to the unmotivated Chinese authorities. Nor was it in the interest of these authorities, appointed by Lin Zexu's predecessor Deng Tingzhen 鄧廷楨, to clamp down on the trade, since they received regular bribes known as "squeeze" to turn a blind eye. Obliged to maintain the appearance of vigilance, they would give half-hearted chase and, in some cases, even stage mock battles with smugglers to satisfy their superiors. They would then turn in opium chests received from the smugglers to convince Deng that their tactics were working.[107]

With Britain effectively out of the way, there were a few means by which Dixwell could exploit the opium trade to Augustine Heard & Co.'s benefit. The most obvious, and safest, was through consignment shipping and brokerage. Dixwell chartered ships to carry British goods to Canton for sale and while there would secure a buyer for British opium being held aboard the American hulks downriver.[108] The firm levied a holding fee, labeled demurrage, on every opium chest secured in the hulks, a brokerage fee on the final transaction, and a shipping fee on the legitimate goods taken to Canton. Dixwell was ambitious, however, and saw further opportunity for expanding the trade. Having used the opportunity afforded by the cessation of British trade to get into the business, Dixwell immediately set about fostering Parsi contacts in Calcutta and Bombay, the most consistent being Kessresung Kushalchand at Bombay, who alongside the prominent merchant Jamsetji Jejeebhoy did a substantial trade with Jardine Matheson & Company.[109] With the situation in China returning to normal in 1844, Augustine Heard & Co. began to act extensively as consignment merchants for the Indian opium trade.

Dixwell wrote enthusiastically to Augustine Heard Sr. in America that opium was the future of business in China and, perhaps inspired by the operations of Jardine Matheson & Co., ordered two ships from America so the firm might carry the drug on its own. Augustine Heard Sr. denounced the move, thinking it foolhardy to invest capital directly in ship ownership, but Dixwell assured him that trade was changing and that the move was a timely one. Besides, the firm would continue to broker trade for its Indian contacts, which was steadily increasing and provided an unparalleled source of revenue.[110] Aboveboard brokering of cotton for Jardine Matheson & Co. secured only a modest return. Dixwell charged the British firm roughly 1 percent on commission and shroffage, earning, for example, $433 on a sale worth $42,410. Meanwhile, on a sale of moderate quality opium for Kushalchand totaling only $6,222, the firm levied fees on demurrage, freight, insurance, and commission, earning $803.[111] The cut on smaller and more regular opium transactions was consistently higher, and by a substantial amount, than any other good the firm could act as agents for.

Dixwell also cannily sought ways to break the British hold over the opium trade. Despite a surplus in opium at Bombay, it was hard to acquire the drug, since British merchants were "keen as sharks" to get it.[112] Jardine Matheson & Co. enjoyed the largest share of this trade, running its own fleet on the "country trade" between India and China. Just as Russell & Co. had been "made" through Houqua's patronage, Jardine Matheson & Co. built its initial success upon the opium trade and the patronage of the Bombay merchant-philanthropist Jejeebhoy.[113] In 1846, however, Dixwell had it from regular client Kushalchand that Jejeebhoy was "far from satisfied" with his business through Jardine Matheson & Co. In a letter labeled "Quite Private," Kushalchand disclosed that the shipment to which the letter was attached was in fact assigned a pseudonym and actually belonged to Jejeebhoy. The latter had decided to test Augustine Heard & Co., and should it perform better than Jardine it might "get into Sir Jamsetjee's good graces." Regardless of performance, it was imperative that "Sir Jamsetjee's present adventure" be "kept secret."[114] The firm's later accounting does not suggest that much came of this clandestine transaction, but the fact that it was even a possibility demonstrates the ability Americans had to simultaneously cooperate with and exploit their British contemporaries.

On the surface, the relationship between the British and American merchant communities was one of gentlemanly competition. Merchants socialized and dined together, treating each other with civility. Such public displays of good faith were important for both the social and commercial well-being of the foreign community, and Dixwell's anxious remarks about one dinner with Alexander Matheson suggest that he was well aware of the importance of such connections. Dixwell assured Augustine Heard Sr. that during the dinner he had taken great pains to "treat the great man

[Matheson] just as [he] would any other guest." Dixwell's colleague "Ryan," the new American supercargo of Jardine's and apparently struggling in his new role, was no less nervous, although far less tactful.[115] His "excess of politeness," "pointless remarks," and "evident dread" seemed to "disgust" Matheson.[116] Much of the firm's early success rode on its partners' abilities to make lasting impressions and the strength of these interpersonal relationships between firms. Augustine Heard & Co. even placed William Jardine's nephew David Jardine in the firm to look on and learn "all he could about it." John Heard recalled years later that the "personal friendship" he formed with Jardine "lasted many years" and "was of much service" when he and Jardine became the heads of their respective firms.[117]

Moving from being agents to trading in their own right, Augustine Heard & Co. transitioned into the opium trade through the relationships Dixwell cultivated with the British traders. The firm's cooperation with the British during the cessations of trade in the 1840s furnished it with the contacts, capital, and know-how to exploit the smuggling networks in the Pearl River Delta. Dixwell then used this knowledge when trade resumed to establish the company's business. Still, American and British firms were competitors, and while they had no issue working together if the circumstances were right, they still struggled to best each other whenever possible. James Murray Forbes recalled years later that such practices were anything but productive. While lauded on the surface as friendly or "gentlemanly" competition, "bitter" rivalries existed below the surface, as did ambitions to undercut competitors.[118]

TWO SIDES OF THE SAME COIN?

Coolidge's and Dixwell's relationships with the British merchant community in the Pearl River Delta represent the Janus-faced nature of Anglo-American collaboration. When analyzed closely, the activities of both individuals reflect the calibrated relationships that existed between American and British merchants and the Chinese authorities. Sociopolitical tensions unearthed through the First Opium War come to the surface through Coolidge's case, while Dixwell's demonstrates the cooperative systems that developed as a result of the same conflict. Neither suggest that there was a strict dichotomy between competition and collaboration among American, British, and Chinese communities in the delta.[119] Each case was made possible through the nuanced relationships and power struggles that developed between the three groups.

Although the British community condemned Coolidge for attempting to benefit from their blood, sweat, and tears during the Opium War, Coolidge was still able to submit his claim for compensation due to the close relationship he fostered with Elliot. Besides, even as Americans denounced British bellicosity, both were generally aligned in their desire to see more concessions extracted from the Chinese. Yet, as Coolidge's claim suggests, Americans could push the boundaries of their relationship with the British too far, resulting in an outpouring of pent-up indignation. Dixwell, too, managed to draw upon the collaborative spirit of the communities to turn a great profit for both his firm and Jardine Matheson & Company. As Robert Bennet Forbes expressed, however, this profit was built upon Sino-British conflict, and it was actually best for the Americans if the hostile situation continued. Americans capitalized on the opportunity to learn the opium trade, seeking new ways to undercut their onetime trading partner and taking an increasing share in what had initially been a British monopoly.

The competition and collaboration that characterized both cases were direct products of Sino-British conflict, and within the tense setting of the Opium War Americans attempted to leverage their standing with both the British and Chinese for personal gain. Their efforts may have been presented as beneficial to their British contemporaries, and in some respects so proved to be, but they were still undertaken in large part for self-serving purposes. Americans thus formed a "mutable" group, variously unified or fractured according to the internal pressures coming from within the foreign community and externally from "Chinese merchants and officials."[120] The Chinese permitted Coolidge to continue trading in Canton as an American individual, but when his property was destroyed, he turned to the British in search of compensation. Dixwell likewise leveraged the neutral position of the United States to carry British trade to Canton, all the while violating anti-opium trading laws and transshipping British goods in spite of the bond the American merchants had signed at Whampoa to abstain from either trade. The legality of their enterprise was tenuous, but Augustine Heard & Co. pressed on regardless of any guilt they might have felt about carrying on trading while the British merchants lay off Hong Kong in their floating community. Their extraterritorial rights gained following the war would only serve to embolden the American merchant community.

The opposing experiences of Coolidge and Dixwell confirm that there was little in the way of a "cohesive" American trading network.[121] A combination of personal interests, beliefs, and commercial aspirations guided each trader. Still, a pattern emerges within both cases of Americans acting according to local conditions, independent of and often in direct opposition to the metropolitan sociopolitical stance toward China.[122] The opium trade and resultant war, condemned in principle among the American public and the U.S. government, was supported implicitly through Coolidge's claim and explicitly through the firm's later business.[123] When compared against the easy partnership fostered between Augustine Heard & Co. and Jardine Matheson & Co., the responses to Coolidge in the *Canton Register* and the *Canton Press* suggest that British anger responded more to the arbitrariness of the American merchants than to their participation in the opium trade itself. That the American public and even some American merchants should continue to denounce the British for propagating a trade and a war from which they openly benefited was absurd to the British community at Canton.

Yet, despite their indignation at the American merchants, there remained room for British gain within Americans' "parasitic" activities. For the Americans, British bellicosity promised future opportunity, while for the British, the Americans provided a convenient means to sidestep the fallout of their country's conflicts with China. It was therefore in the foreign community's best commercial interests to bury the hatchet and cooperate. Besides, the community in Canton was small, and it was necessary that merchants at least put on a show of getting along. Especially in the days of the Hong trade, the same individuals saw each other day in and day out, and the dictates of social life required the interned merchants keep peace. American and British merchants would inevitably be at the same dinners, participate in the same boat races, and work with the same clients.[124] In such a confined space, gossip was among the most practiced pastimes. So, while nationally based tensions existed, the performance of Anglo-American cooperation put a placid face on the China trade.

Coolidge and Dixwell were both active at a time when the China trade was undergoing defining changes. Their narratives pull into focus the ambiguities that existed in the relationships between traders during this transformative period in the Canton trade's history. They further highlight the conditions that would shape the relationships formed within Hong Kong in the years to come. By isolating this brief but complex period through the specific lenses of Dixwell, Coolidge, and their associates, the conflicting interests that affected cohesion and competition between British and American traders emerge. In a sense, both Coolidge's and Dixwell's experiences are extraordinary. The circumstances through which Coolidge formed Augustine Heard & Co. and Dixwell came out to China stemmed from a rift in America's most prominent merchant house, and both were accordingly privileged from the contacts and the capital that the situation afforded them. While Coolidge continued to undermine his own reputation, Dixwell set about establishing that of the firm, and both their paths drew the attention and comments of the wider foreign community. Coolidge's notoriety among the British and American traders and Dixwell's primacy in the opium trade meant that both individuals were thoroughly interwoven into the developing narrative of the China trade.

Coolidge's case became a catalyst for the outpouring of national frustrations but would also not have come about at all had it not been for Sino-British conflict and Coolidge's good standing with Elliot. Dixwell's example was quite the opposite and represented the potential for cooperation and mutual benefit that existed between the two communities. When analyzed further, however, Dixwell's also reflects a more calculating side to American commerce that sought to undercut the British competition. Common to both cases is a fluid relationship that conformed to the specific circumstances of trade and foreign community in the Pearl River Delta.

Coolidge's and Dixwell's efforts to navigate the shifting sociopolitical context of the Pearl River Delta, when contextualized within the triangular relationship between the United States, and the British Empire and Qing Empire, help clarify how American merchants could vilify the British in their letters home even as their actions in China lent implicit support to the activities of Britain's merchants and military. For China and Britain, the activities of these two American merchants explain, in part, the reactions of both communities toward the wider American community, and in the case of the Chinese especially they reveal a calculated response to opium trading that sought to exploit the fault lines apparent within the foreign community. The Americans may have clandestinely traded for the British, justified through a rhetoric of neutrality and amity, but Chinese authorities maintained a close eye on their activities and actively hunted out ways to inflame Anglo-British rivalry.

With the First Opium War's end, foreign enterprises acquired the means to expand their trade in Canton and along the China coast. As an immediate result of the war, the Chinese ceded Hong Kong to the British, and the colony subsequently grew into a regional entrepôt. British merchants, already operating out of Hong Kong Bay, made immediate use of the island, and the small community of Victoria grew on the northern shore. It would be another decade before the Americans moved to the colony en masse. This brief period in Anglo-American, and Sino-foreign relations, however, laid the foundation for the community that eventually developed in Hong Kong. Moving from Canton into an officially British sociopolitical sphere, new tensions and circumstances for cooperation inevitably arose. In this larger and more complex space, Americans would be required to further reconcile their national viewpoints with the standards of the new and diverse community, a process already well underway within the Canton system.

Chapter Two

A HOUSE IS NOT A HOME

The American Merchant House in Hong Kong

On October 8, 1856, Chinese officers at Canton boarded a lorcha called *Arrow*, seized its crew, and allegedly lowered the ship's British flag. Belonging to the Chinese owner Fong Ah-ming, the *Arrow* had previously been registered in Hong Kong as a British vessel and was crewed entirely by Chinese sailors, the exception being the captain, a young Irishman named Thomas Kennedy.[1] While it was true that the ship's registration had expired weeks prior to the incident, it was doubtful whether it had been flying the British flag when seized. To complicate the matter, the ship's crew were suspected pirates. Regardless, the British consul, Harry Parkes viewed the event as a grave insult, insisting that officials had overstepped their authority by boarding a vessel flying British colors. Parkes demanded a public apology and, following a breakdown in communication between the Hong Kong Governor John Bowring and himself, and the Chinese commissioner Yeh Mingchen (Ye Mingchen 葉名琛), used the event as pretext to seize a Chinese warship, a junk, and the forts at Canton in retaliation.[2] By the month's end the British had landed troops outside the city's walls, hostile action escalating into what became known as the *Arrow* or Second Opium War.

John Heard believed that the British "knew perfectly well" that the *Arrow*'s captain was "no better than a pirate." After all, the license for a flag "could easily be bought." The British simply needed "something they could hang a quarrel on."[3] Like other American commenters, John Heard's sentiments reflected the popular U.S. stance toward China.[4] U.S. diplomats and members of the American community who presented themselves as neutral agents in China failed to see why the British were in "such a craze" for "a row" with the Qing. John Heard reproached the British, "all agog for a bit of plunder," musing that the conflict had "all the elements of one of the little wars in which England delights." Still, he fancied himself impartial. He felt, after all, that the Chinese too had been "obstinate" and "conceited," acting without understanding "the military power of foreign nations."[5]

Americans played a small role in the ensuing two-year conflict despite their neutral protestations. In response to Chinese forces' bombarding one of their ships in 1856, American naval forces destroyed the barrier forts at Canton. When British forces stormed the city, U.S. consul James Keenan was seen at the breached walls proudly waving the American flag. Otherwise, involvement was checked.[6] Americans avidly followed the war's progress, not least because concessions that would be secured through the joint Anglo-French campaign against the Qing promised to benefit all Euro-American nations.[7] The new treaties signed in 1858 and ratified in 1860 would expand the privileges of foreign nationals in China and transform Sino-foreign trade, but a more immediate and monumental change was to occur during the war in December 1856. That month, British and French forces blockaded and bombarded Canton, and, as the foreign merchants living and trading there were evacuated, the Thirteen Factories burned to the ground.[8] Returning to the site in 1860, the destruction stunned Albert Heard: "Where three storied houses stood not a brick remains, not a token or sign of the foundations; high piles of rubbish here and there mark generally the position of the foreign factories, but where was our house, the church, the club house, etc.? I could only guess ... but nothing remained as evidence from Canton."[9]

John Heard admitted he was sorry the factories were gone but noted wryly that their destruction "closed a chapter of the most peculiar life that was ever led by white men anywhere."[10] Prior to the *Arrow* incident there had been few Americans in Hong Kong. All the major firms, excepting the British companies Jardine Matheson & Co. and Dent & Co., were headquartered upriver in Canton. After the razing of the Thirteen Factories, the balance shifted, and the upstart British colony became the symbolic center of Sino-foreign trade. The British rebuilt Canton's foreign settlement on Shamian 沙面, a sandbar in the Pearl River, but the damage had been done, and Canton would never again be as prominent as it once was. Anticipating the growth of Hong Kong, Augustine Heard Jr. had begun to prepare a house and office in the British colony two years prior to the Second Opium War. By the time the merchants relocated in 1856, the new lodgings were ready, and trade quickly resumed John Heard described the new house as "commodious and cheap" although "not very spacious or convenient."[11]

This new house provides an appropriate setting through which to explore the "private" lives of Hong Kong's American merchants. The house-as-subject affords opportunities to use the subjective quotidian experiences of those within to interpret the "general," "extraordinary," and "exceptional" within wider urban histories.[12] The history of a house, of necessity, is wrapped in that of its neighborhood, and its neighborhood in that of the town or city. Extrapolated to its broadest limit, it serves as a site where microhistory intersects with national and international histories, providing a setting within which "big themes" can be reduced to granular details.[13] The premise that domestic space provided a retreat in which one could "live out [their] inner lives and family lives" in private, and therefore be "genuinely" themselves, overlooks the unique ways domestic space functioned in a public and globally entangled colonial context such as Hong Kong.[14]

The Heards' experiences of life in the colony suggest that for a time the merchant house continued to serve dual roles as a place of business and a communal residence for partners and clerks as it had in Canton. It was lively, filled with servants, employees, and family and a regular cycle of visiting officials, dignitaries, business associates, and military men. It operated simultaneously as a domestic and commercial space that in many ways anchored the transient foreign society. To onlookers, the company house may have appeared a "seamless community of class and colonial interests," but there were "internal discrepancies" and divisions.[15] Under one roof individuals from distinct racial, ethnic, and class backgrounds lived and worked; wealthy white partners, their aspiring white clerks, native-born compradors, and laborers. As had the factories at Canton, the form (at once public and private) and function (paradoxically transient and permanent) of the domestic spaces Americans such as the Heards inhabited in Hong Kong accordingly mirrored the norms and anxieties of colonial life.[16]

The colonial house was a complex site onto which white settlers projected their imperial anxieties. It came to be imbued with various coded meanings. Among other things, the house was a symbol of prestige and demonstrated colonial control: it reinforced the separation of indigenous and white bodies; it was gendered, considered the refuge of white women; a tense and growing rift between imported metropolitan and developing colonial cultures shaped it and its design demonstrated foreign mastery over the environment. Its symbolic domestic meaning was particular, however, to the unique circumstances of each colony. The American household in nineteenth-century Hong Kong, in particular, was a semiprivate, performative, and transitory space. Within it, the preexisting American identity and conduct was recalibrated according to colonial understandings of race, culture, and class, each reflecting the extent to which British Hong Kong "made" the American household.

COLONIAL DOMESTICITY

Colonizers throughout the British Empire imbued a range of context-specific meanings into domestic space. As such, this private and material setting served as a microcosm within which wider colonial issues arose and played out. How colonial subjects structured private space reflected the tense balance they struck between conforming to metropolitan norms and creating their own distinct identity as they produced or adapted to colonial cultures.[17] Such processes have been most apparent in the ways the British colonial community organized their households across the empire. Where possible, the British in India or in ports such as Shanghai formed closed communities that attempted to recreate a familiar lifestyle.[18] Their homes took on a gendered dimension in which male and female spheres were constructed and contested.[19] In this gendered space, women were considered the "main bearers" of metropolitan domestic life It was believed that under their guidance, the house could represent a feminine "civilizing" imperial mission operating parallel to the masculine "acquisition of territorial power."[20] Yet, while there was a metropolitan character to the colonial household, local influences "permeated" such spaces.[21] The transformative power of these influences depended, in large part, "on the size of the [British] community," which affected its ability to remain self-contained.[22] Greater numbers forming a homogeneous community resulted in an easier time preserving one's metropolitan traits. The ways in which one organized their domestic space thus remained vulnerable to broader societal, colonial, and metropolitan forces.

Comparisons with colonial domesticity as it developed across the empire and in China's treaty ports provide the foundation upon which to understand how Americans structured their household in Hong Kong. Although the American merchant house was a non-British space in a British colony, similar processes of recreating and assimilating nevertheless shaped the merchants' domestic lives. As with the British colonial household, local influences from the surrounding communities permeated the American merchant house, the most prominent communities in this case being the Chinese and British. Although Americans attempted to reproduce their national lifestyle, the small size of the community made them more susceptible to these external influences. Yet, as Augustine Heard & Co.'s house suggests, Hong Kong's domestic spaces differed in a few specific ways from their British India and Canton predecessors, while other characteristics appeared in a magnified capacity. One core breakdown was the binary oppositions of private/public and male/female spheres. Indeed, even in the U.S. and British metropoles, it is unclear that the "home" ever functioned as truly "a private space." The presence of servants and regular social visits brought "the public domain into the private"; private and public spheres were, rather, ideological constructs whose meaning was specific to time and place.[23] The colonial context helped dislodge the "binary oppositions of public and private spheres," while the inherent gender imbalances of white colonial society meant that although the domestic sphere was often conceived of as a female space, men often "contributed to and were shaped by" it in substantial ways.[24]

As in Canton and Macao, the American household in Hong Kong was a space where the public sphere consistently transgressed the private. This "private" realm of the American merchant was one in which life was on display and public norms trumped private behaviors. Because the British formed the majority of Hong Kong's white foreign community throughout this period, they set the standard for what these public norms were, and these standards had to be upheld as a matter of social propriety. Hong Kong further rectified, in theory, the separation between "feminine" Macao and "masculine" Canton that had of necessity taken hold during old China trade days. These spheres merged in the Hong Kong merchant house, even if demographic imbalances meant it retained more masculine than feminine characteristics.[25]

Few American women migrated to Hong Kong for any extended period of time, and as a rule their presence threatened the widely held belief that Hong Kong was a temporary phase in the American merchant's life. The environment of the house reflected this desire for impermanence. According to the precedent set in Canton, life was comfortable for the American China merchant, but few ever intended to stay more than a handful of years.[26] The house was therefore not a home. Communal living, inconsistent lodging, regular absences, and a steady rotation of personnel encouraged transience. It developed what Augustine Heard Jr. perceived as an "entirely masculine" quality, making it inappropriate for settling in and raising a family.[27]

The unique organization of the American Hong Kong household compared with those in more established colonial societies confirms that domesticity evolved independently across the British Empire. To some extent earlier habits such as those formed in Anglo-Indian spaces were reproduced in other colonies, but the case of the American merchant house in Hong Kong suggests that the process of adapting colonial norms was a negotiated one. In some respects the house conformed to British norms, but in others it challenges assumptions about colonial domestic space's function and characteristics. The space's deviations—masculine, transient, public—from the norm suggest an alternative account of how colonial practices were "selectively refashioned to create and maintain the social distinctions of imperial control," or, rather, white prestige and British control.[28] Such deviations were not, however, radical. In establishing themselves, American merchants often adopted, or at least tolerated, colonial ideas about race, class, and culture, reflected in the physical structuring of their houses. In general the organization of the home was a process of negotiation and selective adaptation, for the American merchant lifestyle in nineteenth-century Hong Kong welded together vestiges of habits developed across the British Empire, imported to Canton by the British East India Company, and picked up by the previous generation of American traders at the Thirteen Factories.[29]

THE COMPANY HOUSE

According to their descriptions, the Heards mostly transplanted their Canton factory to Hong Kong. The very designation of the company home as "factory" derived from British India, where such buildings were the residence and offices of the "factor" or trader. Kitchens, treasuries, servants' quarters, and "godowns" or storehouses occupied the factories' ground floors, while offices, parlors, dining rooms, and personal quarters made up the top.[30] Colonnaded archways and a large veranda fronted the Canton factories, an architectural preference of the 1840s that would find favor in Hong Kong.[31] From Augustine Heard Jr.'s descriptions, the company's new house in Hong Kong reflected those styles adapted from the merchants' Canton experiences.

In January 1856 Augustine Heard Jr. hired Kaiping 開平 native, contractor, and entrepreneur Tam Achoy (Tan Yacai 譚亞才) to build a house on a square of land in Victoria, bordered by Staunton road to the north, Aberdeen to the east, Caine Road to the south, and a public road to the west.[32] Situated on "what was then the outskirts of town," the house appeared an imposing three-story building of 82 by 75 feet with two upper floors set upon a foundation enclosing a raised basement housing the servants.[33] The building included an entrance hall, encircling veranda, dining room, pantry, drawing room, anteroom, library, five bedrooms, and three bathrooms. The firm employed Tam again in 1857 to expand the property, and on October 27, 1857, it subcontracted Yang Run 楊閏 to add a billiard room. The initial work cost the company $7,750. In contrast to the relatively open lower floors, the upper story was fortress-like. Augustine Heard Jr. had Tam install iron bars on the windows, trap doors, venetian blinds, and warning bells.[34] At night the partners mounted blunderbusses "on the verandah [sic]" and stashed small arms "close at hand."[35]

Augustine Heard Jr.'s measures seem drastic, but until 1859 Anglo-French hostilities with China continued, and the threat of invasion—not to mention theft and robbery—darkened the minds of the colony's inhabitants. He feared that the isolated house, a mile from Murray Barracks on the foreign settlement's western edge and bordering the densely populated Chinese neighborhood of Taipingshan, was particularly vulnerable. The upper floors, being the refuge of white personnel, were accordingly made defensible, and foreign watchmen or "Manila men" were hired to stand vigil.[36]

A HOUSE IS NOT A HOME

Albert Heard confirmed as much in an 1857 letter home, reassuring that his brother's precautions had "warded off all danger."[37] The space had been made at once a lodging and a bastion. Although no tragedy befell the Heards during the war, emergency legislation such as Ordinance No. 2, passed on December 16, 1856, seemingly justified Augustine Heard Jr.'s paranoia. The measure imposed a harsh curfew on the Chinese community, lending credence to foreign anxieties that the Chinese were hostile while counterproductively nurturing "the very hostility that the colonists found so unsettling."[38]

The defensive construction of the house reflects architectural preferences that first gained purchase in British India. Early British houses at Bengal had two stories, the lower floors serving the same functions as in the Heard house, with the upper floors reserved for living quarters. These lower floors had small windows and a heavy door to discourage thieves, while the upper floors boasted broad, airy, well-ventilated rooms and an open veranda. Over time, as the residential areas in Bengal became more secure, the lower floors became more habitable and the space opened up.[39] Such changes occurred as the foreign community grew more certain about the security of their position, the blueprints for the Heard's Shanghai house (figure 2.1) and for

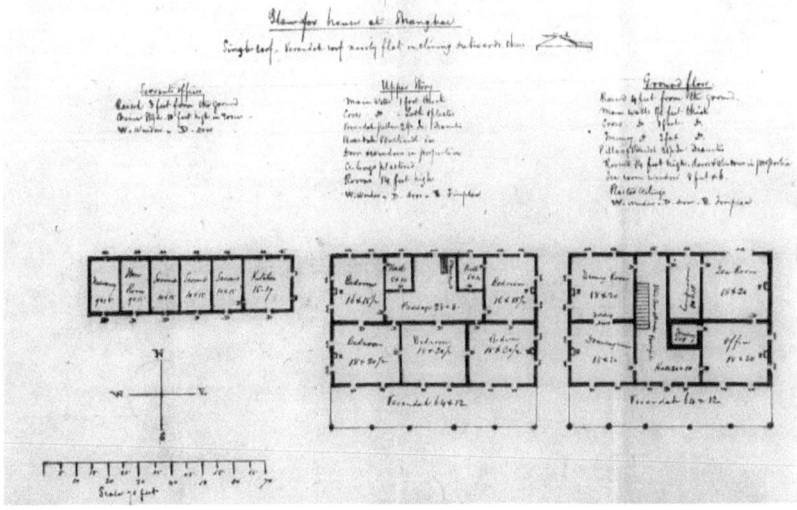

FIGURE 2.1. Augustine Heard & Co.'s Shanghai house. *Source*: Plan for house at Shanghai, Shanghai, undated, Case 30, HBS.

A HOUSE IS NOT A HOME

later properties likely at Kobe and Hong Kong certainly reflecting such confidence, but established in a young colony with the Second Opium War underway and positioned on the margins of the British settlement, the first Hong Kong house conformed more to the earlier iterations of the India houses.[40]

In contrast, the company's Praya Grande and Rua dos Prazeres houses, across the Pearl River Delta at Macao, with its established foreign enclave, were more in line with the later evolutions of the colonial house.[41] One of the houses—although it is impossible to tell which Augustine Heard Jr. referred to—had thirteen rooms, a separate wing, a large garden, thick walls, and an ocean-facing veranda.[42] The grander of the Macao houses, such as the company's at 39 Praya Grande, rented by George Weller in 1873, fronted the beach and were considerably more open than the new structures erected in Hong Kong (figure 2.2).[43] Augustine Heard Jr. noted none of the defensive measures that characterized the Hong Kong house. The initial worrisome location bordering Taipingshan was short lived, however. Augustine Heard Jr. left China for America in 1857, and two years later the

FIGURE 2.2. An idealized sketch of a Western villa at Macao. *Source*: George Chinnery 'Private House at Macao, 1844, pen and brown ink with graphite on paper, asset no. 284621001, British Museum.

FIGURE 2.3. St. John's Cathedral (left), Augustine Heard & Co. house (center), and City Hall (right) in Hong Kong, c. 1873. *Source*: William Pryor Floyd, Wellcome Collection 29663i, https://wellcomecollection.org/works/dpenf74y.

company acquired the former Supreme Court building, located centrally above the parade grounds by Murray Barracks (figure 2.3). This house stood on a "bluff near Queen's Road," propped up by a retaining wall.[44] The property was "beautifully situated," overlooking the harbor, and well integrated into the white foreign community, with something always "going on" at the parade ground below.[45] Here, the lodgings and offices were contained in one building as they had been in Canton. The Heards still maintained their Caine Road property, and over the years they would purchase or rent various other buildings throughout the colony (figure 2.4).

As with those in the Canton factory, the layout of the rooms in the Heards' Hong Kong houses demonstrated "a clear social hierarchy."[46] During Gustavus Tuckerman's 1858 trip to Hong Kong, Augustine Heard & Co. partner Francis ("Frank") Parker provided Tuckerman with temporary lodgings. Tuckerman described Parker's room "over the office, with the

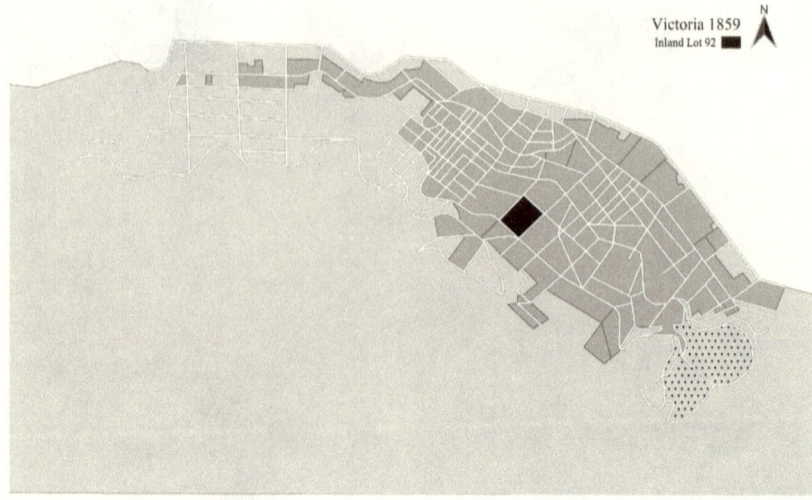

FIGURE 2.4. Location of the Heards' first Hong Kong home (black), based upon "Plan of a Portion of the City of Victoria, Hong Kong, 1859," CO 700, TNA. Image by author.

clerks" as "rather lonely" and "not very aristocratic." The "sahibs," as the Indian-based Tuckerman referred to the partners, lived "top side" while the clerks, with all "their rooms about one," slept below. Tuckerman, struggling financially himself, was quite content with the accommodation and took his meals according to whim with either the "Nabobs" (another of his terms for the partners, commonly used to designate wealthy men who had derived a fortune from Asia), or "down stairs" with the clerks.[47]

The physical layout both Augustine Heard Jr. and Tuckerman described represented a vertical physical hierarchy that mirrored a class one. Parker may have resided alongside the clerks, but, breaking from Canton tradition, the partners and clerks at Hong Kong dined separately. The servants, in turn, occupied the lowest floor of the house, alongside the kitchens and storehouses. Space was finite, however, and tenures were temporary. Regardless of station, rooms shuffled to accommodate the firm's ever-shifting personnel. This reshuffling denied employees the opportunity to settle into the place. When George Heard arrived in Hong Kong in 1873, he set up temporarily "topside," above the billiard room, but he had designs to move "down to [his] old room" over the offices when "Downs" left.[48] In the meantime he shared the upper floor with Albert Heard, Albert's wife Mary Livingston, and their dogs.[49]

The Hong Kong house's internal segregation also mirrored an external one, where, in theory, the 'separation of the native population" from the colony's white inhabitants was "nearly absolute."[50] In colonial or semicolonial spaces such as India or Shanghai, British settlement planners maintained such separation by using the orderly enclosure of "civil lines" to distinguish the supposedly "sprawling," "cramped," "irrational," "savage" natives from the "ordered," "spacious," "rational," "controlled" British.[51] Reproducing this practice, Hong Kong's initial white and Chinese settlements were separated. The former occupied premium land while the latter settled on the surrounding hills and beaches as landowners made efforts to limit the spread of Chinese housing.[52]

Yet, despite these efforts to enforce separation, colonial space relied on regular contact and separate cultures interacting.[53] Strict separation broke down as Hong Kong expanded, confounding attempts to enforce boundaries in both public and private space. Land limitations meant that by 1870, physical distance between the Westerners and the Chinese had begun to disappear. In 1874, "native houses" covered "all the land in front of the next house" over from the Heards. To Albert Heard, it created "perfect pandemonium." Confined to his room with illness, he found new empathy for his wife's distaste for a sequestered life in Hong Kong, enduring "the noises" and "annoyances" of the "native neighbours."[54] Proximity encouraged white foreigners to complain about the "smells and sounds of [the] Chinese," resulting in racism predicated on the self-perception that white inhabitants constituted "members of a special community."[55] Through their opposition to the Chinese, these white foreigners found unity. When articulating their desire to remain separate from the Chinese they formed a single voice. Yet separation broke down in private, where Chinese customers were courted and servants employed. When business required it, or within the appropriate master-servant hierarchy, contact occurred.

In response to the dissolving boundaries between Chinese and white communities in the settlement proper, white elites and the port's upwardly mobile sought alternative means to establish separation. Like other wealthy inhabitants of the port, the Heard brothers purchased property in Pok Fu Lam, reasonably far from Victoria on the island's western shore. Reminiscent, in a way, of the British hill stations in India, residents could reach Pok

Fu Lam by horse-drawn cart or sedan chair, and their estates there offered a respite from the clamor of the city. Owning property in this suburb demonstrated the privilege of wealth, as its remoteness required owners maintain such property at considerable expense. The wealthy Scottish merchant Douglas Lapraik owned the grandest such estate, tellingly dubbed "Douglas Castle."[56] Augustine Heard Jr. also recalled the changes that developing The Peak above the harbor brought about, with houses "built high up on the hill" and linked to the town by a "steam (cable) road."[57] No Chinese were admitted, excepting "servants, cooks, and drivers." The Peak was exclusively white, taking on the style of a "quaint English town."[58]

In the city proper, the house functioned as a closed "American" space that ideally preserved distance between the merchants and the Chinese, but it was never a stable and permanent "home." Families often relocated, "having to buy and sell furniture," adapt to new communities, and establish new networks.[59] In India houses were usually let empty, and homely comforts were furnished at the tenant's expense.[60] The same case existed in Canton, where the necessities to make clerks' bare rooms livable were paid for out of pocket.[61] In Hong Kong too, the Heards imported a variety of products intended to make life more bearable. Albert Heard wrote in 1859 for a steady supply of "Congress Water" (a New York mineral water), a barrel of baked beans, and all the copies, from commencement to the present, of the *Atlantic Monthly* periodical. Like the British, Americans ordered everything from alcohol to their favorite style of trousers. The brothers even sent home for carpeting with "high colors" and "modest patterns" such as "flowers and large figures" to line the 29 × 19 foot billiard and 27 × 20 foot drawing rooms.[62] Life in the merchant house may have been temporary, but it would not do to let national standards of style slip.

The Heards worked to infuse the space with a degree of comfort, but possessions often belonged to the individual, not the house, and "hominess" stemmed from the efforts of whomever currently resided in Hong Kong. On his return in 1873, George Heard found the house clean "but very bare." Augustine Heard Jr. had "carried off all the curios" and John Heard the "big ship pictures in the hall." Dixwell or the "boys" had smashed and abused the furniture, and Dixwell had let "everything go to pot," either not knowing how, or not caring much to "make things look nice."[63] Each brother collected possessions that would leave the house with them. Albert Heard shipped furnishings and collectables home, including Japanese lacquerware, cabinets full of jade, souvenirs from his European tours, Chinese vases, sandalwood goods, and a Chinese atlas. John Heard collected ship paintings, Augustine Heard Jr. acquired Asian curios, and somewhere lost in the shuffle was a series of water colors and a bound album of sketches by the English painter George Chinnery.[64] As the American community throughout China grew, such material interests would be reproduced in elite households at Shanghai, Kulangsu, Hankou, or in remote missionary homesteads, the "stubborn" adherence to home comforts and the "compromise" with colonial fashions reflecting American adaptation to the "social arrangements" of "an overseas colonial community."[65]

Temporary and bare as their house at times appeared, Tuckerman conceded the Heards lived "very handsomely" (but not more so than he and Whitney in Calcutta!), and the items George Heard listed as absent upon his arrival reflect the influence tenures in China and the colony had on the brothers' tastes.[66] These tastes were peculiar to the developing colonial culture in Hong Kong and the treaty ports. Anglo-Indian houses displayed "a particular type of colonial sensibility" through "sporting and hunting trophies," not "books and art," but the British in Canton and the Americans in Hong Kong deviated from this pattern.[67] The East India Company kept a well-stocked library at Canton, and the Heards sought styles and decor that signaled their extensive ties to China and Japan.[68] They were determined to bring this memorabilia home with them as evidence of their experiences. These personal items therefore found their way back to America with their purchasers, filling the mansion parlors of returned China traders such as Robert Bennet Forbes's in Milton, Massachusetts, and in turn shaping how the American public perceived China.[69]

Conflict between transience and permanence recurs throughout these examples. Permanence meant stability, power, and control in a contested space such as Hong Kong.[70] Permanence in Asia, however, was undesirable, so Americans sought alternate means of exercising control. The British colonial household represented a manageable symbol of imperial authority, and American merchants controlled their Hong Kong house to the same effect. The Heards' anxieties over Hong Kong's contested public spaces shaped the ways they fortified their house and spoke of encroaching Chinese neighbors. The house's physical ordering in turn muted anxieties by giving the American merchants a space where they were the central authority. The layout reproduced the desired colonial hierarchy, with the white

American partners on the top, subservient white clerks below, and "othered" Chinese servants occupying the bottom. The house's temporary nature also served as a bulwark against the much-derided danger of "going native," a phrase denoting what nineteenth-century critics considered the debasement of Anglo-European civilization through prolonged contact with local populations and the adoption of native culture.[71] To do so was "unthinkable" because it undermined the image of a superior and cultured white elite. The American experience in Hong Kong suggests they shared British concerns about "going native." Scarcity of possessions (imported American ones at that), impermanent lodgings, communal living, and constant encouragement to return home together underpinned a transitory life. A stark lack of domesticity characterized domestic space. The house functioned, rather, as a temporary shield against interracial contact. It provided a "safe" space where its tenants could reproduce white authority and preserve their lifestyle from unwanted Chinese influences.

LIFE IN THE HOUSE

Life as an employee in the American merchant house was a ritualized and in some ways overindulgent affair. American experiences during the old China trade laid the foundations of a hybrid culture that would develop in Hong Kong and across the treaty ports. The Canton foreigner's lifestyle grew from Anglo-Indian roots, and, because the British made up the most substantial group among Canton's insular community, they shaped the domestic habits of other white merchants. The penny-pinching associated with old China hands, as the senior merchants were dubbed, stemmed from India, where, facing criticisms of their excess, the English East India Company had tried to project a frugal face.[72] Their parsimony, however, was mere rhetoric. In Canton, EIC officers ironically set the same high standard of living they condemned, high spending growing so ubiquitous that even the most fiscally responsible "Yankee soon became accustomed to luxury."[73] An old China hand himself, Augustine Heard Sr. criticized his nephew John Heard's extravagance. John Heard admitted retrospectively that under his watch the company's employees enjoyed an excessive lifestyle.[74] Such had become the fashion by the 1850s, and John Heard was replicating the habits of his fellow merchants. Under the Heard brothers, life in the house was very comfortable indeed.[75]

High levels of expenditure ultimately proved unsustainable. Augustine Heard Sr. described John Heard as "reckless in expenses," and Albert Heard was similarly careless during his tenure as company head.[76] Reflecting on the matter, John Heard explained that any attempt to stymie the outflow of money was equal to "saving at the spigot and letting go at the bung."[77] As the firm's bankruptcy became inevitable in 1875, Augustine Heard Jr. despaired that unless they could bring expenditure "down very much," they would be unable to "go on at all."[78] Therein lay the problem: any sign of retrenchment would wreak havoc on the company's reputation, which was built on the stability of its capital.[79] In the China trade, even appearing to flounder was as good as drowning. And so, Albert Heard spent, with no real change apparent in the account books until 1871, when it was already too late.[80]

Prior to the company's failure, Hong Kong life fluctuated between periods of manic work and monotonous inactivity. The weekly mail ships dictated the ebb and flow of work, with most activity clustered around their arrival and departure. The brothers described the interim period as rather dull. During this downtime, the social ritual of visiting provided entertainment and ensured "cohesion within the community."[81] The regularity of these visits, so ingrained in society, meant they often encroached upon the foreign merchants' lives, requiring merchants to perform public standards of acceptability within the private space of the home. Rounds of dinner parties, given "by Westerners for other Westerners," were also common.[82] John Heard recalled that these dinners were among "the only [kinds] of entertainment possible" in Hong Kong, and someone was always available to share a meal. Augustine Heard Jr. remembered spending "every night of the week" at "some dinner party." Even while sick, Albert Heard managed to attend three dinners in a week.[83]

The merchant house, already a shared space and therefore less private than the traditional domestic sphere, was further laid bare to outsiders through the frequency of these dinners and the visitors they brought. The dinner was a great social occasion where the company men, guests, boarders, and visiting captains gathered together for a long, relaxed meal with many alcoholic beverages and cigars. In the Canton days, almost a dozen partners and clerks would sit down together. These dinners were a habitual occurrence where all would gather at the table, eat and drink a "great deal too much," and afterward sip brandy and smoke under the punkah.[84]

As the practice continued in Hong Kong it developed rather more of a class element, and increasingly the partners of the house dined with other leading members of the community rather than their own staff.

Heavy drinking was a staple of this dining culture, with a bottle of wine accompanying each place at dinner and a generous store laid aside.[85] While no British or American class had a monopoly on hard drinking, the practice grew unfashionable in early nineteenth-century India as the colonial elite came to equate alcohol with criminality.[86] In this matter, Hong Kong and the treaty ports lagged far behind. The acceptability of drinking prevailed, provided it did not interfere with business. Rather, it often provided a necessary lubricant for trade and social relations. Diverse foreigners would come together for drunken binges across the treaty ports or throw lavish receptions for visiting officials with banquets and flowing champagne.[87] Less than two days in Hong Kong, Albert Heard had already managed to find himself hungover on brandy following a night out with some naval officers. George Heard complained after a difficult visit in 1873 that the Russian naval officers could "drink tumblers at a time."[88] John Heard similarly recalled visits from Captain Larkins, described as something of a bon vivant, who drank so prodigiously that the more temperate Augustine Heard Sr. would exploit his insobriety to make him the object of pranks.[89]

Building upon a shifting metropolitan attitude toward drink that can be traced back to the eighteenth century, nineteenth-century British and American upper and middle classes were increasingly critical of drinking culture and habits.[90] Popular colonial attitudes soon followed the metropole's lead, and correspondence reveals a similar shift in nineteenth-century Hong Kong. Augustine Heard Jr.'s 1890 statement that no one fell "a victim of the habit of drinking" was not entirely correct. Within his own house at least two cases of excess are recorded: William J. Loring and George Heard. Augustine Heard Sr. had recommended Loring for a position in China, but the man, it seems, "had not always been right." Loring's "unfortunate propensity" was identified as a family trait and written off as tainted blood.[91] The colonial context made Loring's habit especially concerning, since his was considered a disease of the will, implicitly representing a loss of self-control and undermining the myth of Anglo-European superiority.[92]

George Heard's habit came to light when he fell ill in 1875. In a transparent letter home, Albert Heard admitted George Heard had "got into the way of drinking a good deal," and although he said he felt well "his appearance began to show the effect." Albert Heard justified George Heard's drinking as the product of "his good nature and carelessness" and "his love of the good things of the table." Mary Livingston even enjoyed drinking with him, thinking it "good fun to hear him rattle on."[93] By the mid-nineteenth century, it had become common knowledge that drink contributed to poor health.[94] While drink was not blamed for George Heard's illness, his habit merited attention, and its attribution to his declining health reveals changing attitudes toward consumption.

Health was a constant anxiety in the foreign community, and American desires for short sojourns and prolonged vacations home aligned with broader imperial social practices built upon the premise that southern climes were dangerous. Americans envisioned Hong Kong as a quick fix. The colony was a place to make a handsome living and then vacate. Hearing his brother-in-law intended try his luck in the colony, Albert Heard protested that although he felt the same way at that age, he was "weary of it" and "would so gladly leave forever." He professed a "a year at home" trumped "a cycle of Cathay." The environment was, granted, damaging to American constitutions, and lengthy stays in Hong Kong were considered risky. When an acquaintance of George Heard's, "Miller," passed away on August 6, 1873, it was generally felt that had he stayed in California there was a "chance of his getting to be a well man."[95]

The following summer, Albert Heard sent Livingston home for similar reasons, fearing the effects "another hot season" would have on her health. Albert Heard fell quite ill that same season, remaining bedridden for a couple months.[96] Livingston objected to the arrangement, desiring to remain with her husband, and so returned at the earliest opportunity. Her return caused Albert Heard distress, for he had no doubt she would find the Hong Kong heat and the house uncomfortable. He repeated his request that she "remain patiently at home for the present," and "not think of coming back to China."[97] Albert Heard's motives in sending Livingston to the United States may have stemmed from Augustine Heard & Co.'s imminent and expected failure. Yet, the letters demonstrate themes common in British colonial society: the colonies were considered ill suited for families; the environment disastrous to health; Hong Kong was not safe for permanent settlement. Albert Heard's letters simply reiterated the rhetoric of the time.

Augustine Heard Sr. too obsessed over the Heard brothers' health in his letters. He worried most about the length of their tenure in Hong Kong.

Reprimanding Albert Heard's fiscal excess and lifestyle, Augustine Heard Sr. demanded to know how long he "expected to remain in China." If he "had any economy" he might have come home sooner and not spent "the best part of [his] life" in the colony.[98] Among Augustine Heard Sr.'s recommendations were "giving up the use of tobacco," which he claimed softened the brain and caused "idiotry [sic]," eating well, temperance, avoiding out of door work, and walking and riding daily, but only early in the morning.[99] He placed such importance on riding that he had kept a small pony at Canton that he rode daily "around the square," amusing Chinese onlookers.[100] Albert Heard likewise felt Livingston should have the appropriate accessories on hand so she too could enjoy daily rides in Hong Kong. He had these, of course, imported from the United States. Augustine Heard Sr.'s concerns were not ill placed. George Heard complained he was "getting fat again" in 1873, and although Livingston was in "good apparent health," Albert Heard was "just as fat."[101]

Both the Hong Kong lifestyle and environment contributed to illness and poor health. Excessive consumption was part of the merchant house culture, and, seemingly at odds with foreign anxieties over health, mid-nineteenth-century colonial norms privileged propriety over comfort and well-being. Colonial pressure to play the gentleman had meant "dress moved away from simplicity and lightness to formality and opulence."[102] Participation in such a "self-consciously British" society occurred on "British terms."[103] Ideas about the relationship between dress and health in the tropics circulated throughout the eighteenth and nineteenth centuries, but in the colonies common sense competed with British metropolitan fashions and the "social status and power" that accompanied them.[104] This was particularly true for women, for whom metropolitan fashions were encouraged with only minor alterations, and little effort was made to produce appropriate tropical attire.[105] Americans throughout China thus conformed to colonial norms regarding behaviors and dress, donning socially accepted fashions, British or American, that were inappropriate for the environment. They were comfortable enough in the spring when it was cool—what Albert Heard called "punkah and white jacket weather"—but in the summer one had to be "clad most lightly." A pith helmet might be fine for trekking out of doors, and a light blouse might suit in private, but the heavy clothing that was expected attire for entertaining at home, attending social functions, or venturing into public could cause discomfort and a much dreaded case of "prickly heat" that turned its victim into "a gigantic lobster."[106]

The formality of the American merchants' domestic lives, more public than private, meant they endured these discomforts in their day-to-day lives to maintain appearances. Although there were those Americans who stayed on, almost everything about domestic space and private life in the colony contributed to a culture of transience. The communalism of the house, the coming and going of partners, the absence of consistent comforts, and concerns about health and lifestyle together dissuaded most Americans from laying roots in the colony. For those whose tenures were longer, however, lives took on an increasingly British colonial quality, and for a brief period, at least, they adapted to the local society and culture.

A TRULY PRIVATE SPACE?

In part due to the transient lifestyles of the employees, and in part due to its simultaneous function as a communal living space and an office, a steady rotation of people filled Augustine Heard & Co.'s Hong Kong house. Each of the four Heard brothers served sojourns in Hong Kong overseeing company affairs, sometimes simultaneously and at other times to relieve each other. Other partners such as Parker and Dixwell, and the numerous clerks they employed, lived alongside them. Besides these occupants, a cast of people both visible and invisible in the records intruded upon the house. Servants, family, friends, visiting dignitaries, and fellow merchants occupied the space at any given moment. The diverse individuals who temporarily resided within the house contributed to its open and public character.

Servants were perhaps the most consistent yet least visible group occupying the house. Servants featured in both British metropolitan and colonial households, and it was even commonplace for American ladies to bring servants or employ white attendants, as did the Beal sisters Helen and Elizabeth in 1851 and 1859 respectively when they moved to Shanghai or Lucy Hooper in 1866 when she traveled to Hong Kong. These were usually engaged for a short contract and thereafter replaced with cheaper and more easily obtained Chinese labor.[107] In the merchant houses each member, down to the lowliest clerk, had a "boy," a personal manservant, who acted as their exclusive aide.[108] The tasks of this "boy" appear intimately personal.

He drew the bath, "laid out his [master's] linen," and served only his master at the table.[109] Rarely mentioned by name, the "boy" became an interchangeable character throughout colonial homes in Hong Kong and the treaty ports, and Albert Heard's shared the same traits in letters as his brother John's, Ruth Bradford's at Amoy, Rebecca Kinsman's at Macao, or Francis Blackwell Forbes's at Hong Kong.[110]

Besides the boy, the list of staff the firm employed stretched on. There were butlers, watchmen, water boys, horsemen, market boys, a boy for the "small house," cooks and cooks' mates, chair bearers, doormen, men to operate the punkah, gardeners, grooms, coachmen, boatmen, and a man to tend the cow.[111] In one establishment, split between house and office, the Heards employed fifty-two servants. This was effectively an invisible labor force, no more than numbers on an accounts ledger, but those individuals who were named give some sense of the nonwhite composition of the merchant house. Macanese and Portuguese individuals such as Henrique Catano Victor De Figueiredo and his son José Miguel both carved relatively stable positions within the firm's Hong Kong and Shanghai houses, as did Inácio Pires Pereira Jr., Olímpio Augusto da Cruz, and Franciso António de Seabra.[112] Chinese employees from Hong Kong likewise became crucial to staffing overseas branches, both He Gan 何乾 and Wang Changjie 王昌傑 signing generous contracts in 1866 to serve as cooks in Manila.[113]

At the top of the hierarchy of Chinese in the American merchant houses' employ was the comprador. This man occupied myriad roles, including commercial intermediary, banker, advisor, and manager of household affairs. He hired the servants, "supplied the table," "kept all the private accounts," and in general did "everything there was to be done." The Heards' comprador, Mok Sze Yeung (Mo Shiyang, 莫仕揚) came from Xiangshan 香山. Mok made himself instrumental to the firm's business, and during the tighter years in the 1870s he even extended a large amount of credit to Albert Heard. Besides a monthly salary of $100, he levied a small percentage on every transaction that passed through his hands; John Heard estimates that between 1840 and 1846 these levies totaled $70,000 without the house's being "conscious of losing a cent."[114] Mok carried substantial influence, and upon his recommendation, Butterfield & Swire employed Ng Ahip (Wu Ye 吳葉) and his second son Mok Tso Cheun (Mo Zaoquan 莫藻泉) consecutively as chief compradors.[115]

Mok was also responsible for hiring and managing the conduct of the household servants. The firm held the comprador responsible for the well-being of the firm's employees, and so these servants tended to be those they could trust, such as family, clan members, or those from their home village. This is apparent in company contracts that suggest the Heards hired compradors from Xiangshan to staff both Hong Kong, as did Je Ayu (Xie Yayu 謝亞玉), and more distant ventures.[116] Akow (Chen Yajiu 陳亞九) went to Yokohama in 1860, Ah Chin (Liang Yadian 梁亞甸) and On Acheong (Wen Yazhang 溫亞章) were dispatched with two months advance pay to Saigon that same year, and Ayeung (Ya Yang 亞楊) was sent to Fuzhou "to be installed at that port to serve as comprador for Heard & Co. (*Long shun xing He Gongsi zhuang kou cheng chong maiban* 隆順行喝公司裝口承充買辦)."[117] In short, the compradors made themselves and their network invaluable to the foreign household in China.

Chinese employees, servants, and customers were vital to the merchant house and its day-to-day operations, but how the Heards described the Chinese reflects an ambiguous racial relationship between American and local communities. This relationship in many ways conformed to widespread attitudes in nineteenth-century colonial society.[118] Letters home by George Heard and Albert Heard in 1860 painted the Chinese as "squalid," "human filth," and "dirty celestials." Albert Heard described his amah "Aleen" using equally patronizing language, relating how she had "the most hideous grimace, her usual smile you know," and how having received "cumsha" (a tip) for delivering a package, "went her ways rejoicing . . . delighted at her success." Occasionally such rhetoric was reflected through action. John Heard unapologetically recalled whipping a servant for ignoring his calls, and Albert Heard related thrashing his "boy" for dropping a "Japanese cup and tea." George Heard found that Dixwell and Weller were "discourteous" to Chinese customers but claimed that the Chinese "seemed to like it."[119]

Such comments about and actions towards their servants and the wider Chinese community constituted a means of articulating "everyday tensions," "antagonisms," and difference.[120] If daily contact undermined the "strict separation between coloniser and colonised," language served a converse purpose to reaffirm difference.[121] Daily contact with the Chinese was unavoidable, but American rhetoric and actions represented a growing sense of racialized boundaries, intensifying racism through familiarity. Racialization was part of a complex process where the fear of the "other," and the desire to protect white prestige converged with a "critical class-based logic," appearing in statements "about indigenous subversives" and lower-class Europeans alike.[122]

Yet proximity's power to effect racism was only one part of a more complex racialized environment, and circumstances invariably affected rhetoric. During the Second Opium War, for example, all Chinese were imagined as "potential enemies" and the British and Americans viewed even their own employees with distrust. Real threats, such as the 1857 bread panic, when Cheong Alum of the Esing bakery allegedly doctored bread sold to much of the foreign community with arsenic, only served to justify such fears in the minds of Hong Kong's foreign community.[123] Although such crises were minor (there was only one death, possibly unrelated, during the poisoning), they exacerbated Sino-foreign tensions and played upon the foreign community's sense of vulnerability within the colony. For American merchants, the ongoing war and panics such as the poisoning affair were "the indirect cause of a great change in the relations of foreigners with the Chinese."[124]

In more tranquil times, and when it was advantageous to do so, the brothers heaped praise on the Chinese. For instance, in Augustine Heard Jr.'s 1894 address to the Mercantile Club in St. Louis, he praised the "fidelity and trustworthiness" of the Chinese he had employed. He expressed good faith in their management of the house and wished to commend them at a time "when [Americans] were hearing nothing but evil."[125] The American Ruth Bradford, isolated in the foreign settlement of Kulangsu at Amoy took great pleasure into getting into "flirtations" with visiting Qing dignitaries, entertaining elite Chinese ladies, and staring at beautiful Chinese women in the streets. Her own servant, "Mr. Coolie," was indispensable—at once her "chambermaid, dressing maid, errand boy, and a good many other characters."[126]

Although an innocent inclusion, descriptions such as Bradford's of faithful and "loyal" servants could quickly transmute into "deeply" and "intentionally" patronizing commentaries that reaffirmed racial hierarchies and downplayed the threat of the racialized "other."[127] The American Helen Beal, for instance, described the religious practices of her servants at Shanghai, which she spied upon from the elevated position of her veranda, as "ludicrous" and "absurd." From her perch, Beal literally and symbolically looked down on her servants as she dismissed their obeisance to "some small god."[128] The American Ruth Bradford likewise viewed her Shanghai servants as "beastly filthy," despairing that "one might as well try to stop the waves of the Yangtze with a shingle" as keep them clean.[129] In a letter to his sister, Francis B. Forbes, too, referred to his servants as "poor little Chinamen." He then went on to dehumanize his "boy" through animalistic comparison, even while finding himself despondent as the boy, like others in the community, had left him due to imperial decree.[130] These commentaries demonstrate a unified racist rhetoric that developed across China's treaty ports expressed through adjectives such as "small," "poor," "little," "filthy," and "beastly." Such language infantilized and dehumanized Chinese servants, implicitly justifying their subservient roles.

Even as circumstances encouraged (backhanded) praise they helped cement racial boundaries. Justifying his views on the Second Opium War, John Heard allowed that "it was difficult, if not impossible, to avoid being influenced by" the surrounding atmosphere of wartime Hong Kong. In retrospect, he formed a clear stance regarding the rights and wrongs of the conflict, but he allowed that "one can't help taking sides with the [British] people one is living with."[131] As John Heard's account and his brothers' commentaries demonstrate, racializing the Chinese occurred as a product of two distinct but not exclusive attitudes formed in Hong Kong. The first was the general attitude of prejudice the Americans both developed on their own and conformed to while in China. The second was more nuanced, with Sino-foreign differences producing a sense of white cohesion. If the Americans and British often felt at odds over political policy and social behavior, they found unity by identifying that which they both were not: Chinese. Their belief that the Chinese posed a threat to Anglo-Europeans and Americans "helped bind" the foreign community, breaking down "divisions of class and nationality."[132] An implicitly acknowledged white community developed by identifying a distinct and different Chinese population against which their community could be contrasted.

On the opposite end of the social hierarchy, a menagerie of white guests and lodgers frequently filled the Heard house. These guests were entertained for networking purposes, and the house and its resources became tools for fostering such contacts. As early as 1859 the Heards used their house to leverage social and political connections. May that year the Heards put up John Ward, his brother, and Commodore Josiah Tattnall of the U.S. legation to Peking (Beijing). George Heard joined the legation as Ward's attaché; a "most glorious" opportunity for "seeing all there is to be seen in the best company in China." It seems, from Albert Heard's letters, that this connection had been deliberately fostered during George Heard's voyage to China with Ward, and Albert Heard felt the firm should "derive benefit from his acquaintance." Upon his return from Peking, Ward was offered temporary residence alongside Commander Cornelius Stribling at the Heards' Macao house. The brothers extended the same courtesy to Russian officials in 1873, hosting Grand Duke Alexei Alexandrovich, an admiral named Fedorovich, and their attendants.[133]

The brothers hoped that the efforts put into filling diplomatic roles and extending such courtesies would secure future opportunities. John Heard served as the Portuguese and Russian consul in turn, and Ward personally requested that George Heard join him on a mission to Japan. Augustine Heard Jr. also leveraged his connections to become the American ambassador to Korea following the firm's bankruptcy. John Heard described these honors as having little use, and being Russian consul, in particular, meant the house was often overrun by visiting Russians coming to "eat, sleep, and live" at the house. The Portuguese post, at least, enabled him to contact Chinese officials directly.[134] Despite having little use, the positions were maintained, often at company expense, as it was believed they granted the house esteem in the eyes of the Chinese and others in the colony.

The guests these positions brought, although influential, were largely viewed as a drain on the company's resources and the brothers' personal faculties. By the time Ward's legation left Shanghai for Peking on June 18, 1859, Albert Heard was beginning to show signs of fatigue. The legation's departure reduced the residents of the Shanghai household from eleven to three, and Albert Heard was relieved to "enjoy tranquillity and peace of mind" and have time to see to his own business. Over the course of the next fourteen years George Heard repeated the same sentiments about their Russian guests. In 1870, he expressed frustration at Albert Heard's "damned Russians," as they must have understood that Albert Heard had "other things to attend to." In 1873 the Russians were back, and for all the attention they required, the "office might just as well be shut up."[135]

The presence of so many guests, and for networking purposes at that, meant that the brothers were constantly performing the role of host. The house was further drawn into the public sphere as the brothers' conduct at home around their guests took on new sociopolitical importance. John Heard remembered the whole thing as an "immense bore" that cost the firm "no end of money in the way of entertainment," but Albert Heard, George Heard, and the partners insisted John Heard play the diplomatic role to increase the firm's influence.[136] John Heard retorted that the obligation brought no profit, but as Augustine Heard Jr.'s and Albert Heard's later activities will demonstrate, such connections helped them secure government appointments after the firm folded. Domestic space was therefore leveraged for commercial and political gain and social capital, further blurring the lines between private and public spheres.

The conspicuous absence of white women in China further upset traditional metropolitan understandings of the domestic sphere. In eighteenth- and nineteenth-century Britain, domestic and female spheres were considered synonymous. Women and the home came to represent a civilized side of the Western culture: modest, chaste, pious, compassionate, and virtuous.[137] Cultivating the "home" to display these virtues was considered the "woman's prerogative."[138] In colonial space, however, feminine domestic virtues were increasingly "taken out of doors." Across the British Empire, such virtues were leveraged to justify the imperial mission, as the presence of women in the colonies' private and public spheres helped shape colonial policy.[139] On both a stereotypical and ideological level the domestic sphere was considered feminine, and in overseeing the space's organization according to the standards of Western civility, the colonial woman, and gender relations in general, became inextricable from the politics of authority.[140] Even the etymology of the British-Indian term "memsahib," used to address white married women, served a dual purpose. While it verbally subordinated the white woman's authority to that of her husband, the "sahib," it still signaled her authority over "dark-skinned natives."[141] The cultural virtues, political importance, and relative authority attributed to women and domestic space thus became equated with the performance of imperial authority in colonial spaces.

As in India, the presence of women at Canton took on a broader political dimension. During the days of the old China trade, Chinese officials barred foreign women outright from residing at the Thirteen Factories. To their dismay, the wives of traders, such as Ellen Coolidge or Kinsman, were required to wait out the trading season in Macao.[142] The American Harriet

Low, objecting to this law, took it upon herself to visit Canton in 1830. The outrage her presence sparked fueled a political debate between white foreigners and the Chinese on the importance of women to the home and nation. For the foreign traders, women represented family and were thus "the essence of a moral nation." To the Chinese, however, women and family meant permanence, the threat of the Thirteen Factories becoming a settlement and thus encroaching upon Qing sovereignty.[143] Moreover, the publicness of white women was improper by Chinese social standards. Even attempts to reside modestly, as American Peter Parker and his wife Harriet did in 1842, elicited outrage. Parker blamed the backlash on the British, "who, in the course of the [Opium War], had rendered themselves particularly obnoxious to the Chinese."[144] Relegated as they were to the domestic sphere, colonial women remained crucial to debates of empire, morality, and contact.

Upon moving to Hong Kong, the ban on women residing in Canton became a moot point, but they continued to comprise only a small portion of white foreign society. Most men felt China ill suited for families and looked forward to returning home to find a wife.[145] Albert Heard, a young man in 1854, admitted he possessed a singular monomania, being completely preoccupied with women and the idea of finding a wife. Having just arrived in Canton in 1854, he already registered his intent to marry as soon as he could leave "off for home," although looking back in 1859 he admitted he did not know what he should "have done with a wife out here."[146] Albert Heard's outlook soon shifted, and within a few months he was complaining that he wished he had "brought a wife," since China had "wonderfully changed" by 1860. It no longer seemed "such a heathen land to bring a woman as it formerly was." Where the number of foreign women in the 1850s was negligible, a high society ball in the late nineteenth century could "bring together probably 300 ladies." Aided by its stability as a British Colony, Hong Kong had grown more suitable for maintaining a family. To George Heard, in 1873, it seemed "all the women in [Hong] Kong" were "getting children." George Heard listed Mrs. Wood, Mrs. Heywood, Mrs. Parker, and Mrs. Fearon all as raising families.[147] Still, firms discouraged married life, for the estimated subsistence of a married partner in China was between $8,000 and $10,000, "which the house must pay if he cannot." As Augustine Heard & Co. began to fail, such obligations became a growing concern for the senior partners.[148]

There were alternatives, however, and foreign traders entered into relationships with Chinese "protected women" as part of a quietly accepted but never openly discussed practice. The white community did not often denounce interracial relationships, so long as they were not legitimated in public by marriage.[149] Still, the presence of mixed-race children was considered a "blight" upon the community, threatening the veneer of Anglo-European "prestige and control."[150] While at Canton, John Heard conceded that interracial relationships were an "amiable weaknesses," resulting in "a lot of bastard children kicking about Macao."[151] His letters suggested he personally kept the company of the Macanese woman Lam Kew-fong—mistakenly identified as Albert Heard's protected woman—with whom he had a son, Richard Howard.[152] Upon leaving China, John Heard entrusted the Hong Kong partners of Augustine Heard & Co. to oversee a fund of $6,000 with 8 percent interest per annum to provide for Sai and the boy until he came of age. His letter stressed that this was one of those matters in which "one must rely on his friends" for discretion.[153] John Heard continued to manage this account through the firm even after returning to Boston and marrying, his 1882 drafted will further stipulating that the remainder of the sum be transferred to Richard Howard for his personal use on his twenty-first birthday.[154]

John Heard's experience was relatively common among the American China merchants. John Hartt of Perkins & Co., and Benjamin Wilcocks and William C. Hunter of Russell & Co., for example, all fathered children "by their Chinese or Macanese protected woman."[155] Dixwell likewise had a son with Hu Ts'ai-shun, Charles Sargent, born in 1868 in Shanghai, whose U.S. entry permit noted his "oval" chin and face, his "dark brown" hair, and his "dark" complexion. A marriage registry in 1897 confirmed his birthplace as China.[156] Augustine Heard Jr. also provided for a protected woman, Apook, and their daughter, Anui (likely *aa neoi* 阿女, or "daughter"). Augustine Heard Jr. had set $4,500 aside, administered at $30 monthly for the rest of Apook's life. An additional $10 monthly was provided to care for Anui. Her wedding expenses were covered and a $1,000 dowry granted. The measures John Heard and Augustine Heard Jr. took demonstrate the obligation American merchants felt toward their protected women and offspring, but they also confirm that these cases were potentially embarrassing. All of John Heard's letters were managed through the firm, and George Heard sent his correspondence with Augustine Heard Jr. through their partner Fearon, since he feared sending "it to the club" might attract unwanted attention.[157]

Moreover, these discrete relationships failed to stop Americans involved in them from racializing Chinese women. White observers used gender and sexuality to differentiate the Chinese and the foreigners, and how the Heards described Chinese women certainly underscored established opinions that white women (and thus white foreigners generally) possessed greater civility. To Albert Heard's dismay upon arriving in 1854, "you couldn't pick out a girl" in Canton "that would hold any comparison with the homeliest b—h of five points." His statement hierarchically ordered all Chinese women in Canton beneath the most destitute and lower-class Americans he could imagine. He confided to a school friend that he would have soon heard "of a Mrs Heard," but there were "no pretty girls, white or yellow," anywhere in China.[158] Albert Heard's statements reified the racial and class judgments that found outlet through the medium of female bodies.

Amplifying normative expectations in the metropole, white society demanded its women represent colonial ideals and uphold an idealized image of civility, turning them into pressure points for racist and classist commentaries. Their presence explicitly produced "stronger racial divisions," while the language describing them deliberately "[enforced] the separation between Asians and whites."[159] Women were symbols of the nation's civilization, their "innate domesticating and nurturing qualities" were deemed "essential to the colonial civilising mission."[160] Whether in Hong Kong, Shanghai, Yokohama, or Kobe, those who made the journey were charged with promoting housekeeping, hygiene, and the task of revitalizing an enervated social and cultural life.[161] In their idealized form, they represented the supposed moral superiority of the West. In less reputable contexts—white prostitutes or indigent women in the treaty ports, for example—they threatened that same moral standard. Women's bodies, elite, non-elite, Chinese or white, thus became mediums through which colonial idealisms and difference were crystallized.

Albert Heard eventually managed to find an "acceptable" wife in the United States whom he could bring back to Hong Kong. He married Livingston in 1868, and after a brief tour of Europe the couple returned to China. A woman's home life in such a masculine society, however, was less than ideal. Livingston found her days "lonely and dull" and spent much time alone while the men worked. In a misguided effort to comfort Livingston and against the advice of his brothers, Albert Heard paid for his cousin Eunice Farley to come from Boston to keep her company in 1873. Farley was also miserable in Hong Kong, and the cost of putting her up further strained the firm's little remaining capital. Albert readily admitted he had done a "very foolish thing" and promptly sent her home. He then sent Livingston home, using her health as a pretext. In reality, she was unable to adapt to Hong Kong society, and her unhappiness weighed on their marriage. Francis B. Forbes was not overly fond of Livingston but conceded that it was "hard to judge correctly a woman whose life has been wrecked as hers."[162] Albert Heard's confused actions suggest that while a growing number of American women migrated to Hong Kong, the isolation and social demands caused considerable stress and discouraged prolonged settlement.

Among the brothers' wives, Livingston alone spent significant time in China, and Heard women participated little in the company's affairs. When George Heard wrote Albert Heard about the company's failure in 1873, he stated that although he did not think Livingston "cared about seeing letters on business," Albert Heard ought not open the letters in her presence. George Heard felt the same toward John Heard's wife Alice Leeds, apologizing that he had nothing much to write her about "except business and she doesn't naturally care about that."[163] John too kept business matters separate from his wife. The 1873 letters related the failure of the business, and the brothers' reluctance to keep their wives informed reinforced the division between male and female roles in the American merchant house. Yet those women that did arrive played a vital role in business. As wives of leading merchants, American women such as Ellen Coolidge and Helen Beal managed the social interests vital to company affairs. They hosted, visited, provided entertainment and conversation, and generally represented the civilized face of their husbands' firms. Some individuals, like Kinsman at Macao, managed business affairs, running the house, maintaining business and political contacts, and even handling company correspondence.[164]

These women were exceptions to the rule, and in terms of occupants the merchant house remained a masculine space, even those tasks of housekeeping associated with feminine domesticity being performed by (mostly) male Chinese servants. More women migrated to Hong Kong over time, but the percentage remained heavily skewed toward the men. While Augustine Heard & Co. operated, women comprised a small portion of society.

Although Albert Heard no longer saw Hong Kong as a "heathen land," the 1860 Annual Administrative Report still found just over one-third as many European and American women as men. By 1870 the gap had expanded, listing six times more Western men than women in the colony. In the American community, the 1870 report identified ninety men, seventeen women, and eight children.[165] Hong Kong Society, and by extension domestic space, was fitfully masculine. Women may have been held up as civilizers and paragons of morality, but they also represented permanence. A family meant settling down, and American merchants rarely entertained the idea of staying in Hong Kong. Social propriety dictated that men return home to marry, leaving the wife and children behind during China tenures. Despite Hong Kong's growth, merchants continued to conform to this longstanding social pattern, and the American woman's physical presence remained an irregularity in the mid-nineteenth-century American merchant house. In the meantime, American men entered discrete interracial relationships, even as they attributed white idealisms and social capital to those few American women in China.

Both the physical organization of the Heards' Hong Kong houses and the lifestyles of those therein reflect the sociopolitical tensions and unique circumstances of the colonial environment within which they were built. Architecture and layout reified racial and class hierarchies and anxieties regarding interracial contact, while interior furnishings displayed an ambivalent attitude toward colonial life where merchants balanced competing needs to emphasize their affluence and authority, and to tread lightly, work fast, and return to the United States. The private lifestyle conformed to this culture of transience and to the public sphere's daily transgressions into domestic space. The constant presence of servants and guests and the almost complete absence of women warped the private household into a space that was effectively public and masculine. Merchants were required to constantly perform, while the prospect of starting a family remained incentive to avoid settling too comfortably in China. Concerns over economy and health further encouraged merchants to avoid laying down roots. Still, despite these varying concerns, excess remained commonplace, women arrived in slowly increasing numbers, and lifestyles became increasingly settled into the late nineteenth century.

By upsetting the binary oppositions of private/public and male/female, the Heard household exemplifies how domestic culture shifted from colony to colony. In many ways, the house conformed to British colonial traditions, but it was also a product of unique U.S. influences and the demographic and social specificities of Hong Kong. Transient lifestyles, social practices, servant culture, political and commercial duties, and a masculine population each molded the merchant household into something unique to Hong Kong and in turn shaped how Americans interacted with the colony. The ways the Heards described the space demonstrate that the circumstances of life in Hong Kong significantly affected how they established themselves in the colony and influenced their perceptions of race, class, and British colonial culture.

Chapter Three

LIVES LIVED IN PUBLIC

American Encounters with British Colonial Society

> More intellectual than other races, when they live with other races, they do not take their language, but bestow their own. They subsidize other nations, and are not subsidized. They proselyte, and are not proselyted. They assimilate other races to themselves, and are not assimilated.
>
> —RALPH WALDO EMERSON, *ENGLISH TRAITS* (1856)

Ralph Waldo Emerson's 1856 hagiography of the "English" people continues in this vein for over three hundred pages, valorizing the British and their Anglo-Saxon heritage. It seems ill fitting for an American to have penned such a text in the mid-nineteenth century, but *English Traits* represented an underlying ethos of New England culture, at once proudly independent and nostalgic for the imperial past. Perhaps more significantly, the Anglophilic mentality permeating Emerson's text helps explain American encounters with British society and culture abroad. The British in China had proven, through the First and Second Opium Wars, the crude efficacy of their military at extending imperial power and influence, but while white Americans in Hong Kong and the treaty ports may have found the starkness of such power uncomfortable, the "prevailing spectacle" of empire had its attractions.[1]

This discord shaping American public encounters with British colonial society and the spectacle of empire prompts the questions of why American merchants in nineteenth-century Hong Kong adapted to the port's dominant British cultural norms and what sociocultural fluency they required to do so. Following independence, U.S. society lacked a "titled nobility" and so "socioeconomic categories came to be more useful" status markers.[2] The class system entrenched in Britain was relatively unfamiliar to Americans.³ Americans placed greater emphasis on labor and income when establishing class divisions, tying both to race to determine one's position in the nation's fledgling society.⁴ Emerging at the apex of class hierarchy, the affluent Boston Brahmins of New England formed an elite network based on kinship ties and common values.⁵ Their wealth often came from trade, industrial enterprise, and their skill at marshaling the capital of their peers.⁶ But just as entry into the British upper class required "an acceptable mix" of breeding, education, capital, and culture, acquiring status in the United States meant transcending financial pursuits.⁷ New England elites therefore married well, retired early, and sent their children to Harvard and Yale, where men such as James Russell Lowell and Oliver Wendell Holmes Sr. educated pupils in the English tradition.⁸ These formative student years in turn cultivated social and cultural habits well suited for life among the British. With many members of the Brahmin circle making fortunes in the China trade, such an English-style upbringing eased their assimilation into British communities at Canton, Hong Kong, and the treaty ports.

Emerson's idealization of a superior "Anglo-Saxon" character shared by British and Americans of privileged ancestry failed to account, however, for the divergent paths seventy-five years of U.S. independence and British empire building had taken.⁹ In the British metropole, a sense of "Britishness," refined and ingrained through continental rivalries, a common investment in Protestantism, and the idea that the empire reified Great Britain's "providential destiny" bound together disparate ethnicities and classes.¹⁰ The culture that the New England merchants encountered in Hong Kong merged these metropolitan influences with local ones, contributing to a colonial "British identity" more imperial than domestic and dependent upon a "strong sense of racial difference."¹¹ In some respects British colonial culture and identity were more porous than in the metropole, and class and ethnic barriers could be circumvented, but in others the colonial experience cemented differences, and markers such as race, politics, and religion acquired renewed significance.¹² So, while the American merchants and their families found some aspects of the culture familiar, others felt stifling or alienating. The convergence of metropolitan culture, class anxieties, and race created both social cohesion and tension, affecting the ways Americans integrated with their own, and the largely British foreign communities of nineteenth-century Hong Kong. Through their efforts, American merchants selectively conformed to the dictates of British colonial society while infusing it with American characteristics, contributing to a developing colonial culture that merged diverse metropolitan influences with local Hong Kong ones.

Such was a nuanced processes through which disparate sociocultural influences from Hong Kong and the British and American metropoles converged, and efforts to assimilate—successful or not—were commented upon in both personal and popular representations of the public sphere. Whether within or outside the home, in letters or in newspaper articles, mid-nineteenth-century Hong Kong's American inhabitants came under scrutiny. Such sites provided stages upon which sociocultural tensions emerged, and on these stages Anglo-American interactions acquired a performative nature. These various "publics"—the public home, public space, and public letters and media—exposed and tested the extent to which Americans were willing to assimilate with the British, their visibility in each reflecting the processes through which they made and were made by British colonial society.

THE SOCIAL ROUNDS AND THE HOME AS A PUBLIC SPACE

In 1873 *China Punch*, a satirical publication inspired by London's *Punch* that enjoyed a short run in Hong Kong across the 1860s and 1870s, published an article instructing its readers on the etiquette of "calling culture." The acerbic guide mocked the rigid and disingenuous rituals characterizing the practice. Its author emphasized the importance of presenting a respectable image while in the same breath criticizing the entire practice's banality. The author allowed, however, that "if life [was] to be worth living, residents in China must do the round of calls."[13] By describing the rituals surrounding calling and the various parties' mutual reluctance to participate, the article underscored an unavoidable aspect of treaty port society: the public sphere's intrusion into everyday private life. Social propriety compelled the port's white inhabitants to open their homes to what seemed like the entirety of foreign society. The socialite must always be prepared to host, gossip, entertain, and feed a steady stream of visitors. The few women who accompanied their husbands to Hong Kong formed the nucleus of this culture, offering outsider perspectives of the rituals elite Americans performed in order to participate in colonial society and voicing misgivings about doing so on a "public stage."

Through hosting, entertaining, and visiting, the home, and by extension white women, were increasingly drawn into Hong Kong's public sphere. While domestic life in Hong Kong was in many ways performative in and of itself, the home further served as an appendage of colonial society and public life. Women, by extension, occupied a central role as social facilitators, underpinning "calling culture" and the practices of dining and hosting. Their novelty in the port heightened their significance to the social rounds, and the importance that men and women alike ascribed to the rituals of calling, dining, and hosting in turn recast the home as a public space. Still, this blurring of the lines between public and private space was not without tension, and as Hong Kong's American community increased, its discomfort with certain colonial practices and attitudes triggered, in some, the impulse to retreat from British colonial society.

Hong Kong's foreign community continued to grow and diversify following the 1850s. Improvements in steam technology meant shorter and more comfortable trips from the United States and Europe, encouraging an influx not just of merchants and opportunists, but their wives and children as well. Hopeful new arrivals dreaming of a satisfying social life invariably faced the daunting cultural practice of "calling." Imported from the metropole, the system became entrenched in Hong Kong and the British colonies as a means of socially regulating "the ever-expanding colonial community."[14] Young American and European men, dressed finely and sporting a pocket full of calling cards, would make the rounds from house to house to introduce themselves to the women of the port (and by extension their husbands). Upon arriving at a home, the men presented their cards to the Chinese doormen, who would confirm whether the mistress of the house was receiving visitors at that time, before ushering them into the parlor. Women, if they were receiving, would remain home to host callers for a short social visit. In this manner, new arrivals to the port made themselves known and were granted access to proper society.

By the 1870s the practice of calling in Hong Kong was well established and ritualistic. The 1873 *China Punch* article on calling, posing as a guide, instructed young men unversed in the practice's strict etiquette. The article played upon the concept of respectability in Hong Kong society to pass off a series of missteps as sound guidance to a hypothetical hapless reader.

The article instructed the caller to be patient when brushed off, to utter inane platitudes (but not too many), and to "talk as much trash" as possible.[15] Such "advice" emphasized the practice's performative and obligatory nature and, through obvious satire, the actual etiquette required. The ritual was an opportunity to make a good impression in polite society, during which both the callers' and the hosts' characters came under scrutiny. Testifying to the practice's social importance, the article's one truism was that anything said, even to a friend, would be repeated. The event, ostensibly a private meeting between two individuals, was in fact a public performance. Men used calling to generate social and economic connections, advertising themselves and their business in the port in one move. Yet while it had a similar social function for women, drawing them into or excluding them from elite society, those few that came out to China also endured calling as objects of curiosity.

The Boston, New York, or Philadelphia elite arriving in China were well acquainted with the practice of calling, but the activity's scale in Hong Kong surpassed anything they had experienced at home.[16] Theirs was a society that valued social interaction within rigid norms; networks were primarily based on kinship, and modesty in conduct and lifestyle was expected.[17] Newly arrived American women accordingly found the steady pulse of social life in Hong Kong and the treaty ports novel. Some, such as Helen Beal, approached it with enthusiasm, writing home about all the graces of calling and the manners that had to be practiced upon a new lady's arrival in China. She basked in the attention, bragging that "few ladies" had been "as much the objects of notice."[18] Others, such as the irrepressible twenty-year-old Ruth Bradford, who accompanied her father and brother to Amoy in 1862, found the fawning less beguiling. Bradford recorded receiving "a great many callers" in her diary, musing that as "the only American lady" and "the only young girl" she had become "an object of some curiosity." Bradford referred to the ordeal of calling as "[passing] muster."[19] But if her novelty invited scrutiny, Bradford still found opportunities to play within and push the boundaries of colonial gender mores, using the attention she attracted to make "fools" of those determined to intercept her in public or to "dress up," go out, "astonish" the bachelors and "have a big fuss made over [her]."[20]

Describing Amoy, where the gender imbalance was more pronounced, Bradford's case demonstrates how calling allowed eligible bachelors in Hong

Kong and the treaty ports to introduce themselves to eligible ladies, but also how women manipulated the practice. Still, an expected code of conduct underlay the practice and could be quite restricting. *China Punch*'s 1872 comic entitled "Our Social Miseries" depicts a Chinese servant who, unfamiliar with cultural mores, leads the male caller directly into the private quarters of his mistress (figure 3.1). The comic made light of calling culture and the potential for cultural incomprehension to cause embarrassment, its humor stemming both from the naïve mistake of the servant and the absurd violation of a man being introduced into a woman's private quarters. In doing so it drew upon real concerns about proper conduct. Bradford's father, for example, "came down on [her] very hard" in 1862 for receiving a caller in her room at Hong Kong. She argued it was acceptable as the room was "just a private parlor" and "the drawing room [was] too public," but a line of respectability had been crossed.[21] That same year at Amoy Bradford related the anger she felt when her servant brought her the cards of visiting gentlemen as she was preparing to go out for a walk. She "threw the cards at the coolie, and wished the gentlemen to Guinea," but went down to meet the callers nonetheless. Social propriety in mid-nineteenth-century Hong Kong and the treaty ports demanded that Bradford, like others in her situation, submit to entertain when called upon, and to do so respectably.

The emphasis placed on women's respectability in *China Punch* and in Bradford's diary reflected shifting attitudes toward women's roles in colonial spaces in the mid- to late nineteenth century. Women and the home had become symbols of imperial progress and white civility by the midcentury.[22] Yet conflating women and the home produces a circumscribed model for describing their roles within colonial society.[23] The colonial context rather encouraged a breakdown in domestic responsibilities, freeing women to take on new public roles.[24] With few domestic duties and in high social demand, they participated in a gamut of visits, evening drives, and dinner parties, facilitating the colony's social life from within their respective households. They were not freed, however, from critics' comments on their conduct. Articles in the *China Mail*, for example, reprinted from across the empire instructed readers on what constituted appropriate conduct for British and American women.[25] Together, white men and the media commodified women's company while attempting to regulate their conduct, and so women's public activities acquired new sociocultural significance.

FIGURE 3.1. China Punch comic satirizing the daily grievances of Western women. *Source*: "Our Social Miseries," *China Punch*, November 2, 1872. Courtesy of the Hong Kong Baptist University Library.

White women had always been outnumbered in Hong Kong, the 1860 Annual Administrative Report listing only 279 European and American women to 755 men. Considering the imbalance, their social importance was disproportionate to their numbers. Hong Kong grew rapidly—by 1870 its total European and American population had more than quadrupled—and by 1872 Albert Heard found it had "changed and grown much more European," with life revolving more around "home ideals."[26] Given the port's increasing suitability for habitation, women became more conspicuous figures in everyday life. Their centrality to the social rhythm of the colony is evident from their presence in American letters home. Writing to his wife, Mary Livingston, in June 1874, Albert Heard described a typical "monotonous" week in Hong Kong. He dined with the Forbeses twice; a "great bore." He visited the new judge and his wife and attended the "usual service" at church. "Mrs Forbes," likely Deborah Perry Forbes née Delano, took him for a drive one day, but otherwise "everyone repeats the same formula." The women present at these events, "Mrs Snowden," "Mrs Bertrand," and "Mrs Forbes" were among the few attendees Albert Heard bothered naming, and were central to how he remembered and related his week. Augustine Heard Jr.'s wife, Jane deConinck, had made a similar impression on the foreign community, and Albert Heard boasted to her that "the days of Mrs Heard's reign" were "often most pleasantly alluded to" by others in the port. He was pleased to relate that Livingston, too, "made quite an impression" on the Russian delegation in 1873, and that she found the excitement of entertaining these visitors a respite from the "ordinary dull nature of Hong Kong life."[27]

While Albert Heard's letters emphasize the influence of American women on Hong Kong society, they are unique among merchant correspondence for the attention they devote to everyday life.[28] Far more detailed and candid accounts of how American women experienced colonial society can be drawn from letters of the women themselves. Albert Heard mentioned to deConinck in 1872, for example, that his wife was fascinated with neither Hong Kong or its people. A later letter stated, "Mary does not fall in love with Hong Kong or the society here, and the days to her seem long and weary." Both letters refracted Livingston's perspective through that of her husband, but comparison to other experiences of Hong Kong and China's treaty ports suggests that some women shared her ambivalence about social life. Foreign women may have enjoyed a central place in the social practices of calling, hosting, and visiting, but newly arrived Americans could find the stress of constantly performing disheartening and alienating. Bradford despaired, upon returning to China in 1871, that "everybody loses their spunk out here, and subsides into a sort of automation." Writing from Shanghai, even the more optimistic Helen Beal wondered at the "mortifying" politics of calling culture, where "ladies merely sen[ding] their cards" to a new arrival rather than calling first was a fatal snub. This was a "ceremonious kind of visiting" that Beal dismissed as "English," although she conceded that with a powerful husband and "well known and highly esteemed" friends life could be much happier.[29]

The social experiences of deConinck, Livingston, Beal, and Bradford were unique to their elevated social status. Both deConinck and Livingston, from respectable families in their own right, had married into the Heard Family and lived in Hong Kong. Beal, the daughter of the lawyer Thomas Prince Beal from Kingston, Massachusetts, married the doctor

George Hall, arriving in Shanghai in the 1850s.[30] Bradford was the daughter of the 1862 American consul to Amoy, later marrying Captain Ira Crowell, who acquired employment with Augustine Heard & Co. in the 1870s, and residing in Hong Kong and Shanghai. Their connections to the Heards and to high society in Shanghai, Amoy, and Hong Kong conferred a degree of stature upon these women, easing their entry into the social fabric of the ports. They may have found aspects of the culture unsettling, but they enjoyed numerous opportunities to exploit their familiarity with it for social capital.

For Americans of more precarious standing, the practices of calling and visiting could be tense. When pirates murdered Captain Benjamin P. Howes near Hong Kong in 1866, his widow, Lucy Lord Howes Hooper, found herself lodged at the expense of the British government, awaiting arrangements to return to the United States. Staying at the Stag Hotel, she engaged in a social life as busy as that of the higher society women. Yet Hooper found public scrutiny of her activities stifling. While Beal and Bradford enjoyed the attention and bustle, Hooper felt social practices left little room for privacy or error. She felt particularly conscious of being a single American among British women, whom she considered lofty and unfairly critical of American people and culture.[31] As Americans developed a larger presence in China, critiques such as Hooper's became commonplace. Beal, writing from the 1850s, was diplomatic in the ways she described British colonial practices, but over the next two decades, women such as Hooper, Bradford, and Livingston (filtered through Albert Heard) had fewer reservations about highlighting the dissimilarities between the British and American communities.

The quotidian practice of dining demonstrates this shifting relationship between the British and Americans in Hong Kong. In the Canton days, when trustworthiness, kinship ties, and sociability were imperative to trade's success, American and Anglo-European men strove to maintain and expand personal networks. Dining together provided one such opportunity. At the Thirteen Factories, American merchants frequently dined with their British peers.[32] Dixwell had gone to great lengths to host and impress prominent British merchants such as David Jardine, who stayed with the Heards, and Alexander Matheson.[33] Robert Bennet Forbes even acted as the master of ceremonies at William Jardine's 1839 goodbye dinner, drinking tea to keep his wits, settling rows between the Parsis and Scottish clerks, and proudly toasting his own "scotch blood."[34] The presence of Parsis at such an informal party owed credit to William Jardine's long and productive history with their mercantile community, but otherwise the party, like most casual dinners, was sufficiently "Anglo-Saxon."[35]

Nineteenth-century contours of "Anglo-Saxonism" were imprecise, but to the American elite it encapsulated an ambiguous set of traits believed to be shared with their British peers.[36] Although from separate nations, the British and Americans found camaraderie through their supposedly common heritage, their shared use of English, and their whiteness made explicit by the small size of their community. With so many commonalities, they had few reservations about toasting each other's company.[37] Formal dinners did occur with Chinese and other European nationals, and the Chinese particularly hosted extravagant affairs, but the day-to-day social network of the American China traders was British.[38]

Dinner parties with the Chinese declined in the years leading to the First Opium War, and following 1856 mixed dining in general followed suit.[39] Formal dinners imbued with sociopolitical importance continued in Hong Kong for the benefit of visiting dignitaries and business associates; in the case of the Heard brothers, they became a necessary part of their duties as Russian and Portuguese consuls, but as China's American community grew and expanded, elite gatherings becoming more nationally exclusive. Over time, the casual dinners that American women described in letters home were less and less frequented by the British.[40] These more intimate gatherings "agreeably reminded" Americans of home and helped foster nostalgia for the United States.[41] This was due, in part, to the merchant house's decentralization. Less often confined to a single house turned office, married partners and clerks lost the communalism of the old China trade dinners, instead taking turns hosting each other's families.[42] These events came to rely upon the metropolitan networks of the merchants, and even rivals such as Albert Heard and John Murray Forbes frequently mentioned dining with each other. In this sense, at least, Hong Kong's American community turned inward as it expanded.

The ready availability of American companionship from the 1850s on augmented a growing sense of cultural difference between Americans and their British neighbors in China and shifted attitudes toward social life. Elizabeth Warden, née Beal, Helen Beal's younger sister, found that "English people" in the ports were poor company, ignorant regarding matters of American culture and politics. Helen Beal too felt politically and culturally disconnected from the British community, while Bradford avoided the British, full of "dash and swell." Bradford preferred "solid" Germans, or better yet Americans newly arrived in China; it seemed "a breeze from home to catch a real live American just from the sod." For those such as Livingston, without such a community, "no children, no friends," and a husband toiling away at the office, life could be miserable.[43] Although three of these women mostly wrote from Shanghai, the circumstances of all four were similar. Their desire for home comforts and distaste for British culture affected their experiences in China and Hong Kong. Rather than struggle to assimilate, as Ellen Coolidge or Rebecca Kinsman had before them at Macao, these women, and by extension their husbands, turned to internal networks for social fulfillment.

A growing national sense of class propriety likewise shifted American attitudes toward hosting culture. Many American merchants in China came from the Boston Brahmin class in New England—"an East Coast establishment that discreetly but effectively dominated academia, trade, politics, and the arts"—or could claim equivalent status.[44] Nineteenth-century Brahmins adhered to a strict set of social traditions and norms, including church membership (some designated Unitarianism the "Boston Religion," but there were Protestant revivalists and evangelicals as well), attendance at appropriate schools, and marrying within the same class.[45] Their religious and social beliefs valued, in theory, rational thought, a "capacity for moral action," and by the century's end a distaste for commercialism, which favored "not the self-made business man but the idle man" devoted to culture.[46] Temperance and parsimony were celebrated; public notoriety was not. One of Augustine Heard Sr.'s earliest lessons to his nephews had been that a gentleman should not associate with "hangers-on in tap rooms" or "be seen in such places."[47] Public consumption of spirits had acquired a class element in America, and contemporary British and colonial observers likewise associated overconsumption with the "lower orders."[48] Vices such as drinking and smoking "threatened to undermine the carefully cultivated impression of the superiority of Western institutions."[49] In theory, the successful American merchant in China avoided vice, worked hard to make a quick competency, and retired early, shrugging off the unseemly quest for capital to cultivate cultural interests.

Rounds of dining and hosting contradicted the American merchants' values, and an extravagant life in China could ruin the aspirations of a prospective American elite.[50] Helen Beal described the folly of young clerks in China, who kept "a body-servant of necessity," imbibed "a variety of wines" at dinner, and acquired "all kinds of luxuries and indulgent habits." These clerks developed "sentiments and opinions which they never would have formed in life in the quiet of home."[51] Heading Augustine Heard & Co. in 1873, Albert Heard received similar critiques from his brothers, who denounced his decadence. He explained that Hong Kong's social life necessitated some overspending.[52] Maintaining status in the port required demonstrating wealth, but excessive luxury deviated from metropolitan ideals and the purpose of tenure in China. The dilemma was so endemic that it became a regular theme in the *China Mail*, where opinion pieces attacked the "romance" of "expensive living." As had Albert Heard, responders blamed demanding social pressures that required merchants and clerks alike return the hospitalities of fellows, or else live "like a hermit."[53]

In an ironic twist, New Englanders' sociocultural habits, fashioned as they were upon "a reservoir of [British] tradition and prestige," encouraged the American merchant community's seclusion from certain social practices.[54] From the 1850s until the community's decline in the 1880s, American homes continued to function as public spaces, but as more Americans inhabited the port their retinue of guests became more exclusive. Throughout this period hosting and dining remained characteristically American, providing a refuge for cultivating metropolitan sociocultural values that in turn affected one's status upon their return from China. Americans by no means sequestered themselves from China's British or other foreign communities; through calling culture and in Hong Kong's formally public spaces they continued to assimilate with and contribute to colonial culture. The growth of their community, however, from a handful of men at Canton to several families enabled them to recall and preserve some aspects of their metropolitan culture.

Yet even as American writers underscored Anglo-American differences throughout their commentaries on calling culture, dining, and hosting, they took the racial homogeneity of these activities for granted. As in other colonies, domestic laborers formed the backbone of colonial life, and in most cases domestic laborers in Hong Kong were Chinese.[55] These Chinese staff employed in British and American households undergirded the social world of their employers. When calling, a Chinese doorman took the visitor's card, an amah assisted the expecting hostess, Chinese cooks prepared the tea (or for privileged guests, tiffin), and Chinese staff served the party. On route, Chinese "chair-coolies," as they were termed, bore their employers up and down the mountain. When dining, either at home or with friends, a "body servant" accompanied their employer to act as their personal attendant at dinner.

These domestic servants had "privileged access to the private lives of Europeans," and being the "only Chinese with whom Europeans in Hong Kong came into extended contact" these servants became the basis of "negative stereotypes of "the Chinese character."[56] When American letters mentioned the Chinese staff, writers described them as curiosities. Letters related Chinese "peculiarities" to friends and family for amusement, while barely accounting for their centrality to social life. The descriptions in these letters infantilized Chinese servants, construing them as "other," "impotent," to mitigate the "dependency on and vulnerability to the Chinese" that foreigners in Hong Kong felt.[57] Such infantilizing discourse was a common feature with regard to white servants as well in the British metropole, but in the colonies its racial edge was honed.[58]

Through such representation, American writers perpetuated negative racial stereotypes and obscured the agency of their Chinese employees, erasing them from the public life of a port predominantly populated by Chinese subjects.[59] It was scarcely acknowledged, for example, that without Chinese men to bear them up the hills American men and women would hardly be visiting anyone. Arriving at Hong Kong in 1863, Martha Green complained of being "obliged to walk" to the house of a merchant who would not supply her party with chairs. She noted that all ladies in the port kept their own, "covered with cloth and ornamented with tassels," doors and "venetian shutters."[60] She spent much more time describing the chairs than those who bore them. By neglecting to acknowledge the servant in social life, Green's account idealized a segregation impossible to achieve.[61] While Green never explicitly advocated segregation, she and other writers circumvented the matter of public racial contact through omission. Those Chinese or Indian pedestrians Green did describe were observed from her chair on evening drives to or from dinner with members of the foreign community.[62] The social life American men and women related to those back home was white, energetic, and occurred within the prescribed boundaries of colonial acceptability.

SOCIAL PARTICIPATION AND THE PUBLIC EYE

While calling, visiting, and dining occurred in the home, most social contact between Americans and the wider colonial community took place through daily interactions in Hong Kong's public spaces and institutions. Hong Kong's foreign community habitually used the port's public sites, congregating on the parade ground below the Heard house, walking Queen's Road to Happy Valley each evening, or picnicking at The Peak and Pok Fu Lam.[63] Besides mitigating the boredom of "seeing the same people day after day," these spaces provided opportunities for observing and being observed, for bumping into friends and peers and participating in the port's colonial culture.[64] For the elite and socially mobile, clubs, committees, and the church constituted primary sites to network. Membership in the Hong Kong Club, the Hong Kong Yacht Club, the Victoria Cricket Club, the Freemasons, and other organizations conferred a degree of respectability and social capital. They provided prestige and networks, with benefits extending across the British Empire. These varied forms of social networking reached their most fevered at Hong Kong's pinnacle social event: the annual races held every February at Happy Valley Racecourse. All attended, the elite displayed their wealth, and Hong Kong's many communities used the opportunity to demonstrate their status within society. As the Americans' experiences within these public sites suggests, their success at assimilating with the British depended on their whiteness and their ability to perform the sociocultural norms of the elite class. Still, social, political, and cultural differences created tensions. Americans straddling elite colonial and elite metropolitan societies had to balance the competing impulses to conform while assuring those back home that they were still, in fact, American.

Although designated "public," one's admissibility in Hong Kong's common spaces hinged on race and class. Public spaces were not welcoming to all, and American merchants' capacity to navigate these spaces relied upon their whiteness and their cultural connections with the British elite. As a colonial entrepôt at the edge of the Qing Empire, the presence of nonwhite migrants, indigent sailors, and soldiers within Hong Kong was inevitable. These groups affected foreigners' perceptions of Hong Kong's public spaces.

By performing prescribed roles as Sikh police officers, Chinese sedan chair bearers, or amahs tending white children, the public activities of the nonwhite communities reinforced entrenched colonial hierarchies that affirmed the authority of empire, even as visual markers of alterity such as the turbans of Sikh officers uncomfortably symbolized their exotic "otherness" and inspired racial prejudice.[65] Unlike "othered" groups, American merchants appeared no different than their elite British counterparts and were culturally fluent. In Hong Kong they increasingly leveraged such similarities to assimilate into the colony's elite foreign public life.

Hong Kong's social spaces that rendered "non-bourgeois" whiteness visible were, however, problematic for a colonial society that determined status through "imperialist politics of race" and "bourgeois politics of class."[66] Commenters denigrated spaces such as Queen's Road as a "tempting locality" for white transients to get "publicly intoxicated" and predicted in 1862 that the proposed Praya would gain a similar reputation.[67] Sailors, soldiers, beachcombers, and others who upset the socioracial order of things were especially problematic to the elite. American prostitutes, for instance, established themselves around the center of Victoria, and the poorer of them lived in the vicinity of Wan Chai.[68] These women possessed the "ambiguous status of privileged pariah," protected by their race but still embarrassing to the colonial elite.[69] Even the most "wretched members" of white society shared "a status higher" than those who could lay no claim to whiteness.[70] Accordingly, those areas at the far end of the spectrum with heavy Chinese populations, such as Taipingshan and Sai Ying Pun, barely registered in the social consciousness of the port's white community, except as neighborhoods of poverty and crime.[71] Americans may have enjoyed unobstructed access to all Hong Kong's public spaces, but preserving their image required confining their activities to respectable locales while avoiding contemptible streets and nonwhite neighborhoods.

If Hong Kong's size prior to the 1898 acquisition of the New Territories denied the foreign community the freedom to hunt, paper chase, and "trample" all over the countryside as their countrymen did in the northern treaty ports, reputable public spaces offered Americans opportunities to engage with and perform colonial culture.[72] Although small, the dusty parade ground provided adequate space for meeting. Here cricket matches (British and Americans competing together), military tattoos, and concerts performed for the foreign community's enjoyment punctuated the monotony of colonial life.[73] Americans even brought their own national flair to these spaces through annual Fourth of July celebrations. Initially such affairs were muted. Writing in Amoy in 1862, Braford wished more than anything "to hear a good brass band play 'Dixie'"—the de facto Confederate anthem enjoyed popularity among Northerners and Southerners alike prior to the Civil war—and complained of the otherwise poor showing in comparison to Queen Victoria's earlier birthday celebrations.[74] That same year Hong Kong's *China Mail* reprinted a British editorial from *The Times* that read "to us [the Fourth of July] is like any other day, to them it is a festival solemnly set aside for gratifying . . . a national vanity the most inordinate and the most exacting the world has ever seen."[75]

The article's tone is unsurprising. As America waded further into its civil war in 1862, a series of political blunders strained the relationship between the British and American communities. Following the war relationships normalized, and reports on the Fourth of July from 1873 at Shanghai and 1877 at Canton described extravagant celebrations hosted by American firms and officials.[76] British Hong Kong, however, was less jubilant. An 1868 edition of the *China Mail* marked the day with a report about Americans disturbing the peace by illegally launching fireworks from the Praya East.[77] Even an editorial about America's 1876 centenary describing the nation's history concluded with the lackluster statement, "the usual 4th of July reception will be held at the United States Consulate from eleven a.m. to two p.m."[78] The various reports suggest that while Americans imported aspects of their culture to China, transnational rivalries limited their success in Hong Kong.

Other rituals, such as the habitual morning and evening rides to Happy Valley, provided Americans less abrasive opportunities to infuse the port with their metropolitan culture. Affluent Americans, familiar with riding back home, kept horses in Hong Kong at considerable expense for recreation and to pull carriages, but James Murray Forbes recalled that upkeep of the animals was well beyond the average clerk's means.[79] Augustine Heard Sr.'s lectures to his nephews on the benefits of riding were well heeded, and Livingston, particularly, adhered to the practice. Albert Heard would meet her at the stables in the evenings after work and lead her to Happy Valley for a turn around the course, which he bragged was "turfed over . . . according to English custom." Bradford, of somewhat lesser means, noted in 1870 that the "saddle & bridle" in Hong Kong cost more than the horse.

LIVES LIVED IN PUBLIC

Still, she kept a pony named "Bob" (short for Robert le Diable), which, despite its penchant for biting, she rode daily.[80]

China Mail's "Light Litterateur" exaggerated in 1863 that "almost everyone in Hong Kong" kept a horse for daily use, but by the 1870s the popularity of riding and driving among both men and women had earned the port a reputation.[81] In an 1873 caricature notably foregrounding Heard house as the iconic view of Hong Kong, *China Punch* jested that women such as British broker Atwell Coxon's wife, Louisa Coxon, were notorious throughout China (figure 3.2). "Mrs Atwell Coxon," who flouted social etiquette and drove her own carriage, was "a force of nature," and "Mr. Punch" suggested that only the fear of appearing in *China Punch*'s pages could induce such Hong Kong ladies to drive respectably.[82] American men and women embraced Hong Kong's riding culture as an extension of their national

FIGURE 3.2. *China Punch* comic depicting Louisa Coxon driving with her husband Atwell Coxon. *Source*: "Manners and Customs of Hong Kong," *China Punch*, February 1873. Courtesy of the Hong Kong Baptist University Library.

culture and the enthusiasm with which they participated in all things equestrian undoubtedly helped build the reputation the *China Mail* and *China Punch* alluded to.

Besides riding, Americans exploited their familiarity with other forms of British recreation to assimilate with Hong Kong's elite British society. Many of the Britons coming to the colonies found they could sustain a lifestyle reserved in the metropole for the upper class and participated in leisure activities inaccessible to them back in England.[83] For many of the American merchants, however, the very act of coming to China was a product of privilege. Clerks and business partners were drawn from local kinship networks and often came from the same class and social circles.[84] Of elevated status, these merchants acquired the necessary skills for assimilating into elite colonial society at home and through college experiences at Yale or Harvard that emphasized sporting culture and a healthy social life.[85] Such sporting culture featured cricket, yachting, horseracing, golf, and tennis and functioned as one of the ways "affluent Anglo-Americans" separated "themselves from the masses."[86] Their familiarity with the use of leisure to demarcate their elite status in the metropole gave the American elite an edge in Hong Kong's social life.

The ease with which Americans integrated themselves into Hong Kong's British community underscores their comfort with elite forms of colonial social interaction, and they used this know-how to enmesh themselves completely in elite colonial society. Any American with sufficient status joined the Hong Kong Club. The club was a main vessel for facilitating the port's elite networking, making membership in it essential. Club culture was not new to American merchants: such institutions had a rich history in Boston and New York. Membership in Boston's exclusive Somerset Club on Beacon Street, or the Union Clubs on Boston's Park Street and New York's Park Avenue indicated a merchant's social capital.[87] Membership in these invitation-only clubs likewise affirmed others' recognition of one's upper-class pedigree. The Hong Kong Club held similar importance, with the added benefit of easing the American merchants' entry into elite British society. Formed in 1846, the club limited membership to civil, naval, and military officers as well as "any gentleman received in good society in China."[88] George Heard even served on the Hong Kong Club Committee while in the colony.[89] Applicants were admitted through ballot, and prohibitive fees meant that membership in the club equated to membership among the colony's wealthy elite.[90]

Moreover, membership in the Hong Kong Club was transnationally recognized, cementing its centrality to the extension and maintenance of colonial networking and granting its holders access to a wider club network across the Empire. John Heard described how his Hong Kong Club affiliation secured him access "to all the Indian clubs" while traveling in Calcutta, and he lodged at the Bengal Club during his month-long stay in the city.[91] The Somerset Club in Boston and Knickerbocker Club in New York provided similar services, and both were used by repatriated American merchants from Russell & Co. to host annual "Keechong Club" dinners. This closed group of returned traders included such illustrious members as John M. Forbes, J. Murray Forbes, Warren Delano, Joseph Coolidge, Gideon Nye Jr., and Augustine Heard Sr.[92] Through such functions, the Hong Kong, Bengal, Somerset, and Knickerbocker Clubs became anchors within the transnational networks of the American merchant elite.

The Hong Kong Club provided a space to network outside the formal business world of the merchant house. *China Punch* satirized that the club was a place to meet for dinner and "endure drinks" with "insufferable friends" or to hold celebratory parties such as the annual Scottish St. Andrew's Dinner.[93] Yet despite being carried out in private, such gatherings of cultural pride were made public by the port's print media. *China Punch*'s ribbing of the St. Andrew's proceedings is unsurprising, since the periodical's producers, J. B. Coughtrie, W. N. Middleton, and Edward Beart, were members of the club and knew the attendants personally.[94] Even the *China Mail* could not resist teasing the sixty or so "Caledonians" and "one or two English guests" about the "enthusiasm, or seeming enthusiasm" with which they celebrated their "cultural peculiarities."[95] In fact, the *China Mail*'s egalitarian 1861 editor, James Kemp, took aim at every aspect of the club, noting sarcastically that only "vulgar people" found the sight of "so many good-looking young gentlemen" together "smoking their cigars in an amiable manner" irritating.[96] Kemp found issue with the performance of aloof exceptionalism the club inspired in its patrons. For its members, the club conferred the benefits of an elite transnational network, but its exclusivity and class pretensions made it a site of social tension, and so easy fodder for the satirists and social commenters of the port. In joining the club American merchants aligned themselves with its values, came increasingly under the public eye, and received similar scrutiny from papers such as *China Punch* and the *China Mail*.

Although *China Punch* and *China Mail* editors lambasted the Hong Kong Club and its members for superficiality, decadence, and drinking, the club served a wider social purpose for its members, connecting them to sporting clubs, institutions, and public events in the colony; social worlds in which the editors were themselves participants. By the 1860s elite social life unmoored itself from the club, as distinct societies, committees, and sporting clubs appeared. Still, many of these new institutions maintained ties to the Hong Kong Club, and for the American merchants the club's external connections provided opportunities to participate in Hong Kong's British society and politics on a wider scale.

Americans did so through sport and through civic institutions. Colonial inhabitants felt that a healthy sporting culture demonstrated the "Anglo-Saxon" race's national spirit and vigor, and by participating, Americans lay claim to the same energy.[97] New England merchants, well acquainted with sailing and rowing, took especial interest in these aspects of the port's sporting life. During the Canton days, Americans established the Fah Kee Yacht Club—the name a transliteration of the Cantonese term for the United States, *fakei* (*huaqi* 花旗), or "flower flag"—and later joined Hong Kong's Victoria Regatta Club upon its creation in 1861.[98] The latter was fully open to Hong Kong Club members as well as British Army and Navy officers, and it hosted an annual regatta in November and races in which George Heard and William Howell Forbes competed.[99] American merchants also joined the Hong Kong Cricket Club, became involved in institutions such as the General Chamber of Commerce (George Heard was a committee member), practiced Freemasonry (Albert Heard served as junior warden), and acquired various consular appointments across Hong Kong and the treaty ports.[100] Each club, institution, and society they joined integrated Americans further into the port's elite society, providing opportunities to contribute to its social administration.

Breaking the tedium of daily social rituals, drinks at the club, and civic obligations, the annual spring horse races run at Happy Valley since 1846 were the much-anticipated highlight of Hong Kong's social calendar.[101] Newspapers and letters home documented the races in great detail. The *China Mail* inflated the races, a multiday affair occurring every Chinese New Year, as "the sole holiday" for the colony's businessmen, and American merchants made the most of the surrounding weeks.[102] Albert Heard wrote his father-in-law in 1873 that he and Livingston had enjoyed a "fortnight" of "gaities" [sic]. He listed a different event every day of the week, including the Race Ball, dinners with the Russian Grand Duke Alexei Alexandrovich, dances, and parties. Drawn to all this revelry, Albert Heard cared little for the races themselves.[103]

With the balance between women and men in Hong Kong skewed noticeably in favor of the latter, women found themselves in high demand during the weeks' events. Two hundred men vied for the attentions of fifty women at one 1873 event. American women wrote home of being run off their feet during the foreign community's various balls, and *China Punch* weighed in on the scarcity of women and the lengths men went through to impress them (figure 3.3).[104] Balls in general encouraged American women to draw cultural comparisons between themselves and the British. Describing several such events thrown by Augustine Heard & Co. partners, Helen Beal relished contrasting American "grace and elegance" with the "stiff and reserved" conduct of "English ladies."[105] While the festive atmosphere of the races, balls, and parties promoted the intermingling of Hong Kong's foreign communities, these events also exposed cultural differences and inspired participants to comment upon distinctions between the cultures they encountered and their own.

Differences of class, race, and culture were especially explicit at Happy Valley, where attendance was not limited to Europeans. The *Illustrated London News* provided metropolitan readers with a calibrated and racialized vision of the diverse groups attending the 1858 races, an event that brought all in the colony together "regardless of creed or class," but where "order and social boundaries were maintained" (figure 3.4).[106] While the metropolitan paper worked through stereotypes, local articles likewise depicted the social disparities that characterized the festivities. The port's well-to-do inhabitants patronized merchant booths and the mat-shed grandstand, while the rest of the white population congregated on the ground in front. "A large crowd of well-dressed Chinese" always attended, and the Chinese community put up their own race, with Chinese riders "on native ponies."[107] South and Southeast Asian picnickers dotted the slopes surrounding the course, their marginalized presence emphasized in the papers. The *China Mail*'s correspondent could not resist mocking the "Lascars and Manilamen," noting that the event brought out "an interesting collection of the

FIGURE 3.3. *China Punch* comic joking about the influence Western women held over Western men in society. *Source*: "Manners and Customs of Hong Kong & Ball-Room Manners at Hong Kong," *China Punch*, February 20, 1873. Courtesy of the Hong Kong Baptist University Library.

FIGURE 3.4. Sketch for the *Illustrated London News*, showing a range of nonwhite and lower-class white patrons crowding the one-shilling stand at the 1858 Hong Kong races. *Source*: "The One-Shilling Stand," *Illustrated London News*, May 15, 1858.

picturesque and the grotesque," and publishing derisive caricatures of them based solely on the pseudoscientific racism of the time.[108] Still, those communities that could accrued some social clout by sponsoring a cup, and all found ways to participate in the revelry.

Europeans especially used the opportunity to show off. American men and women donned stylish or outrageous outfits to make a splash, merchants contributed subscriptions to present a "Fahkee" cup—the "most magnificent in point of design and execution"—and the great trading firms turned out large tiffins each day.[109] American merchants erected private booths, offering guests flowing champagne and the best food Lane & Crawford could supply.[110] Augustine Heard & Co. was among those firms that hosted tiffins, and John and Albert Heard used the opportunity for "hobnobbing" and "entertaining."[111] For Albert Heard, the event was electrifying. His 1860 letter home to his parents about the week of partying invoked the energy of the day. He described lavish suits and military regalia adorning the port's elite and officers, dressed in "Red coats and blue coats, lace and embroidery." The Heards invited associates, dignitaries, and military officers to join them in dining, partying, and watching the races. The event was an expensive but vital opportunity to generate social capital. By acting the gregarious host, the Heards hoped to signal their business's success to the port's inhabitants, buy themselves a place within elite British society, and instill confidence in the stability of their company. But while the races brought communities together, they also inspired "petty nastiness of one kind or another."[112] The Heards' performance was in many ways an obligation and failing to meet it could be as disastrous as meeting it was productive. John Heard recalled being loathe to the idea of showing his face at the races and subjecting himself to ridicule following the firm's 1875 bankruptcy.[113] If lacking the adequate means, the publicness of events such as the annual races could have adverse effects on the social reputation of the port's white inhabitants.

Class and race were ever-present themes in accounts of the festivities, and like the *China Mail* correspondent, Albert Heard fixated on differences. He complimented the American officers invited to tiffin at their 1860 race booth and felt the British soldiers attending the race ball cut a "gallant" bearing of "bewildering loveliness," while the ladies and rooms were "tastefully adorned." He applauded the colony's British pageantry, contrasting it to "dull and gloomy" Shanghai. Yet if he found British pomp appealing, it was offset by what he described as "squalid" crowds of "Chinese, Parsees, Jews, Malays, Congalese [sic]," and "siamese."[114] The contrasting language in his letter reflected a wider mid-nineteenth-century ideological shift whereby exclusionary obsessions with the primacy of white "virtues" supplanted the assimilative idea that nonwhites could learn "Victorian values."[115] As scientific racism became entrenched in mid-nineteenth-century British and American thought, adherents came to believe in rigidly defined ideas of racial virtues and flaws.

White British and Americans thus bestowed upon themselves the peak position within emerging racial hierarchies, both laying claim to a supposedly privileged Anglo-Saxon heritage. For white New Englanders, this heritage evoked nostalgia for the "tradition, ornament, and ritual," of British imperial forms; a nostalgia apparent in Albert Heard's descriptions of the British soldiers at the race ball.[116] Such reverence helped smooth over contradictions, positioning American values of "freedom and liberty" as core tenets of the "Anglo-Saxon" alongside the contradictory belief that Anglo-Saxons were "natural rulers of other races."[117] Race remained the most visible marker of one's status, but within British colonial society the added ability to perform the sociocultural role of the English-speaking "Anglo-Saxon" eased entry into the elite ranks.

American confidence in their Anglo-Saxon virtues was self-reflexive, bolstered through comparison, and Albert Heard's racial juxtaposition of the British with the Chinese and others, stemmed from his latent desire to conflate the Americans with Hong Kong's elite white community.[118] His point of comparison hinged upon not just Anglo-American similarities but also articulations of difference.[119] His description of the races provided the perfect medium to do so, as transnational encounters helped familiarize American merchants with the relationship between "racial diversity and social complexity." Merchants such as Albert Heard acquired a heightened awareness "of how"—they believed—Asians and Africans perceived them as white gentlemen, and of their relative place atop colonial social and racial hierarchies.[120] For Albert Heard it did not matter that the diverse groups attending the race events celebrated in European style; his denigration of the nonwhite communities sharpened his veneration of the British, implicitly conferring an elevated status on his brothers and himself as they intermingled with the British revelers present in these elite spaces. Albert Heard's letters used the explication of racial difference to equate the British and Americans as forming two parts of a single colonial social elite, placing the Americans, on paper at least, on par with their British counterparts.

Involvement in one notable social institution, however, damaged Anglo-American relationships. The church occupied, in theory, a central position in colonial society, and weekly attendance was necessary for much more than spiritual fulfilment. Through church attendance women could enter the public sphere, and men and women could be observed performing respectable norms.[121] The first church in Hong Kong was, unexpectedly, a small chapel established by the American Baptist mission in July 1842 that accepted both European and Chinese members. The mission's members preached throughout the region, but in 1860 the mission closed and moved to Swatow.[122] Yet as a British colony, Hong Kong's main church for the foreign community, St. John's Cathedral, established 1849, was Anglican. By the 1850s there were little more than two hundred Protestants in Hong Kong, and of these some, such as the Americans, were dissenters disinclined to attend an Anglican service.[123] Choices were, however, limited, and the small American community could either attend the British preachers' Anglican sermons or forgo church. Bradford recorded just one instance of a good sermon while at Amoy, which she credited to the visiting American missionary, Rev. Leonard W. Kip.[124] Both Bradford and her future husband, Crowell, were outspoken about the role of Christianity in general in China, writing home about the "intrusion of missionaries into Chinese life" and relating with pleasure the difficulties missionaries encountered in the interior.[125]

The upper-class Americans, many of them New England Unitarians, took particular issue with secular topics in British sermons.[126] The intermingling of reverence to both God and the queen in British preachers' rhetoric sat uncomfortably with Americans, and women especially wrote home that it was unpleasant to hear "prayers offered three times every Sunday morning to 'Our Gracious Queen and Governor Victoria.'" Moreover, New Englanders felt that, especially among "Englishmen and English women," the Unitarian faith was held "in contempt" and so avoided the church more than they might at home.[127] Ironically, they registered their complaints on account of both their republican and religious sensibilities, merging, in their own way, church and state. These women equated their religious identity to their republican pride and used both to differentiate themselves from the British community.

Despite social pressure to attend weekly sermons, the ramifications of forgoing church were minor. Writing from Shanghai in 1850, Helen Beal commented that "not all foreigners go to Church," and in 1852 wrote that her husband never found the time to attend. Nor were American elites overly concerned with proselytizing, as Bradford's and Crowell's distaste for missionaries suggests. The complaints New England women registered about religion in China rather reflected insecurities about the standing of American religion and politics within British society. They used both topics to reaffirm their republican pride by juxtaposing their beliefs against those of the British. Their commentaries articulated more than just religious difference, merging critiques of British social habits and political sensibilities into accounts of colonial life. When referencing religion at least, they exposed the fault lines that existed between Hong Kong's American and British elite. Race and language may have unified both, but through sensitive subjects such as religion, deeper issues emerged. Accounts of "visiting culture," extravagant dinners, regattas, race days, and the club all demonstrated the willingness of Americans in Hong Kong and the treaty ports to assimilate with and contribute to British colonial society and culture, but comments on religious and by extension political and social differences helped remind the writers and those back home of "the fact" that they were "American," with "home endearments," and "love of Country." "You must not fear," wrote Helen Beal in 1852, "that your child is growing anti-republican—I thank god I was born an American."[128]

GOSSIP, SATIRE, AND THE MEDIA

American merchants largely endeavored to participate actively in Hong Kong society. Their relationship with the British was not always placid, but they tended toward aligning themselves with the port's dominant Anglo-colonial culture, distancing themselves from "other" communities in the process. The extent of their public engagement, however, had its own dangers. Being so conspicuous, American merchants became easy targets for social critiques in the port's newspapers and satirical publications. *China Punch* satire and *China Mail* articles alike targeted the United States, and even Augustine Heard & Co., whose bankruptcy served as a lightning rod for unwanted attention. *China Punch* used whimsy and satire to recreate China in the British idiom, but the publication's satire also presumed "a one-to-one correspondence between real individuals or classes" that thrived on picking at their reputation. The articles about Americans in Hong Kong that *China Punch* and the *China Mail* published toyed with the community and its place within elite society, their satirical or critical content demonstrating the precarity of social status in the colony, and how public visibility was double-edged.[129]

Published by the *China Mail* office, *China Punch* enjoyed only a limited and nonconsecutive run from 1867 to 1876.[130] The magazine was read widely by and often featured commentaries on elite members of the foreign community. Francis Blackwell Forbes wrote in 1874, for example, that Mrs. Bramston, whom he evidently did not care for, considered the paper "intensely vulgar," as it had dubbed her husband "Mr Treacle Brimstone."[131] The paper likewise lambasted "Wm F. Orbs" (William H. Forbes) for idly watching his goods and offices burn, only to submit a heavy claim to the government for remuneration.[132] George Heard even submitted jokes to the paper, at least one of which was accepted.[133] Whether Americans scanned the paper for references to themselves or were earnest subscribers, the community was aware of the content being written about them.

As in the Bramstons' case, the way the paper represented elites could inspire indignation and provoke reactions when the subjects being mocked were sensitive. Indeed, in later issues the Heards appeared in several satirical articles. These articles, targeting the firm through the pseudonym "Messrs Disgustine Bird & Co.," were increasingly frequent as the Heards fell upon financial difficulty and ultimately bankruptcy.[134] If John Heard was sensitive to the effect the firm's failure would have on his public image in 1875, the paper's jabs salted the wound.

China Punch even featured George Heard, the most public of the brothers, multiple times by name, and his political "reaching" and bon vivant demeanor inspired his depiction through both text and caricature. Likely depicting Richard Rowett, who succeed George Heard as vice commodore of the Hong Kong Yacht Club following the latter's 1874 promotion to commodore, a *China Punch* comic, for example, questioned the "Naval Intelligence" behind the promotion (figure 3.5). The caricature, at least, was likely in good humor, as the *China Punch* editor Ed Beart worked beside both men as secretary of the Yacht Club.[135]

It is difficult to gauge how George Heard received these jokes, and he continued to read the paper following their publication. The attacks levied on the firm's failure, however, were more critical. Merchant decadence was a recurring theme throughout the paper's short run, juxtaposed to the "hard times" of business in the port.[136] Augustine Heard & Co.'s bankruptcy, and the lavish public style with which Albert Heard and George Heard conducted themselves, therefore fit comfortably within the paper's range. Their struggling ventures, such as the Hong Kong and Macao Steamship Company, became the fodder for critique, and the sale of their properties was underscored in the paper's mock-advertisement section.[137] The most barbed piece, however, took the form of a thinly veiled poem about four nephews dragging the respectable name of their uncle through the dirt.

Whose name will help us when we tell
The shareholders we love so well
Their Capital is all a "sell?"
Our Uncle's

We'll say our first desire will be
From liabilities to free

FIGURE 3.5. *China Punch* caricature poking fun at the 1873 appointment of a new commodore and vice commodore in the Hong Kong Yacht Club. *Source*: "Naval Intelligence," *China Punch*, October 8, 1873. Courtesy of the Hong Kong Baptist University Library.

The highly-honoured name of thee,
Our Uncle

Our partner too—unlucky youth—
Who's in the self-same boat, forsooth,
Will "*go* with us," and that's the truth,
Our Uncle

Through years of work the task entails,
Affection's holy claim prevails,
And we will clear, whoe'er assails
Our Uncle

Whose memory did we most revere
While spending thousands year by year
(*Whose* thousands wasn't very clear,
Oh, Uncle!)

Whose reputation free from stain
Will we endeavour to maintain
Since we our own can not retain?
Our Uncle's

And if our creditors do scout
And turn us to the right about
Thy name we'll never cease to spout
Our Uncle.[138]

The poem drew upon a familiar style, made popular by William Henry Wills's 1845 poem "The Uncles of England," published in *Punch*, in which the charitable "Uncle"—slang for pawnbroker—helped the layabout author retain his good name by generously offering cash for goods, thereby keeping the author's creditors at bay.[139] The roles in the *China Punch* poem channeled this relationship, the "Uncle's" good name being the credit upon which the brothers drew. "Our Uncle" made it clear that while the Heards had spent three decades in China building up their company, the public was aware that they had achieved their success through Augustine Heard Sr.'s reputation. Considering the company's founding circumstances, the article was an ironic eulogy. The brothers having briefly resurrected their enterprise as Heard & Co. in 1875, *China Punch* trumpeted that "by a late *August* arrival," (they referred here to Augustine Heard Jr.'s return to China), "Erred & Co." was ready to "Commence the Duty of CLEARING THE NAME of THEIR LAMENTED UNCLE."[140]

It would seem the Heards took the brunt of *China Punch*'s broadside on Hong Kong's American community, but the paper directed more general articles at "Brother Jonathan" as well. It would be a mistake to distort "the relative severity" of such criticisms, as many reflected "the idiom of their time."[141] A brief survey of 1867, 1870, and 1873 runs of *Punch* in London turns up interspersed articles providing similar political commentaries about post– Civil War tensions and Anglo-American cultural differences.[142] Still, during *China Punch*'s brief run, such differences provided more consistent content than in contemporary runs of its London cousin, and the regularity of certain local topics suggest that, through the paper, fraught sociopolitical relationships between China's Anglo-American communities not only existed but also found public platform.[143] An 1867 address directed at the Americans at Canton, for example, picked at the Opium War tensions of the 1840s and 1850s, patronizing the Americans for reestablishing themselves at that port "after lending 'tin' to the Chinese" to help keep the British out.[144] The article reminded Americans it was the first time since the Second Opium War that they had "set to work independently," condescending that the British—"who opened the way"—would bear "no objection."

Other articles mocked American social pretensions, reinforcing the primacy of British etiquette in colonial society. Responding to an American correspondent who complained in 1867 that "contemptible little [American] clerks" in China would "drawl in their speech, part their hair in the middle, and ape English manners" the instant they landed in Hong Kong, *China Punch* retaliated that doing so was better than acting the "unkempt," "dirty," and uncouth "Yankee."[145] *China Punch*'s evocation of this final term "Yankee" was especially barbed. The term had a conflicted past, adopting a range of meanings since the American Revolutionary War. Although Americans claimed the moniker as one of veneration, signifying revolutionary valor, in the mouths of the British it was an epithet of derision.[146] An 1874 article, still, mused that Hong Kong must be the British Crown's "most Royal Domain," as evidenced by the "number of expatriated princes from Europe and America" settled there acting as "humble and honest traders."[147] The tropes *China Punch* deployed in these two articles, separated by seven years, suggest a progression of the American in the eyes of Hong Kong's British. In the first article, the contemptible clerk, by aping English manners, elevates himself above his unkempt Yankee brethren so that by the second article the American merchant in Hong Kong has assumed the airs of an "expatriated prince."

The tone of articles in the more respectable *China Mail* legitimized the statements published in *China Punch*. By printing and reprinting content similarly critical of America and Americans, the *China Mail* indirectly sharpened the satire in its offshoot. If the *China Mail* occasionally had a pro-American slant, Americans still remained a favorite target, evident through the frequency with which the paper published critiques of the United States and Hong Kong's American mercantile community.[148] Writing at a time when Anglo-American relations suffered over their respective politics during the Second Opium War, for instance, commenters attacked the American national press, its "low language," and its "abuse or deprecation of England," arguing that its readers were "average" or "working class," "an inevitable consequence" of its questionable quality.[149] When compliments were bestowed on their American cousins, merits stemmed from their "Anglo-Saxon" heritage or their shared sociocultural practices. The paper even reprinted entire blocks of text from Emerson's Anglophilic *English Traits* in 1857.[150] Commentators reserved particular criticism, however, for American celebrations of their nascent cultural and political identity. An editorial reprinted from Britain took issue, for example, with Fourth of July celebrations. The author felt Britain the unfair target of "invective and vituperation," while the holiday's purpose had "uniformly been to elevate the opinion which [Americans] entertained of their own merits."[151] Just as Americans were concerned about British opinions of their culture and politics, so too were the British concerned about the Americans, and these concerns were cemented in regular articles attempting to undercut Americans' national pride.

The *China Punch* articles had different tones and mocked separate aspects of society as those published in the *China Mail*, but both reflected British perceptions of the United States and Americans. The *China Mail* also served as a window into the world beyond Hong Kong, reprinting articles from Britain and the United States to inform the port's inhabitants of global politics, conflict, and culture. If the colonial press affected metropolitan perceptions of the empire, the inverse was true of colonial society.[152] Hong Kong's media published and reprinted articles discussing national politics and society, disseminating news about wider Anglo-American relations to the port's isolated communities. Americans behaving within prescribed colonial norms formed an acceptable part of Hong Kong's foreign society, but when American politics and culture, either in Hong Kong or at home, diverged too noticeably from the British, they were criticized. Therefore, while Americans might act the part of the British colonial elite, political and cultural tensions simmered, and Americans felt there was a palpable distaste among the British for the culture and republican ideals of the "Yankee." Colonial etiquette could be adopted and a place within elite society assumed, but "Brother Jonathan" and "John Bull" remained, through it all, rivals.

The most significant social critiques, however, came not from the pages of *China Punch* or the *China Mail* but from letters to friends and family back home. The American China merchants and their families were tied to insular social networks in the metropole, reproduced in Hong Kong and the treaty ports due to the influence kinship and personal relationships had in securing employment in China. The names of China merchants were well known, their activities and personal quirks fueling gossip spread through letters passed between eager readers at home. The publicness of private letters affected the nature of the information conveyed and language used in correspondence. These nineteenth-century writers had little faith in the privacy of letters, assuming unintended or interested parties would open and read them.[153] Helen Beal, aware of this eventuality, begged her father "regard [her] caution and not make [her] letters too public."[154] The Heard brothers, too, included quips to each other in French and experimented with ciphers in telegrams. Regardless of their precautions, the impulse to gossip could be strong; offhand remarks found their way to the page, and these remarks could be damning.[155]

Albert Heard, for example, found himself the topic of side conversations regarding his political ambition and the apparent scandal of his and Livingston's marriage. Tackling the topic more directly than *China Punch*, which mocked the wider community's fawning over Alexandrovich in 1873, Alethea Moller wrote from Shanghai to a friend in Massachusetts that Albert Heard's chaperoning of the Grand Duke was "absurd."[156]

Meanwhile, Francis Blackwell Forbes spread gossip about Albert Heard's relationship with Livingston. Although not overly fond of Livingston, calling her "frivolous and flippant," Forbes speculated that her departure from Hong Kong on account of her ill mother was a pretext.[157] Forbes's gossip had multiple implications, suggesting Albert Heard had caused his wife's misery, and evoking "gender prejudices" that generalized women in colonial ports as "irresponsible," "disorderly" socialites, thus betraying "anxieties and insecurities" about women's public activities.[158]

Such scandals and gossip provide alternative perspectives on the American China merchants' social world. Moller, Forbes, and the recipients of their letters were members of the New England and New York elite, and merchants, recognizing their transience in China, toiled to cultivate a respectable image among these metropolitan networks. Albert Heard confirmed as much when he described his later divorce from Livingston. He told his brothers that the marriage was troubled the entire time the two resided in China, observers clearly sensing the couple's estrangement.[159] He wrote in a coinciding letter of his reluctance to divorce her, as he had a "dislike to publicity and a horror of scandal," preferring his "personal affairs could remain hidden from all." His stress over "saving face" in marital matters reflected metropolitan preferences for discretion and the social power of gossip.[160] While Augustine Heard Sr.'s reputation (also cemented through his peers' correspondence) was infallible, the Heard brothers, with their uncertain business ventures, bankruptcy, and divorce to their name, had a less stable standing within Boston society.[161]

CALIBRATED PERFORMANCES

Local, colonial, and transnational traditions converged in Hong Kong, affecting how Americans experienced and contributed to the colony's growing foreign society. Whether within the home, the colony's public spaces, or the pages of the local press, Americans in China came under sustained public scrutiny. Raised in similarly hierarchical societies, the American merchants and their wives met this scrutiny as a matter of fact and proceeded to carve a space for themselves among Hong Kong's upper echelons. They were able to do so because of their whiteness, sociocultural background, and belief—shared with the British—in the virtues of the Anglo-Saxon race. They were less prepared for the resistance they would meet due to concerns over religion and politics. Conforming to British society, Americans nonetheless proudly retained aspects of their nascent culture, including their religious and republican beliefs, and their professed distaste for extravagance. On paper they upheld their values to those back home while critiquing contradictory British practices. In practice, however, American men and women enthusiastically engaged in Hong Kong's vibrant and often excessive social life.

In both the home and public spaces, Americans practiced a calibrated performance that aligned with colonial mores. More than a carbon copy of British metropolitan culture, Hong Kong's social practices stemmed from Britain's colonial past and from the various other foreign communities converging in the multinational entrepôt. American men and women arriving in the port thus encountered an exhausting calling culture and constant rounds of dining and hosting. Such practices could be exciting, and some found the increased attention flattering, but the culture also deprived the port's inhabitants of privacy. As a result, tensions could rise, and small matters assumed greater significance as unintentional or targeted slights. Americans, aware they constituted a small group within a British society, therefore grew defensive of their social, cultural, and political values.

Public spaces offered greater opportunities still for men and women to experience the colony's culture and society. A habitual life of public activity developed outside the parlor and dining rooms, and here Americans found wider acceptance among the British elite. They took evening rides, joined suitable clubs and committees, and used conspicuous events such as the Hong Kong Races to accrue social capital and standing. In these spaces they visibly assimilated with the white British elite while distancing themselves from "othered" communities such as the Chinese, Sikhs, or Portuguese. Anglo-American differences dissolved in favor of a racial dichotomy between "white" and "other," and, as active participants in the former community, Americans cemented their claim to elite status. Yet public spaces such as the church remained tense sites, and religious or secular differences could have divisive effects on the community. Religion catalyzed a variety of other anxieties, and through complaints of religious difference, cultural, political, and class concerns came to the forefront.

Such publicness had further drawbacks, and Americans' increased activity in the port mirrored their increased presence in the press. Both satirical and legitimate news targeted the United States and the conduct of

Americans. In the case of *China Punch*, these critiques cohered to a wider theme of class critique woven throughout the paper. But *China Punch* could also be malicious, as its attacks on Augustine Heard & Co. demonstrate. The publicness of the American community and the contentious success of its merchants made it an easy target for diatribes about elite society. Transnational Anglo-American tensions filtered into local publications such as the *China Mail* and reinforced *China Punch*'s satire. Cultural, political, racial, and religious themes affected American experiences of Hong Kong, while their activities in China and distant interactions between Britain and America could inspire salvos of indignant articles and editorials to be published and reprinted from papers across the empire. Such critical media contributed to the fragility of American social status, underscoring that while they may have been nominally accepted members of the colony's foreign elite, they were still, in their own way, outsiders.

Race, class, and culture affected the position of Americans within Hong Kong's social hierarchies and their participation in its public sphere in complex ways. In some respects, Americans fit the appropriate profile of the elite, as evidenced by their conspicuousness in port society, their success as merchants, and their status upon returning home. But port life also laid bare Anglo-American differences. Elites in the metropole may have felt some affinity for British culture, if not politics—some sense of the "Anglophilia" that Emerson so passionately espoused—but in Hong Kong, transplanted from the United States into a rigid and hierarchical society, Americans became acutely aware that they were not British, and that long-standing tensions persisted between the two groups. Still, they participated, assimilated, and rebranded themselves, implicitly at least, as members of the elite community. They took advantage of their social upbringing, their language, and their skin color to become de-facto colonial elites. Through such efforts they contributed to the port's social development, joined clubs, sat on committees, hosted balls, and sponsored race cups. American merchants, already members of the elite back home, used all the resources at their disposal to entrench their status in Hong Kong.

Chapter Four

MISSED OPPORTUNITIES

Balancing Metropolitan Politics and Private Interests in China

An "unusual zest" marked the 1871 Fourth of July in Hong Kong. American houses "were lively in their bunting"; ships in the harbor were likewise adorned. The central point of the festivities, the U.S. Consulate, "was buried in flags of the most cosmopolitan description," and, most tellingly, "the flags of the United States and of England were intertwined." The *China Mail* congratulated U.S. Consul David Bailey for bringing together Americans and non-Americans alike "in the most friendly manner possible, to celebrate the day held in honour."[1] The environment could not have differed more from the previous decade's celebrations that had invited the *China Mail*'s mockery.[2] Bailey reported these positive accounts to U.S. Secretary of State Bancroft Davis, claiming the "good feeling" resulted from the "happy adjustment of all differences between Great Britain and the United States."[3] The signing of the Anglo-American Treaty of Washington that May had "cleared away" the difficulties existing between the two nations, establishing "an *entente cordiale* . . . welcomed in no part of the world more thoroughly and sincerely than in Hong Kong."[4]

The Treaty of Washington concluded a convoluted narrative of Anglo-American rivalry and friendship in China. Since the First Opium War there had been a clear divergence between America's professed neutrality and the interests of its merchants, who stood to gain from the British belligerence they so vehemently denounced. Ambition often trumped rhetoric as American merchants and consuls in China became supporters—in action, at least—of the British imperial project. By the end of the Second Opium War, Americans were positioned to exploit their supposed neutrality and British-won concessions, extending their businesses northward and along the Yangzi River into China's interior. But before they could capitalize on the opportunities acquired through the Treaties of Tianjin, ratified in 1860, the intraregional and transnational instabilities of China's and their own civil wars converged, ruining their commercial interests. As the wars escalated, rumors of imminent Anglo-American conflict reached Hong Kong and the treaty ports, freezing American shipping. Yet while commerce suffered, the exigencies of colonial and treaty-port life mitigated the potential conflict's threat to the Anglo-American sociopolitical order in China. With the signing of the Treaty of Washington in 1871 and the British payment of a $15,500,000 indemnity for the British-made Confederate ship *Alabama*'s damages to American shipping, the spirit of cooperation could return, Bailey hoped, to Hong Kong's foreign community.[5]

Although there existed antecedent sources of tension, and minor issues would continue to develop between the two communities into the twentieth century, the narrative of Anglo-American rivalry in mid-nineteenth-century China followed a clear arc, beginning with their divergent policies toward the 1839 and 1856 Opium Wars, reaching its apex at the height of the American and Taiping civil wars in the mid-1860s, and resolving with the 1871 Treaty of Washington and the *Alabama* indemnity. Within this narrative it is clear that not only immediate sociopolitical circumstances but also regional and transnational political developments modified American experiences of Hong Kong.[6] The activities of merchants such as the Heards and Forbeses, or American consuls such as James Keenan, Horace Congar, and David Bailey, represent attempts to reconcile the American government's relationships with China and Britain with the realities of life in Hong Kong and the treaty ports.[7]

Radiating from Hong Kong, China's expanding American community became invested in commerce and society throughout the treaty ports, their overall success affecting their lives in the colony. It is therefore crucial to expand the scope of the narrative to engage with the changing world within which American merchants operated. Trade might have benefited from

Sino-foreign contests and integration with the British, but there was a cost to interdependence, and the American sociocultural position within Hong Kong was potentially vulnerable to the macropolitics of the nineteenth century. Indeed, conversations about wider political contests proliferated, even if their reception was distorted in Hong Kong. From a local vantage point, trade interests trumped national policy, the question of Yangzi access dominated Taiping concerns, and whispers about the American Civil War threatened disproportionate repercussions. Yet despite their frequency in the record, crises such as the Taiping and American civil wars had minor tangible effect (save commercial) on American lives in Hong Kong. Instead, imagined slights spread through slow-moving mail and local and foreign papers shaped their social environment; American investments and political considerations were driven forward, by "fallible calculations of a still unrealised future."[8] How, then, did individual agents and communities make sense of their national interests in light of distant events, and how malleable were these interests to colonial influences?

THE PARADOX OF AMERICAN DIPLOMACY

Throughout the twenty-one years between the outbreak of the First Opium War and the resolution of the Second Opium War, American, British, and Qing relations grew increasingly convoluted as contact between the three countries' agents produced more nuanced understandings of each other's motives. For the United States, the period between the two wars revealed inconsistencies between official rhetoric and its citizens' activities that would transform the nation's relationship with Britain and China. To understand these shifts and the commercial and political circumstances they brought about, it is necessary to outline how America's diplomatic approach to China contrasted with the activities of its merchants and consuls; the influence of the latter bolstered through their status as men "on the ground."[9]

Before 1839, American mercantile interests in China carried little weight in the United States, but from the First Opium War onward merchants' experiences of China informed their government's knowledge of and policies toward the Qing.[10] Lin Zexu's destruction of foreign opium at Humen and the resulting British declaration of war thrust America's own China trade into the spotlight in the metropole. Unlike the British Whigs, who were pushed to declare war amid accusations that they had failed to protect their citizens' interests, American officials ignored their merchants' demands for retaliation. Oriented instead toward local concerns, politicians such as Caleb Cushing refused to act due to a pervading fear of and distaste for British militancy. Domestic parties remained deaf to merchant pleas for a military force to defend Canton, preoccupied, instead, with their "opposition to Great Britain" in the Atlantic theatre from 1839 through to the end of the war.[11] When pressed, Congress cited the evils of opium and Britain's unjust spread of the trade to justify its antipathy.[12] Its opposition reflected a blind conviction that American merchants in China had no hand in the trade.

Americans at home and in Canton alike remained critical of the hard-fisted approach through which the British defended their interests in China. But if Americans denounced the British Empire, their own Treaty of Wanghia secured the means to extend commercial and legal power under the guise of "amity"; their actions confirming that the "humanitarian" republic's goals were not antithetical to those of empire.[13] Such early forms of "liberal imperialism" sprouted from the transimperial experiences of Americans abroad who in turn deployed hybrid ideas of a "universal democratic republicanism" to support their drive for the United States nation to emulate overseas European imperial expansion.[14] Such overseas interests built upon a tradition of westward expansion along the U.S. frontier—imperial in practice—where the "internal contradiction" between constitutional freedom and political or commercial penetration into occupied land threw the constitutional dynamic into a "crisis."[15] These competing impulses toward liberty and empire comprised an "unstable" logic that Americans used to advocate for the expansion of their political and commercial interests abroad.

The overseas drive toward empire was not a state-led initiative. It was pursued instead by private individuals without imperial motives but increasingly comfortable operating within imperial spaces and benefiting from the territorial and commercial fruits of imperial power. Americans in such spaces brandished neutrality pragmatically to advance their enterprises while preserving their patriotic sensibilities, but the fact remained that the concessions they desired were products of imperial aggression.[16] Recognizing this, American merchants and officials in Hong Kong and the treaty ports adapted their values to the local and regional environment, either discarding or suppressing the anti-British, anti-empire rhetoric so prevalent in the U.S. metropole.[17] As with American émigrés in London, one sees, in these colonial and semi-colonial spaces between 1840 and 1880, the roots of a pro-imperial discourse that diverged from metropolitan American republicanism and anti-imperialism and became part of the justification for the American imperial project's expansion.[18]

As George Dixwell's and Joseph Coolidge's experiences of 1840s Canton, discussed in chapter 1, suggested, American merchants initially benefited from the ambiguity of their relations with the British and Qing empires. Sino-American relations were especially placid in the years immediately following the First Opium War, the Qing implementing a strategy of placating the American community through concessions. Officials preached caution, however, that the Americans, although "outwardly respectable and submissive" (*wai sui gongshun* 外雖恭順), were simply biding their time.[19] Both Coolidge's claim for indemnification and Dixwell's opium smuggling confirmed suspicions that such favor failed to inculcate Americans with respect for Qing regulations.[20] Edicts and letters issued by Lin Zexu, Deng Tingzhen, and Qiying during and after the Opium War reprimanded Americans for flouting trade regulations and warned Chinese merchants against trading with perpetrators.[21]

Making American transgressions explicit, the Manchu general Yilibu 伊里布 complained that American merchants colluded with the British by carrying their trade, that British and American ships were virtually indistinguishable, and that Americans had no problems raising false flags to gain access to China's ports.[22] Despite such reservations, scholars such as Wei Yuan argued foreign relations should be manipulated to "keep England in check."[23] Wei's approach made sense in the immediate context of the 1840s where such policies gained some traction in undermining Anglo-American relations, but Yilibu's warning that trade in China ultimately bound British and American interests was ultimately better founded.

Effectively justifying Yilibu's concerns, articles in Hong Kong's *Xia'er guanzhen* 遐邇貫珍 (The Chinese Serial) recast Anglo-American relations in a positive light in the 1850s. Produced by the missionary James Legge's students and financed by foreign and Chinese subscribers, *Xia'er guanzhen* targeted an "educated Chinese readership in Hong Kong" and the treaty ports.[24] Given its patronage, the editor's choice to publish articles more flattering about the state of foreign politics is unsurprising. Articles such as "The History of Foreign Intercourse with China" ("Xiguo tong shang su yuan" 西國通商溯源) and "The Discovery of America and Independence of the United States" ("Jixi kai huang jian zhi xi guo yuanliu" 極西開荒建治析國源流) stressed that, despite their past, both America and Britain now enjoyed peace, "utmost harmony" (*jimu* 極睦), and a magnificent trade.[25]

Xia'er guanzhen articles extolling Anglo-American cooperation reflected the shifting dynamic between the U.S. nation and the British and Qing empires, and each instance of commercial gain, consular indiscretion, or racial and cultural tension from the Canton days through to the 1860s resurrected the question of whether Americans stood with the British or the Chinese.[26] The apparent efficacy of Britain's diplomatic obstinacy softened the American merchants' attitudes about British belligerence and encouraged them to lobby their government to extract further concessions from the Qing.[27] Hardly satisfied with their initial treaty, they demanded its revision and increased access to China's abundant interior. Dismissive Qing officials preoccupied with internal instabilities frustrated them on both counts.[28] The threat of these instabilities to foreign commerce and foreign bodies, in particular the Taiping Civil War, which had broken out in 1850, further soured American opinions of the Qing Empire.

Arriving in China in 1853, Albert Heard was disappointed by what he saw. His reports of the Chinese were unflattering and encounters with rebellion around Canton did little to endear him to the Qing administration. He would later record similar frustrations about the Taiping in Shanghai.[29] Still, if the threat of war at Canton added a sense of excitement to his work, he trusted the British to protect the foreign community.[30] Albert Heard's observations suggest that on both interpersonal and political levels contact with the Chinese alienated Americans. Conversely, as the American merchants integrated into the foreign community, they discovered common goals and sociocultural similarities with the British, the realities of life in China aligning the interests of the two nations' merchants.

By the Second Opium War in 1856 there was no longer any question that American merchants and consuls in China had thrown their lot in with the British. From their Hong Kong vantage, the ensuing conflict acquired a threatening character.[31] As early as 1844, the American consul Thomas Waldron had written to Augustine Heard & Co. from Hong Kong that the Chinese unsurprisingly bore the colony a "heavy grudge."[32] A decade later the panics of 1857 that had driven the Heards to fortify their Hong Kong house further polarized the American and Chinese communities in the

British colony.³³ Although the British officials had effectively instigated the Second Opium War and its conflicts were fought in Canton and to the north, a fearful atmosphere and largely misplaced paranoia directed at the Chinese community persisted among the colony's foreign community. Swayed by such fears, the American merchants worried that, should the Chinese invade the port or be incited to uprising, the assailants would indiscriminately attack all foreigners. So they lauded the British cause and anticipated the concessions and rights that an inevitable Anglo-French victory would secure.

The change in local attitudes is apparent in the scandal surrounding the conduct of James Keenan, Hong Kong's American consul from 1853 to 1861. Access to Canton, within its capacious walls, was a contentious issue between foreigners and the Qing. Foreign merchants at the Thirteen Factories had petitioned Qing officials for city access since the First Opium War, meeting rebukes such as Qiying's in 1846 that refusal of access was for the foreigners' own safety.³⁴ An opportunity to enter arose during the Second Opium War on October 29, 1856, when Keenan, alongside "forty or fifty" of his voyeuristic countrymen, followed British forces into the besieged city.³⁵ Keenan strolled through the streets to the Governor's Palace with "many other spectators," in "unofficial costume and smoking [his] usual cigar," and although he insisted he participated as a member of the public, witnesses reported observing him brandishing an American flag atop the destroyed city walls.³⁶

Keenan's actions alarmed the U.S. government, for if true, they threatened the legitimacy of U.S. neutrality. U.S. Secretary of State William L. Marcy launched an investigation, demanding that the missionary-turned-diplomatic agent Peter Parker, who was in China seeking treaty revisions, verify the rumors, and remove Keenan should they be true. Keenan weathered the inquiry and kept his post, supported by the British and Americans in Hong Kong, who were pleased that he was not "quite as scrupulous in maintaining the United States' strict neutrality as his predecessors had been."³⁷ Keenan responded to the Department of State that his alleged conduct was no less contradictory than the "appearance of American men of war" opposite the breach, the presence of U.S. naval officers in uniform "within the city," the "loaded American cannon pointing up New China Street," or the intermingling of U.S. marines and British troops.³⁸ It was obvious to Keenan that American neutrality was a facade.

The rift between U.S. official rhetoric and the actions of its diplomatic agents, so explicit through Keenan's actions, was hardly an isolated incident. American merchants, for example, had wasted no time converting Waldron to their cause. Consulting with Augustine Heard Sr. in 1844, Waldron sought advice on engaging a comprador, business matters, Hong Kong housing expenses, and outfitting his watchmen. Heard obliged and took further steps to align the consul's interests with the community he represented. He pressed Waldron to enter the opium trade, assuring him that their "communications upon business" would remain "individual and confidential." Augustine Heard Sr. placed Dixwell and his "connections" at Waldron's disposal, recommending these "side operations" be given "discretion" despite assuring this very first U.S. consul to Hong Kong that it was "usual for the consul [in the port] to transact such business."[39]

Augustine Heard Sr.'s hobnobbing stemmed from a world where private interests were well placed to influence diplomatic policy. Hong Kong's second consul was, fittingly, the American merchant Frederick Busch, and members of the merchant elite generally went through great efforts to assume U.S. or third-party country consular offices throughout China's treaty ports. Such positions were leveraged to support merchant interests, acquire much-needed trade intelligence, and assure, in theory, that diplomatic policy would follow local interests.[40] Where merchants could, they also ingratiated themselves with members of official U.S. diplomatic missions, as did the Heards with U.S. minister John E. Ward or U.S. Consul General George Seward, in hopes that they might benefit from such privileged relationships and sway official stances toward China in the metropole. Their efforts often worked, the activities of U.S. officials such as Keenan, Waldron, or Ward implicitly supporting the British-inspired interests of China's U.S. merchants.

As the Second Opium War drew to a close in 1859, Americans followed the British to the mouth of the Bai He 白河 (White River) to ratify the Treaties of Tianjin. Ward, as William Bradford Reed's successor, led the mission to ratify the American treaty that Reed had secured in 1858.[41] George Heard, having met Ward on his voyage to China to join the family firm, was invited to join the American mission, serving as Ward's attaché in 1859 and again in 1860.[42] During the first mission Chinese forces barred foreigners from sailing up the river to Beijing, dealing an unexpected blow to the British. In response, the British engaged the Dagu forts and on June 25 moved to deploy troops. During the action, the British Admiral Hope's ship *Plover* ran aground on the mud banks below the forts. American Commodore Josiah Tattnall, encouraged by Ward, disregarded his country's politics and rushed to Hope's aid. Reported to have shouted "blood is thicker than water," Tattnall sailed the *Toey-Wan* into the fray to tow Hope from the bank.[43]

Observing such Anglo-American cooperation in this and the following mission, and no doubt prejudiced by his contemporaries, George Heard became convinced that the British were justified in fighting the Chinese, whose resistance he considered "impertinent and insolent." And the environment at Hong Kong reflected such Anglophilic sentiments.[44] William Wood recalled after visiting the port that although James Armstrong, commander of the U.S. East India Squadron, had ordered the American community to neither engage in hostilities or enter "into any alliance" with the British during the Second Opium War, the "considerations and impulses" of the port had caused most Americans to freely "fraternize" with their British neighbors.[45] Still, there were inherent tensions in such fraternizing. Like many of George Heard's countrymen, he paradoxically admired Britain's bellicosity while upholding the holier-than-thou morality of Americans in refraining from the "slaughter" of Chinese.[46] Anglo-American interests in China coexisted uneasily with official national policy. Such unity was imperfect, and while it helped recalibrate Sino-American relations, it would soon be subject to its own stresses.

American alignment with the British further recalibrated relationships with the Chinese. Qing reform efforts following the Opium Wars required a degree of Sino-American cooperation, but rhetoric of a special Sino-American relationship gradually dissipated.[47] Although the Qing requested American assistance in technical and political reforms due to the strong ties that two decades of American noninterventionist posturing had produced, it would be a mistake to assume friendly rhetoric was solely responsible for their cooperation, thereby downplaying such rhetoric's mutually superficial purposes. Through their "declared . . . respect for China's territorial integrity," a fiction made obvious through merchants' opium smuggling, Keenan's belligerence at Canton, Tattnall's military interventions, and a host of other transgressions, U.S. diplomats and merchants reaffirmed their brand of morally superior benevolent republicanism on an international stage while continuing to pursue their private

MISSED OPPORTUNITIES

interests.[48] Qing officials, in turn, accepted that the Americans shared many of the British designs for China.[49] Their deferral to American expertise on technical and political matters was rather a calculated course designed to achieve specific aims.

The diplomatic language of the 1860s may not have changed since the First Opium War, but each of the parties involved bore no false pretenses about the other's aspirations. Leading up to the 1860s, the "neutral" course Americans adopted set the tone for their relationships with both China, and Britain in China. By maintaining a moderate rhetoric, Americans managed to affirm their republican identity, even as they carried on their clandestine opium trade and benefited from British military campaigning. This rhetorical trick enabled Americans to distance themselves from the British imperial project and validate their "special relationship" with the Qing. The Chinese, in response, manipulated Americans to maintain amicable ties, offering special privileges to American merchants to weaken support for Britain and keep America from joining the other belligerent nations. In a sense the Qing succeeded. Americans never formally entered the wars, and Qing diplomatic maneuvering provided Americans the handicap they needed to compete with British mercantile interests. Throughout the 1850s, however, exposure to Sino-British economic and political contests within China bound American and British interests. Eager to share in the spoils, American merchants and diplomats alike sidestepped neutrality. In spaces such as Hong Kong Americans thus became politically untethered from their government, adhering instead to the popular feeling and commercial interests of the colony.[50] With the Second Opium War's advent, while one American waved his flag tellingly from atop Canton's ruined walls, American merchants watched eagerly from the sidelines, anticipating China's opening and planning their next steps.

OPENING UP THE YANGZI

Excepting Keenan's excitement during the siege of Canton, and Tattnall's intervention at the Bai He, Americans mostly managed to maintain a neutral course during the Second Opium War. There was no need to participate. The First Opium War proved that they could avoid overt hostilities and still enjoy the benefits of European-won treaties.[51] As the Treaty of Wanghia had done, Reed's Sino-American Treaty of Tientsin (1858) extended Americans' legal and commercial advantages without conflict.[52] In any case, most favored nation status guaranteed any benefits granted to one power were shared by all.[53] The treaties opened eleven new ports to foreign merchants and the Yangzi to foreign navigation, confirmed the opium trade's legality, and expanded systems of extraterritoriality.[54] For the Heards and other Americans in China, Hong Kong was the jumping-off point from which to access this expanding treaty-port world. The enterprises they established throughout became entangled parts of expansive intraregional and transnational networks overseen from the British colony. Emboldened by the new opportunities these treaty ports promised to unearth, American merchants in Hong Kong fixed their gaze upon the China coast, past Shanghai—by 1860 already an important entrepôt—and along the Yangzi, preparing for the opening of China's interior that the British and French would surely secure through treaty ratifications at the Convention of Peking.

In November 1860, soon after the convention, Albert Heard wrote to his uncle from Shanghai: "You know the Yangtze river had been a promised land for foreign commerce . . . and we have all looked to this treaty and the peace as the commencement of its exploration."[55] Now that the treaty was resolved, John Heard prepared his steamer *Fire Dart*, ordered from America against his uncle's warnings. The ship had reached Hong Kong in the spring of 1861, and on April 14 John Heard departed Shanghai for the Yangzi. While he ostensibly intended to sail upriver to assess the state of trade at Hankow and install C. D. Williams as Augustine Heard & Co.'s agent there, he also sought to gauge the commercial prospects of trading with the rebels at Nanjing.[56] There had been scattered trade with the Taiping rebels in the 1850s, but John Heard's voyage signaled a sustained American commercial interest in the Yangzi, spurred by visions of great potential profit.[57] These visions prompted the remodeling of American companies from commission agents to shipping firms, as steamships were ordered from New England and New York to ply the river. Before these ships made it to China the American Civil War broke out in 1861, and many were repurposed to carry troops and goods for the Union along America's inland waterways. By the war's 1865 resolution American commerce had stagnated, enthusiasm for Yangzi shipping had mellowed, and, facing loss, China trade merchants looked to jettison these ships where possible. The "disruption of American trade during the Civil War years" and "the failure of commerce in the Yangtze Valley to increase as expected" would eventually lead to retrenchment and bankruptcy for the established American firms.[58]

There was, throughout the mid-nineteenth century, a complex convergence of political and commercial developments along the Yangzi and abroad that helps explain America's stagnated enterprises.[59] The evolving political relationships between foreign powers, the Qing, and the Taiping, and the ongoing conflict between the latter two destabilized and then reshaped commercial systems throughout the region. Such shifts had serious repercussions for American trade, and the changing political and commercial landscapes in China and the United States bore unanticipated consequences. American failure upon the Yangzi, to which so many mercantile aspirations had been fixed, hit China's American elites hard, and among a predominantly British foreign community in which they had grown invested, matters of commerce and politics would become increasingly sensitive topics.

The Heards' and other American merchants' initial enthusiasm over the Yangzi stemmed, in part, from the river's geopolitical situation. The river's upper reaches, close to tea-producing regions in the interior but partially controlled by Taiping forces, promised immense gain. The Yangzi entrepôt Hankow was "well known to every Chinese as the seat of the most extensive commerce in the interior of the country," and the *North China Herald* predicted it would become "an important seat of foreign trade" once steamships unlocked the river.[60] Such promise drew Chinese and foreign entrepreneurs alike into Taiping territory to observe firsthand the prospects of trade in teas, opium, and foreign manufactures.[61]

Numerous obstacles, however, blocked the river's efficient use. First was the question of access. Prior to the Treaty of Tientsin's ratification, the Qing denied foreigners permission to carry their trade to interior ports. Second was the question of the Taiping Heavenly Kingdom, whose stronghold at Nanjing blocked the river's upper reaches, and whose peculiar religion and obtuse politics cast doubt on the profitability of establishing relations.[62] Finally, there was the question of navigation. The river was treacherous, flowing fast and silting seemingly at random; only the most skilled pilots could navigate it safely.

The first and second of these obstacles potentially negated each other. There is no doubt that Taiping campaigns along the Yangzi were destructive, altering demographic patterns and commerce. Just as "socioeconomic dislocations" in Guangdong following the outbreak of the Taiping Civil War had bolstered Hong Kong's population, nearly 500,000 Chinese refugees filtered into Shanghai between 1853 and 1862, boosting the city's economic significance.[63] Foreigners and Chinese traveling from Shanghai toward the Yangzi and on to Nanjing, occupied in 1853, had "grown almost accustomed to a range of sombre sights."[64] By 1860 "the abject state of Nanjing" and the "destruction caused by lower Yangzi fighting" turned foreigners from the Taiping cause.[65]

In the early days, however, foreign merchants had few pretentions about trading with the Taiping or capitalizing on instability to access the river and skirt duties owed to the Qing government.[66] As a result, Nanjing enjoyed an "impressive volume of international trade" during its early occupation, importing goods such as food, commodities, opium, munitions, and arms. The duties the rebel administrators levied on this trade were an important source of revenue, collected inconsistently at Nanjing, Wuhu, Anqing, Wuxue, and Wuchang. In theory, Taiping control granted foreign merchants access to interior ports, and the Taiping policy of encouraging local and international trade resulted in an "infamous" black-market "sale of arms to the Taepings [sic] by Hong Kong firms" willing to breach their countries' neutrality.[67]

In practice, trade with the Taiping frustrated the British and American merchants, and rumors of the war's progress had far-reaching effects on East and South-East Asian markets.[68] When the Taiping occupied the coastal city Ningbo, Taiping commanders assured the foreign community there that trade would continue as usual. The British consul, Frederick Harvey, worried, however, that despite their best efforts, "commerce would never come back."[69]

If the conflicts of 1860 hardly diminished foreign trade, contemporary American reports still betrayed dismay that the state of the Yangzi proved no better than Ningbo.[70] Arriving at Zhenjiang on April 19, 1861, John Heard observed no trade "to be done for the very simple reason that there was no one to do it with." The market at Nanjing, too, seemed "very slim." Reaching Wuhu three days later behind the British firm Dent & Co., things appeared no better. A visit from Yung Wing, who had arrived to probe the possibility of exporting tea for the Taiping, did little to reassure the American merchant.[71] Yung Wing would recall in his memoirs that the potential profit from Taiping teas was negligible. In six months at Wuhu he had hardly moved "a tenth part of the entire stock."[72] The *Fire Dart* continued its voyage up the river. With imperial forces invested around Anqing there would be no stopping there, and although at Kiukiang Dent's comprador and Endicott's old shroff Atong expressed faith that the city "must become a great green tea district," John Heard observed "but a small market at present."[73]

From a political standpoint, the situation should have been more promising. The supposed Christian sentiments of the Taiping, their support for free trade, and their willingness to treat with foreigners inspired early British and American efforts to establish formal ties. U.S. President Franklin Pierce even predicted in 1853 that the rebellion would benefit U.S. commerce with China. The resulting race to send diplomatic missions triggered Anglo-American rivalries, the American commissioner, Humphrey Marshall, competing with Hong Kong's governor and British plenipotentiary George Bonham to reach the Taiping at Nanjing in 1853. Marshall lost the contest, his steamer *Susquehanna* "ingloriously" running aground outside Shanghai.[74] His successor Robert McLane eventually succeeded in reaching Nanjing. Taiping arrogance toward the foreigner diplomats, however, disillusioned Bonham and McLane, the latter falling victim to a "dramatic example" of "American wishful thinking about China."[75] Trade persisted, but "normal relations with the Taipings were ruled out."[76]

The Qing termed these missions, the contraband trade, and the opportunistic "neutrality" of the foreign powers "*nei you wai huan*" 內憂外患 (trouble from within, threats from without). Embroiled in the American Civil War, the parallels were obvious to American politicians; their rival Britain allegedly propping up the Confederate states "diplomatically, and even militarily."[77] Aware of the hypocrisy of condemning Britain's Civil War policies while U.S. diplomats treated with Taiping rebels and American merchants smuggled wantonly, Union Secretary of State William Seward recommended in 1862 that the American minister to China, Anson Burlingame, follow the British and French in declaring for the Qing.[78] The decision rendered American subjects' profiteering and adventuring particularly embarrassing, and in 1863 Qing military commanders Zeng Guofan 曾國藩 and Li Hongzhang 李鴻章 petitioned the Emperor to halt foreign trade around Nanjing until the city was recovered. The foreign powers at Shanghai complied with the request.⁷⁹ The Qing's internal instability, initially cause for speculation, had become an impediment to the Yangzi trade American merchants had envisioned.

Even before Zeng's and Li's petition, John Heard's exploratory voyage effectively ruled out trade with the Taiping. The war had become another obstacle, the resolution of which merchants eagerly awaited so that normal trade might resume. Reaching Hankow on May 1, 1861, John Heard noted the Taiping had not taken the place, which looked "populous & active." He soon realized that trade was "very dull," and that the people had not shaken "the funk they [were] in about the rebels." Finding the port's prospects "heart-breaking," he set about acquiring a plot for the firm's warehouses. He complained that the best land was reserved in the British concession for British buyers (a regulation that persisted until 1867), and that, the British firms Dent & Co. and Lindsay & Co., had snapped up "all the best lots outside" as well.⁸⁰ He eventually settled on a plot just outside the concession limits.

Despite his misgivings, John Heard left Hankow optimistic that the port would "become a great commercial emporium." He even leveraged a chance encounter with the commander-in-chief of the U.S. East India Squadron, Cornelius Stribling, aboard the USS *Saginaw* on his return trip downriver to plant the idea of Williams serving as the port's U.S. consul.⁸¹ Such appointments were falling out of favor as Chinese and American officials realized they disadvantaged other traders and provided "a degree of immunity in carrying out illegal business activities."⁸² These may have been the very advantages John Heard envisioned, he and his brother Albert holding Russian Consulships in Hong Kong and Shanghai respectively in 1860 for similar reasons.⁸³ John Heard's lobbying was successful, and Guanwen 官文, the governor general of Huguang, reported after a "gentle and amiable" (*heshun* 和順) meeting with Stribling that Williams (*Wei'liang'shi* 韋良士), "presently living at Augustine Heard & Co's factory in Hankow," would assume the role.⁸⁴

John Heard's record suggests that despite disappointing Taiping encounters, a depressed state of trade, and the devastated countryside flanking the river, Americans maintained a steadfast belief that the Yangzi would yield profit. British and American merchants thus directed their political lobbying to the question of river access. On their behalf, Lord Elgin and his brother Frederick Bruce impressed upon Prince Gong (Yixin 奕欣) that opening the river "would help revive commerce" and assist efforts to suppress the Taiping by "increasing the dynasty's revenues." With the river open, American merchants commissioned more vessels from U.S. dockyards, believing the trade would "justify the considerable expense of building and fuelling steamships."[85] Over the next couple years, Augustine Heard & Co. added *Shantung* and *Cortes* to their roster.[86] Russell & Co., using the opportunity to springboard the Shanghai Steam Navigation Company (1861–1877), commissioned *Antelope, Flambeau, Huquong,* and *Kiangse*.[87]

These new steamships, innovatively designed and constructed in the United States, enabled the merchants to surmount the third obstacle of river navigation. The ship designs, refined through trials on America's internal waterways, incorporated low drafts and sidewheels perfect for navigating the Yangzi and provided American merchants technical advantages over their British contemporaries (figures 4.1 and 4.2).[88] But technology alone was insufficient. To succeed, detailed geographic knowledge and a pilot skilled at traversing the river's shifting sandbars, strong currents, and narrow bends were required. During the *Fire Dart*'s 1861 trial voyage, for example, the "ignorant" and "obstinate" pilot, barely out of Shanghai, twice stuck the ship on shoals.[89]

Even with a competent pilot steam technology was troublesome, and accidents happened. In June 1862 Heard's *Cortes* caught fire, the front half burning to the water. Another American steamer exploded after departing Shanghai killing almost all aboard, the *Pembroke* was reported invalided, and Russell & Co.'s *Kiangse* broke her cylinder, making "four steamer accidents within a week." Exiting the Huangpu and sailing up the Yangzi, the latter river's swift currents and dangerous moorings threatened both safety and the overall speed of the voyage. The *Fire Dart*'s first round-trip voyage to Hankow took a month, and speed became something of an obsession for John Heard. He kept detailed records of the voyages of *Shantung, Fire Dart,* and *Cortes*, rejoicing when six-day round trips were achieved in 1862.[90]

Mastering the river meant shorter voyage times and safer travel, and with the Taiping losing ground "foreign capital expanded notably in China."[91] As the market at Hankow rebounded, American firms such as Augustine Heard & Co., Russell & Co., and Olyphant & Co., expanded operations. By May 1861, the *China Mail* reported "about a dozen fine steamers already trading" on the river.[92] Writing in 1862, John Heard's father George W. Heard commented that "steamboat property" appeared to be "the rage" in

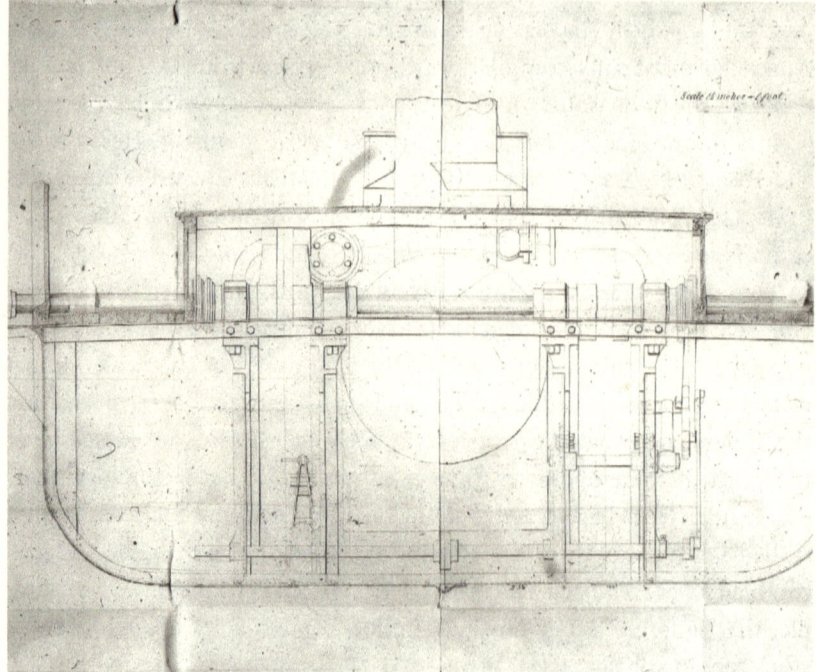

FIGURE 4.1. Cross-section of an American river steamer, built by the Atlantic Works, Boston, c. 1863. *Source:* American river steamer side view, c. 1863, case 30, HBS.

the United States as well and would likely remain productive for a while.[93] By 1863 Brooklyn dockyards were repairing and constructing twenty-nine steamers, at least four of which had been intended for China.[94] The next year, some sixteen steamships plied the Yangzi, ten belonging to Americans. But while George W. Heard praised his son's luck and foresight in turning a profit with the *Fire Dart*, he cautioned that a turn was coming, and "a very rapid decline must of course be the consequence." He warned John Heard to "expect this to come at some perhaps not very distant day," and to "be ready to trim [his] sails accordingly."[95] The prophecy proved uncannily accurate.

While American merchants in China explored the Yangzi and tested the Taiping, their kin in America were being pulled into their own vicious fratricidal conflict. As the Union and Confederacy scrambled to raise armies, China-bound steamships attracted the Union navy's attention. Many ships

MISSED OPPORTUNITIES

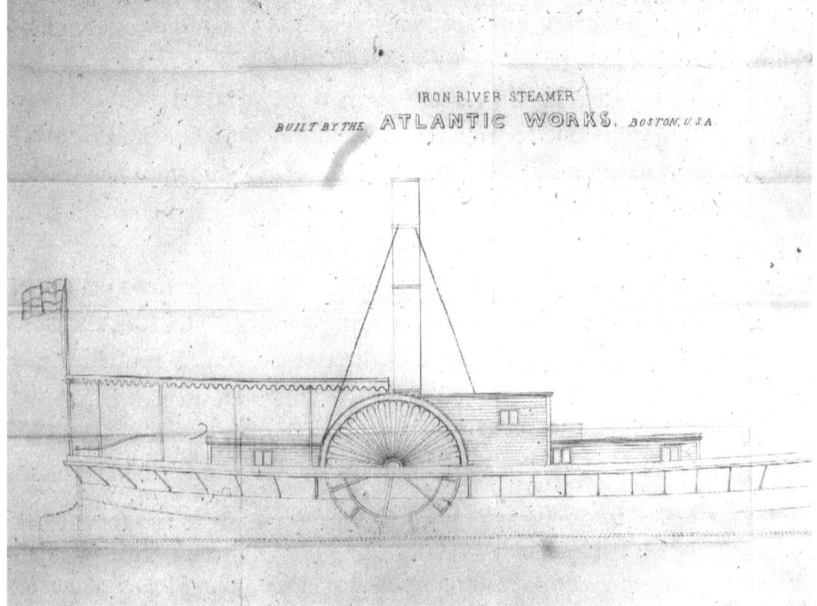

FIGURE 4.2. Side view of an American river steamer, built by the Atlantic Works, Boston, c. 1863. *Source*: American river steamer cross-section, c. 1863, case 30, HBS.

commissioned for the China trade were bought and reoutfitted to fight or carry supplies and troops in America. Augustine Heard & Co.'s *Suwonada* spent its first couple years as a troop transport, to be "sent at once to China" following the war.[96] Russell & Co.'s *Antelope* and *Flambeau* were redirected to the war effort before they could sail for China.[97] *Ta-Kiang*, eventually run by Olyphant & Co., was built in 1862 for the China trade, operating for two years before being chartered by the Union Navy in 1864.[98] The *Fahkee*, built in 1862, and the *Howquah* were both bought by the Union in 1863.[99] And it was not just merchant ships that were redirected. Qing authorities commissioned Henry Ward, brother of the infamous Frederick Townsend Ward, to construct and deliver five steamers from America for military use. The three ships built for the contract, the *Dai-Ching*, *Chih-Kiang* (renamed USS *Tulip*), and *Kiang-Soo* (renamed USS *Fuchsia*), were sold instead to the Union Navy in New York.[100] Redirecting steamers to the federal government may have been no more profitable than sending them to China, but the demands of the Union war effort clearly influenced the merchants' choice to sell.[101] Reversing the status quo prior to the 1860s, U.S. merchants' interests, so far removed from the conflict, came second to the Union government and the American Civil War.

The war effected a rapid increase of American naval forces and following 1865 decommissioned merchant ships and men-of-war became available for use in East Asia.[102] The Chinese market for steamships had leveled off, however, with Russell & Co. initially emerging as the dominant firm, but later ceding ground to Chinese and British navigation companies.[103] For those edged out of the trade, offloading these now-available vessels at a price equal to the costs of purchase and outfitting became a challenge. Despite the Shanghai bubble bursting, some of these vessels found profitable new homes in the China trade. Of the thirty-two American steamships operating in China in 1866, at least six had seen military service.[104]

Many ships long active in China, such as the *Shantung*, changed hands multiple times, suggesting considerable financial stress accompanied ship ownership at this time, and that commercial priorities were shifting. With the *Suwonada* intended for China upon discharge, John Heard requested that "if she could be sold on the way than all the better."[105] But a buyer was hard to come by, and financial prospects in China continued to decline. Other merchants, encountering similar pressures, commissioned the Heards in 1868 to sell the former gunboats *Pawtuxet*, *Kankakee*, and *Ashuelot*.[106] The boats were sent to Japan, where the company hoped the instability of the Sonnō-jōi movement would encourage buyers eager for foreign weapons. Ironically, Japan's own civil war had reduced prospective customers "to the verge of bankruptcy," and between January and July 1868, only two of the ships were sold.[107] By 1871, Dixwell complained that Chinese customers had stopped coming, that shipping and speculation were ruining the company, and that all the firm's money was tied up in real estate and the ships *Venus* and *Suwonada*.[108]

U.S. commerce increased steadily in the post–Civil War years, rising 56 percent higher than it had been before the war, but the percentage of this trade made up by China actually shrunk. Trade with China had stagnated, growing the years following "in tiny increments or not at all."[109] George W. Heard's warning had been realized. The shipbuilding craze had abated in China. Not only had the American Civil War redirected steamships, thereby resulting in missed financial opportunities, but in its immediate wake decommissioned vessels flooded the market. For many, the days of commercial potential had passed. The Yangzi had quickly saturated with American steam shipping, and then just as quickly Russell & Co. had taken the whole business, until the British trader John Samuel Swire successfully challenged their hegemony in 1873.[110] The other onetime competitors were left reeling; Augustine Heard & Co. lost the head start that John Heard's astute moves of 1861 had afforded.

THE AMERICAN CIVIL WAR IN CHINA

While Americans struggled to turn a profit on the Yangzi, American Consul to Hong Kong Horace Congar described grim prospects in the British colony to Seward. The Taiping Civil War, by now firmly opposed by the foreign powers, had been "disastrous to trade and commerce," and lacked a "reforming aim or purpose."[111] And if regional markets seemed anemic to foreigners generally, the outbreak of America's domestic Civil War and the subsequent rise in Anglo-American tensions crippled the American mercantile enterprises in China and Hong Kong.[112] Four months earlier, Congar had reported, "the entire stagnation of shipments and trade at this port on account of rumors which are in circulation in regard to hostilities between the United States and Great Britain. Some of our American vessels are changing owners, some are seeking security in Chinese ports, and all are anxious for intelligence from home so that they may act with prudence and discretion."[113]

Already concerned about the meagre returns realized through the Yangzi trade, American merchants became especially conscious of how the progress of the war affected their relationship with their British neighbors in the immediate context of Hong Kong. Incidents such as the *Trent* affair (1862) and the *Alabama*'s privateering were reported in Hong Kong newspapers and related in letters from the United States. These flashpoints, sharpened by clear political differences emphasized in metropolitan and colonial papers, helped develop imagined conflicts between Hong Kong's American and British communities.[114] I use, here, the term "imagined" because the threats sensationalized by the papers were never realized in Hong Kong.[115] An Anglo-American war never broke out, the *Alabama* never entered the port's vicinity, and no overt conflict between Hong Kong's British and American communities ever materialized. Still, although these events and debates unfolded in distant theaters, the war loomed in the minds of the foreign community, threatening the colony's society and commerce.

Transnational politics might instill imaginary divisions, but the circumstances of Hong Kong helped its foreign community overcome disparities that in other contexts would "separate and often set [its] members in conflict."[116] Domestic politics clashed, but as in Shanghai fifty years later, foreigners did not want war; for better or worse "they were partners, colleagues, friends."[117] In such an environment, political differences, social slights, commercial failings and even transnational conflicts were negotiated. National interests were weighed against local social ties and discarded when prudent.

But while three decades trading in China had separated American private interests from those of the nation, the Civil War sparked widespread processes of national reaffirmation, reminding those Americans in China that local interests had to be reconciled with national sympathies. Civil War information reached Hong Kong's Americans through local British-run newspapers and through family correspondence. Both relayed a volatile mixture of national and personal sentiment that threatened to antagonize tensions already escalating within the colony's Anglo-American community. Both inspired reactionary speculation about the inevitability of an Anglo-American conflict. For an American minority within a British colony far from the United States, rising tensions were keenly felt. Commercial failings, in particular, although a result of their nation's instability, were blamed on British interference, and so threatened to degrade the Anglo-American social alliances that had slowly been forming.

The *Trent* affair of November 1861 constituted the first real threat to Anglo-American peace in China. The USS *San Jacinto*, known to Hong Kong's American community for its year of service in China and brief involvement in the Second Opium War, boarded the British mail packet *Trent*, detaining the Confederate diplomats James Mason Murray and John Slidell on board.[118] Following the episode, war became an anticipated possibility. The Union claimed the British had breached their neutrality by transporting belligerent diplomats, and the British responded that the act had transgressed British sovereignty.[119] Family letters to the Heards from New England, accompanied by frenetic reporting and telegraphs, stoked these fears, drawing the brothers into "a social setting dominated by the spirit of war."[120] Their mother, Elizabeth Ann Farley, wrote from Ipswich,

Massachusetts, that immediately following the incident the British press and people "[broke] forth with violent denunciations and abuse" of the Northern states. The British government was rumored to be pouring "troops and munitions of war" into Canada "with every demonstration of hostility." Farley's letter and a later one from her husband, described how the whole event "produced a profound sense of scorn and disgust" in the North. Augustine Heard Sr., writing from Boston, informed Albert Heard that one "cannot find a man or woman [in America] that does not pray for a time when" the United States might "punish [Britain] as she deserves."[121]

While distance lessened the war's severity, the *Trent* affair "came to a boiling point" in China.[122] The social makeup of China's white community catalyzed such tensions: most Americans in China were Northerners, the British were pro-South, and without a navy to defend them American merchants "were forced to depend on [British] warships for protection" (a fact, given the circumstances, they resented). Anticipating trouble at Shanghai following the *Trent* affair, Admiral Hope prepared to "seize the assets" of the American community there should war break out.[123] The scene was reproduced in Hong Kong and across the treaty ports. For American merchants in the British colony, vulnerable and loath to rely on the British for protection, news and letters from home threatening war froze American shipping so completely that even already chartered vessels remained in port.[124]

American vulnerability in China had been a persistent anxiety, and prior to the war Albert Heard had recounted the "disgraceful condition of the American navy" at Hong Kong. A twin letter to New York begged that the city's influential magnates lobby on the China traders' behalf for more protection. If they did, they failed. At the war's start the one sloop Albert Heard had mentioned, the *Hartford*, was recalled. Commander-in-Chief Stribling and Commander William Radford of the *Dacotah*, under scrutiny as citizens of southern states, were reassigned to America, where they fought for the Union. Americans in China were now "without either protection or minister." The only remaining war steamer in the East, the *Saginaw* floated crewless off Macao and Congar begged Seward send forces "to defend American honor and interests."[125] But while Admiral Hope and Congar feared trouble, the foreign community's common interests prevailed. One British editorial in Hong Kong stated that, should Americans require protection, British naval commanders were duty-bound to "stand by [their] brethren."[126] As Tatnall had declared in 1860 at the Bai He, for many foreigners in China blood was thicker than water.

Yet a cursory survey of the *China Mail* suggests the mounting crisis polarized the Anglo-American community. The *China Mail*'s London correspondent reported "great excitement" in Britain as both sides armed for conflict, articles encouraged Britain to support the South, and one bizarre commentary, reprinted from the *Economist*, invited the Americans to attack Canada.[127] These reports were gathered or reprinted from metropolitan papers and, in the interest of sustaining debate, the *China Mail*'s editors published a range of stances. Their selections represented the diversity of British opinions about the war and Anglo-American relations.[128] The August 29, 1861, supplement reprinted from the *Spectator*, for instance, sought to educate readers on the cause of the Americans' bitterness toward Britain, acknowledging problems of Southern recognition and American beliefs that the British possessed "false pretences of liberality" and "a wicked delight in the suffering of the states."[129] A counterpoint, taken from *The Times*, expressed joy that "the pedestal on which Americans have been placed has been knocked from under them," that they were not "the paragons of enlightened rule that they had been constantly made out to be."[130]

Cutting to the underlying matter, an editorial published on February 6, 1862, requested both parties consider each other's perspectives of the *Trent* affair, hoping "against hope" for a peaceful solution.[131] But even as the author preached moderation, the paper's editors reprinted reports from Britain describing preparations for an Anglo-American war.[132] News of the *Trent* affair faded and tensions in Shanghai subsided following the winter of 1862, but Hong Kong's *China Mail* published incendiary materials throughout the war, the resulting anxieties bleeding into everyday life. The Fourth of July the following summer, for example, merited articles criticizing the celebration, and months later a British commenter's caustic editorial rejoiced at the mutual destruction of both the slaveholding Confederates and the "ignorant and debased" Union.[133] Within the *China Mail*'s pages, at least, Anglo-American rivalries were sustained.

It is significant to note, however, that while a minority of *China Mail* articles preached moderation, the majority of those that did were locally written editorial and op-ed articles. Although the editors preferred incendiary pieces from metropolitan papers, the local communities themselves, when in dialogue, demonstrated a capacity for understanding in the face of

MISSED OPPORTUNITIES

baiting journalism. Hong Kong society's dictates diffused metropolitan tensions and transnational political conflicts, the inhabitants keeping peace among themselves out of necessity.[134]

For a time, relations did normalize, with few references to local unrest appearing in merchant letters home. Augustine Heard Sr.'s comments to his nephew suggest that while merchants such as Albert Heard initially shook "from fear of a war with England," recent reports made it evident that the situation in China was relaxing. Dixwell wrote from Shanghai, October 1863, that the port's cosmopolitanism afforded a balanced view of Anglo-American troubles in the Atlantic, and with access to papers from Boston, New York, and London, the American community was not "liable to the influence" of reactionaries. James Murray Forbes reported a similar thaw in Hong Kong the same month, where arriving war news was "so very old" that he found "little interest reading the papers."[135]

Despite the merchants' apathy, potential threats of war spilling into the East Asian theater continued to fray American nerves in China. Although debunked as rumor, reports trickled in early as 1861 that Confederate privateers were visiting ports such as Shanghai, resulting in a general "indisposition" to ship under the American flag.[136] These rumors resurfaced in 1863 through accusations that British-made ironclads intended "nominally" for "the Emperor of China" were in fact built for the Confederacy. An article reprinted from London confided that the term "Chinese" was code in Liverpool's shipyards for Confederates, and the "Emperor of China" meant none other than Jefferson Davis.[137] Although conspiratorial, these rumors were based upon the construction in Britain of what would become the Confederate's most notorious privateer in China: The *Alabama*.

In 1862 the *New York Times* reported that Seward accused the British of producing a fleet of steamers "to run the [Union] blockade" and prey on Union shipping.[138] Shipwrights in Liverpool, "the most pro-Confederate place in the world outside the Confederacy itself," were charged with outfitting a number of vessels such as the *Labuan*, *Emily St. Pierre*, *General Miramon*, and *Oreto*, but the sister sloops-of-war *Florida* and *Alabama* became the focal point of Union outrage.[139] American commentators denounced Britain's breach of neutrality, going so far as to advocate that Union raiders raise the Taiping flag to "prey on British commerce, *a la Florida, Alabama, &c.*"[140] The entire episode reignited Anglo-American hostilities in the Atlantic, prompting American demands for indemnification that would only be resolved by the Treaty of Washington in 1871.[141] In the meantime, fears of piracy and questions of lost commerce would drive a new wedge between China's British and American communities.

Reports reached Hong Kong in autumn 1863 that the *Alabama* had sailed eastward round the Cape of Good Hope to raid in India and the China Sea. As in 1861, these reports undermined confidence in "the use of American tonnage," and American vessels in the port busied themselves changing flags.[142] By December, unproven rumors the *Alabama* had taken the "favourite American steamer *Fokkien*" further impaired confidence in American vessels. With the flag becoming even "less in demand than before in Chinese waters," owners were encouraged to sell their ships.[143] A reprinted *New York Times* article suggested such fears affected a transnational market, speculating that four Confederate steamers were operating in the East Asian theater and observing only one ship in Liverpool "loading under the American flag." Others had swapped flags for those of "Peru, Prussia, and Portugal," as Eastern insurance offices "point blank refused" American risks.[144] It is estimated that the Union lost one-third of its total shipping tonnage as American ships reregistered to escape Confederate raiders, high insurance rates, and Union service.[145] *Alabama* rumors, widespread and damaging, were short-lived, and by the following spring the *China Mail* reported the ship's departure "from eastern seas" and subsequent defeat by the USS *Kearsarge* off Cherbourg, France.[146]

Hong Kong's American and British officials handled such reports of Anglo-American tensions rationally. In March 1864, for example, Hong Kong's colonial secretary, W. S. Mercer, wrote to Congar that the USS *Wyoming* had abused British neutrality by refueling within the colony's territorial jurisdiction and that its arrival should have been "intimated to the government."[147] Unlike the war's transnational outrages, decried by antagonistic politicians in the metropole, Hong Kong's officials engaged in a measured correspondence, it being both the British Governor Hercules Robinson's desire to underscore the port's neutrality respecting the American conflict and Congar's to dutifully and lawfully comply.[148] Fears of the *Alabama* might have sparked international outrage and destabilized American shipping in China, but Hong Kong's intimate context begged a more diplomatic touch.

The *Trent* affair, the *Alabama*, and American fears of British interference soon faded in Hong Kong and the treaty ports. Letters and news articles from home exported hostile rhetoric, but if Hong Kong's American inhabitants felt anxious about their relationship with their British neighbors, they rarely voiced it. Instead, they wrote home about dinner parties, races, excursions, and balls. They spoke of China's political instabilities, their own rebel problems, Yangzi navigation, and the opening of Japan. There was a life-goes-on quality to their reports home. The lives described in these letters were overwhelmingly active. Whatever anxieties afflicted the community, Americans participated in the port's society, the social decorum of the colony repairing the rifts caused by the two nations' volatile relations.

Anglo-American conflicts evaporated following the war as other China concerns attracted the attention of Americans. Congar's successors applied to the U.S. Department of State for an increased hand in Chinese commerce and an expanded China policy. Isaac Jackson Allen combatted piracy, C. N. Goulding brought up the question of revising the Treaty of Tientsin, and the injustices of the "Coolie trade" became something of a personal crusade for Bailey.[149] But for American merchants emerging out the other end, the reality remained that business stagnated and shipping suffered.

Then, on September 18, 1873, the U.S. bank Jay Cooke & Company failed, sparking the "Panic of 1873" and plunging the United States into a long depression that lasted until the century's end. Radiating from New York, international commerce flagged, and the country entered "the longest contraction of business in its young history."[150] The various conflicts of the 1850s and 1860s provided convenient scapegoats to explain American shipping's decline, but following these wars the old merchant houses soon realized that the China trade had changed and, facing a national depression, there was little hope of generating new capital.[151] Between 1870 and 1874, George Heard wrote his brothers that the coastal trade and the China Sea business were "about played out." The firm was "hard up" for funds, and even their unwavering rival Russell & Co. was ceding the Yangzi trade to the British firm Butterfield & Swire.[152] Merchants continued to struggle, and the depressed period between the mid-1860s and 1880s would see widespread commercial failure, even if the sociopolitical turmoil of the American Civil War dissipated.

Bailey's 1871 report of the jubilant Fourth of July celebrations attended by all in the colony resolved Anglo-American Civil War tensions in Hong Kong. Considering that the "nationalist and colonialist instincts of different foreign nationalities coexisted uneasily" in such spaces, the success of the 1871 celebration was remarkable.[153] The Treaty of Washington, ratified a month earlier, secured an apology from Britain for allowing the *Alabama* and "other vessels" to "escape" its ports, reaffirmed the meaning of neutrality for both parties, and, possibly most relieving for Americans in China, made allowances for the arbitration of claims against commercial loss.[154] With its ratification, the "long-standing difficulties to a complete understanding between England and America, had been practically cleared away."[155]

AN "ENTENTE CORDIALE"

Throughout the mid- to late nineteenth century, Hong Kong's American merchants occupied tenuous commercial and political positions relative to the British and the Chinese. Early political intercourse between the three powers had produced a "man on the spot" mentality whereby American merchants and select diplomats became unaligned with the U.S. state. While these Americans fashioned themselves as neutral bystanders in China, their rhetoric of republicanism, free trade, and self-determination was mostly performative. Contradictions between U.S. politics and American interests in China undermined the legitimacy of such claims, but in the context of Sino-British conflict Americans remined largely inconsequential. The British and Chinese courted American sympathies, rather, as a means of bolstering their positions in their own rivalry. To the Chinese, the United States was a power that had resisted the British. Technologically and politically it had much to emulate, and preexisting Anglo-American tensions might be exploited to diminish the threat of foreign militancy. To the British, the American community was a convenient ally as, by the Second Opium War, their interests aligned.

The intraregional and transnational environment of the 1860s threatened, however, to polarize the respective communities. Contributing to the instability of the Qing Empire, the Taiping Civil War in the 1850s encouraged American merchants to flout their neutrality once again in the pursuit of profit. Initial interactions with the Taiping, while generating profit for merchants, left British and American officials disillusioned about the prospects for normal relations. They thus declared support for the Qing, making the clandestine trading and adventuring of American subjects embarrassing. Support for the Qing, official condemnation of smuggling, and the flagging momentum of the Taiping undermined the profits generated through contraband goods. Still, Americans remained admirably placed to profit from the stabilization of China's interior and wasted no time planning their moves along the newly opened Yangzi. But just when they should have been best situated to dominate the market, the outbreak of their own Civil War denied them the required resources and ships. The Yangzi's promise had spurred a shipbuilding boom, but the subsequent reality of China's internal instabilities and America's Civil War just as quickly ruined the profitability of such moves. Seemingly distinct transnational and intraregional narratives thus converged through this initial episode in America's Yangzi speculation.

While American merchants struggled to turn a profit in China amid the destruction of the Taiping Civil War, their own country's mounting tensions with Britain provided new threats to Hong Kong's sociopolitical and commercial stability. Concerns over British interference in the American Civil War produced rumors of inevitable hostilities between the two Anglo-Saxon nations. These rumors, in Hong Kong at least, revolved around particular flashpoints that brought American and British communities into conflict. But there was a marked disparity between metropolitan and colonial reactions to flashpoints such as the *Trent* affair and the *Alabama*. National predispositions, in the form of divergent political and sociocultural discrepancies, competed with colonial society's assimilative power, resulting in an environment that paradoxically heightened and mitigated transnational conflicts. Such episodes were part of an "imagined" war, rumors and conjecture causing more damage to social order and commerce than the crises themselves. Thus, while metropolitan sentiments inspired momentary indignation, antipathies were easily forgotten. American commerce struggled to rebound from lost opportunities on the Yangzi and the ephemeral crisis of Confederate privateering, but local affairs and the immediate context of Hong Kong competed for the attention of China's American communities. According to their letters home, life went on.

At each instance, then, American merchants negotiated between the political identity adopted and espoused by their government and their personal interests in China. Both were reconciled according to American experiences on the ground. National interests continued to determine the course of American commerce and politics in China, but there was a changing relationship between American merchants and the metropole. Their experiences in China and Hong Kong were instrumental in defining a more nuanced overseas American identity adapted to the requisites of colonial life. One could thus be both republican and pro-empire, neutral and belligerent, American and a member of a British colonial society.

The overarching narrative here has been one of American commercial collapse within the context of intraregional and transnational political crises. Although Augustine Heard & Co. expanded rapidly throughout China in the early 1860s, by the Civil War's end, it had closed three prospective offices in Tianjin, Kiukiang, and Amoy. Those that remained open did so at a greatly reduced capacity, and company registries show that, excepting Shanghai and Hong Kong, the remaining offices employed skeleton staffs of one or two agents, possibly a clerk, and a shroff.[156] The company appeared to have overreached and underperformed, failing to generate the capital necessary to sustain its ambitions.[157] The firm's remaining offices gave the impression of success, with agents operating in Canton, Fuzhou, Hankow, Amoy, Yokohama, and Hiogo until its bankruptcy, but it lacked the energy—the confidence of the community—that it had enjoyed in the 1840s and 1850s.[158] Augustine Heard & Co. persisted for a decade following the Civil War, but the intraregional and transnational circumstances of the mid-1860s portended its decline.

Interwoven into this overarching narrative is a consideration of how nonstate actors strategically deployed their political identities and of the resilience of such identities within foreign spaces. Incongruities between letters to and from American merchants during periods of domestic upheaval reveal a unique set of concerns that do not cohere as one might expect to the political trajectory of Sino-American contact. American opportunity in the 1840s and 1850s was a nonstate project, often at odds with official rhetoric; relations with the Qing and the Taiping in the 1860s were significantly more multifaceted than a tale of embarrassing wartime adventuring would suggest; experiences of their own Civil War were far less emotional and reactive than might be supposed from metropolitan letters and news reports. These various flashpoints, traced onto the rise and decline of the first wave of American commerce in China, demonstrate at once the complex and opportunistic nature of American merchants and politicians and the power of colonial society to diminish the impact of transnational sociopolitical tensions.

Chapter Five

FRIENDS NEAR AND FAR

Creating and Maintaining Global Networks
Through Hong Kong

In 1871 the four Heard brothers traveled from Hong Kong and New England to Paris to discuss the difficulties facing their business in China. John Heard blamed excessive spending, implying that Albert Heard's high living and mismanagement of funds had overstretched the firm.[1] George Heard had, in fact, written to Albert Heard in March 1873 that the firm was "hard up" and liable to run a deficit by September, without enough revenue to meet salaries, expenses, or pay shareholders.[2] Albert Heard agreed that high expenses had been prohibitive but failed to adjust the house's personal accounts or rein in the partners in China. Looking back from 1894, Augustine Heard Jr. explained to the Mercantile Club in St. Louis that the market in China had simply changed. Local banks, the rise in steam shipping, and telegraph cables crossing the ocean floor from Shanghai to London rendered the China trade unrecognizable to the old China hands.[3] New firms with more agile business models and astute Chinese entrepreneurs once employed by the foreign firms they now competed with flourished in this new world, while the major American firms made anemic attempts to evolve. As the Heard brothers and their peers discovered, the old mode of business was no longer sustainable, and by the 1880s each of the remaining American firms founded in Canton thirty or forty years prior collapsed.

Each of the brothers would leave China in their own time and would reconcile Augustine Heard & Co.'s coming failure in various ways. At first glance, the business's looming failure foretold the end of the Heard brothers' relationship with Hong Kong. The colony would continue, however, to exert its influence over the brothers' lives, as would the firm over the lives of those left in China. Thirty-five cumulative years' experience of China had drawn the Heards into an expansive transnational network. Whether in transit, in Hong Kong, or through other opportunities the China trade generated, the Heards accumulated numerous social, political, and business contacts upon whom they could rely long after Augustine Heard & Co. failed.

Hong Kong lay at the center of the Heards' transnational networking. The colony has been described as a contact zone: a space of "different mobilities" where distant people, cultures, and identities collided.[4] The colony would become the sum of these sometimes competing and sometimes cohering parts, each of which contributed to a unique Hong Kong identity and to society's development.[5] But while the port was a contact zone, or "meeting place," it was also an "in-between" space, a "transitory point where multiple migratory trajectories intersect."[6] For the inhabitants of Hong Kong, contact with diverse migrant communities produced favorable conditions through which individuals created and maintained expansive transoceanic networks.[7] Efforts to establish these networks integrated the port's foreign community and in turn shaped American merchants' lives both in Hong Kong and long after they returned to the United States.

American merchants' tenures in China were typically short. Each Heard brother's overriding goal was to earn a competency so that they might retire in Boston. The work was a quick means to this end and brought them into contact with networks of like-minded individuals. When merchants returned to the United States, they brought their contacts back with them. Their contacts similarly moved on, thereby extending social networks established in the British colony throughout the empire and to their respective home countries. Through such far-reaching channels John Heard, traveling home from Hong Kong in the 1840s, could easily secure entry to the Bengal Club in Calcutta, meet with friends to travel overland from Suez to Cairo to Alexandria, dine with Russell Sturgis at the Star & Garter Hotel in Richmond-upon-Thames, and enjoy good credit while touring France and the German and Italian states.[8] By these same channels, dozens of young American men traveled in the opposite direction, relying on kinship networks and social connections to secure promising employment in China.[9]

Situated at the conflux of imperial migratory paths, Hong Kong provided vital opportunities for individuals to integrate into and cultivate such transnational networks. For American merchants, their nation's underdeveloped diplomatic infrastructure in China and their adaptability to British sociocultural norms multiplied opportunities to do so. The Heard brothers capitalized on their knowledge of China to connect themselves with American diplomats and pursue political ties that would outlast their commercial success and pay off long after leaving Hong Kong. At the same time, they used their commercial success and their shared sense of purpose with their British peers to insert themselves into British colonial society, joining elite social clubs and committees. Mercantile interests further encouraged the brothers to spread their trade throughout China's treaty ports, into Japan, and even to the Philippines. It was hoped this expansive network, rooted in Hong Kong, would afford power, influence, and stability as it drew American merchants into an increasingly transnational world.

The Heard brothers' social, political, and business networks grew steadily between the 1840s and 1870s. While sometimes organic, this was often a strategic growth, as they pursued particular relationships to elevate their social and commercial positions. More than a pragmatic strategy for surviving Hong Kong, the networks they had established through the China trade in turn steered the decisions the brothers made and the opportunities available to them across the world. Personal ties had brought the Heards to China, were exploited to expand their business, and influenced the directions their lives took long after leaving. Their lives, and the lives of those like them, became thoroughly globalized in the process. As a contact zone, Hong Kong was instrumental in drawing Americans into global networks, just as the preexisting networks Americans arrived with contributed to the global character of Hong Kong.

WELL-CONNECTED MERCHANTS

The networks American merchants formed in China adapted to preexisting ones connecting the region.[10] Despite the Qing's *haijin* 海禁 (maritime ban), reintroduced in the seventeenth century following the Ming model to restrict Chinese coastal settlement and overseas trade, Fujian merchants had long cultivated trade networks extending throughout East Asia and Southeast Asia during the following centuries. Their activities formed a mainstay of the Nanyang 南洋 (south sea) trade American merchants were so eager to penetrate.[11] Well-placed contacts both in China and transnationally were therefore vital if Americans hoped to succeed in China. Throughout China's port cities, Chinese and foreign merchants alike established widespread relationships, both with bureaucrats linking state and commerce and socially between merchants themselves. The most stable ties, however, were among direct kin.[12] Kinship could in turn be leveraged to create stable interfamilial ties that extended beyond racial, and cultural barriers, such as the privileged relationship between Houqua and the Forbeses in Canton.[13] The Forbeses, understanding the advantages of the leading Hong merchant's patronage, took great care grooming family members as ambassadors of sorts. Their efforts to win the influential trader's trust displayed their own sensitivity to the importance of familial hierarchies in Chinese business.[14]

Such intermingling of local and foreign networks was crucial to trade, but differences encountered in China affirmed for foreign merchants the importance of preserving strong financial, social, and cultural links with the home country. The metropole provided the capital and manpower merchants felt necessary for their firms' stability in China.[15] This imported manpower formed the upper strata of the company hierarchy, while select outgroups filled rigid occupational categories: Macanese shroffs and clerks, the Chinese comprador, a variety of Chinese house staff and personal servants. Excepting the comprador, mobility and opportunity within these positions were limited, reserved instead for the young clerks who arrived from the metropole bearing letters of recommendation from some leading partner's uncle, cousin, or friend.

These clerks integrated with the community, met important business contacts, and should they prove adept or well connected, became leading partners in the firm. Great emphasis was placed on establishing ties to their own kin or to the dominant British community, with its social, cultural, and racial similarities. Intricate familial and social relationships interlinking Hong Kong's American community and the "self-conscious" bonds between the Americans and the British bore the greatest influence over the shape of the Americans' networks in such colonial spaces.[16] Relationships with Chinese merchants were, of course, essential, but they went unmentioned when Americans thought of and recorded their commercial relationships and were virtually nonexistent in American social circles.

FRIENDS NEAR AND FAR

The Heard brothers' experiences were largely representative of these network-building patterns. From their earliest arrivals in Canton, and in George Heard's case Hong Kong, the brothers were embedded in a sociocultural and commercial environment built upon informal networking. As a Boston Brahmin–adjacent family, apprenticed in Thwing & Perkins on Boston's India Wharf or educated at Yale and Harvard, the Heards recognized networking as an essential fixture of their elite social worlds.[17] Family ties secured their training in America, and family ties brought them to China, where their first and closest contacts were naturally members of the "Boston Concern," names they were already well-acquainted with such as Forbes, Perkins, Sturgis, and Endicott.[18] The members of these families (although not the Heards) formed an endogamous group centered in Boston and New York and reproduced in Canton and Hong Kong.[19] Such insularity was not unique to Americans, and other merchant communities such as the Chinese and the British likewise prioritized the trust and security afforded through such kinship networks.[20]

Business demanded outreach, however, and to expand their firm's position the Heard brothers cultivated social and commercial ties outside the Boston Concern. Through Augustine Heard & Co.'s founding partners Augustine Heard Sr. and Joseph Coolidge, for example, the firm benefited from a tense but profitable relationship with Robert Bennet Forbes of the leading American firm, Russell & Company. Robert Bennet Forbes's influence and Augustine Heard Sr.'s reputation helped the family penetrate the trading networks of the leading Chinese merchant Houqua and his son Chongyao (Yang Haoguan 央浩官) of the E-wo Hong (Yihe Hang 怡和行) and establish ties with the leading British firm Jardine Matheson & Company.[21] From the First Opium War onward Augustine Heard & Co. collaborated further with British companies, entered the opium trade under the guidance of George Dixwell, and spread their network to India through businessmen such as Kessresung Khushalchand and Jamsetji Jejeebhoy.[22]

Following the firm's founding, Augustine Heard Sr., who gave the company his namesake, turned to family, bringing his nephews to China. John Heard had already acquired some experience through his uncle, accompanying him on voyages to Havana and St. Petersburg. Following a brief Boston apprenticeship, he arrived at Canton in 1841, rising to the position of partner and becoming prominent within the Thirteen Factories compound. During his first tenure he helped entrench the firm's position and spread their social and commercial networks, linking Macao, Calcutta, and Bombay. Augustine Heard Jr. joined him in March 1847, inherited John Heard's contacts, and helped establish the firm's Shanghai and Hong Kong branches. John Heard left China in 1852 and the second youngest brother Albert Heard replaced him, sailing from Boston in October 1854. Business was an unnatural enterprise for Albert Heard, but he participated readily in treaty-port life while maintaining a lively correspondence with Yale alumni, friends, and family from home.[23]

The firm's operations remained rooted in Canton until 1857, when the business migrated to Hong Kong. From this new base the brothers integrated with the colony's social fabric, acquiring a growing list of political contacts and diplomatic appointments. Soon after establishing the Hong Kong house, Augustine Heard Jr. returned home, and John Heard replaced him. As Sino-Western conflict opened China further, John Heard and Albert Heard established agents in numerous ports and prepared to spread up the Yangzi. George Heard arrived in 1859 and wasted no time securing a position as attaché to the American minister, John Ward, visiting China to negotiate the Sino-American Treaty of Tientsin.[24]

The four brothers rotated through Hong Kong for the next decade, filling diplomatic posts, joining Hong Kong's important social institutions and committees, and pursuing business ventures. By the company's peak between the mid-1860s and early 1870s the Heards had established a business network linking Boston and New York to China through London. As illustrated in the introduction, from Hong Kong they managed houses in Shanghai, Amoy, Fuzhou, Hankow, Kiukiang, Tientsin, and Canton.[25] They installed agents in Yokohama and Hiogo (Hyōgo) in Japan, traded between India, Vietnam, and the Philippines, and consigned goods to San Francisco via the Pacific. Their travels to and from China took them variously through Aden and Suez, to France, and to London. John Heard toured Europe, George Heard studied in Geneva, and each of the brothers was magnetically drawn to Paris. Their experiences during Augustine Heard & Co.'s thirty-six years of operation resulted in peripatetic lives, as reflected in the variety of contacts found in their social, political, and commercial networks.

The Heards' mobility stemmed from the idea that China was a temporary venture for American merchants. Hong Kong, like other locales throughout East Asia and Southeast Asia, was considered deleterious to the white constitution, and doctors and family in the metropole discouraged lengthy tenures there.[26] Heeding this advice, the Heard brothers shared the work, returning to China only to relieve each other. Their average trip between the United States and China included stops in London, Marseilles, Valletta, Alexandria, Suez, Aden, Galle, Bombay, Calcutta, Penang, Singapore, and finally Macao or Hong Kong. Such arduous journeys took as long as three months in the early 1840s, but by 1847 P&O steamers completed the journey between Southampton and China in seven weeks, and six by the 1860s.[27] The Heards made the most of time in transit, using voyages to network with other prominent Americans, Europeans, and British and to develop "personal connections to and knowledge of many places around a rapidly globalising world."[28] These steamships, like other technologies such as telegraphy, effectively shrunk the globe in the mid-nineteenth century, making it easier to maintain ties over once prohibitive distances and bringing an increasing variety of individuals—and thus ideas and cultures— into contact. Often the community aboard these steamships running between Europe and Asia reflected the British Empire in "microcosm," and two to three months confinement provided the perfect chance to meet peers traveling to fill similar roles in rival or allied firms or occupy important political posts.[29]

From the 1860s the Pacific route to America became viable, further embedding Hong Kong into transnational migratory and commercial networks. "Connective infrastructures" competed, however, with the subjective needs that shaped how people navigated imperial space.[30] The Heards still favored the circuitous voyage via Suez, since they had commercial dealings and social ties in London and Paris.[31] Maps tracking their respective paths during Augustine Heard & Co.'s operations confirm these hubs' importance (figures 5.1–5.5). In the United States, New York and Boston were central to the Heards' lives; London and Paris and Hong Kong and Shanghai formed the nucleus of their worlds in Europe and China.

The European connection was crucial. Beyond commerce, each brother traveled to and lived in Europe at some point. John Heard completed a grand tour of the German and Italian states in 1853–1854, Albert Heard attended school in Geneva before enrolling at Yale, as did George Heard upon dropping out of Harvard in 1855. And the cities of London and Paris were embedded in the Heard brothers' business networks. Augustine Heard & Co. banked with the London firm Baring Brothers & Company and its

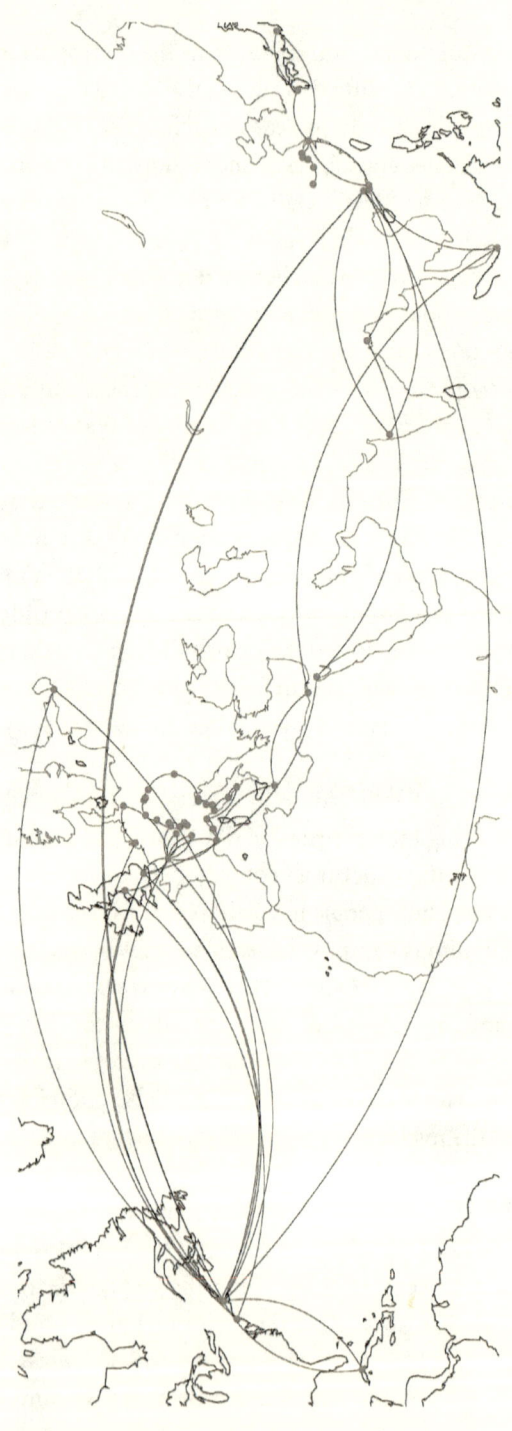

FIGURE 5.1. John Heard, travels, 1839–1877. Image by author.

FIGURE 5.2. Augustine Heard Jr., travels, 1846–1893. Image by author.

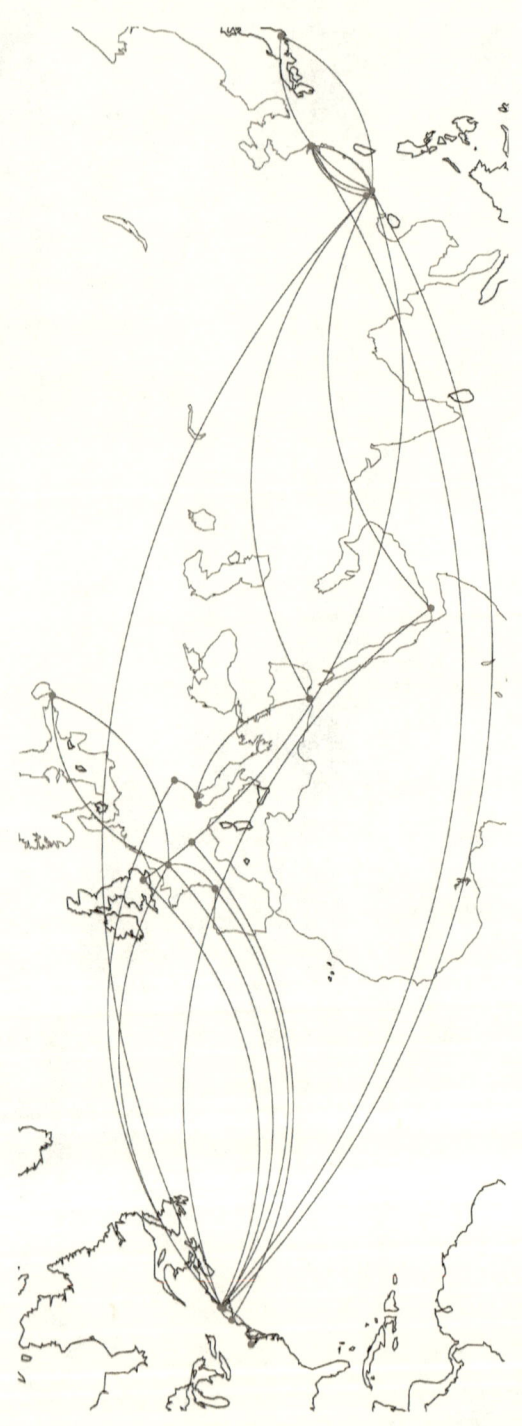

FIGURE 5.3. Albert Heard, travels, 1845–1889. Image by author.

FIGURE 5.4. George Heard, travels, 1854–1875. Image by author.

FIGURE 5.5. Core cities, 1839–1893. Image by author.

senior partner, the American China merchant Russell Sturgis. Paris, too, exerted pull as both a meeting point and a city of opportunity. John Heard, Augustine Heard Jr., and Albert Heard each spent time living in Paris (the brothers all spoke French), they reunited there to discuss the firm's troubled future in 1871, and following the firm's bankruptcy, Augustine Heard Jr. and Albert Heard both returned to Paris and worked in France. The country functioned as a go-between space where their migratory paths to and from China intersected.[32]

Through each of these spheres, America, Europe, and China, the Heard brothers developed and stitched together a transnational network. Although not all their contacts from this time were made in Hong Kong or even China, many were acquired through the Heards' travels between Asia and the United States. Some 498 of these connections from their time trading in China have been traced and grouped according to rough naturally occurring—although not necessarily geographically contingent—community clusters to demonstrate the characteristics and contours of the brothers' networks (figure 5.6). Each point on the graph represents an individual, the varying sizes reflecting the number of unique connections they have with others in the network. The dark cluster John Heard is embedded in mostly represents contacts made through his grand tour of Europe, or, directly above him, Canton merchant networks that dissipated by the time his brothers arrived. His location within the graph places him proximate to the same Canton cluster as his uncle. This placement represents his period of greatest activity in China, reflecting his deeper relation to the old China trade than to newer networks developing in and through Hong Kong. The position of the firm's founding partner George Dixwell, equidistant between John Heard, the Canton cluster, and the bulk of Augustine Heard & Co.'s staff comprising the left half of the graph, reflects his longevity with the company. Albert Heard is located centrally at the intersection of Hong Kong's social cluster (right half) and Augustine Heard & Co.'s Hong Kong and Shanghai staff (left half), having been embedded in each of these worlds. George Heard sits toward the bottom of the graph as an explicit intermediary between the company's Hong Kong staff (bottom left) and Hong Kong society, his position reflecting his active role in the colony's social and civic life. Augustine Heard Jr. wrote sparsely about nonbusiness matters and is accordingly underrepresented in the graph.

Heard Network: Modularity

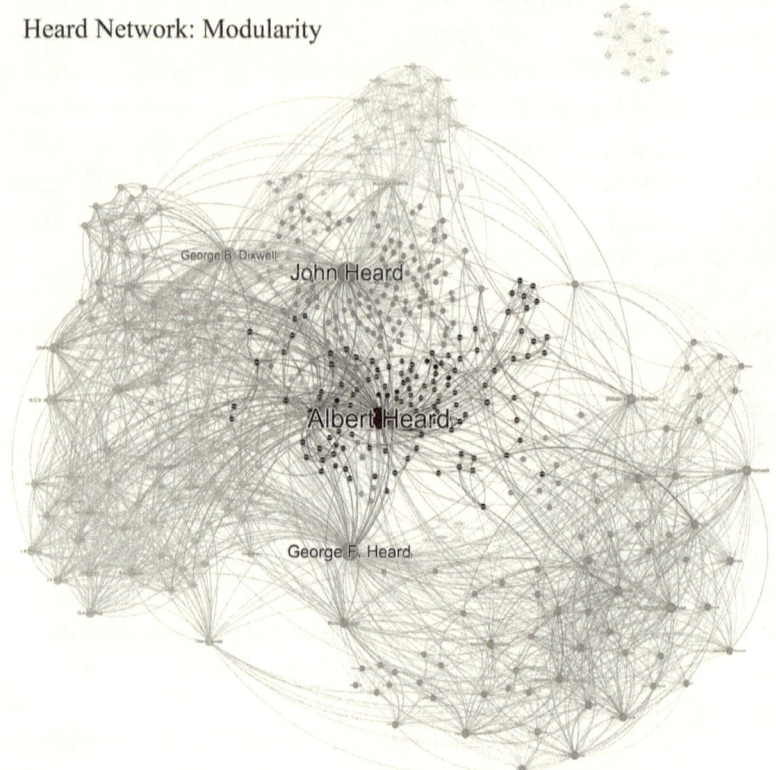

FIGURE 5.6. Augustine Heard & Co. networks in and beyond Hong Kong. Image by author.

That distinguishable groups appear despite clustering's tendency to dissipate as networks grow larger reinforces both delineations and interconnections between China's separate communities and between outliers.[33] Although clear links occur between defined clusters, each comprises a bounded location or period within the Heard network. While the lower-left gray cluster represents the firm's Hong Kong employees, for example, and the upper-left gray cluster mostly represents Shanghai employees, the two tighter groups within the Shanghai cluster depict consecutive waves of staff that cycled through the port. There are numerous ways the groups intersect, but there are also defined boundaries indicating both geography and time.

This network was predicated upon a combination of commercial, political, and social connections (figure 5.7). These categories should not be considered rigid, and social and business worlds often overlapped, but they are organized according to the primary relationships between the Heard brothers and their contacts. Two distinct types of connections are immediately apparent. The large social cluster (dark gray) is made up of contacts from institutions such as the Hong Kong Club, the Hong Kong General Chamber of Commerce, the Sailors Home, the Freemasons, and the Hong Kong Yacht Club, demonstrating the brothers' sustained efforts to participate in Hong Kong's elite public social spheres. Although the business cluster (light gray) is geographically varied, spanning Hong Kong, the treaty ports, and Japan, it shows the internal networks permeating the company. Scatterings of official relationships (black), significant

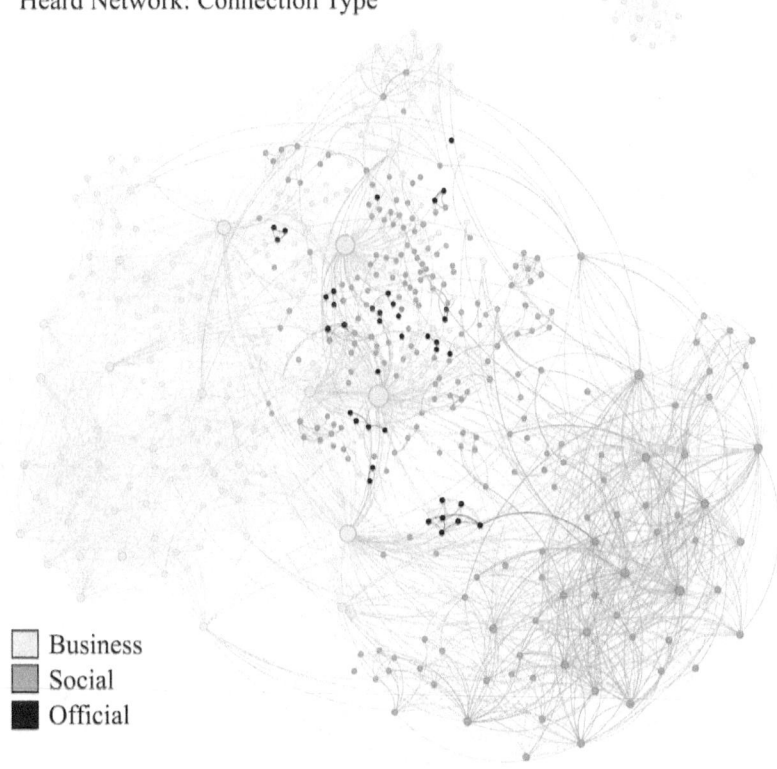

FIGURE 5.7. Heard network: Connection type. Image by author.

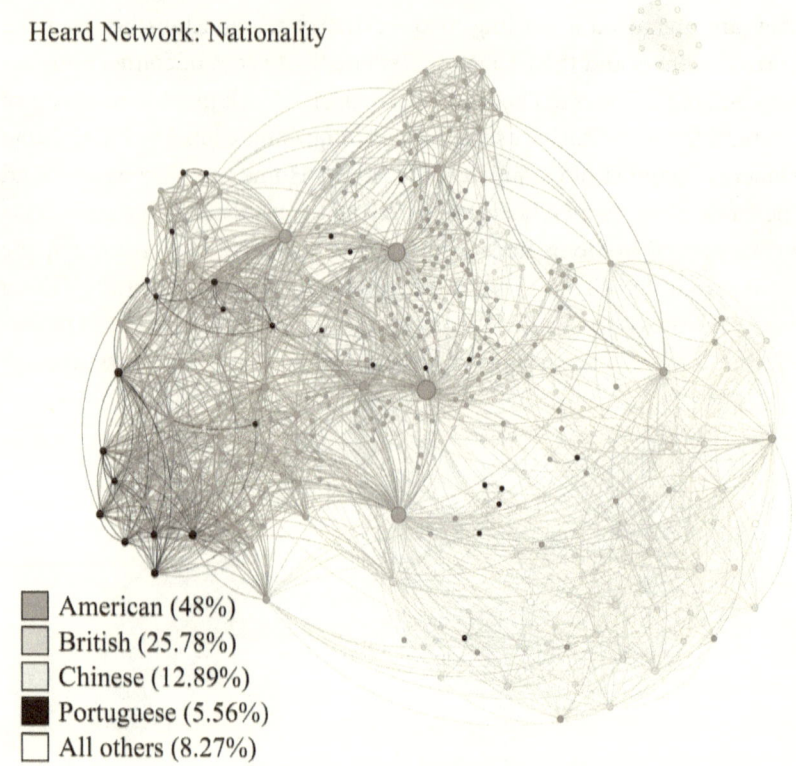

FIGURE 5.8. Heard network: Nationality. Image by author.

enough to indicate sporadic efforts at maintaining ties with influential persons, suggests that such efforts were inconsistent.

The clean division between social and business connections mirrored divisions drawn according to nationality (figure 5.8). Two nationalities, British and American, dominated the Heards' networks, confirming the homophilic tendency (a pattern of those with similar traits bonding) within the Heards' mercantile network. That most business contacts, whether from Hong Kong, Shanghai, or Canton, were American suggests a "bias" toward "similar individuals" according to nationality and kinship.[34] British contacts, in contrast, monopolized the brothers' social networks in Hong Kong, a product of British prominence in the colony. This does not necessarily mean that homophily defined the apparently British social world or suggest that relationships between Americans lacked a social element. It emphasizes, rather, that for American elites, commerce formed an essential part of their intranational relationships within China. The Portuguese are the exception within the American-dominated business world, occupying a central spot in Augustine Heard & Co.'s business networks. Portuguese agents were enmeshed in both the Hong Kong and Shanghai networks, and the relative size of their nodes confirms their stability within the company roster. The minority of Chinese individuals the Heards documented are isolated, absent, as expected, from the Heards' social world.

Whether ties were social or commercial, British or American, a simplified survey of occupation (figure 5.9) reveals that merchants dominated the Heards' China network.[35] Although they fostered ties with officials

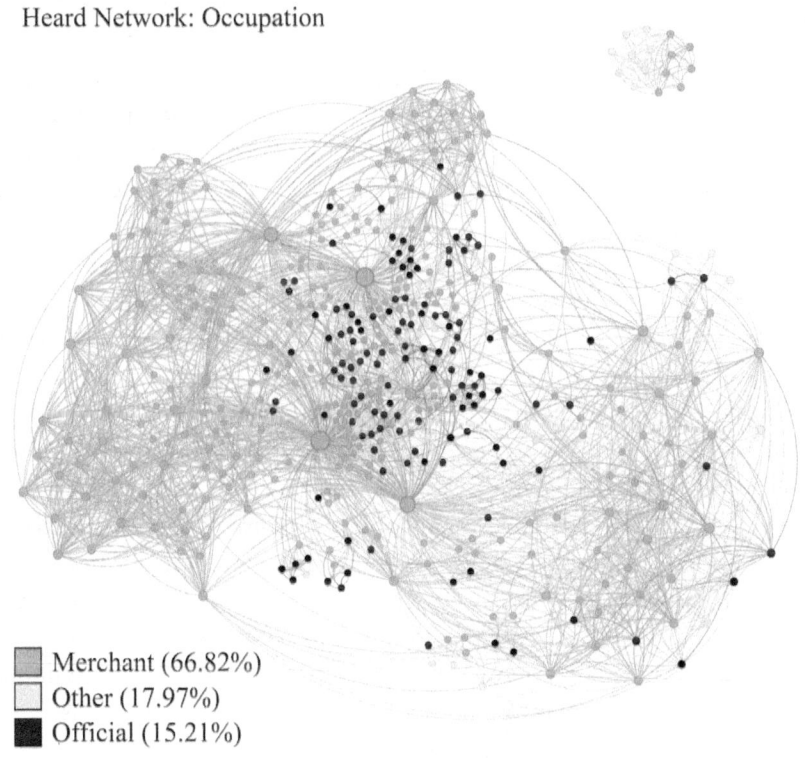

FIGURE 5.9. Heard network: Occupation. Image by author.

and "others"—doctors, missionaries, captains, tradesmen, or military figures—the network was largely homogeneous. As members of elite society this is a predictable but important confirmation of the prominence of merchants amongst Hong Kong and treaty-port elites.[36] Still, the graph risks conflating class with occupation, as the term *merchant* has been applied to cover a wide range of roles within the merchant firm. Considered alongside the connections graph, it is evident that leading partners such as George Heard and Albert Heard, Richard Deacon, or David Jardine enjoyed the strongest ties to Hong Kong society. If being part of the merchant class afforded some mobility, elite status was reserved for those individuals through which the separate spheres of commerce and society converged. Even so, few members of a foreign firm could be considered lower-class, and even a clerkship afforded proximity to networks that drew together individuals from the upper reaches of the colonial hierarchy.[37]

The closest networks were formed, however, through family ties or according to employer. Limiting the analysis to those subgroups with at least a moderate presence in the Heard network reveals the contours of a significant—if insular—network that confirms assumptions about the origins of Americans in China and the extent to which leading firms were entangled. Augustine Heard & Co. was, of course, the primary employer of individuals within the Heard network (figure 5.10). Among the firms, Russell & Co. enjoyed the next highest position. The progenitor of Augustine Heard & Co., Russell & Co.'s employees hailed from similar regional and sociocultural backgrounds. Despite their underlying rivalry with the Heards, the Forbeses, their partners, and their staff remained present in the Heards' social and commercial worlds throughout Augustine Heard & Co.'s history. Two British firms, Jardine Matheson & Co., and Gibb, Livingston & Co., were also prominent within the Heard network. The former's partners, central within Hong Kong's elite society, were linked to the Heard brothers through social institutions and commercial relationships extending back to the old China trade. The Heards' fate, moreover, was tied to Jardine's who served as trustees for Augustine Heard & Co.'s 1875 liquidation.[38] Gibb, Livingston, & Co.'s members, on the other hand, were active participants in Hong Kong society, connected through clubs and committees such as Charles Nunn's and George Heard's memberships in the Hong Kong Yacht Club in 1874/75, and Henry Lowcock's and Albert Heard's joint 1875 involvement with the Sailor's Home.[39]

Heard Network: Employer

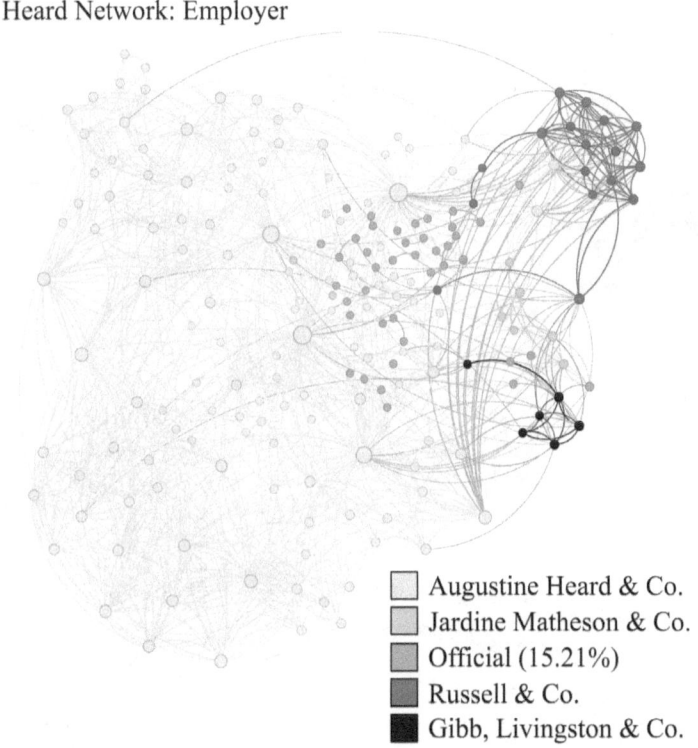

☐ Augustine Heard & Co.
☐ Jardine Matheson & Co.
☐ Official (15.21%)
■ Russell & Co.
■ Gibb, Livingston & Co.

FIGURE 5.10. Heard network: Employer. Image by author.

The families present (figure 5.11) within the Heard network naturally leaned toward the brothers' extended family. The remaining clusters were all American, underscoring the links that existed within and between New England kinship groups, for familial ties guaranteed security in business.[40] The extended network of affiliated families with members connected to the Heards were predominantly New Englanders, demonstrating how, as family members were inducted into and inherited the networks of their kin, a microcosm of elite metropolitan society formed in China. Included in this family network were two children, Anui and Richard Howard, fathered by Augustine Heard Jr. and John Heard respectively. Both children were born to protected Chinese women, Apook and Sai Louey, who existed outside the strict confines of the group as they were neither related to the Heards by blood or marriage.[41]

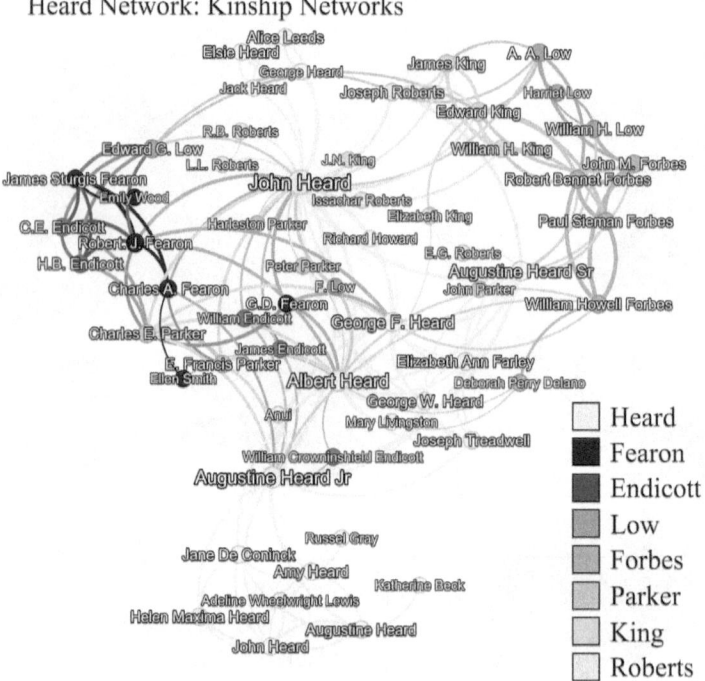

FIGURE 5.11. Heard network: Kinship networks. Image by author.

Through the course of business in China the Heard brothers formed a broad social, political, and commercial network. Associations occurred within a limited set of parameters and while varied individuals filled the network, the bulk of the Heards' social and commercial worlds tended toward homogeneity. Defined subcommunity clusters within this network demonstrate that, while time and space separated the various groups, the insularity of foreign life in China made such boundaries porous as pervasive ties formed between the members of each cluster. The overall network encompassed two dominant groups: an American commercial sphere and a British social sphere. As significant outliers, the Portuguese represented a central and stable fixture in Augustine Heard & Company. Regardless of nationality or relationship type, merchants monopolized the network, suggesting the mercantile class's primacy both within Hong Kong society and to other merchants. Other significant firms—Russell's, Jardine's, Gibb

Livingston's—were accordingly intertwined with Augustine Heard & Co., the first laying the conditions for Heard's foundation, the second overseeing Heard's demise, and all three comprising pockets of their social world. Yet the presence of significant family clusters suggests that despite the expansiveness of the Heard network and the variegated contacts therein, New Englanders relied upon kinship to reproduce metropolitan sociocommercial worlds in distant Hong Kong.

BUILDING NETWORKS IN HONG KONG AND CHINA

While the Heards cultivated expansive networks, each of the four brothers had subjective priorities while living in China that shaped their ideas of what constituted a productive relationship. For John Heard and Augustine Heard Jr., brought up on the cusp of the old China trade, commercial relationships were paramount. John Heard toiled to establish contacts within the business worlds converging in Canton and Hong Kong that might benefit the firm. His travels while doing so took him around the world, and many of those he traveled with, stayed with, or gladhanded along the way were either friends from China or introduced through China contacts. Augustine Heard Jr. continued John Heard's work, integrating into both Hong Kong and American business networks throughout his life. The two older brothers inevitably left China, settling in the United States and France, but their networks remained. The Chinese compradors and Portuguese clerks they hired contributed to Hong Kong's developing multiethnic milieu, their agents spread throughout China's treaty ports, their brothers inherited their contacts, and in the practice of many China hands they left behind children born to Chinese women, their kinship, social, and commercial networks extending across the world.[42]

Preoccupied less with economic concerns, Albert Heard valued diplomatic relationships. Although he grew to regret the distraction, he remained convinced throughout most of his Hong Kong and Shanghai tenures that pursuing diplomatic offices would benefit the firm and the family's private interests. This idea so ensnared him that he accepted the post of Russian consul to Hong Kong and even convinced the more pragmatic John Heard to occupy similar posts. George Heard was also less engaged in the firm's business, spending more time expanding the family's sociopolitical influence in the colony. His relationship with the American minister Ward represented his first experiences of China, and later activities as member to Hong Kong's various clubs and committees raised the Heard family profile within the British colony's social world.

Whatever the brothers' priorities, the ties they maintained to the metropole, to colonial society, and within the company reflected their insecurities and aspirations for their transnational lives. Their key relationships fall roughly into four categories. Their strongest impulse was to preserve links to home, which they did by exporting metropolitan social dynamics, habitually writing home, and participating in philanthropy that remitted the wealth of China to the United States. Colonial life also triggered the impulse to cluster with similar groups. Race and culture determined many of the relationships the Heards formed (or did not, for that matter). As a result, their prominent Hong Kong social connections were to the British merchant elite or to other Americans. There were, of course, exceptions to the rule. The Chinese comprador was crucial to the firm, and through him Western and local networks converged, even if the respective members operated in separate spheres. Interracial relationships, too, transcended sociocultural barriers, anchoring foreign merchants to local society. Finally, looking forward, the Heards courted diplomats and officials to leverage their expertise in China for advantages there and in the metropole. The pursuit of these various relationships embedded the Heard brothers into Hong Kong society, while also drawing that society into a broader transnational network. Many ties, particularly those to other American merchants, diplomats, and officials, would outlast the firm and continued to be drawn upon long after the Heards returned to the United States.

For Hong Kong's American merchants, the most important relationships were metropolitan ones. These distant links in their networks were also their most stable, with family being paramount. The Heard brothers sustained steady correspondence with their parents, George W. Heard and Elizabeth Ann Heard, née Farley; their uncle Augustine Heard Sr.; and of course with each other. The brothers sent and received letters at each biweekly mail service, but because it took nearly three months to contact home and another three to receive a response, concurrent conversations were common. Through these letters the Heards remained anchored to family members in Ipswich and Boston.[43] They were apprised of politics, commerce, and gossip; they ordered sundries; they managed their private affairs.[44] Such letters perpetuated a sense of belonging, reminding the brothers that they were Americans, and New Englanders no less.[45] Their absences were felt, "the idea of so many old friends at home" and "all of them" neglecting to write causing much anxiety.[46]

For these same reasons, Americans abroad maintained contact with stateside friends.[47] In doing so they performed and were reminded of their identity and their cultural traditions. Albert Heard's efforts to preserve contact with fellow alumni of Yale's secretive Skull & Bones society exemplify this impulse. In January 1853, barely in Canton twenty-three days, he sent fourteen letters to his peers. The letters were in honor of "322," the "day of days" (a Thursday), which bore some significance within the club's apocryphal lore. Their content was standard, describing the journey to China, his new occupation, and reminiscing about college days. Albert Heard vowed in three letters to donate to the club's fund for a new temple. In each he begged for responses and to be remembered at home.[48] The letters' recipients were varied and, despite their youth, navigated elite circles in the United States. Henry Babcock would go on to become a successful industrialist, George A. Johnson was already a professor in Kentucky and eventually became the attorney general of California in 1886, and William Henry Gleason was, in succession, a lawyer, minister, and candidate for the U.S. Congress.[49] Beyond reinforcing his sense of belonging to this elite group, writing these letters helped Albert Heard remind others of his achievements and preserve his space in high society.

Kinship and friendships represent just two facets, however, of the metropolitan networks exported to Hong Kong. The Heard brothers also remained connected to their home through their sense of civic and social responsibility. Philanthropy provided opportunities to perform their success for those at home while cementing their elite status. New England traders in China demonstrated national pride through support for causes such as the "Union League, civilian defence groups, and Lincoln's presidential campaigns."[50] The Heard brothers also donated to relief funds and community projects. In 1862 they provided charity for the Civil War soldiers' benefit and considered setting up a subscription "among American houses & residents" in China to assist families of the wounded and sick. The brothers joined fellow American merchants in China to send relief funds following the Great Boston Fire of 1872 (John Heard lived in Boston at the time). Augustine Heard Sr. purchased the land for and funded the construction of the Ipswich Public Library.[51] A unitary sense of national and racial identity sharpened through the colonial context encouraged such charitable acts.[52] Yet personal agendas, such as fabricating a positive public image, also guided philanthropy, as John Heard's complaint that the soldiers' benefit generated no "acknowledgement" from "the many that must have benefitted" suggests.[53] Through such acts, the brothers leveraged their success in China to guarantee their position within the elite United States society.

The social and kinship ties that linked American merchants to the United States also resulted in the reproduction of metropolitan networks within Hong Kong. The Heard brothers' own induction into the China trade stemmed from their uncle. Augustine Heard Sr.'s reputation in Canton with the Boston Concern ensured that despite the inauspicious conditions of Augustine Heard & Co.'s founding, the tight-knit and insular American merchant community still accepted the Heard brothers.[54] Such positive relationships were necessary, as status in elite Hong Kong society accordingly translated into status among the Boston Brahmins.

Within such an insulated clique, a gregarious disposition served merchants well, but rivalries and personal animosities existed as they did in any network. Still, these arose mostly within private letters between trusted confidants. Such a rivalry developed between the Heard and Forbes families. The conditions of Augustine Heard & Co.'s foundation, and the subsequent competition between the firm and Russell & Co. preconditioned the members of the two families to resent each other.[55] As a hopeful clerk destined for Russell & Co., James Murray Forbes had sailed for Hong Kong with his friend Jim Jackson, the latter slated for Augustine Heard & Company. James Murray Forbes remembered, later in life, that the "bitter rivalry" between the two firms kept him from seeing much of his friend.[56]

Still, Hong Kong was small, and appearances were everything. Some relationships, such as those between James Murray Forbes and Charles Orne or Jim Cunningham of Augustine Heard & Co., transcended rivalries in good faith, while others were more calculated.[57] Robert Bennet Forbes, for example, maintained his good name and peace within the Anglo-American community by referring to Coolidge the contracts that secured Augustine Heard & Co.'s start in 1839. He maintained a productive relationship with Coolidge to prevent scandal—in private he felt the man to be "supremely ridiculous" and "excessively mean"—and despite their differences spoke fondly of Augustine Heard Sr. as a courageous and honest man in his

Reminiscences.[58] His family members, James Murray Forbes, William Howell Forbes, and Francis Blackwell Forbes, showed less tact.

As two of the handful of elite American merchant families in China, the Heards and Forbeses had various opportunities to interact socially. By the 1860s and 1870s, the two families grew entangled in each other's social and business networks, getting along, for all appearances, amicably. Tiffin and dinner invitations, trial runs aboard each other's steamers, and drives about town put a placid face on an otherwise superficial relationship.[59] Such politesse preserved peace within Hong Kong's American community, as Robert Bennett Forbes had done in Canton and Macao thirty years prior. Face mattered among elite colonial networks, and it was important to inspire admiration if one wished to maintain one's status. The exercise of maintaining these ties stopped, however, at the public sphere. In private, rivalries and gossip were given traction. In letters, frustrated Heards denounced Forbeses, Forbeses spread rumors about Heards, and while the situation in Hong Kong was stable, onlookers from the metropole were privy to a much more fractious world. Forced "friendships" between the Heard brothers and the Forbeses would not survive the return to America, where prominent members of the Boston Concern, with their strong ties to Russell & Co, formed a closed clique.

Americans had only a small presence in Hong Kong, and to secure a place within elite colonial society, it was necessary that the Heards move beyond the American community and cultivate ties with the British. To do so they leveraged their cultural fluency for networking. Socially mobile white Americans, educated to revere the idea of Anglo-Saxon racial and cultural solidarity, assimilated well with the colony's British elite.[60] Although there were exceptions, nonwhite or non-Anglo-Saxon individuals rarely disrupted the homophily of this elite social world.[61] A handful of Europeans, such as the German Adolf Zimmern, born in Heidelberg, the Dane Peter Karberg, or the Norwegian George Helland were linked to the Heards through notable civic and social organizations. Exceptions included, as well, the Portuguese U. S. da Silva and Baron do Cercal, the Baghdadi Jewish Sassoons, and the Anglo-Indian Malcolm Straun Tonnochy (figure 5.9), but the Heards encountered these men through committees and advisory boards.[62] There are only brief, if any, reference to nonwhite contacts in the Heards' private social lives.

While each of the brothers leveraged the firm's prestige to situate themselves among Hong Kong's elite foreign community, none were so engaged as George Heard. Alongside his peer William Howell Forbes, George Heard performed several social and civic roles that brought him into contact with the colony's elite. In 1870 both joined British merchants William Keswick of Jardine Matheson & Co., Hugh B. Gibb of Gibb, Livingston & Co., and American Gideon Nye as members of the Medical Missionary Society.[63] In 1873 George Heard was also a member of the Seaman's Hospital and had ties to the China Sea, Saigon, & Straits Company Ltd.[64] George Heard and William Howell Forbes were both members of the Hong Kong Yacht Club in 1874, George Heard a concurrent member of the Victoria Regatta Club, and that same year serving on the board of the Hong Kong, Canton, & Macao Steamboat Company Ltd., and the Hong Kong General Chamber of Commerce alongside the wealthy Baghdadi merchant, Solomon David Sassoon.[65]

William Howell Forbes and Albert Heard joined the philanthropic Sailors' Home initiative, again in connection with Sassoon, Dent & Co.'s John Dent, and a roster of British officials and merchants from the influential firms of Jardine Matheson & Co., Holiday Wise & Co., Gibb, Livingston & Co., and the P&O.[66] And while Albert Heard did not serve on the Hong Kong Club House Committee, George Heard, Dixwell, and Deacon represented the firm. Inclusion in these networks supported the brothers' social and commercial aspirations, such visibility alongside the British elite a testament to the influence American merchants enjoyed in the colony.[67] Of the brothers, George Heard participated most actively in society. He cultivated the widest range of ties, connected with the port's influential merchants and officials, and generated enough notoriety to appear in the pages of *China Punch*.[68] George Heard best exemplifies how Americans interacted with Hong Kong's elite foreign society. His premature passing, however, makes it impossible to gauge how useful these ties would have been to him in later life.

Although most American relationships were formed with the British or with other Americans, a few of the most significant contacts the Heards acquired crossed racial barriers. Compradors such as Mok Sze Yeung, and their kinship or same-place networks were crucial contacts through which white foreign and Chinese worlds converged. Inconsistent record keeping means the majority of the Mok's Xiangshan network is obscured in the archive, but through him the Heards strategically tapped into an entire world of Chinese commerce that enabled their business to run smoothly.[69] Mok and the other Heard compradors oversaw Chinese staff, met with Chinese vendors, and even lent money to the firm's partners.[70] Through these same channels, Mok worked to aid those within his own kinship network, establish commercial and social relations with "a number of foreign businessmen and authorities," and extend his own business interests and those of his family.[71] This was a symbiotic relationship, and while the comprador was crucial to the American firm, extending its network through a world of unseen Chinese agents, he benefited in his own right, using his foreign contacts to cement his position amongst Hong Kong's Chinese elite.[72]

Less acknowledged than the comprador but no less indispensable, the firm's Portuguese and Macanese employees were likewise central to the success of the Heards' business. These men never appeared in letters or diaries describing China, but while their presence was elided their longevity in the firm's company rosters attests to their importance. Employees such as Henrique Caetano Victor de Figueiredo, his son José Miguel Victor de Figueiredo, Inácio Pires Pereira Jr., Olímpio Augusto da Cruz, and Francisco António de Seabra reappeared in directories year after year as their American coworkers cycled through the port, their presence remarkably stable in a society and business model built upon transience.[73]

As with the comprador, the benefits of this relationship flowed both ways. Portuguese and Macanese clerks used their stability within the firm to secure opportunities for family, as Figueiredo did for his son, and to establish their wider community within a comfortable middle-class niche. Doing so was part of a negotiated process whereby the community strategically adapted to the culture, society, and politics of Hong Kong. Such efforts could be tenuous, and race still mattered in the ways society saw these men and their families. They were successful often enough, however, and Portuguese and Macanese accountants and clerks became generally well-regarded fixtures of the American merchant house.[74]

While this mix of transnational, social, and interracial relationships represents the range of ways the Heards pursued, maintained, and contributed to networks within Hong Kong, some of the most important and controversial ties were those fostered through diplomatic postings. The American government made few provisions for consular officials in China during the early to mid-nineteenth century. Consular posts in ports such as Macao were self-financed, and typically only independently successful merchants applied.[75] Political connections enabled merchants to acquire these posts, and once in them they used their power to appoint fellow merchants to positions in "less important treaty ports." Congress criticized the system for giving merchant-consuls a political edge to augment their mercantile activities as early as 1833, but in Hong Kong it persisted for another twenty years.[76] In more remote treaty ports like Hankow, the system of merchant-consulships lasted well into the 1860s.

As Hong Kong's foreign community in China continued to evolve, other nations offered similar opportunities that were, importantly, open to Americans. Albert Heard became Russian consul in Shanghai (1862, 1864–1865), a post that, despite the pomp of the title, bore little power. He later acted in the same capacity in Hong Kong, encouraging his brothers to do the same.[77] John Heard accordingly was recorded as Canton's Portuguese consul in 1862, and concurrently listed as Hong Kong's Russian consul, and George Heard served as Hong Kong's Russian vice consul in the 1870s.[78] The brothers found consular duties distracting, but Albert Heard believed the posts afforded the house "face" and privileged access to powerful individuals.[79]

Albert Heard used his Russian consulship to become well acquainted with Russian Grand Duke Alexei Alexandrovich. He leveraged the firm's resources to host Alexandrovich and spent most of his time during the grand duke's visits chaperoning Alexandrovich around the treaty ports. During Alexandrovich's September 1862 visit to Hong Kong, Dixwell assured John Heard that while his presence gave a "good deal of work to the consulate" it did not interfere with business. In his memoirs, John Heard recalled that the partners of the firm felt that through such activities they might as well "be adopted into the [Russian] Imperial Family." He ultimately condemned the move, however, as entertaining Russians cost "no end of money" while not "bringing in one cent of profit."[80]

If consular duties disillusioned John Heard, courting the imperial family and high officials consumed Albert Heard. Despite asserting the contrary, Albert Heard's efforts to entertain the Russians distracted from business (although Dixwell had assured it would not) and appeared absurd to onlookers. Even Albert Heard despaired at being "overrun with distinguished foreigners." Still, he justified the expense of upkeeping these relationships. His proclivity survived the firm's bankruptcy and his departure from China. Returning to Boston in 1875, Albert Heard made plans "to renew many of [his] former acquaintances with Russian friends."[81]

Political office was not, however, the only inroad to official networks, and other diplomatic links would prove more lucrative than those to the Russians. The paucity of the American community in China and the inexperience of the American government in Sino-American diplomacy granted merchants greater influence in political affairs than they might enjoy elsewhere. American consuls, commodores, and diplomats consulted the Heards and other merchants about commerce and politics in China. And the Heards, for their part, groomed these relationships, as they had when they inducted Thomas Waldron into illicit business in the port in 1844.

Such efforts extended to every level of the U.S. political presence in East Asia. Albert Heard predicted in 1859 that the firm would benefit from George Heard's ties to the American minister Ward's mission, since George Heard was traveling "in the best company in China." Prior to Ward's mission, Albert Heard accommodated the minister and Commodore Tattnall at Hong Kong. Such familiarity allowed the Heards to voice concerns about naval protection and the coming Treaty of Tientsin. Ward, in support, encouraged Albert Heard to marshal his domestic networks to "bring pressure 'upon the government.'" John Heard, using a similar opportunity, accompanied the American minister Townsend Harris to Japan in 1859, claiming to have been the first American civilian to visit the island nation.[82] The mission provided John Heard with the chance to outpace his competitors in assessing trade prospects in the Japanese treaty ports.

While such networking provided economic advantages, social motivations also guided the Heards' efforts. Accompanying historic missions or being the "first" to visit a country or port contributed to the brothers' sense of pride. The Heards collected these experiences and relationships as a form of social capital. Other Americans, such as Henry Warden of Russell & Co., who hosted former U.S. Secretary of State William Seward and his entourage at Shanghai during their 1870 tour of East Asia, did the same.[83] Such activities confirmed the status of the firm both self-referentially to the Heards and publicly to the wider foreign community. There was also the potential to leverage these relationships in the metropole, an outcome that both Albert Heard and Augustine Heard Jr. desired following the firm's bankruptcy.

THOSE LEFT BEHIND

By 1875 Augustine Heard & Co.'s imminent bankruptcy faced the Heard brothers. High expenditure, overdrawn accounts, and their Boston agent Percival Lowell Everett's poor fiscal management rapidly dismantled an enterprise that had taken decades to build.[84] Signs of trouble had been mounting between the mid-1860s and early 1870s as local and transnational conflicts, new systems of banking and capital investment, and global recession transformed foreign commerce in China.[85] Like the other great American firms, the Heards held on until it was impossible to continue, but as the end grew apparent they prepared their retreat from China.

Each of the brothers left China with an expanded network of contacts that they would draw upon as they navigated bankruptcy back in the United States. Yet they also left behind the remnants of networks that they had cultivated. Children born to their protected women, a cousin electing to remain in Japan, and American employees marooned in China without work each represented the ways the firm's influence continued to be present after its failure. For many connected with the firm, life in China or the surrounding region marched on long after the Heards pulled up stakes. This diverse cast of those left behind in turn continued contributing to the developing social, cultural, and commercial milieu of (semi)colonial enclaves throughout East Asia.

Protected women and illegitimate children comprised one such interracial, if ambiguous, side of the Heard network that anchored the brothers to China long after they left. American men established funds to provide for these women and their Eurasian children until a specified age and entrusted power of attorney to reliable but discrete partners still in China.[86] Provisions were made for their children's marriages, and possibly future careers.[87] In the case of the Heards, the intimate transnational relationships that sustained business also provided avenues to support protected women and children left in China. These children in turn adapted the ambiguity of their parentage, cultural upbringing, and racial identity to establish themselves in unique ways.

John Heard's son Richard Howard Heard remained in China. In 1882 he married the Irish-born Mary Purcell in Hong Kong, who had come out to China as a young girl and had been educated in the colony.[88] Perhaps owing to the Heards' long-standing ties to Jardine, Matheson & Co., Richard

Howard Heard secured employment in Jardine's China Sugar Refining Company at East Point.[89] Toward the turn of the century, the couple moved to Shanghai, where Richard Howard Heard worked for the Soy-Chee cotton mill (Rui ji fangzhi gongsi 瑞記紡織公司). Their son, Augustine John "Johnny" Purcell Heard, bore a name evoking his father's pedigree.[90] He became China's best-known jockey, departing Hong Kong for Europe in 1935 having "won more races than any other rider" and ridden "on every race course in China."[91] One daughter, Emily, married the Scotsman Kenneth W. Campbell, Chief Engineer of the International Settlement's Fire Brigade, on November 16, 1905. Another, Theresa Agnes, married Albert Leon Chapeaux of Lyons.

Richard Howard Heard died in Shanghai in April 1913, well respected among the international community. His wife died thirteen years later, in December 1926. The family they had raised in China testified to the global circuits that collided in Hong Kong and the treaty ports. This Eurasian man, born to an American father and Macanese mother, had married an Irish woman raised in China. Their China-born daughters married Scottish and French migrants, and their son became a celebrity throughout the sporting world. Richard Howard Heard had leveraged his upbringing for success in a British business in Hong Kong, and then a German one in Shanghai.[92] He was remembered as "highly popular," a Mason; "a son of one of the principals" of Augustine Heard & Company. He was by all accounts a product of transnational networks.[93]

If Richard Howard Heard integrated with foreign society, his cousin, Augustine Heard Jr.'s daughter Anui, took an opposite path. While Richard Howard Heard's mother settled in Hong Kong, bought property, and provided her son opportunities to interact with foreign society, Anui's spent her time living in the countryside, coming into the colony only to conduct business. Augustine Heard Jr. had made provisions for his daughter's betrothal, and George Heard reported that on December 5, 1868, she had been engaged to the son of a "respectable" and "well to do" Chinese man from Canton, whom she married four years later.[94] As with Richard Howard Heard, the funds made available to Anui and her mother had provided commercial and social leverage, enabling them to navigate between Macao, Hong Kong, and Guangdong's countryside. But rather than mix with white society, they reinforced their belonging within the Cantonese community. Mixed parentage might have invited ostracization from white and Chinese communities alike, but for those children left behind in China it could also be brandished to gain access to either.[95]

George Dixwell's Eurasian son Charles Dixwell took an alternative path still accompanying his father to the United States, where he would be educated in an American fashion. His mother, Hu Ts'ai-shun, remained in Shanghai, an anchor to the treaty-port world of his birth. As with other Eurasian children, the change in scenery ensured Charles Dixwell would become sufficiently "anglicized."[96] His ever-shifting self-identification reflected, however, certain immutable aspects of race in the nineteenth century as U.S. attitudes toward Chinese migrants shifted. Charles Dixwell had an American father, but to look at him would have betrayed his mixed parentage.[97] He accordingly tweaked details in his passports, in the census, and in shipping manifests to cement his status as an American citizen. He returned to China to visit his mother but spent the rest of his life living in the United States and, briefly, in Paris.[98]

The three paths these Eurasian children took represent the complex ways interracial relationships shaped local networks even after foreign men returned home. Some, such as Richard Howard Heard, "asserted European or Eurasian connections and identities." Others, such as Anui were "absorbed into the fold of Chinese communities."[99] Still others, such as Charles Dixwell, used the opportunities their parentage afforded to navigate transnational networks back to America. This latter route had its own set of complications. Race functioned as an unpredictable barrier, Charles Dixwell's 1889 passport reiterating that he was the son of a native-born U.S. citizen in five places.[100] In each instance these Eurasian offspring reflected and challenged the "shifting markers" demarcating race and nation.[101] The "discreetness" of their ethnicity and race permitted them to straddle local Chinese and foreign American networks should they successfully "pass" as either.[102]

As their enterprise crumbled throughout East Asia, the Heards left more than children behind. Clerks caught off guard, partners in Hong Kong, and branch managers each worried over their futures in China and Japan. Their cousin and tea taster Gustavus Farley anxiously awaited information in Yokohama, weighing options as others in the house panicked. Working with Augustine Heard Jr., Farley helped attempt to reestablish the firm under a new name, but his letters betrayed financial precarity.[103] Yet his cousins' hardship was an opportunity for the enterprising Farley. He and his British peer Jack Fraser endeavored to start the new Fraser, Farley & Co in Yokohama, 1876, as a British firm trading with Boston and dealing in insurance. The two had, after all, ten years collective experience in East Asia, preexisting credit with their peers, and "sufficient support to warrant [their] starting."[104]

Farley went home after establishing the business to take leave and drum up support in Boston. In the United States he met Katharine Cheney and the two were married in 1880. Cheney accompanied Farley back to Yokohama via San Francisco.[105] Her descriptive letters home could have been those of Bradford, the Heards, the Forbeses, the Kinsmans, or the Beals. The scene had changed, but foreign life was familiar: making friends on the boat over, dining with other foreigners (with many servants to help), entertaining calls in the afternoon, and driving about the foreign neighborhood with her husband.[106] Through their cousin Farley and his new wife, the cycle the Heards had inherited from their uncle at Canton and exported to Hong Kong and the treaty ports found new life in Japan, as Americans continued to "make" foreign society in East Asia.

Augustine Heard & Co. employees throughout East Asia had a less certain future. From roughly the start of their Yangzi speculation in the early 1860s the Heards hit peak numbers in employees. Excluding Chinese employees—accurate numbers are impossible to obtain, but one house alone maintained upward of fifty-four in 1859—the firm supported roughly forty rotating foreign and Macanese staff at any given time until their failure. From their foundation to their bankruptcy the Heards had employed and connected more than 120 foreign individuals in China and Japan, the last cohort of which were set adrift in 1875. In 1876, under the refreshed moniker of "Heard & Co." they retained some thirteen foreign agents, but these too were forced to find new employment by the year's end.[107]

Augustine Heard Jr. made some provisions to find new postings for employees waylaid by the bankruptcy. He offered to refer one dejected employee at Yokohama to Butterfield & Swire's Shanghai office should they need an agent in Japan, but the employee proved inflexible, and nothing much came of the efforts. Upon firing Charles Endicott at Shanghai in 1875 he likewise offered to provide any assistance that he might.[108] For those who could, the question remained of whether or not to return to the United States, while others sought posts in new firms. The latter efforts were made easier due to the close local relationships that had supported the business in the first place. Those in the firm unburdened by bankruptcy—such as Robert Fearon and Edward Gilchrest Low, who entered into business together—exploited their position to build upon the wreckage of the Heards' old commercial networks.[109] Whether employees from any stage of the firm elected to stay in China or return to the United States, Britain, or Europe after their tenures, they too diversified foreign society and culture in China, expanded (or sought to at least) Sino-foreign commerce, and helped strengthen the interpersonal networks that connected China to the wider world.

The Heards' China networks long outlasted the firm, continuing to shape the social, cultural, and commercial landscape of Hong Kong and the treaty ports. The presence of the brothers, the individuals they had brought to China for business, and the impact of the firm itself produced new forms of interpersonal networking, new opportunities for trade, and new pathways between the United States and China that individuals exploited to move both ways. In the absence of these American men, their Eurasian children still used the circumstances of their parentage to navigate foreign and Chinese communities and to migrate to the United States. They established themselves in either through the joint capital, contacts, and culture that they inherited from their Chinese or Macanese mothers and their American fathers. In a similar manner the firm's employees found new work in Augustine Heard & Co.'s absence through the sociocommercial networks that had buttressed their firm. The void the firm's failure produced in turn provided new spaces throughout China and Japan for a growing community of British and American traders to operate, as Fearon, Low, Farley, and Fraser built their livelihood using the contacts and expertise they had acquired as employees of Augustine Heard & Company. The legacy of Augustine Heard & Co. accordingly lived on in China.

In a similar manner China continued to exert influence over the Heard brothers, as the course their lives took after returning to the United States will demonstrate. John Heard, who had always remained tangentially connected to elite Brahmins, found it easier to reintegrate into life in the United States. Augustine Heard Jr. relied on a network of school peers, fellow merchants, and social relations as he attempted to relaunch himself as a businessman before settling into a diplomatic posting. Albert Heard stayed abroad for a time, soliciting friends and contacts in France, Germany, Britain, Russia, and the United States for political patronage while he worked as a commercial agent, scholar, and governmental aide in turn. In the United States or Europe each of the brothers would continue to tap into the networks they had built through the China trade as they attempted to rebuild their lives.

THE FAILURE OF AUGUSTINE HEARD & CO.

Examination of these three epilogues to the narrative of Augustine Heard & Co. will demonstrate the transnational reach of nineteenth-century American mercantile networks, but the importance of Hong Kong as an in-between place where these networks converged, expanded, and then spread globally cannot be overemphasized. Boston networks, transplanted from the shores of New England to Canton's Thirteen Factories, brought merchants such as Augustine Heard Sr. and Coolidge to China and led to the latter's founding of Augustine Heard & Co. in Augustine Heard Sr.'s name. Augustine Heard Sr. introduced each of his nephews into the firm, combining the stability of kinship networks with his varied connections among the British, Chinese, and American communities to establish the company in China.

As a transnational enterprise, the firm linked traders, bankers, and financiers in America, Britain, continental Europe, and China, but on a personal scale, the partners also linked the social and domestic worlds of China, the United States, and the British Empire. These partners each contributed in their own ways to making Hong Kong a transnational society. Some, such as John Heard and Augustine Heard Jr., were key figures among the merchant elite, bridging the gap between the old China traders and the new cohort of American merchants in Hong Kong and Shanghai. Others prioritized different interests. Albert Heard chose to focus on official relationships and diplomatic postings, while George Heard embedded himself comfortably into the elite Anglo-American society.

Networks both in and through Hong Kong were expansive and their analyses, as this case of the Heards demonstrates, reveal how and to what extent communities such as the Americans integrated with colonial society. Although there were exceptions to the rule, the Heard network, as might be expected, was composed of merchants, mostly white. Some of these relationships were of vital importance and others were ephemeral, but each contributed to a homogeneous elite Anglo-American community. Still, as the data suggests (in some cases through omission), there were spaces for other communities to operate within the network, and even entire communities invisible within the archive. The most important feature, however, for understanding Hong Kong society, is that the individual communities that together comprised such networks were porous. Whether separated by time and space, occupation, race, or class, a high level of interconnection existed within the Heard network between individual actors.

Still, some relationships carried more weight than others, and it is impossible to gauge the strength of ties through quantitative network analysis alone. A more qualitative approach reveals that those ties that carried the most weight occurred between family members and close friends in Hong Kong or the metropole. Through letters and furloughs American merchants remained rooted to family and metropolitan society; through Eurasian children and subsidies, returned merchants remained rooted to Hong Kong. These latter ties required a more discrete sort of maintenance in the form of stipends managed by trustworthy partners still in China. Metropolitan social networks bridged the gap in a different but still influential way. The insularity of the Americans' transnational networks compressed space to the point where Hong Kong and Boston society functioned as natural extensions of each other. Everyone knew everyone else's affairs, and issues in one port often extended to the other. Hong Kong's insularity had a soothing effect on underlying rivalries, but conduct and scandal in one place could influence social standing in the other.

Other relationships that figured less prominently in the Heard network, such as those with the comprador or with diplomats, bore disproportionate influence on their affairs both in Hong Kong and after the firm's failure. The comprador bridged the homogeneous Anglo-American network and local Chinese networks. Although his presence and the contacts he cultivated are underrepresented in the Heard records, Augustine Heard & Co. would not have succeeded without his expertise and contacts. In a similar manner, the moves the Heard brothers took following the firm's bankruptcy relied on a few key relationships with diplomats and officials that were fostered in Hong Kong but appeared, outwardly, to be minor figures in their networks. Of questionable consequence in Hong Kong, relationships acquired through consular duties such as Albert Heard's with the Grand Duke Alexandrovich and through opportune meetings such as George

Heard's and Ward's helped determine the opportunities available to the brothers upon their retreat from China.

The communities they left behind when they returned to the United States likewise leveraged their relationships with the Heards and with the company to produce their own opportunities and expand their own networks in China. John Heard and Augustine Heard Jr. personally left Macanese protected women and Eurasian children who helped contribute to the transcultural character of (semi)colonial society. The women used the funds provided them to selectively assimilate with Hong Kong or Guangdong, their children following similar paths as they became members of "white" or Cantonese societies respectively. Others traveled migratory routes back to the United States, strategically shedding aspects of their Chineseness along the way. In each case they reflected the merging of cultures and identities unfolding along the China coast. Others still—stranded American employees and kin—used the firm's failure to build new lives, perpetuating their own networks in turn as they continued to live and trade in China.

As these entanglements between China and the United States suggest, Hong Kong was "made" by Americans. They helped draw Hong Kong into a social, cultural, political, and commercial world crisscrossed by transnational networks. Americans brought preexisting relationships, adding to the complexity of Hong Kong society, and extending the commercial and private interests of U.S. merchants to the colony. Often, they conformed to the sociocultural dictates of the port, and in doing so they helped entrench the position of the colony's white, predominantly Anglo-Saxon, merchant elite. Americans joined the clubs, served as consuls for other nations, expanded their business interests throughout China, and supported each other through kinship and metropolitan ties. Although their community was comparatively small, they enjoyed a prominent place among elite foreigners that reflected their ability to at once contribute to and navigate British colonial society. When they departed, they left behind communities that continued to be shaped by those personal ties that bound China to the United States, their significance reified through the ways these communities in turn contributed to the continued development of Hong Kong and the treaty ports.

Chapter Six

WEALTH OR EXPERTISE

The Social and Professional Paths of Returned American Merchants

> Formerly a young man went to China with the expectation of returning in ten or twelve years, if not with fortune, at least with a competency.
>
> —AUGUSTINE HEARD JR. (1894)

> We left China in February last and after numerous trials, including loss of fortune, and the death of my brother George, we are again in America.
>
> —ALBERT F. HEARD (1875)

Misfortunes never come single. The year 1875 brought with it consecutive tragedies for the Heard family. The solemn year began when Dr. Richard O'Brien recommended that George Heard leave Hong Kong for his health. Albert Heard bundled his ailing brother onto a steamer for home where it was hoped a change of air would reverse his condition. George Heard was the first Heard brother to leave China for good. Telegraphs arrived in February that somewhere in the Gulf of Aden he had succumbed to his illness. The passing of the youngest and by many accounts most gregarious of the Heard brothers weighed heavily on the family. But the remaining brothers lacked the time to dwell upon their grief, for in the summer Augustine Heard & Co. formally declared bankruptcy. Almost immediately after he had seen off his younger brother, Albert Heard too left China with his wife, personally declaring bankruptcy in Boston on August 10, 1875.[1]

The couple faced the daunting reality of returning home to few prospects. Albert Heard had failed to earn the competency emblematic of the China trader. He had squandered his brothers' funds, which should have been secure investments that would carry them through a comfortable retirement in the United States. Instead, the bankruptcy took a toxic turn, as various creditors claimed what they could from the now-liable partners of the firm. All three brothers would be forced to turn elsewhere to generate a living, and all three would face the prospect of returning to New

England society having wasted the opportunity bestowed upon them by their venerable uncle.

The more successful New England China traders expected to retire in Boston with the means to reintegrate seamlessly into the elite society from which they had come. Families such as the Forbeses, the Russells, and the Sturgises redeployed their wealth and the leisure time an early "retirement" afforded to them to become leaders in Brahmin society, shapers of New England culture, and political influencers on both state and federal levels. Such recalibrating was necessary, for elites returning to post–Civil War Boston encountered a Brahmin society in which the commerce that had uplifted their families was fast becoming an unfashionable marker of status.[2] In their efforts they were aided by both a strong network of preexisting contacts—a product of their upbringing—and new ties to a web of like-minded returned traders with similar sociopolitical agendas. Not all achieved this elite status at home. Throughout Europe and America there were many partners of middling firms or clerks who returned home without a competency or a reputation to support such a path. But most aspired to it.[3]

For a time, it seemed that retiring upon a competency would be the Heard brothers' natural path. Their uncle Augustine Heard Sr., passing long before the firm's bankruptcy, had enjoyed such a life of wealthy bachelorhood. He had occupied a prestigious home opposite the Boston Common at 3 Park Street just steps from the Massachusetts State House and Beacon Hill's upscale south slope. He remained connected to a core cohort of Brahmin families despite the schism between Russell & Co. and Augustine Heard & Co., and he was well regarded among elite society. Resettling in Boston in 1863 and marrying Alice Leeds in 1867, John Heard's life looked much the same for twelve years, as would Augustine Heard Jr.'s after he handed control of the firm to Albert Heard in 1871. John Heard enjoyed a comfortable life in Boston that resembled his uncle's—even renting the Park Street property himself until 1875.[4] Augustine Heard Jr. divided his time between the United States and France, a common destination for the New England elite, where he lived with his wife, the daughter of a Belgian diplomat, and their French-educated children.

The bankruptcy, however, diverted this comfortable trajectory. Each of the brothers managed to protect a portion of their assets by transferring ownership to their wives, but they no longer possessed the means to emulate the style of the returned merchant elite. Commercial success had, besides, been "virtually closed as an avenue to [Brahmin] class membership" from the 1830s.[5] All three brothers scrambled to find new business ventures, struggling for the next decade to reclaim a semblance of the success they had once enjoyed. John Heard remained in Boston, progressively downsizing his living arrangements and expenditure. Augustine Heard Jr. worked in Biarritz and New York, trying to launch new investment ventures in his own name before eventually securing a diplomatic posting in Korea. Albert Heard served as a sales agent for an American firm in Russia until his and Mary Livingston's divorce proceedings, following which he returned to Boston and played the part of bachelor-scholar. He eventually found employment that suited his long-suppressed political aspirations in Washington, DC.

These unconventional paths offer an opportunity to explore returned China traders' gilded lives from an alternative perspective—from the outside looking in. The anxieties, successes, and frustrations articulated in the Heards' letters to each other both reinforce the desired standard that returned merchants aspired to and the ways they adapted their experiences in China to open new doors. Boston's local elite may have derided commerce, but U.S. China merchants returned home with more than wealth; they arrived with an influential and tightly interwoven network of peers linked together by their shared lives in Hong Kong and the treaty ports; they arrived with insider knowledge of the culture and politics of a country that had the potential to be one of the most important trading partners of the United States; and they arrived with the confidence of an overseas community accustomed to molding political and diplomatic policy to suit private interests. If the ideal product of a tenure in China was a competency with which one might retire back home in style, even those who failed in this goal returned to America with experience and contacts that proffered new opportunities.

LEAVING CHINA

Only nominally the end of Augustine Heard & Co., Albert Heard and Livingston's retreat from Hong Kong was rather the beginning of a year-long effort to resuscitate the company. As the couple sailed west, John Heard and Augustine Heard Jr. returned to China, launching an unenthusiastic and ill-fated attempt to resurrect the company under the shortened moniker "Heard & Co." John Heard would later recollect that the whole scheme had been the idea of the "last admitted partner to the house," Charles Edward Parker, who, having gotten John Heard there, "bolted from China."[6] Whatever his motives, Parker stuck around long enough to sign a contract with the Heard brothers, witnessed by company veteran Henrique Caetano Victor de Figueiredo before being sent on to Albert Heard in the United States. On April 28, 1875, Heard & Co. was formed.[7]

Many in Boston, including Francis Parker, Gordon Dexter, John Griswold, and Jefferson Coolidge, offered to underwrite the new venture, but within the year both Augustine Heard Jr. and John Heard came to understand that the effort was futile and set about closing down the business properly.[8] As fathers, committed to children and wives back home, neither brother desired to remain in China unless they could "lay up something beyond earning mere bread and butter," and the likelihood of this was slim.[9] High expenditure, overdrawn accounts, and their Boston agent Percival Lowell Everett's poor fiscal management rapidly dismantled the enterprise that had taken decades to build and undercut the family's good name.[10] The signs of trouble, apparent since the mid-1860s when local and transnational conflicts and new systems of banking and capital investment transformed foreign commerce in China, grew more ominous in light of the Panic of 1873.[11] Over the next decade the number of U.S. firms active in China would drop from 15 to 5 percent of total foreign firms.[12] Returning to Hong Kong within this context of U.S. commercial decline, John Heard and Augustine Heard Jr. found society unfamiliar, their positions within it no longer secure.

Augustine Heard Jr. remained in China a few months longer than John Heard in the hope that something might be done. Even as the brothers resolved affairs in Japan and New York, Augustine Heard Jr. toured Hong Kong, Manila, and Shanghai in search of any opportunity. At the former, he briefly considered the propriety of manufacturing painkillers (likely from opium), an interest that bore some overlap with George Dixwell's ongoing efforts to leverage his experience and possibly assuage his guilt by developing an "opium cure" in New York. Augustine Heard Jr. even used a missed connection at Shanghai to explore the prospect of getting into the much-derided "Coolie" trade. While waiting for the *Alaska* to depart, he met with one "Hoh-yan-ki" of Canton, whom he described as "just the man we have been wanting to find for years." "Hoh" had another Cantonese man in his employ who had visited the United States during the 1876 Centennial Exposition and could help establish a trade in "Chinese laborers," having identified Virginia as a potentially lucrative market. The scheme amounted to nothing. Leaving China in April 1877, Augustine Heard Jr. began a circuitous route home, which included business in Biarritz to gauge a coal mining interest and a stop in Paris before returning briefly to the United States in November 1877.[13]

John Heard's recollections of leaving China reestablished that while Hong Kong and the treaty ports had changed since the days when he and his uncle had enjoyed success, wealth remained an important marker of status. Without this wealth, and eight years absent from the social circuits of Hong Kong and Shanghai, John found himself an outsider. Few of his old contacts remained, and while he reminisced about dining with William Keswick of Jardine Matheson & Co. and Thomas Francis Wade, now British minister at Beijing, he mostly shunned contact with the wider community. He made a special point of avoiding Hong Kong's annual races outright out of fear of being snubbed by what he perceived to be a judgmental Anglo-American community.[14] Feeling thoroughly out of place in China, John Heard returned to the United States in the autumn of 1876 to set about reorganizing his life around the coming financial trials.

The bankruptcy dragged on for the remainder of the decade. In May 1878 Butterfield, Swire & Co was still pursuing litigation against the Heards regarding property in Hong Kong, and London's Baring Brothers & Co likewise applied pressure. John Heard supposed the affairs with both companies were undermining his and Augustine Heard Jr.'s opportunities in the United States and France—a fact he resented, given that neither brother had much to do with either. Rumors plaguing Albert Heard surrounding his departure from Hong Kong that he and Livingston had fled with money and valuables while the firm sank fed such anxieties over the brothers' reputations.[15] The proceedings were resolved, in theory, the following December. William Howell Forbes, serving as trustee for Baring Brothers, authorized the final dividends on both Augustine Heard & Co. and the general estates, forwarding the check for this sum to the brothers. Forbes sent this claim, seconded by W. W. Ray, to Theophilus G. Linstead, who had been overseeing the proceedings, and it was signed off by James Whittall and Keswick, thus closing the ongoing legal action.[16] In the meantime, the brothers set about rebuilding their lives.

While the bankruptcy derailed the Heards' lives in the United States, each had taken precautions to protect their assets. At some point prior to the firm's failure, John Heard recognized the direction things were headed and set about cataloguing and calculating the value of his private holdings and inheritance in Boston and Ipswich.[17] Albert Heard had taken similar measures during Augustine Heard & Co.'s final couple of years. A collection of sundry items at the Tremont Row house, kept initially by Augustine Heard Sr. but occupied at various points by the brothers, were registered as Livingston's personal possessions, as were items stored at Ipswich.[18] Shares in Hong Kong had likewise been purchased in Livingston's name.[19] Doing so ensured some funds would remain available to the family in lieu of new ventures.

In one especially suspect move, John produced a legal document backdated April 12, 1872, in which he had "sold" all his property and assets to a third party—William Dixter—for the sum of one dollar. Dixter "sold" the property and assets to John Heard's wife for an equal sum.[20] John Heard's lawyer William Russell then tallied Leeds's private assets the same month Albert Heard declared bankruptcy. Russell's audit further accounted for other miscellaneous investments made by John Heard in Leeds's name, making the explicit point that when such gifts were made "John Heard had retired from the active management of the affairs of Augustine Heard & Co in China, but remained the senior Partner in the House." Through the "1872" sale and 1875 audit Leeds was confirmed to be, according to Commonwealth law, "entitled to hold without marriage settlement" all property acquired before marriage "or which she may have subsequently acquired, except by direct gift" from her husband. Having purchased it for one dollar, Leeds was argued to be the sole legal recipient of John Heard's estate in a manner that protected her from his creditors. According to Russell's estimation, her portfolio of holdings in luxury goods, real estate, investment bonds, and insurance totaled roughly $24,300.[21]

In the habit of the China traders, John had also collected over the years a large inventory of art and curios that he supposed had been come to market following the Anglo-French forces' looting of the Yuanmingyuan 圓明園 northwest of Beijing. The pillage and razing of China's imperial Summer Palace, occurring over roughly a week between October 7 and 19, 1860, had scattered rare and valuable objects of interest snapped up by foreign merchants on the black market.[22] Many more of these objects, consisting of "silk, pearls, gold, ivory or jade," "objects for personal use such as furs or watches," and memorabilia including "state robes or seals" became part of royal collections and have since made it into museum collections throughout the world.[23]

A large portion was diverted, however, into private hands. "Kept as souvenirs and curios in family collections," the grandeur of their origins heightened their value and desirability.[24] Although not present at the looting itself, the acquisition of such collections reflected the global extent of the Brahmins' capitalism. Such items from "the Orient" bore great influence both within and beyond the residential neighborhoods of Boston's upper classes, allowing those who imported them to advertise their cultural refinement and "strike back at the pretensions of the Old World."[25] An expose on the Heard House at Ipswich effused about the treasures therein—a "trove of fine antiquities" from China and Japan—many of which were still unpurchasable decades later in the United States.[26]

The rarity and exoticism of such items drove interest in them, as the aesthetics promoted through these private holdings worked in tandem with globalization to reshape consumer appetites. Such consumerism merged with a developing national identity that centered the United States within a global context, the viability of supply producing wider demand for Chinese imports, Chinese-style recreations, and "oriental" products.[27] American consumers would ultimately conflate nation-building with the expansion of the American imperial project, as the ability to secure foreign commodities justified their belief in the global ascendency of the United States.[28] For John Heard, however, the most important matter was that the public sought Chinoiserie with enthusiasm.

Others' inventories provide an impression of what John Heard had accrued. Typical collections might include blue and white porcelains, hand-painted wallpaper, silks, decorated fans, and even "white or red-dyed ivory" chessmen.[29] Albert Heard's 1872 list of possessions stored at Ipswich, Park Street, and Tremont Row included a dizzying array of goods from China and Japan: tea sets, mahogany tables, armchairs, and stands, Japanese screens and lacquerware, old China vases and dinner sets, and countless porcelain and jade pieces.[30] John Heard's holdings included a collection of Chinnerys, having been a contemporary of the artist, and miscellaneous paintings besides.[31] As with other assets, these had been clandestinely protected by being purchased in Leeds's name. Upon his return to

Boston he consented to open his house for auction, overseen by a friend, Susan Swett. Testament to the elite community's enthusiasm for authentic China manufactures, the sale of his collection of East Asian curios and objets-d'art secured Leeds, in John Heard's estimation, an additional $50,000.[32]

Through such plans the couple preserved enough assets to sustain a comfortable lifestyle, but the reality of Augustine Heard & Co.'s losses still forced them to reduce expenses. The winter following John's return, the brothers dispensed of the Park Street property, each counting one third its $26,666 valuation as part of their assets.[33] It also seemed likely that the Heards would lose the family estate at Ipswich. Writing to his uncle, John Heard's son lamented the loss of the "old house and stables" of which he had so many "pleasant recollections." Indignant at its sale, he declared it "the home of the Heards, and though they have sustained a hard reverse just now, their name is unstained and God willing will ever remain so."[34] John Heard Jr.'s optimism was well founded and, in testament to the Heard's longstanding ties to Ipswich, friends in the wider community pooled together to repurchase the property and gift it back to the family.[35] Other family and friends would provide financial aid in their own ways.[36]

While John Heard remained in Boston, his brothers' letters suggest that they were more vulnerable to the financial stresses the bankruptcy brought about. In the following years Augustine Heard Jr. struggled to find a scheme that would resuscitate his wealth. There is little to indicate he had shared John Heard's foresight to protect his family's assets through legal loopholes. What stands out was that he redeployed his keen business sense and the networks that he had formed in the United States and through the China trade to find employment in France before settling down in New York. Between 1877 and 1880 Augustine Heard Jr. split his time between his family in Biarritz, his managerial duties at a foundry in Bayonne, and regular trips back to the United States to wrap up family affairs. Having sustained this lifestyle for three years, he followed the lead of other wealthy merchants from Massachusetts and settled down in New York, where he hoped to reintegrate into the elite society of a city on the rise in the 1880s and 1890s, and find some scheme that would guarantee returns on his investments.[37] New York, which by 1892 boasted "a staggering 27 percent of the nation's millionaires" seemed an appropriate place to do so.[38]

Augustine Heard Jr.'s activities in the following years reveal much about returned merchants' social, commercial, and political aspirations, but his letters to Albert Heard related feelings of financial insecurity and frustration concerning his U.S. ventures. His office at 32 Nassau Street, far from the "center of bourgeois life . . . well above 14th Street," was closer, rather, to the immigrant Chinese communities that clustered in the Fourth and Sixth Ward.[39] While in some ways a participant in elite white society, he still worked, at this time, on its margins. He endeavored to rectify this by exploring alternative means of reclaiming elite status. Meeting William Crowninshield Endicott, Augustine Heard Jr. hoped the newly appointed secretary of war would offer something by way of a stable official post with a steady salary, preferably the Paris consulate earning $12,000 per annum. Endicott informed Augustine Heard Jr. that his recent vote for the presidential candidate James Blaine would "count against [him]" in the new administration. His own chances shot, Republican Augustine Heard Jr. vowed to try and find something for Democrat Albert Heard, chasing up old contacts such as John Ward from China. The following five-year correspondence between the brothers settled into a cyclical rhythm, oscillating between discussions about potential influential connections, complaints of being "hard up" for funds or work, and speculations about new ventures.[40]

Albert Heard and Augustine Heard Jr. eventually achieved their goals of political office, but in the interim, Albert Heard's post–Hong Kong life was far more uncertain than that of his brothers. Returning to Boston, he and Livingston took up lodgings in a "pleasant and comfortable enough" boarding house, "the cheapest place" they could find at $250 for the summer. Still, he despaired that bankruptcy voyeurs would deem it extravagant. Writing to Augustine Heard Jr.'s wife, Jane deConinck, he admitted to having little idea what his "movements and situation" would be going forward. Though he would find work in time, he wondered in the moment whether he should ever "look forward to a house" or "to a life" in any place but Hong Kong.[41]

In 1877, the Lowell Gun Company employed Albert Heard to "represent [their interests] in Russia."[42] He and Livingston departed for Europe but lived separately even when in the same city. They returned to the United States in the summer of 1878 where they set about resolving their finances with help from John Heard. The couple mostly looked to dispense of the possessions Augustine Heard Sr. had bequeathed to them, but they also tried selling a number of luxuries—silverware and a piano included. Although not formalized until 1881, their coming divorce was evident in Livingston's handling of her estate. In a move unfathomable to John Heard, Livingston intended to keep a collection of silverware and family portraits, for instance, including one of George Heard, for whom she had been particularly fond, since they were gifts. An 1879 draft of her will left a diamond ring to William Howell Forbes, whom she had been close to in Hong Kong, as well as a package of letters and a handkerchief to be delivered directly into the Russian Grand Duke Alexei Alexandrovich's hands.[43] The latter, a known womanizer whom Livingston had become close with in Hong Kong, regularly vacationed in Paris and Biarritz, where she spent the final years of her estrangement from Albert Heard.[44]

Albert Heard again departed Boston for Europe in December 1878.[45] Comfortable with Paris, equipped with a range of contacts throughout Britain and Russia from his Hong Kong days, and granted power of attorney for Lowell, Albert Heard returned to France with Livingston, on whom he had been dependent until that point, to set about negotiating arms contracts with the Russians.[46] While in Paris, Albert Heard too contacted Ward, inquiring about government posts that he might be able to occupy. He wrote to John Heard months later as well, asking him to call upon friends to help him secure a post with the American Legation in Paris, Vienna, Berlin or London. In the meantime he sold guns for Lowell. While Livingston remained in Paris, Albert Heard traveled between the city and St. Petersburg, where he subcontracted the Russian Eugene de Zelenkoff to find buyers within the Russian Navy.[47]

Albert Heard also reached out to his old Hong Kong networks and classmates for support. In the summer of 1879, he wrote to Julian Pauncefote, a British barrister he had met in Hong Kong, then employed in the British Foreign Office, with the aim of signing a contract with Britain's War Office and Admiralty. Pauncefote, happy to reminisce about the "old sunshine and good pay of China," could not provide much help and recommended Albert Heard write the War Office directly. Albert Heard then contacted Rawson, a merchant also met in Hong Kong who was evidently connected in Britain, for a letter of introduction to the British General "F. A. Campbell" and "Admiral Hamilton." An old classmate, "White," in Hamburg with the American Legation Society, also promised to put a word in with Hamburg officials.[48]

Meanwhile, business continued to be an uncomfortable fit for Albert Heard. The Russian contacts he hoped would open doors in St. Petersburg failed to come through. Although he insisted he could further Lowell's Russian interests, Albert Heard's letters to Admiral Stepan Lessovski (which Heard rendered as Lassoffski) and the aide-de-camp to the Grand Duke, "Baron Schilling," amounted to little.[49] Albert Heard was reunited with Alexandrovich briefly at Tsarskoye Selo in June 1878, but while the grand duke was "very friendly," their long-standing relationship did not secure a contract. Albert Heard spent the remainder of the year attending the odd social function in St. Petersburg and giving irregular and uninspired gun demonstrations. Still, he insisted he could make the deal happen, writing Lowell for more funds, and a higher commission on sales. His requests achieved nothing more than drawing the ire of his employers, who Augustine Heard Jr. felt had "meant to get rid of [Albert] anyway as soon as [he] had given them the introduction." DeWitt Clinton Farrington wrote to Albert Heard in the spring of 1879 revoking the funds to support his work abroad, providing only what was necessary for his return and hoping he would "understand" that this meant the end of his role as commission agent.[50]

Albert Heard terminated his agreement with Lowell Gun Company in 1879 and with Augustine Heard Jr.'s aid became manager of a metallurgical foundry near Bayonne, France. He remained in this position for several years, splitting his time between Bayonne, Biarritz, and Paris. Meanwhile, Livingston engaged her own apartments and servants in Paris, where she lived apart from Albert Heard. From 1879 her health declined, Albert Heard relating her condition to her father. From this time, however the couple formally separated short of a legal divorce. Livingston passed away in 1881, Albert Heard not having been in contact with her since June the previous year.[51] He left Europe in 1882, arriving back in New England an unemployed bachelor.

A COMPETENCY

Returning to Boston after having failed in China, the Heards lived in notably different ways from the tight social web of repatriated merchants forming the "Boston Concern."[52] Yet their aspirations for the same level of social prestige and financial stability remained. Because such aspirations drove their activities for the next two decades, the courses they took as they reeled

WEALTH OR EXPERTISE

from, and fought back against, their insolvency provide useful counternarratives through which to assess the China trade's influence over the metropolitan lives of those who had lived and worked in Hong Kong and the treaty ports. Their material holdings, social worlds, networking, business ventures, and political goals each demonstrate the standard to which China merchants held themselves and strove to maintain.

The two paths that adhered closest to those of the more successful New Englanders who extracted a fortune from China before returning home to "practice their ethics" were those of the firm's founding partners, Augustine Heard Sr. and Joseph Coolidge.[53] Benefiting from the firm's meteoric early success, but either passing away prior to the bankruptcy, or being far enough removed to be protected, their lives followed a path which most young Americans heading out to China aspired to. Augustine Heard Sr. retired to Boston a bachelor, acquiring a reputation as a socialite, philanthropist, and gentleman. Coolidge, by contrast, traveled widely with his wife, living an international life that would take the couple to France and England. In both cases these men enjoyed an elite Brahmin lifestyle.

A supercargo, ship's captain, and partner of Russell & Co. in turn, Augustine Heard Sr. embodied the successful Brahmin merchant.[54] Upon his 1844 retirement from China, he settled in central Boston's Tremont Row and Park Street respectively (figure 6.1). From Boston he contributed capital to local business ventures, such as the Ipswich Cotton Mill, donated to philanthropic causes including the establishment of the Ipswich Public Library, and offered his nephews sage advice as they attempted to steer Augustine Heard & Company.[55] In the New England elite fashion, he was a temperate man, socially reserved and fiscally conservative.[56] He passed away at the age of eighty-three on September 21, 1868, at the family home in Ipswich. He was remembered for his "munificent" gifts to charitable and benevolent societies, and for being the "model of a high-minded, honorable and enterprising merchant."[57]

Augustine Heard Sr. established, during his Boston retirement, a comfortable life in the manner of returned China merchants. John Heard's record of Park Street's renovation and furnishing costs upon renting it from his uncle in 1863–1864 indicates the style in which the family would have lived while the firm enjoyed success. Admittedly restored at an inopportune time, it cost John Heard and his uncle $104,000 to prepare the home.[58] The inventory, valued at $21,397, showcased a life of international trade:

FIGURE 6.1. Looking south down Park Street from the Massachusetts State House. *Source*: Photograph, Boston, c. 1860, Photos-XL 008, MHS.

plated ware from Smith, Nicholson & Co. and silver from Hunt and Roskell in London, Turkish carpet-laid rooms adorned with blankets from Boston's C. F. Hovey department store, Briggs glassware, Lincoln & Foss furnishings, jardiniers, and over $1,000 in chinaware. Outstanding bills on packages included freight from Europe, "Arabia," Canada, and Africa.[59]

Russell & Co.'s Francis Blackwell Forbes took a similar inventory upon leaving Shanghai, listing countless items intended as mementos, curios, and demonstrators of success and expertise. Forbes shipped porcelains, stone wares, jade, and bronze pottery with gold inlay. Furnishings included Japanese lanterns and hanging baskets, kakemonos—or "hanging things"—and wood screens, bamboo étagères and chairs, rattan tables, straw baskets, and embroideries from Beijing, Shanghai, and Kyoto. Some items were calibrated to reflect his elite status in China; race and steeplechase cups from Hong Kong and Shanghai, for example. Others projected the persona of a cultured and learned Brahmin gentleman; Fra Angelico oil paintings, Chinnery watercolors, and a library of more than 825 books on history law, science, horticulture, and mountaineering. Chinese classics, maps of the Peiho, and transactions of the Asiatic Society shared crates with Machiavelli and Rabelais.[60] Such goods played an important role in both displaying and—as John Heard's and Leeds's bankruptcy schemes suggest—preserving the China traders' wealth and prestige.[61]

A life of affluent retirement in the metropole was not, however, the only path returned merchants pursued. Upon resigning from Augustine Heard & Co., Joseph Coolidge and his wife Ellen Randolph Coolidge split their time between Boston, where they had kept a home at Beacon Hill's Pemberton Square, and lengthy tours of Europe. The couple's 1868–1870 correspondence with their children related the life of mobile socialites. Coolidge described reunions with extended family in Rome, where they toured ruins and St. Peter's church, before heading for Florence. Their travels took them through Nice, where they reconnected with their children; Monaco, where Lucien Bonaparte's daughter and granddaughter were guests at the same hotel; and onward to Florence, Bologna, Parma, Milan, Turin, and Aix-les-Bains. Pau in Southern France had "many Americans," including Robert Bennet Forbes and his wife, and while Ellen Coolidge abstained from the "grand balls" and "amusements" the Russian princes and princess hosted, she enjoyed observing fox hunting and steeplechases from the comfort of her carriage.[62]

In 1869 they found themselves in Paris—the epicenter of their European life—lamenting their absence from the boat race between American and British students upon the Thames (an event attended by "all the Americans in London"). A year earlier, the Coolidges had themselves been in Britain. They traveled with New York friends, toured Bristol before ascending from the harbor to the "open air" and "beautiful scenery of Clifton," and headed north to Great Malvern. Edinburgh they thought the most attractive city they had seen "excepting Paris," which they felt "the most beautiful in the whole world."[63] In this manner they enjoyed a retirement split between France, Italy, Switzerland, and Britain, returning—as most Americans did—to Paris between each excursion.[64]

Beautiful though she thought it was, Ellen Coolidge took little interest in Paris, going out "sometimes to concerts, seldom or never to the theatre." Yet Paris was not without an American society of its own. Between the autumn of 1865 and 1866, Ellen Coolidge described a "pleasant society" of

Boston friends including William and Susan Swett (who would auction John Heard's China collection) and the Lowells. In 1870 society was much the same, inundated with elite Americans who occupied "conspicuous places everywhere and [spent] a vast deal of money." Although part of this community, Ellen Coolidge distanced herself from her compatriots in letters to her daughter-in-law. While she avoided society, her countrywomen—"very rich or very reckless"—bought more dresses and paid more dearly for them "than the ladies of any other nation," she believed, "in the civilized world." Less in the know than Ellen Coolidge, these women were "also more cheated by their servants and more imposed upon by tradespeople."[65]

Reflecting the elite New Englander tendency to straddle the worlds of Boston and Paris, she emphasized to her daughter-in-law the importance of impressing upon her children a mastery of French, "as the intercourse between America and Europe is always on the increase." Ellen Coolidge's letters suggest that as a member of the entrenched American elite she felt herself a class above the American nouveau riches who filled the French capital's boulevards. Tiring of this transient society, she conceded that a relative of hers had bought her and Joseph Coolidge property on Milldam Creek in Virginia and that the couple planned to return to the United States in the summer of 1870.[66]

Replies from their children related life in the United States. Algernon Coolidge provided necessary news of society: deaths in the Boston community, the refreshing presence of English actors performing at the theater ("you insensibly forget what good acting is if your experience is confined to the American stage"), his desire to send Algernon Jr. to dancing school. He described to his parents in Paris the arrival of Burlingame's Chinese embassy in Boston, which left an overall dignified impression, and the reception that was given them at the newly opened St. James Hotel in the South End.[67] Such letters ensured that his parents, despite their travels, remained well informed of Boston's social ebbs and flows in the event they should encounter acquaintances abroad or choose to return to the city.

Whether electing to remain in Boston as Augustine Heard Sr. had or using wealth to retire abroad like the Coolidges, commercial success enabled returned China merchants to maintain a comfortable (and expected) standard of living, but as in Hong Kong acceptance into elite society also relied upon public and civic engagement. Returned China traders maintained contact with each other by joining socially elite clubs and associations such as the Somerset Club in Boston and the Union Club and Knickerbocker Club in New York.[68] Through such membership they committed to advancing culture and practicing philanthropy. Their activities, sometimes born of a sense of civic duty, were calibrated to enhance their prestige.

Despite financial insecurity, Augustine Heard Jr. made a point of reviving such associational ties upon his return to the United States in May 1880. Upon settling in New York, he joined the prestigious Century Association, similar in purpose to Boston's Somerset, Union, and Knickerbocker Clubs and the Hong Kong Club. The Century claimed to bring together "scholars, philanthropists, scientists, soldiers, explorers," politicians, and, begrudgingly, businessmen such as Augustine Heard Jr.[69] Politically, the members were "almost by instinct" Mugwumps, supporting their fellow Centurion Grover Cleveland for president in 1884. And, if not members outright, "Bostonians were always dropping in," as were the odd "British cousins."[70] Through membership, Augustine Heard Jr. rekindled vital metropolitan networks and blended them with those cultivated in China.

Augustine Heard Jr. in turn leveraged his own membership to advance his family's sociopolitical interests. While he hesitated to petition for Albert Heard's admission as member of the Century, friends informed him there would be no impropriety in doing so. He described his brother as a "valuable man," well regarded in the United States and Europe and possessing a "wide experience of men and things." He lauded Albert Heard's bilingualism—having been many years a resident of Paris—and his "intimate acquaintance" with that city's "literary and artistic men."[71] In doing so Augustine Heard Jr. refashioned his once-merchant brother as a scholarly and cultured individual whose values were in keeping with the wider membership of the association. Such was an important move, for while Centurions nominally possessed lofty cultural interests they remained—as did Brahmin members of Boston's elite associations—shapers of politics, commerce, and society in the United States. Through the combined clout of such club members, Augustine Heard Jr.'s Harvard-days friendship with William Crowninshield Endicott, and the influence of the returned network of China traders, both he and Albert Heard would springboard their official careers.

Boston's Saturday Club, first organized in 1855, gained similar acclaim as a space for social meetings and conversation upon "historical, literary, scientific, and artistic subjects," and for the disbursement of funds to promote such topics.⁷² Membership provided China traders socially respectable avenues through which to spend their wealth and time that were divorced from their indecorous mercantile scrambling. In such groups they reimagined themselves as arbiters of an American literary, artistic, and intellectual tradition.⁷³ The names of members with China trade pedigree including Endicott, Bowditch, Everett, Forbes, Peabody, and Loring were entered in the roll call alongside such eminent thinkers as the writer Oliver Wendell Holmes Sr. and his lawyer son Oliver Wendell Holmes Jr., essayist Ralph Waldo Emerson, the biologist Louis Agassiz and scientist-engineer Alex Agassiz, poet Henry Wadsworth Longfellow, and Harvard's president, Charles William Eliot.⁷⁴ Testament to their commitment to such institutional culture, John Murray Forbes's and Sarah Hathaway Forbes's son John Malcolm Forbes bequeathed in 1900, on behalf of his late mother, a gift of $5,000 (or higher, if necessary) to top up the club's discretionary fund of $15,000.⁷⁵

If these private clubs offered returned merchants an avenue to reintegrate into Brahmin society, they also preserved insular China networks in Boston and New York. Such was especially true for the prominent members of the Boston Concern who formed a closed social group.⁷⁶ These men met annually though the Keechong Club. Membership was restricted to repatriated Russell & Co. partners. Some members were familiar to the Heards: John Murray Forbes, A. A. Low, Robert Bennet Forbes, James Murray Forbes, Henry Warden, and Paul Siemen Forbes.⁷⁷ Their own uncle, who had remained friends with John Murray Forbes for "many years" and was a onetime member of the firm, was invited irrespective of the Heard/Forbes rivalry, and although he passed away before the club's first meeting, he was remembered fondly by those in attendance.⁷⁸ The less popular Joseph Coolidge, also invited, was conspicuously absent from the first meeting and passed away before the second.⁷⁹

The Keechong club served a dual purpose for returned merchants, reinforcing the ties between the firm's members and providing support for struggling peers who were "friends" of the house, such as Gideon Nye Jr., still in China and destitute by 1879.⁸⁰ In doing so, it extended the interests of American merchants both within and without Russell & Co. back to the metropole. But if social protocols, racial anxieties, and political interests in Hong Kong and the treaty ports created a setting that bound American merchants together in solidarity, such anxieties were of lesser importance in the United States. The Heard brothers, also struggling, were afforded none of the same considerations as merchants such as Nye. The Forbses accused the Heards of undercutting Russell & Co.'s Yangzi trade to remain solvent in in the 1860s and 1870s, so that both firms "lost money hand over fist." Although James Murray Forbes evidently remembered all the brothers well, "Augustine, John, George, and Robert [Albert]," this rift between the younger members of Augustine Heard & Co. and Russell & Co. prevented the Heard brothers from drawing upon the same elite Boston networks their uncle mingled in for aid.[81]

Socially marginal to the Brahmin "Boston Concern," and without the same support network as Nye, John Heard's and his brothers' lives over the next decade demonstrate the difficulty with which they reestablished themselves in the United States. As early as 1873 John Heard had shown signs of financial stress that diminished his ability to participate in elite society. Writing his brothers that he was "very hard up for money," he requested the funds owed to him as a partner in the firm. In the meantime he tallied the total of his uncle's estate for future reference, sold his private yacht, and began to offload properties he had invested in with Albert Heard.[82]

By 1875 the extent of John Heard's retrenchment emerged through a series of resignations he submitted for various clubs, societies, and subscriptions. While he renewed the contract for Alice's possession of a pew in Trinity Church's new edifice, he deemed other expenses frivolous. He wrote the New York Yacht Club's skipper to cancel his and George Heard's memberships, and likewise resigned from Boston's Beverly Yacht Club and Marblehead's Eastern Yacht Club, which he had helped found five years prior.[83] His role as Commodore of the Eastern Yacht Club was passed to a member of the Brahmin Sears family and then John Murray Forbes, in turn.[84] He excused himself from civic responsibilities, resigning from the Massachusetts Humane Society's board of trustees, and from the board of trustees for the Sailor's Snug Harbor, a nonprofit retirement home for sailors that Russell & Co.'s Robert Bennet Forbes initially presided over. The most socially damaging for a returned aspirant to elite Boston society, however, were John Heard's resignations from the Wednesday Evening Club, one of Boston's oldest and most exclusive social clubs, and from the prestigious and selective Somerset Club opposite the Commons on Beacon Street, from which he took the liberty of excusing all three of his brothers.[85]

John Heard's series of resignations tells a narrative of financial instability, but it also reveals the wider social landscape of returned China merchants. Prior to Augustine Heard & Co.'s bankruptcy, John Heard had been an active participant in New England life, as had his uncle and fellow China traders.[86] His and George Heard's membership in various yacht clubs reflected a continuity in the types of recreation they—as young boys who had spent all their pocket money hiring boats at Boston's no. 7 wharf—and their fellow U.S. elites had exported to China and resumed in the metropole.[87] His trusteeship for the Sailor's Snug Harbor initiative was strikingly similar to his and his brothers' support of Hong Kong's Sailor's Home. And while he may not have had access to the selective Keechong Club as had his uncle and Coolidge, he still enjoyed membership in the Somerset and Wednesday Evening Clubs as he had the Hong Kong Club while in China. This merging of recreational, associational, and philanthropic culture comprised the social program of many returning elites.

As John Heard retreated from club and associational life, the bankruptcy disrupted his life in other, arguably more pressing ways. Unable to sustain the expense of the Park Street house which between 1872 and 1875 had accumulated $3,153.18 in outstanding rent, John sold the property and moved to the Back Bay neighbourhood.[88] Here again John Heard's course offers deeper insight into the social world of China merchants, irrespective of his and his family's financial stresses. As the progression of John Heard's dwellings suggest, his family sustained something of the respectable urban life returned China merchants sought by cycling through a range of properties in what were still, he admitted, respectable neighborhoods. Park Street may have been the pinnacle of prestige, occupying a conspicuous central position in Boston, but lodgings on West Cedar and Beacon remained central within the Boston Brahmins' social world.

John Heard moved through numerous properties, first being a small house at 277 Clarendon Street, then 214 and 295 Beacon Street in the fashionable Back Bay neighborhood, the first of which he secured at a "very cheap rent" through his ties to the owner, Dan Curtis. The house at 214 was similarly economical, but while large and fine it was "furnished but sadly." The family moved in just over a month to 295.[89] When 295 became too expensive, they moved to "a most forsaken tenement" at 19 West Cedar Street, escaping the city in the summer for Bar Harbor. West Cedar Street proved too disagreeable, so upon their return from Bar Harbor he and Alice

FIGURE 6.2. The Hotel Oxford on Huntington Avenue, Boston. *Source:* Photograph, Boston, c. 1920, Boston Pictorial Archive, Boston Public Library.

took up apartments at Boston's Hotel Oxford on Huntington Avenue around 1886 (figure 6.2).[90]

Before Back Bay's development, Beacon Hill's South Slope was the heartland of elite Boston society and residence in its orbit was essential.[91] The properties John Heard occupied on Tremont Row and West Cedar Street were within a short walk of the Somerset Club, the Commons, theatres, and restaurants. West Cedar was, however, rather close to Beacon Hill's North Slope, notorious among a prejudiced Brahmin society as the onetime center of Boston's Black community.[92] Testament to the racial barriers that divided the city, these two slopes, in close proximity, were effectively separated for much of the nineteenth century, with only two through-streets linking them. Yet by the time John and later Albert Heard resettled in Boston, Black and Brahmin families alike had migrated from Beacon Hill, a bohemian community of artists, writers, and thinkers springing up in their stead. The best-known Brahmin families—Lawrence, Forbes, Cabot, Saltonstall, and Standish—had been enticed from their perch by the wide lanes and modern amenities of Back Bay.[93]

Back Bay came into its own in the wake of Boston's Great Fire, which had "led to vast reconstruction of the city." Filled completely by 1882, the grounds Back Bay reclaimed "provided space for the grand dwellings of the city's expanding gentry," as well as for new cultural monoliths (figure 6.3).[94] The Museum of Fine Arts, Trinity Church, and the Boston Library, all built in Copley Square, became sociocultural anchors for the Heards and for Boston's wider elite.[95] The conjoined neighborhoods of Back Bay and Beacon Hill, converging at Charles Street running between Boston Common and the newer Public Garden composed Brahmin Boston's habitable zone, their red-brick rowhouses satirized decades later as relics of "the values that had been lost in the passing of this world of old Boston money, manners, and morality."[96]

Returning from Europe to Boston, Albert Heard naturally took up residence at 13 Walnut Street, an equidistant three-hundred meters from 3 Park

FIGURE 6.3. Cropped image of Back Bay, looking west from Beacon Hill, 1890. *Source:* Photograph, Boston, 1890, Ms 272.07, MHS.

and 19 West Cedar, and so similarly well situated. His entries over the next three years mapped the social habits of a man who, while upended by the bankruptcy a decade prior, still performed the role of returned China merchant. As his niece, Elsie Heard, related, "the charming" Albert Heard reclaimed in Boston his Hong Kong reputation as a socialite. A typical day for Albert Heard included a short walk to the Athenaeum to spend the morning researching for his book, or, alternatively, Sunday morning spent at Trinity Church, followed by an afternoon of cards at the "club."[97] As he had for years in Hong Kong, he spent much time obliging callers, entertaining visits from family and dining at friends' homes. While holidays took him to Ipswich and he traveled periodically to Washington, DC, in search of a diplomatic or political posting, his life revolved around a four-square-kilometer area of central Boston (figure 6.4).

As Elsie Heard grew older her letters to her father depicted a gilded account of the Heards' lives in Boston unmarred by the bankruptcy scandal. Residing at the Hotel Oxford, she related attending the opening of the Art Museum, and performing volunteer work at Trinity Church sewing "for the Indians" of North or South Dakota. She described meetings with green-clad friends on St Patrick's Day, lunches with Nora Winthrop and her second cousin Christine Farley, a ball at Mechanics Hall on the corner of Huntington Avenue and West Newton Street, and leisurely walks along Commonwealth Avenue to Westchester Park.[98] As her extended family reestablished themselves in the city, she spent her time socializing with the other young women from Boston's elite families and years later would realize her own ambitions as an artist.[99]

While his brothers resettled in Boston, Augustine Heard Jr. attempted to rebuild his life first in France, then New York and, briefly, Korea. Characteristic to his correspondence from China, Augustine Heard Jr.'s letters were pragmatic, concerned almost entirely with businesses affairs and telling little of New York's social world. Speaking frankly with Albert Heard, Augustine Heard Jr. conceded that he was having difficulty making things work in the United States. By October 1885 he was "literally cleaned out" and by the month's end would have "used up more than everything." Still, he maintained the expense of Century Club membership, expedient as it gave him access to influential peers who might effect a job for Albert Heard or himself.[100] He would eventually succeed in securing a posting to Korea, his family's accounts of their second encounter with East Asia telling far

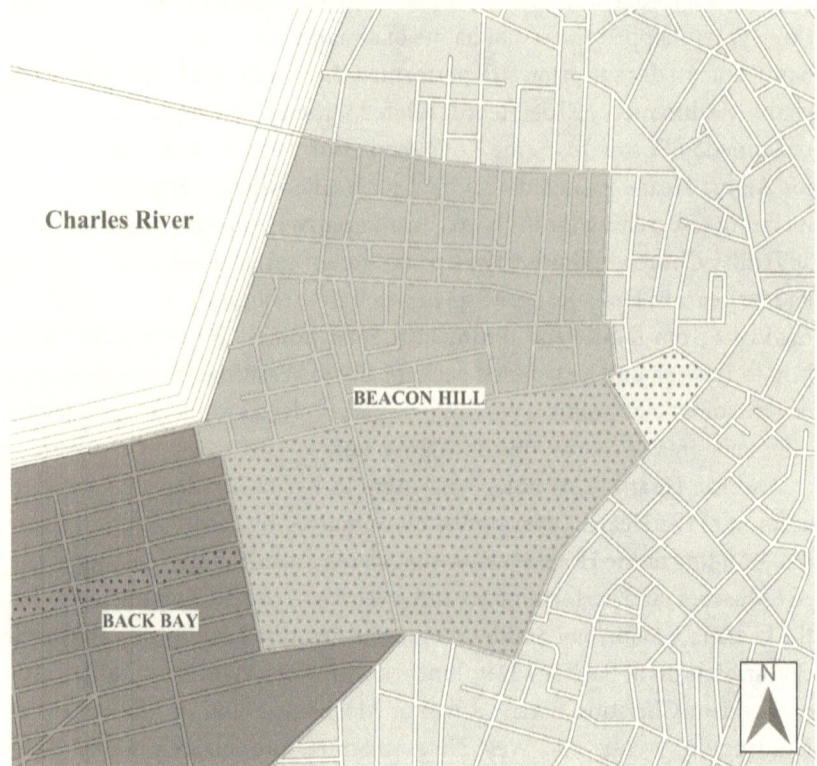

FIGURE 6.4. Portion of central Boston bordering Boston Common, based on a map of Boston from 1880. Image by author.

more about the transnational social world of China merchants than Augustine Heard Jr.'s erudite letters.

By Helen Maxima Heard's account, her life in China and "Löel" (Seoul) was as charmed as her father's and uncles' had been twenty years earlier. Accompanying her father east for his posting, Helen Heard's letters to John Heard described a life shaped by the simultaneous glamour and tedium of diplomatic duties. Her audience with Korea's Queen Regent, "interesting and peculiar to a certain extent" was the peak of a social season that saw her family entertaining the "usual distinguished travelers." During the former, she and her mother were gifted finely quilted silk, ordinary needlework, lacquerware, mats, and other items. Regular entertaining was, in addition, "a pleasant change in [an] otherwise quiet life." Tennis and riding provided further respite from the monotony.[101]

Helen Heard thrived especially among East Asia's Euroamerican communities. She quickly found herself a potential suitor in Shanghai, who she had courted first at Chefoo (Yantai 煙台) and who was sufficiently elite ("I shall laugh the first time I am addressed as 'your excellency'"). She and the suitor, the German diplomat and minister to China Maximillian August von Brandt, soon married, but their haste was his undoing. The couple had failed to secure the permission of Kaiser Wilhelm II, and so "B" was forced to resign his post, which Helen felt "a cruel blow . . . and such a case of ingratitude."[102]

Marriages and royal audiences aside, Korea was not to the family's taste, and months of chaperoning missionaries in Seoul failed to match the allure of Hong Kong or Shanghai society. Winter was dreadful "in all respects" and Helen Heard appraised her uncle of the family's desire to return home on account of her father's health. Her own discomfort inspired an outpouring of racist vehemence as she despaired of having a "Jap dentist"—her following epithet growing more colorful—treat her toothache. Although in April 1893 the prospect of a contract renewal remained on the table for Augustine Heard Jr., the following month the family was already preparing to return to the United States.[103]

SELLING EXPERIENCE

John Heard's family carried on using the savings he had transferred to Leeds. Augustine Heard Jr. and Albert Heard were, by contrast, unceasing in their hunt for ventures or employment that would suit their sensibilities. Both drew from their past in China, redeploying the networks they had developed, the diplomatic experience they had acquired, and their firsthand knowledge of East Asian politics and commerce to emphasize their aptitude for the posts they sought. In such efforts, they were hardly unique. Robert Bennet Forbes, famed China trade captain, became heavily involved in ship construction and naval innovation, for example, upon returning to Massachusetts. Returned China traders Asa Whitney and John Murray Forbes reinvested China capital into transcontinental railroads to advance American continental and global imperial ambitions.[104] Russell Sturgis of

Russell & Co. pedigree retired to Boston until the merit of his commercial success secured him a partnership in London's Baring Brothers bank, financing the future generation of China traders. The wealth and experience such men accrued through the China trade eased their reentry into U.S. society, opened new doors for further investment, and cemented their elite image.

Commerce being the pursuit that had given them their start, the Heard brothers naturally first sought new enterprises related to trade and manufacturing. Their bankruptcy reduced access to investment opportunities but failed to block them entirely. While Augustine Heard Jr. spent a substantial amount of time in the United States lobbying for a diplomatic posting that might guarantee income, he also tried to play the part of investor. Five years following his return, his letterhead read:

> Loans on Railway and other Negotiable Securities.
> Purchase and Sale of Same.
> Loans on Bond and Mortgage.
> General Financial Business.[105]

His progress was, however, stunted. His meetings with Endicott had failed to produce the desired diplomatic office in Paris and he was struggling to find viable investment opportunities.

By 1889 Augustine Heard Jr. renewed his efforts, lobbying old political contacts and merchants to support his campaign to become the American minister to Korea or Beijing. Albert Heard's new position as librarian to the War Department proved indispensable to the campaign, and Augustine Heard Jr. asked that he "bring his influence in his position to bear" to support the candidacy.[106] As with the earlier consuls in China, "true diplomatic" experience was not necessary, and "well-to-do gentlemen amateurs" often found their way into such posts.[107] Augustine Heard Jr. achieved his goal in 1889 and was deployed to Seoul the following year. A glance at his later campaign to secure reappointment in 1893 provides a sense of what such lobbying entailed.

Francis McNeil Bacon, of Bacon & Co., New York, an acquaintance Augustine Heard Jr. made through Korea and a fellow Centurion, contacted John Heard in January 1893 to pledge support for Augustine Heard Jr.'s bid.[108] While in Seoul, Bacon met Edward Low of Shanghai, and William

Rockhill, who would become the third assistant secretary of state in 1894.[109] Low, "a warm friend of [John's] brother" and onetime partner of Augustine Heard & Co. had returned to Boston to work for Fearon, Low & Co., and Bacon recommended that John Heard write him for support. John Heard sent similar requests to the influential lawyer and Harvard alumnus Russell Gray of Boston, and to the Boston Brahmin Leverett Saltonstall II, asking both to write Assistant Secretary of State Josiah Quincy on Augustine Heard Jr.'s behalf.[110] Bacon personally lobbied Centurions including Josiah Choate (who had nominated Cleveland as member for the Century), the poet Richard Watson Gilder, and Edwin Lawrence Godkin of the *Evening Post*. Bacon's and John Heard's efforts were for naught, and even as the two built Augustine Heard Jr. a promising support base, the mail carried news that he had resigned.[111]

Following his return, Augustine Heard Jr. drew upon his tenures working in China and Korea to reimagine himself as a resident East Asia specialist. He had already once tried his hand at publishing on the region on the merits of his lived experience. His 1886 article "France and Indo-China" commissioned by the *Century Illustrated Monthly Magazine* gave a sketch of French missionary interest in "Annam," providing little practical knowledge and attempting to justify France's colonial claims to the region before launching into an overview of its commercial potential. Augustine Heard Jr. defended the economic benefits of colonialism in general, using imprecise comparisons with events he had witnessed in China to argue that French stewardship would invigorate the region.[112]

Upon returning from Korea, he again agreed to share his expertise in an 1894 talk entitled "Old China and New" for the St. Louis Mercantile Association. For this second talk he deferred to John Heard to fill in knowledge gaps. Twenty years after the bankruptcy and many more since he or his older brother had been in China, their memories were fallible and both challenged the other's claims about their achievements and experiences. He likewise became an armchair critic of secondhand tracts on China, contesting on the basis of memory James Harrison Wilson's account in *China: Travels and Investigations in the "Middle Kingdom"* that Russell & Co. won the race to the Yangzi (Dent, he thought, was first, followed by John Heard aboard the *Fire Dart*). He was particularly keen to clarify this point with John Heard as he had been invited to meet Wilson and wished to refute it and Wilson's claim that Chinese men were illiterate.[113]

His "Old China and New" talk, especially, provided a public forum through which Augustine Heard Jr. could advocate for a revived American presence in East Asia. In his own words, his "whole life (so to speak) [had] been devoted to the consideration and study of things of China."[114] His posting to Korea strengthened this claim to expertise. By the 1890s his interests had migrated, however, from mercantile to official circuits as he advocated for political reform. He had encountered enough "merchant-prince" consuls (he had been one himself) to be convinced that the only course for a productive relationship with China was to follow the British model and deploy "a regular, trained, foreign service, Diplomatic or Consular."[115] Augustine Heard Jr.'s initial failures and final success in pursuing a diplomatic posting impressed upon him the importance of political posturing. While the support of old China hands and fellow Centurions was a boon, it amounted to little if one lacked political contacts or toed the wrong party line.[116] Accepting this, Augustine Heard Jr. adopted the course Albert Heard had advocated all along and navigated the realm of political networking.

Albert Heard, too, would eventually meet success in his campaign for a political position. While his interlude in Boston following his return from Europe was spent doing the social rounds and researching his book *The Russian Church and Russian Dissent*—a "well written" study of an "unpopular" subject—he spent considerable time chasing supporters for diplomatic or political postings.[117] Leverett Saltonstall II had allegedly promised Albert Heard that he would do all in his power to support a consulship pending an application "endorsed by friends" and "expressing preference and willingness to serve." Albert Heard cast widely for advocates, calling upon Yale friends such as Henry Babcock and fellow China traders including the Russells and the Forbeses.[118]

Albert Heard gathered his signatures and proceeded to Washington, DC, on March 30, 1885, to present his credentials directly to Thomas Bayard at the State Department, who skimmed the materials before condescending to pass on the application. Albert Heard then did the rounds, bringing copies to William Collins Whitney, secretary of the navy, and calling at the English and Russian legations. An advocate supposed that Albert Heard should have an office if a strong friend would only ask for it. He applied himself for a week, meeting no success and many excuses ranging from his political camp (he insisted he "voted for nobody") to the ill-timing of his presentation to Bayard. Albert Heard returned to Boston on April 7, 1885, having failed in this first foray, succeeding, rather, in 1887 when Endicott appointed Albert Heard as his private secretary.[119]

The new position provided Albert Heard a respite from the stress of finding employment and his diary suggests that he took full advantage of the new role. He used the time to hobnob in Washington, developing and strengthening a new network of peers who provided social fulfillment and might further help him down the line. And while he relocated to Washington he remained tied to New England and New York through family, friends, and regular trips. He dutifully listed those visited while in both, and even found time to rekindle ties to "322"—Yale's Skull & Bones Society—on a birthday trip to New Haven in October 1888.[120] As he had while pursuing a consulship, Albert Heard made sure he maintained an expansive web of peers from his university days, his time in China, and his links to elite society in Boston, New York, and Washington. He applied the sociability he had learned to cultivate in Hong Kong and Shanghai to endear himself to an influential and interconnected network of friends and patrons.

Albert Heard remained in his secretarial role for two years until the administration changed. His record of Washington during this upheaval related anxieties about health and job security. While the sociopolitical scene shifted in the capital, Albert Heard's friends committed to help him where possible. Following roughly a month of conversations and oblique promises, he was encouraged to both make a bid for the role of librarian within the War Department and to take the Civil Service examination. He studied for both, but upon taking the examination on January 18 and 19, 1889 found the "questions puzzling," the language requirements intense, the work hard. He left the trial "disgusted."[121] Within days rumors clerks spread of his poor performance made the result all but guaranteed.

Albert Heard's cohort of supporters set about contesting the results and reminding him of the War Department opportunity. The group determined that much of the previous exam covered the content of the exam for "clerk of the 4th class in classified service," and Albert Heard hastened to sit the second on January 28. As he waited for the results, he was further advised to press the matter of the War Department librarian as soon as he had them to hand. Albert Heard was certified on January 31, 1889, and the next day began his work in the War Department library.[122]

In their own ways, the post-China ventures Albert Heard pursued, including his book and his political office, extended from his experiences in Hong Kong and Shanghai. The book's title page included the qualifier "formerly Consul-General for Russia at Shanghai," and Albert Heard judged his "own experience" in connection with the Russians adequate proof of his expertise in the subject.[123] The same sense of experience motivated him to seek a political role. His efforts to acquire a consulship in Europe and his service to the U.S. War Department were natural moves for one who had been so enthusiastic about diplomatic work and official relationships in China.

In turn, these positions provided Albert Heard the social capital to reclaim a lifestyle in keeping with other returned China traders. Less than two weeks into his librarian role, Albert Heard had already acquired permission to conduct a scouting trip in Boston, staying in the Tremont Street house, visiting with John Heard and Augustine Heard Jr. on his return trip through New York, and "investigating"—on official business—his favored haunts, the Athenaeum and the Boston Public Library. In both social and official respects, Albert Heard was again a representative member of the New England elite. Experience and networking in China had proffered the ladder to a new life in Washington, and by extension Endicott and Albert Heard's cohort of peers secured for him his new post, which he would occupy for the remainder of his life.[124]

LEGACIES OF THE CHINA TRADE

Albert Heard's health rapidly declined over the next year. While his letters to John Heard tried to reassure his family, he conceded in February 1890 that he felt "as if broken in two." He passed away the following month, his resuscitated reputation evident in the outpouring of sympathy his death inspired. Elsie Heard wrote of many in Boston dropping in to express regrets. Various contacts from throughout Albert Heard's life, including the fellow Bonesman George W. Baldwin, the Boston merchant Samuel Endicott Peabody, and acquaintances from London wrote the family. Leaving little behind in terms of an estate, friends remembered him, rather, for his "kindness, patience, and intelligence." John Heard was the third brother to pass away just years after penning his autobiographical memoir about his life trading in China, and ten years later, in 1905, Augustine Heard Jr. would follow.[125]

Though the bankruptcy had unbalanced the Heard brothers at first, each regained footing by leaning on the experience, knowledge, and contacts they had gained trading between China and the United States. Their lives may not have progressed parallel to the paths of their more fortunate peers, but their aspirations remained the same. Through their pursuit of new opportunities, they sought to reclaim space within elite society, whether in Boston, New York, or Washington. The experiences of those who came before them provided the benchmark for success. The lives of their uncle Coolidge, the first generation of Forbeses, or even John Heard himself in the early days of his retirement set the standard to which they aspired. As such, whether within or without elite social circles, the the Heards' trajectories following their return from China provide insight into the ways their unique experiences, contacts, and expertise shaped the lives of China traders in the United States and generated new opportunities for social, political, and commercial advancement.

In material ways, the China trade provided some protection from the disaster of bankruptcy. John and Albert Heard had both hedged their finances through the gifting of valuables, curios, property, and shares to their spouses. Yet their tenures also had less obvious, equally important, benefits. Each brother at some point turned to the communities they had fostered while in China to launch new ventures. Augustine Heard Jr. recalled old contacts while in China in 1876 to try and resuscitate the firm. John Heard kept possession of the Ipswich house through the ties—philanthropic and social—that Augustine Heard & Co had allowed the family to build with the local community. Albert Heard merged his experience in business with knowledge of Russia fostered in Hong Kong to try his hand at both new commercial and academic undertakings.

For the first decade following the bankruptcy, at least, the Heard brothers met limited success, but their progressive retrenchment itself illuminates the sociopolitical world that China traders found themselves reintegrated with in the United States. The volume of activities that John Heard retreated from testified to the social and civic persona that elite merchants sought to project, as did Augustine Heard Jr.'s decision to maintain membership with the Century Association, or Albert Heard's to continue performing the role of Boston socialite. Even in retreat, John Heard never moved far from the fashionable nucleus of Boston's Brahmin community. While lacking the resources of their Keechong Club rivals, the Heards still clung to the elite social worlds of Boston and New York.

In time Albert and Augustine Heard Jr. gained momentum, finding new applications for their expertise in commerce, their diplomatic experience, and their knowledge of East Asia. Augustine Heard Jr.'s appointment as U.S. Consul General to Korea was a combined result of the elite networks he maintained in the United States and his China-trade pedigree. Even his activities as an expert lobbyist for American interests in "the East" were justified on the merits of his consular duties and firsthand experience of foreign imperial systems in China, Korea, and Japan. With Augustine Heard Jr.'s guidance, Albert Heard too found an official post that suited the diplomatic role he had always sought to play in Hong Kong and Shanghai. By marshaling his wide network of supporters and his professed aptitude for political work, he managed to secure a post in Washington and a place within its community that suited his sociopolitical aspirations.

As the afterlives of the Heard brothers suggest, the history of Hong Kong is not just about Hong Kong. In one sense it is about how individuals experienced the colony, how the space shaped those who visited, lived, and traded within it. It is also, however, about how Hong Kong continued to be present in both overt and covert ways in post–Hong Kong lives. Hong Kong "made" American merchants and continued to "make" them long after they left. It afforded them opportunities and introduced them to new cultural forms, testing their values and what it meant to be "American" in a transnational context. It brought together a transnational world of contacts, creating tightly knit networks that transcended social, cultural, and even racial barriers, before sending the innumerable agents back into the world. The ties the brothers formed in the process were carried home with them, influencing their lives in America and Europe. Although not all the brothers exploited these networks to their full extent after leaving Hong Kong, the relationships they developed, maintained, discarded, or strained in the colony and in China shaped the Heards lives in varied ways in America and Europe as they rebuilt themselves from the ruins of their firm.

CONCLUSION

Lives of Consequence

"What is writ is writ, would it were worthier!" John Heard concluded his 1891 autobiography with Lord Byron's melancholic words. John Heard confessed he felt disappointed looking back over his life, that it had "seemed to contain much more incident" than when "brought to the test of analysis"; that it appeared "very poor and meagre when put on paper."[1] He might perhaps have finished the quotation: "But I am not now That which I have been." His life may have appeared lackluster in hindsight, but like his brothers, and indeed like many Americans who had followed a similar path, it was full of incident, and John Heard was changed because of it. In a literal sense, he was older, worn down perhaps, at the end of a long life peering backward through time.[2] Yet in the abstract sense he and an entire generation of American China traders had been shaped by their experiences living in Hong Kong and trading in the Qing Empire. There they made and lost fortunes, were present as its history unfolded, left their mark on it and China, and in turn wove China into the history of the United States. As individuals they had benefited from the interchange and in the process helped make firm the social and cultural identity of Hong Kong's foreign community.

Large American firms such as Augustine Heard & Co. formed the nucleus of American mercantile life in China. From its founding to its bankruptcy, Augustine Heard & Co. brought more than one hundred

CONCLUSION

Americans to China, where they joined the growing foreign community in Hong Kong and in treaty ports such as Shanghai, Hankou, and Fuzhou. At first glance, the firm and the company houses encouraged Americans to cultivate and preserve ties within a closed American group. Yet they soon found themselves participants in colonial or treaty-port society, influenced by all the attendant prejudices and attitudes. The unique circumstances and political turmoil of nineteenth-century China, Sino-foreign contact, and the colonial context informed both the mercantile activities of the firm's partners and their lifestyles. In Hong Kong Americans learned to mirror colonial practices and conform to sociocultural and racial hierarchies that, while not altogether unfamiliar, were sharpened in the colonial setting. And through their participation the society and culture Americans encountered in Hong Kong acquired a distinct form, adapted to the sometimes tense and sometimes cooperative relationship between the port's white, Chinese, and other communities. Faced with these hierarchies and norms, American merchants capitalized on the British community's and their shared language, race, and culture to navigate colonial society and carve a space among the port's white elite.

Hong Kong was not, however, a crucible. Americans were free to selectively adapt to the port's culture, and local interests often remained in flux with national ones. The national and cultural predispositions that accompanied Americans to China limited the extent to which they conformed to local systems. The merchants' sense of what it meant to be American, conditioned by their U.S. upbringing and their understanding of their young nation's history, combined with their administration's political interests to inflect the ways they interacted with the Chinese and other foreign communities. The same racial and cultural criteria through which Americans identified with their British neighbors were repurposed to denigrate Chinese people and their culture. Still, there remained antecedent sources of tension with the British that proved difficult to suppress through a superficial Anglo-Saxon racial-ethnic affinity. Although the Americans performed the appropriate roles in public, in private they voiced frustration with British politics, society, and pretensions. Through these rhetorical acts they signaled to friends and family in the metropole that while they might be changed by their experiences in the colony, they were still proudly American at heart. Their success in Hong Kong reflected their ability to balance these competing colonial and metropolitan interests.

CONCLUSION

In general, however, Americans worked within the boundaries of the colony's sociocultural norms, and their private interests in China led them to encourage British militancy and the extraction of further concessions, by force if necessary, from the Qing. Complicit in the clandestine trading of opium and arms, calculated participants in colonial life, and privately ambitious, Americans helped drive forward the privileged and often exploitative foreign presence in China. Their enterprises helped mold the coastal and riverine China trade; their merchants and consuls, reluctant at first, raised their voices in support for Britain during the Opium Wars; and their community bolstered and solidified the position of the white colonial elite in Hong Kong. Face-to-face with the unfamiliar Chinese communities, and operating on the margins of their monolithic empire, Americans in China and Hong Kong turned to the familiar if sometimes despised British community. The power, confidence, and experience of the latter lent surety to the underrepresented and underdefended American merchants.

This book has used Augustine Heard & Co. to argue that within British colonial society, the American community reconciled national and metropolitan influences, and in doing so reinforced colonial racial and social hierarchies, exploited imperial systems, and contributed actively to developing the British imperial world. While unique unto themselves, the Heards' experiences underscore the need for more nuanced histories of how the varied groups that inhabited colonial spaces contributed to and were shaped by those spaces' society, culture, politics, and commerce.[3] Theirs and the other large American firms of the nineteenth century played prominent roles in Hong Kong, and in the process their partners helped reconfigure Sino-American and Anglo-American relationships, adapting their own American identity to the immediate imperial context. John Heard's 1891 misgivings about the gravitas of his history therefore might be corrected on two accounts: as a member of the nineteenth-century American community in China, he and his peers effected real change, helping "make" Hong Kong; in turn China and Hong Kong indelibly marked these Americans, both in their immediate lives, and well after leaving the colony. In both overt and subtle ways, the British colony "made" those Americans who experienced it.

Augustine Heard & Co.'s rise and decline further reveals how global and microhistorical scales, when brought into dialogue, nuance understandings of colonialism and empire. The history of Americans in Hong Kong is, at first glance, a transimperial one, but it is also just as often a local and insular one. Hong Kong's Americans remained aloof from their metropole as much as they were swayed by it. The colony shielded its foreign population. It drew their attention inward and wrapped them in the immediate concerns of port politics, society, and culture. Global influences remained present, but as the Chinese saying goes, "the mountains are high, and the emperor is far away" (*shan gao huangdi yuan* 山高皇帝遠): the politics of the metropole were often a distant concern. National interests were frequently weighed against local ones, and they usually lost.

Augustine Heard & Co. and the Heard brothers represent these varied scales through which Americans made and were made by British colonial society, their narrative offering, on multiple levels, new and essential perspectives on the American experience in China. Where typically the intensification of Sino-American contact has been understood through diplomatic missions, consular officials, and the lens of the old China trade, the Heard narrative reveals the extent to which nonstate actors guided formal relations throughout the nineteenth century. As American trade expanded following the war and the American community continued to grow, the merchants involved and the informal diplomacy they practiced were crucial in exporting knowledge to the metropole about the Qing Empire and in bringing China and the U.S. into contact. This study has looked past the 1840s and reached beyond the records of diplomats and politicians. It has taken the themes of race, class, contact, and commerce abundant in the Canton narratives and applied them to a holistic account of the first wave of American commerce ending in the 1880s. It has likewise redeployed the history of high politics as much-needed context against which to measure the experiences of those nonstate actors with less patriotic goals.

Central to American commercial and social worlds in East Asia, the British colony of Hong Kong has been integral to this effort to restore Americans to their place in the history of nineteenth-century China. Hong Kong was a springboard for American commerce in East Asia and American engagement with the Qing Empire and the British Empire, but it was also a space shaped by the convergence of diverse groups with distinct interests. Thus, while the "in-between place" paradigm popular in Hong Kong studies has been a useful framework, the dominant paradigms of Hong Kong as a "meeting place" or "contact zone" have had more conceptual heft.[4]

CONCLUSION

Although just one of the groups that came into contact in the colony, the ways American elites structured and conducted their lives in the privacy of homes and in the colony's public spaces complicate the overall picture of Hong Kong society and culture. While some remained outsiders, others such as the Heards adapted and integrated, and their story often confirms the notion of colonies as assimilative spaces. Difference, however, also mattered, whether British and American difference inspiring agitated declarations of the latter's Americanness or Chinese and American difference driving the Americans together with the British in a self-perceived white Anglo-Saxon solidarity. Like grouped with like, and while Americans may not have supported all of Britain's activities in China, they still felt more secure in the company of other whites than they did with the Chinese.

Thus, while the Heards' history augments the picture of Hong Kong specifically, it helps demarcate the criteria through which "out" groups located their place within British colonial society. Some criteria—such as race—were common to other colonial spaces. The colony's unique character determined others. In Hong Kong, with its free trade policies and mercantile origins, wealth reigned, and it often served as the primary marker of one's class within the colony. Provided one had enough wealth and influence, a claim to elite society could be staked, regardless even, in some cases, of racial status. Other markers, such as language, religion, politics, or conduct, each worked in flux to determine one's position within the society's hierarchies. These criteria affected one's ability to assimilate, contributing to the complexity of colonial societies and colonial identities by making them more than British, and more than Chinese.

My secondary interest in undertaking this study has been to frame Hong Kong within comparative historical scales and to locate the colony within its global historical context. Such spaces may be peripheral within the history of empire, but they were central to the histories of those who migrated to, were born in, or made their fortunes through them. The Americans at the core of this narrative often possessed little more than a transitory relationship with Hong Kong, but their experiences in the colony affected the rest of their lives. Hong Kong occupied a central place in their business, in their social and commercial networks, and in the ways they defined themselves long after their firms failed. The Heards, like other Americans, spent just as much time in Hong Kong as they had in Boston and would in Europe. Just as their upbringing in New England shaped their encounters within the British colony, their experiences in China and Hong Kong shaped their encounters afterward.

The Heard narrative has emphasized the need to continue experimenting with the relationships between microhistorical and macrohistorical scales. Although both perspectives have their strengths—particularly in relation to contact zones and meeting places such as Hong Kong—neither proves on its own to be a wholly satisfactory unit of analysis. Moving from one to the other and back again, however, results in a more accurate, nuanced, and granular history.[5] Individuals rarely behaved as expected and often cared not a whit for the great changes that constitute grand historical narratives, but this does not mean the influences of those narratives were not felt on a local or personal level. As in the example of the American Civil War, the internecine conflict had little bearing on how China traders engaged with their environment beyond the odd brief panic. Those matters that did filter into their consciousness such as the *Alabama*'s privateering received disproportionate attention. Indeed, those reading the Civil War through the Heards' letters alone would be surprised to learn there were parts of it more important and more destructive within the grand scheme of things than a lone Confederate privateer. Still, the effects of the war were real, and even if they failed to appreciate it at the time, American merchants were effectively ruined by the conflict.

Both scales are therefore integral to the reading of such episodes. The macrohistorical, often represented in this book by political developments in the Atlantic or by the overarching narrative of Sino-Western contact, provides the context required to understand both the origins and long-term impact of distant or abstract sociopolitical developments. It establishes as a backdrop the flow of history, which, even if relevant to an episode's outcome, remained invisible to its actors. It permits both the historian and the reader omniscience, which they might use to better make sense of local complexities. Meanwhile the focus on small spaces reorientates the history so that matters that mattered most or perhaps not at all are given precedence or appropriately done away with. It enables the bounded case study of a single merchant firm to reflect the experiences of a community and the broader systems within colonial society, even while recognizing the subjective experiences of the firm's partners and employees. Both scales have proved indispensable to the telling of the Heards' history.

CONCLUSION

As more attention continues to be directed toward the complex composition of colonial and semicolonial communities, the need is growing for future studies to attend to the nuanced experiences within these contact zones and meeting places. The case study of Americans in Hong Kong exemplifies one such community, rendered uniquely accessible through the rich company archives the Heard family generated and preserved. Theirs is just one story, however, and a narrow elite and masculine one at that. As other research on racially ambiguous groups such as the Macanese or Eurasian communities, largely invisible groups such as the China coast's Black community, or non-elites such as sex workers or beachcombers suggests, there are many narratives subsumed under the mainstream British or Chinese elite ones that might further explain the sociocultural development of Hong Kong and the treaty ports.[6] Any number of criteria, from race to ethnicity, class, and gender, affected relationships in unique and often subjective ways, and emerging research building upon this history and others like it would do well to acknowledge these variables.

On the surface, this has been the history of the American Heard brothers and their firm, Augustine Heard & Company. This story is interesting in its own right, but its significance lies in the more abstract themes it touches upon. More than the story of a firm and its partners, it is the history of how the first wave of American merchants in China helped make and were made by British colonial society. At the end of the nineteenth century, with American prospects in China looking anemic, John Heard's 1891 regrets are understandable. Had he been privy to the bigger picture, however, he would be stunned by how full of consequence his life had been. Yes, the company had failed, but its presence in China, like that of Russell & Co. or Olyphant & Co., played a significant role in shaping American, and more generally foreign, interactions with the Chinese. Their and their countrymen's enterprises lay the groundwork for American politics and commerce in the Pacific, established the fortunes of many of Boston's and New York's elites, brought China to the American public, and affected the individual courses each merchants' lives took both during and after the trade. Looking forward from 1854, Albert Heard's diary entry "truly I am changed" was perhaps more apposite and certainly more predictive of the collective American experience than the young man, newly arrived in China, could ever have imagined.

NOTES

INTRODUCTION

1. Dael Norwood, *Trading Freedom: How Trade with China Defined Early America* (Chicago: University of Chicago Press, 2022), 16.
2. Jacques Downs, *The Golden Ghetto: The American Commercial Community at Canton and the Shaping of American China Policy, 1784–1844* (London: Associated University Press, 1997), 325.
3. For Britain's acquisition of Hong Kong, see Robert Bickers, *The Scramble for China: Foreign Devils in the Qing Empire, 1932–1914* (Sydney: Allen Lane, 2011), 84; Stephen Platt, *Imperial Twilight: The Opium War and the End of China's Last Golden Age* (London: Atlantic Books, 2018), 406.
4. Qiongji in Mandarin. Given the Cantonese pronunciation, the name was likely meant as a transliteration meaning "Augustine's."
5. Elijah Cole Bridgman and Samuel Wells Williams, *Chinese Repository, Vol. 11* (Canton, 1842), 55–58.
6. *An Anglochinese Calendar for the Year 1845, Corresponding to the Year of the Chinese Cycle Era 4482, or the 42d Year of the 75th Cycle of Sixty; Being the 25th Year of the Reign of Ta'ukwa'ng* (Victoria, Hong Kong: The Chinese Repository, 1845), 17–23.
7. *Historical and Statistical Abstract of the Colony of Hong Kong* (Hong Kong: Noronha & Co., 1911), charts 1–4. Hong Kong population records rarely differentiate between European and American communities. While difficult to gauge how many Americans there were in Hong Kong toward the nineteenth century's end, it is reasonable to assume their population remained low compared to the port's British community.
8. See Stephen Tuffnell, *Made in Britain: Nation and Emigration in Nineteenth-Century America* (Berkeley: University of California Press, 2020), 56–59, 74–75, for

INTRODUCTION

an account of how American emigrants to London defined and solidified ideas of nationalism and the American character.

9. Downs, *The Golden Ghetto*, 143; Paul A. Van Dyke, "Smuggling Networks of the Pearl River Delta Before 1842: Implications for Macau and the American China Trade," *Journal of the Hong Kong Branch of the Royal Asiatic Society* 50 (2010): 84–85; James Fichter, *So Great a Proffit: How the East Indies Trade Transformed Anglo-American Capitalism* (Cambridge, MA: Harvard University Press, 2010), 278; Norwood, *Trading Freedom*, 12.

10. Thomas H. Cox, " 'Money, Credit, and Strong Friends': Warren Delano II and the Importance of Social Networking in the Old China Trade," in *The Private Side of the Canton Trade, 1700–1840: Beyond the Companies*, ed. Paul A. Van Dyke and Susan E. Schopp (Hong Kong: Hong Kong University Press, 2018), 132–47; Platt, *Imperial Twilight*, 418; Mao Haijian, *The Qing Empire and the Opium War: The Collapse of the Heavenly Dynasty*, trans. Joseph Lawson, Craig Smith, and Peter Lavelle (Cambridge: Cambridge University Press, 2016), 456–61.

11. John M. Carroll, *Canton Days: British Life and Death in China* (Lanham, MD: Rowman & Littlefield, 2020), 299.

12. Kwang-ching Liu, *Anglo-American Steamship Rivalry in China, 1862–1874* (Cambridge, MA: Harvard University Press, 1962), 61.

13. Sebing He, "Russell and Company and the Imperialism of Anglo-American Free Trade," in *Narratives of Free Trade: The Commercial Cultures of Early US-China Relations*, ed. Kendall Johnson (Hong Kong: Hong Kong University Press, 2011), 98; Michael H. Hunt, *The Making of a Special Relationship: The United States and China in 1914* (New York: Columbia University Press, 1983); Jerry Israel, *Progressivism and the Open Door: America and China, 1905–1921* (Pittsburgh, PA: University of Pittsburgh Press, 1971); Teemu Ruskola, "Canton Is Not Boston: The Invention of American Imperial Sovereignty," *American Quarterly* 57, no. 3 (2005): 859–84; Eileen P. Scully, *Bargaining with the State from Afar: American Citizenship in Treaty Port China, 1844–1942* (New York: Columbia University Press, 2001), 48, 81; Eileen P. Scully, "Taking the Low Road to Sino-American Relations: 'Open Door' Expansionists and the Two China Markets," *Journal of American History* 82, no. 1 (1995): 62–83.

14. See Stacilee Ford, *Troubling American Women: Narratives of Gender and Nation in Hong Kong* (Hong Kong: Hong Kong University Press, 2011); Jane Hunter, *The Gospel of Gentility: American Women Missionaries in Turn-of-the-Century China* (New Haven, CT: Yale University Press, 1984); Eileen P. Scully, "Prostitution as Privilege: The 'American Girl' of Treaty-Port Shanghai, 1860–1937," *International History Review* 20, no. 4 (1998): 855–83; Rachel Tamar Van, "The 'Woman Pigeon': Gendered Bonds and Barriers in the Anglo-American Commercial Community in Canton and Macao, 1800–1849," *Pacific Historical Review* 83, no. 4 (2014): 561–91.

15. Ann Laura Stoler, "Rethinking Colonial Categories: European Communities and the Boundaries of Rule," *Comparative Studies in Society and History* 31, no. 1 (1989): 135–36.

16. For gender, race, and class, see Eadaoin Agnew, *Imperial Women Writers in Victorian India: Representing Colonial Life, 1850–1910* (Basingstoke, UK: Palgrave Macmillan, 2016); Antoinette Burton, "Archive Stories: Gender in the Making of

INTRODUCTION

Imperial and Colonial Histories," in *Gender and Empire*, ed. Philippa Levine (Oxford: Oxford University Press, 2004), 281–94; Claire Lowrie, *Masters and Servants: Cultures of Empire in the Tropics* (Manchester: Manchester University Press, 2016). See also Robert Bickers, *Getting Stuck in for Shanghai, or Putting the Kibosh on the Kaiser from the Bund: The British at Shanghai and the Great War* (Sydney: Penguin Books, 2014); Catherine Ladds, "Imperial Ambitions: Russians, Britons, and the Politics of Nationality in the Chinese Customs Service, 1890–1937," in *Russia and Its Northeast Asian Neighbors: China, Japan, and Korea, 1858–1945*, ed. Kimitaka Matsuzato (Lanham, MD: Lexington Books, 2016), 33–48.

17. Robert Bickers, *Empire Made Me: An Englishman Adrift in Shanghai* (London: Allen Lane, 2003); Catherine Chan, *The Macanese Diaspora in British Hong Kong: A Century of Transimperial Drifting* (Amsterdam: Amsterdam University Press, 2021); Chen Zu'en, *Xunfang Dongyangren: Jindai Shanghai de Riben Juliumin* 尋訪東洋人: 近代上海的日本居留民 (Looking for Orientals: Japanese Residents in Modern Shanghai) (Shanghai: Shanghai Academy of Social Sciences, 2006); Vivian Kong, *Multiracial Britishness: Global Networks in Hong Kong, 1910–45* (Cambridge: Cambridge University Press, 2023); Catherine Ladds, "Eurasians in Treaty-Port China: Journeys Across Racial and Imperial Frontiers," in *Migrant Cross-Cultural Encounters in Asia and the Pacific*, ed. Jacqueline Leckie et al. (Abingdon, UK: Routledge, 2016), 19–35; Sarah Abrevaya Stein, *Extraterritorial Dreams: European Citizenship, Sephardi Jews, and the Ottoman Twentieth Century* (Chicago: University of Chicago Press, 2016), 97.

18. Carl Smith, "The German Speaking Community in Hong Kong, 1846–1918," *Journal of the Hong Kong Branch of the Royal Asiatic Society* 34 (1994): 1–2; Bert Becker, "Western Firms and Their Chinese Compradors: The Case of the Jebsen and Chau Families," in *Meeting Place: Encounters Across Cultures in Hong Kong, 1841–1984*, ed. Elizabeth Sinn and Christopher Munn (Hong Kong: Hong Kong University Press, 2017), 119.

19. John M. Carroll, *Edge of Empires: Chinese Elites and British Colonials in Hong Kong* (Cambridge, MA: Harvard University Press, 2005), 3, 12. See also Chan, *The Macanese Diaspora*, 167; Wai-kwan Chan, *The Making of Hong Kong Society: Three Studies of Class Formation in Early Hong Kong* (Oxford: Clarendon Press, 1991), 15; Vaudine England, "Zindel's Rosary Hill—Hong Kong's Forgotten War," *Journal of the Royal Asiatic Society Hong Kong Branch* 57 (2017): 38; Jung-fang Tsai, *Hong Kong in Chinese History: Community and Social Unrest in the British Colony, 1842–1913* (New York: Columbia University Press, 1993), 10–13.

20. Christopher Munn, *Anglo-China: Chinese People and British Rule in Hong Kong, 1841–1880* (London: Routledge, 2001), 58.

21. John M. Carroll, *A Concise History of Hong Kong* (New York: Rowman & Littlefield, 2007), 4–5.

22. Elizabeth Sinn, "In-between Place: A New Paradigm for Hong Kong Studies," in *Rethinking Hong Kong: New Paradigms, New Perspectives*, ed. Elizabeth Sinn, Siu-lun Wong, and Wing-hoi Chan (Hong Kong: Hong Kong University Centre of Asian Studies, 2009), 251–52. See also John M. Carroll, "Colonial Hong Kong as a Cultural-Historical Place," *Modern Asian Studies* 40, no. 2 (2006): 519.

23. Elizabeth Sinn, "Introduction," in Sinn and Munn, *Meeting Place*, ix.

INTRODUCTION

24. Carroll, "Colonial Hong Kong as a Cultural-Historical Place," 540. See also Johnathan Goldstein, "Philadelphia's Old China Trade and Early American Images of China," *Pennsylvania Legacies* 12, no. 1 (2012): 9.
25. Platt, *Imperial Twilight*, 420–21.
26. Fichter, *So Great a Proffit*, 17; Alain Le Pichon, *Aux origines de Hong Kong: Aspects de la civilisation commerciale a Canton—Le fonds de commerce de Jardine, Matheson & Co., 1827–1839* (Paris: L'Harmattan, 1998), 39.
27. Downs, *The Golden Ghetto*, 300.
28. Mao, *The Qing Empire and the Opium War*, 461.
29. Stephen Platt, *Autumn in the Heavenly Kingdom: China, the West, and the Epic Story of the Taiping Civil War* (New York: Vintage Books, 2012), 288. See also Kenneth Bourne, "British Preparations for War with the North, 1861–1862," *English Historical Review* 76, no. 301 (1961): 600.
30. David Killingray, " 'A Good West Indian, a Good African, and, in Short, a Good Britisher': Black and British in a Colour-Conscious Empire, 1760–1950," *Journal of Imperial and Commonwealth History* 36, no. 3 (2008), 364. For an introduction to whiteness in relation to the imperial and colonial spaces, see Bridget Byrne, "The Crisis of Identity? Englishness, Britishness, and Whiteness," in *Empire and After: Englishness in Post-Colonial Perspectives*, ed. Graham Macphee and Prem Poddar (New York: Berghahn Books, 2007), 139–58.
31. Douglas Lorimer, "From Victorian Values to White Virtues: Assimilation and Exclusion in British Racial Discourse, c. 1870–1914," in *Rediscovering the British World*, ed. Phillip Buckner and R. Douglas Francis (Calgary: University of Calgary Press, 2005), 111.
32. Albert F. Heard to his parents, Hong Kong, February 23, 1860, HL-33A, HBS; George Heard, *Diary on Board the U.S.S. Hartford*, August 8, 1860, JP-2, HBS, 36–37; Elisa Tamarkin, *Anglophilia: Deference, Devotion, and Antebellum America* (Chicago: University of Chicago Press, 2008), 118.
33. John Heard, *An Account of His Life and the History of Augustine Heard & Co.* (1891), FP-4, HBS, 127.
34. Munn, *Anglo-China*, 58; Francis Wood, *No Dogs and Not Many Chinese: Treaty Port Life in China, 1843–1943* (London: John Murray, 1998), 116. See also Radhika Mohanram, *Imperial White: Race, Diaspora, and the British Empire* (Minneapolis: University of Minnesota Press, 2007), 177.
35. Heard, *An Account of His Life*, 172.
36. A handful of core texts on the relationship between global and microhistories have influenced my approach. See Jeremy Adelman, "What Is Global History Now?," *Aeon Essays*, March 2, 2017, https://aeon.co/essays/is-global-history-still-possible-or-has-it-had-its-moment; David Bell, "This Is What Happens When Historians Overuse the Idea of the Network," *New Republic*, October 25, 2013, https://newrepublic.com/article/114709/world-connecting-reviewed-historians-overuse-network-metaphor; Richard Drayton and David Motadel, "Discussion: The Futures of Global History," *Journal of Global History* 13, no. 1 (2018): 12; Carlo Ginzburg, "Microhistory: Two or Three Things That I Know About It," in *Theoretical Discussions of Biography: Approaches from History, Microhistory, and Life Writing*, ed. Hans Renders and Binne de Haan (Leiden: Brill, 2014), 141; Dale Tomich, "The Order of Historical Time: The Longue Durée and Micro-History,"

in *The Longue Durée and World-Systems Analysis*, ed. Richard E. Lee (Albany: State University of New York Press, 2012), 26.
37. Achim von Oppen and Silke Strickrodt, "Introductions: Biographies Between Spheres of Empire," *Journal of Imperial and Commonwealth History* 44, no. 5 (2016): 718.

1. A VERY PROFITABLE CRISIS

1. "Editorial," *Canton Press*, May 29, 1841.
2. Hsin-pao Chang, *Commissioner Lin and the Opium War* (Cambridge, MA: Harvard University Press, 1964), 148.
3. For further reading on the episode, see Robert Bickers, *The Scramble for China: Foreign Devils in the Qing Empire, 1932–1914* (Sydney: Allen Lane, 2011), 78–87.
4. E. W. Ellsworth, "Introduction to the Journal: Journal of Occurrences at Canton During the Cessation of Trade at Canton, 1839," *Journal of the Hong Kong Branch of the Royal Asiatic Society* 4 (1964): 9–36, contains a transcribed version of William Hunter's account of the affair.
5. William C. Hunter, *The "Fan Kwae" at Canton: Before the Treaty Days, 1825–1844* (Shanghai: The Oriental Affairs, 1882), 145.
6. "Editorial," May 29, 1841.
7. Stephen Platt, *Imperial Twilight: The Opium War and the End of China's Last Golden Age* (London: Atlantic Books, 2018), 420.
8. Platt, *Imperial Twilight*, 416–21.
9. John Heard, *An Account of His Life and the History of Augustine Heard & Co.* (1891), FP-4, HBS, 31.
10. Jacques Downs, *The Golden Ghetto: The American Commercial Community at Canton and the Shaping of American China Policy, 1784–1844* (London: Associated University Press, 1997), 196.
11. John M. Carroll, *Canton Days: British Life and Death in China* (Lanham, MD: Rowman & Littlefield, 2020), 4–11; John M. Carroll, "The Canton System: Conflict and Accommodation in the Contact Zone," *Journal of the Hong Kong Branch of the Royal Asiatic Society* 50 (2010): 62.
12. Jonathan Goldstein, "Philadelphia's Old China Trade and Early American Images of China," *Pennsylvania Legacies* 12, no. 1 (2012): 7.
13. Thomas F. Waters, "Augustine Heard and His Friends," in *Publications of the Ipswich Historical Society*, XXI (Salem, MA: Newcomb & Gauss, 1916), 12–30.
14. Downs, *The Golden Ghetto*, 229–33.
15. Katharine Hillard, ed., *My Mother's Journal: A Young Lady's Diary of Five Years Spent in Manila, Macau, and the Cape of Good Hope, From 1829–1834* (Boston: Geo. H. Ellis Co., 1900), 76–78.
16. Heard, *An Account of His Life*, 31–49.
17. Heard, *An Account of His Life*, 54–57. See also Albert F. Heard to his mother, Canton, October 2, 1854, HL-1, HBS.
18. For what are arguably the most complete descriptions of the Hongs themselves, see Johnathan A. Farris, "Thirteen Factories of Canton: An Architecture of Sino-Western Collaboration and Confrontation," *Building & Landscapes: Journal of Vernacular Architecture Forum* 14 (2007): 66–83; Johnathan A. Farris, *Enclave*

1. A VERY PROFITABLE CRISIS

to Urbanity: Canton, Foreigners, and Architecture from the Late Eighteenth to the Early Twentieth Centuries (Hong Kong: Hong Kong University Press, 2016). For global histories of confinement see Ravi Ahuja, "Mobility and Containment: The Voyages of South Asian Seamen, c. 1900–1960," in Coolies, Capital and Colonialism: Studies in Indian Labour History, ed. Rana P. Behal and Marcel van der Linden (Cambridge: International Review of Social History, Supplement 14, 2006), 113; Matthias van Rossum, "The Dutch East India Company in Asia, 1595–1811," in A Global History of Convicts and Penal Colonies, ed. Clare Anderson (London: Bloomsbury Academic, 2018), 157–58.

19. For examples of Anglo-American cooperation and friendship, see Augustine Heard Jr., Old China and New (1894), GQ-2-2, HBS, 42; Heard, An Account of His Life; Hunter, The "Fan Kwae" at Canton; Robert Bennett Forbes, "Rambling Recollections Connected with China," in Personal Reminiscences, 2nd ed. (Boston: Little, Brown, and Company, 1882), 346–54.
20. Farris, Enclave to Urbanity, 35.
21. Downs, The Golden Ghetto, 321; James R. Fichter, So Great a Proffit: How the East Indies Trade Transformed Anglo-American Capitalism (Cambridge, MA: Harvard University Press, 2010), 280.
22. Heard, An Account of His Life, 172.
23. Richard J. Grace, Opium and Empire: The Lives and Careers of William Jardine and James Matheson (Montreal: McGill-Queen's University Press, 2014), 289–91.
24. Downs, The Golden Ghetto, 192, 229–54.
25. Heard, An Account of His Life, 31.
26. Family data drawn from Downs, The Golden Ghetto, 364–70.
27. Joseph Coolidge to his father, Canton, April 27, 1833, Ms N-2404, MHS.
28. Downs, The Golden Ghetto, 155, 164; Forbes, "Rambling Recollections," 344.
29. Heard, An Account of His Life, 31.
30. Joseph Coolidge to Augustine Heard Sr., Canton, December 13, 1839, EM-12-2, HBS.
31. Downs, The Golden Ghetto, 193; Robert Bennet Forbes to Rose Forbes, Canton, October 11, 1838, in Letters from China: The Canton-Boston Correspondence of Robert Bennet Forbes, 1838–1840, ed. Phyllis Forbes Kerr (Mystic, CT: Mystic Seaport Museum, 1996), 59; Heard, An Account of His Life, 22.
32. John D. Wong, Global Trade in the Nineteenth Century: The House of Houqua and the Canton System (Cambridge: Cambridge University Press, 2016), 72, 81, 148.
33. Farris, Enclave to Urbanity, 156; Forbes, "Rambling Recollections," 369–74.
34. Augustine Heard Sr. to Joseph Coolidge, Boston, June 29, 1839, EM-12-1, HBS.
35. Joseph Coolidge to Augustine Heard Sr., Canton, December 13, 1839, EM-12-2, HBS; Robert Bennet Forbes to Rose Forbes, February 22, 1839, in Letters from China, 96.
36. Joseph Coolidge to Augustine Heard Sr., Tengkao Bay, Lintin, December 19, 1839, EM-12-2, HBS.
37. Downs, The Golden Ghetto, 194; Forbes, "Rambling Recollections," 2nd ed., 352; Heard, An Account of His Life, 22.
38. Heard, An Account of His Life, 31.
39. Grace, Opium and Empire, 278.
40. Editorial, "Supplement to the Canton Press," Canton Press, July 31, 1841. It is likely that the amounts listed are in Spanish dollars. The Press editorial draws a distinction between "$" and "£" but provides no further clarification.

1. A VERY PROFITABLE CRISIS

41. Editorial, "Supplement to the Canton Register," *Canton Register*, July 20, 1841.
42. Heard, *An Account of His Life*, 31; Editorial, "Supplement to the Canton Register," *Canton Register*, 20 July 1841.
43. "Supplement," *Canton Press*, July 31, 1841.
44. Editorial, "Supplement to the Canton Register," *Canton Register*, July 20, 1841.
45. "An Englishman," Letter to the Editor, *Canton Press*, August 14, 1841.
46. "Anonymous," Letter to the Editor, "Second Supplement to the Canton Register," *Canton Register*, July 27, 1841.
47. Joseph Coolidge, Correspondence, *Canton Press*, August 7, 1841.
48. "Supplement," *Canton Press*, July 31, 1841; Heard, *An Account of His Life*, 32.
49. "Supplement," *Canton Press*, July 31, 1841; Mao Haijian, *The Qing Empire and the Opium War: The Collapse of the Heavenly Dynasty* (Cambridge: Cambridge University Press, 2016), 238–39.
50. "Supplement," *Canton Press*, July 31, 1841; "Anonymous," Letter to the Editor, "Second Supplement to the Canton Register," *Canton Register*, July 27, 1841.
51. "Supplement," *Canton Register*, July 20, 1841.
52. Platt, *Imperial Twilight*, 416.
53. Caleb Cushing and Keying, "Articles I & XXII," Treaty of Wanghia: Treaty of Peace, Amity, and Commerce Between the United States of America and the Chinese Empire, Wangxia (1844).
54. Cushing, Keying, "Article II," Treaty of Wanghia. See also Eileen P. Scully, *Bargaining with the State from Afar: American Citizenship in Treaty Port China, 1844–1942* (New York: Columbia University Press, 2001), 21–80.
55. Michael A. Hunt, *The Making of a Special Relationship: The United States and China to 1914* (New York: Columbia University Press, 1983), 50, 51.
56. James Hevia, *English Lessons: The Pedagogy of Imperialism in Nineteenth-Century China* (Durham, NC: Duke University Press, 2003), 13.
57. Jane Kate Leonard, *Wei Yuan and China's Rediscovery of the Maritime World* (Cambridge, MA: Council on East Asian Studies, Harvard University, 1984), 9. See also Jenny Huangfu Day, *Qing Travelers to the Far West: Diplomacy and the Information Order in Late Imperial China* (Cambridge: Cambridge University Press, 2018), 8; James Hevia, *The Imperial Security State: British Colonial Knowledge and Empire-Building in Asia* (Cambridge: Cambridge University Press, 2012), 17; Xue Zhang, "Imperial Maps of Xinjiang and Their Readers in Qing China, 1660–1860," *Journal of Chinese History* 4, no. 1 (2020): 116.
58. Frank Dikötter, *The Discourse of Race in Modern China* (London: Hurst & Company, 1992), 35–38.
59. Matthew Mosca, *From Frontier Policy to Foreign Policy: The Question of India and the Transformation of Geopolitics in Qing China* (Stanford, CA: Stanford University Press, 2013), 238–39.
60. James M. Polachek, *The Inner Opium War* (Cambridge, MA: Harvard East Asian Monographs, 1992), 137.
61. "*Zui qiang da er wei Ying'ji' li suo wei zhe* 最強大而為英吉利所畏者," in *Chou ban yi wu shi mo* 籌辦夷務始末 (The Record of Organizing Barbarian Affairs), vol. 62, c. 1842, 70a, ed. Wenqing 文慶 (Beijing: Gugong bowuyuan, 1930).
62. R. David Arkush and Leo O. Lee, "Exotic America," in *Land Without Ghosts: Chinese Impressions of America from the Mid-Nineteenth Century to the Present*,

ed. R. David Arkush and Leo O. Lee (Berkeley: University of California Press, 1989), 16.

63. Michael Lazich, "Placing China in Its 'Proper Rank Among the Nations': The Society for the Diffusion of Useful Knowledge in China and the First Systematic Account of the United States in Chinese," *Journal of World History* 22, no. 3 (2011): 538; Xu Jiyu 徐繼畬, *Ying huan zhi lüe* 瀛環志略 (A Short Account of the Maritime Circuit) (1849); Wei Yuan 魏源, *Haiguo tuzhi* 海國圖志 (Illustrated Treatise on the Maritime Kingdoms) (1844).
64. Refer to the concept of "strategic formation" in Edward Said, *Orientalism* (London: Routledge & Kegan Paul, 1978), 21–22. See also Leonard, *Wei Yuan*, 153; Liu Xincheng, "The Global View of History in China," *Journal of World History* 23, no. 3 (2012): 497–98.
65. Bickers, *The Scramble for China*, 20; Lazich, "Placing China in Its 'Proper Rank Among Nations,'" 539; Liu Jianhui 劉建輝, "Birth of an East Asian Information Network," in *Demon Capital Shanghai: The "Modern" Experience of Japanese Intellectuals*, trans. Joshua A. Fogel, *Sino-Japanese Studies* 16 (2009): 69.
66. Hunt, *The Making of a Special Relationship*, 51.
67. Xu, *Ying huan zhi lüe*, 773–77.
68. John K. Fairbank, *Trade and Diplomacy on the China Coast: The Opening of the Treaty Ports, 1842–1854* (Stanford, CA: Stanford University Press, 1964), 284. For further reading, see Li Ding-yi 李定一, *Zhongmei waijiao shi*, vol. 1, 中美外交史第一冊 (The History of Sino-American Diplomacy, vol. 1) (Taipei: Qingshui Publishing, 1960).
69. Mao, *The Qing Empire and the Opium War*, 458.
70. Fichter, *So Great a Proffit*, 287.
71. Downs, *The Golden Ghetto*, 46.
72. "*Sheng nu* 聖怒" (His Majesty's anger), in *Chou ban yi wu shi mo* 籌辦夷務始末, vol. 45 c. 1842, 44a–44b.
73. Hugh Hamilton Lindsay to Lord Palmerston, Berkley Square, 1840, FO 17/41, TNA; Robert Bickers, "The *Challenger*: Hugh Hamilton Lindsay and the Rise of British Asia, 1832–1865," *Transactions of the Royal Historical Society* 22 (2012): 146.
74. Downs, *The Golden Ghetto*, 198.
75. See Consul Macgregor to the Governor General of Liangguang and the Governor of Canton, Canton, July 29, 1846, FO 17/120, 7:3, TNA; Sir John Davis to Consul Macgregor, Hong Kong, August 3, 1846, FO 17/120, 7:4, TNA; Mr Campbell to Consul Macgregor, Canton, July 30, 1846, FO 17/120, 7:5, TNA; Mr Campbell to Consul Macgregor, Canton, August 4, 1846, FO 17/120, 7:7, TNA; American Consul to Keying, (translation), Canton, August 11, 1846, FO 17/120, 31:1, TNA.
76. Robert Bennet Forbes to Rose Forbes, Macao, August 21, 1839, in *Letters from China*, 162–63.
77. Robert Bennet Forbes to Rose Forbes, Macao, August 14, 1839, in *Letters from China*, 158; Robert Bennet Forbes to Rose Forbes, Hong Kong Bay, September 2, 1839, in *Letters from China*, 166.
78. Robert Bennet Forbes to Rose Forbes, Macao, August 27, 1839, in *Letters from China*, 165.
79. Robert Bennet Forbes to Rose Forbes, Macao, August 29, 1839, in *Letters from China*, 165.

1. A VERY PROFITABLE CRISIS

80. Joseph Coolidge to Augustine Heard Sr., Canton, December 13, 1839, EM-12-2, HBS.
81. Robert Bennet Forbes to Rose Forbes, Hong Kong Bay, September 18, 1839, in *Letters from China*, 168.
82. Tim Sturgis, *Rivalry in Canton: The Control of Russell & Co. 1838–1840 and the Founding of Augustine Heard & Co.* (London: The Warren Press, 2006), 80.
83. Joseph Coolidge to Augustine Heard Sr., Canton, December 13, 1839, EM-12-2, HBS.
84. Augustine Heard Sr. to Thomas W. Waldron, Canton, March 24, 1844, EL-6-4, HBS.
85. Sebing He, "Russell and Company and the Imperialism of Anglo-American Free Trade," in *Narratives of Free Trade: The Commercial Cultures of Early US-China Relations*, ed. Kendall Johnson (Hong Kong: Hong Kong University Press, 2011), 97.
86. Joseph Coolidge to Augustine Heard Sr., Canton, December 13, 1839, EM-12-2, HBS; Augustine Heard Sr. to Joseph Coolidge, Boston, May 8, 1840, EM-12-1, HBS; Joseph Coolidge, George Dixwell, and Augustine Heard Sr., Partnership Agreement, April 28, 1842, EA-1-2, HBS.
87. Chang, *Commissioner Lin and the Opium War*, 183–84.
88. Robert Bennet Forbes to Rose Forbes, Canton, December 1, 1839, in *Letters from China*, 188.
89. Account Sales, Canton, March 4, 1841, vol. 215, HBS; Calendar, Whampoa, 1843–1845, A-3, HBS; Journal, Canton, January 1, 1840–June 1, 1843, v. 1, HBS. See also Paul A. Van Dyke, *Americans and Macao: Trade, Smuggling, and Diplomacy on the South China Coast* (Hong Kong: Hong Kong University Press, 2012).
90. For a cursory account of Dixwell's early responsibilities, see Downs, *The Golden Ghetto*, 196–98, 330. Coolidge, Dixwell, and A. Heard Sr., Partnership Agreement, Canton, April 28, 1842, HBS; George Dixwell to Augustine Heard Sr., Canton, November 8, 1844, EM-3-2, HBS.
91. Stephen Tuffnell, *Made in Britain: Nation and Emigration in Nineteenth-Century America* (Berkeley: University of California Press, 2020), 119. See Daniel Immerwahr, *How to Hide an Empire: A Short History of the Greater United States* (New York: Vintage Books, 2020), 79–81.
92. William Henry Low to Seth Low, Canton, October 27, 1839, in *The Canton Letters, 1839–1841 of William Henry Low*, ed. James Duncan Phillips (Salem, MA: Essex Institute, 1948), 34; William Henry Low to H. Hillard, Canton, February 14, 1840, in *The Canton Letters*, 41; William Henry Low to Seth Low, Canton, April 29, 1840, in *The Canton Letters*, 42–43.
93. Nathan Allan, *An Essay on the Opium Trade Including a Sketch of its History, Extent, Effects, Etc., as Carried on in India and China* (Boston: John P. Jewett & Co., 1850), 59–63. See also Thomas W. Knox, *John, or Our Chinese Relations: A Study of our Emigration and Commercial Intercourse with the Celestial Empire* (New York: Harper & Brothers, 1879), 19; Aaron Haight Palmer, *Letter to the Hon. John M. Clayton, Secretary of State, Enclosing a Paper, Geographical, Political, Commercial, on the Independent Oriental Nations; and Containing a Plan for Opening, Extending, and Protecting American Commerce in the East &c.* (Washington, DC: Gideon & Company, 1849), 34.
94. Hans Derks, *History of the Opium Problem: The Assault on the East, ca. 1600–1950* (Leiden: Brill, 2012), 748. See also Charles C. Stelle, "American Trade in Opium to China, 1821–39," *Pacific Historical Review* 10, no. 1 (1941): 74.
95. Allan, *An Essay on the Opium Trade*, 13.

1. A VERY PROFITABLE CRISIS

96. Platt, *Imperial Twilight*, 414–15.
97. Heard, *An Account of His Life*, 94.
98. Gordan H. Chang, *Fateful Ties: A History of America's Preoccupation with China* (Cambridge, MA: Harvard University Press, 2015), 49; Joseph Coolidge to Augustine Heard Sr., Canton, December 13, 1839, EM-12-2, HBS; George Dixwell to Augustine Heard Sr., Canton, December 3, 1844, EM-3-2, HBS; Robert Bennet Forbes to Rose Forbes, Canton, April 11, 1839, in *Letters from China*, 117.
99. Allan, *An Essay on the Opium Trade*, 46. See also Heard, *An Account of His Life*, 36; Hunter, *The "Fan Kwae" at Canton*, 94; Forbes, "Rambling Recollections," 144.
100. Norwood, "Trading in Liberty," 271.
101. Fairbank, *Trade and Diplomacy on the China Coast*, 208.
102. George B. Dixwell to Augustine Heard Sr., Canton, January 19, 1844, EM-3-2, HBS.
103. Statement of the Imports and Deliveries of the Opium at Woosung Station, Shanghai, c. January 1852, Case 19, HBS.
104. Paul A. Van Dyke, *The Canton Trade: Life and Enterprise on the China Coast, 1700–1845* (Hong Kong: Hong Kong University Press, 2005), 132.
105. For more comprehensive accounts of the opium smuggling networks in the Pearl River Delta, see Paul A. Van Dyke, "Smuggling Networks of the Pearl River Delta Before 1842: Implications for Macau and the American China Trade," *Journal of the Hong Kong Branch of the Royal Asiatic Society* 50 (2010): 68; Dael Norwood, *Trading Freedom: How Trade with China Defined Early America* (Chicago: University of Chicago Press, 2022), 66–68.
106. Chang, *Commissioner Lin and the Opium War*, 32; Hunter, *The "Fan Kwae" at Canton*, 39.
107. Chang, *Commissioner Lin and the Opium War*, 47.
108. See: Account Sales, Canton, March 22, 1840–March 12, 1845, vol. 215, HBS. Alternating accounts between January and June 1842 show the Heards earning a substantial commission trading Jardine Matheson & Co. cotton while also moving opium for the British firm's Indian contacts. For the latter they earned demurrage, and occasionally also a commission on the sale.
109. Dwijendra Tripathi, *The Oxford History of Indian Business* (New Delhi: Oxford University Press, 2004), 82–83.
110. George Dixwell to Augustine Heard Sr., Macao, May 30, 1845; George Dixwell to Augustine Heard Sr., Canton, November 17, 1844; George Dixwell to Augustine Heard Sr., Canton, January 19, 1845, all EM-3-2, HBS.
111. Account Sales, Canton, March 4, 1841, and March 1842, both vol. 215, HBS.
112. George Dixwell to Augustine Heard Sr., Canton, November 17, 1844, EM-3-2, HBS; Tripathi, *The Oxford History of Indian Business*, 79.
113. Alain Le Pichon, *Aux origines de Hong Kong: Aspects de la civilisation commerciale à Canton—Le fonds de commerce de Jardine, Matheson & Co., 1827–1839* (Paris: L'Harmattan, 1998), 57; Tripathi, *The Oxford History of Indian Business*, 83.
114. Kessressung Kushalchand to Augustine Heard & Co., Bombay, April 9, 1845, EM-1-7, HBS.
115. Sturgis, *Rivalry in Canton*, 80.
116. George Dixwell to Augustine Heard Sr., Canton, March 19, 1845, EM-3-2, HBS.

2. A HOUSE IS NOT A HOME

117. Heard, *An Account of His Life*, 51.
118. James M. Forbes, *Recollections and Events from the Threshold of Eighty-Five* (Boston, 1930), 23.
119. See Marlene Kessler, Kristen Lee, and Daniel Menning, eds., *The European Canton Trade 1723: Competition and Cooperation* (Oldenburg, Germany: De Gruyter, 2016); Carroll, *Canton Days*.
120. Lisa Hellman, *This House Is Not a Home: European Everyday Life in Canton and Macao, 1730–1830* (Leiden: Brill, 2018), 28. See also He, "Russell and Company," 96.
121. Jonathan Goldstein, "Nathan Dunn (1782–1844) as Anti-Opium Trader and Sino-Western Cultural Intermediary," in *The Private Side of the Canton Trade, 1700–1840: Beyond the Companies*, ed. Paul A. Van Dyke and Susan E. Schopp (Hong Kong: Hong Kong University Press, 2018), 112.
122. Hellman, *This House Is Not a Home*, 35, argues that the groups foreign traders formed in Canton were "relational and conditional."
123. Gregory Blue, "Opium for China: The British Connection," in *Opium Regimes: China, Britain, and Japan, 1839–1952*, ed. Timothy Brook and Bob Tadashi Wakabayashi (Berkeley: University of California Press, 2000), 36; Goldstein, "Nathan Dunn," 105. See also Song-chuan Chen, *Merchants of War and Peace: British Knowledge of China in the Making of the Opium War* (Hong Kong: Hong Kong University Press, 2017), 140.
124. Robert Bennet Forbes to Rose Forbes, Canton, December 30, 1838, in *Letters from China*, 79; Robert Bennet Forbes to Rose Forbes, Canton, January 25, 1839, in *Letters from China*, 87–89. See also May-bo Ching, "Chopsticks or Cutlery? How Canton Hong Merchants Entertained Foreign Guests in the Eighteenth and Nineteenth Centuries," in *Narratives of Free Trade: The Commercial Cultures of Early US-China Relations*, ed. Kendall Johnson (Hong Kong: Hong Kong University Press), 99, 112.

2. A HOUSE IS NOT A HOME

1. J. Y. Wong, *Deadly Dreams: Opium, Imperialism, and the Arrow War (1856–1860) in China* (Cambridge: Cambridge University Press, 1998), 43.
2. Robert Bickers, *The Scramble for China: Foreign Devils in the Qing Empire, 1932–1914* (Sydney: Allen Lane, 2011), 141.
3. John Heard, *An Account of His Life and the History of Augustine Heard & Co.* (1891), FP-4, HBS, 111.
4. See, for instance, Augustine Heard Jr., *Old China and New* (1894), GQ-2-2, HBS, 11–13.
5. Heard, *An Account of His Life*, 112.
6. Wong, *Deadly Dreams*, 64.
7. Caleb Cushing and Keying, Article II, Treaty of Wanghia: Treaty of Peace, Amity, and Commerce Between the United States of America and The Chinese Empire, Wangxia (1844).
8. Johnathan Farris, *Enclave to Urbanity: Canton, Foreigners, and Architecture from the Late Eighteenth to the Early Twentieth Centuries* (Hong Kong: Hong Kong University Press, 2016), 80.

2. A HOUSE IS NOT A HOME

9. Albert F. Heard to his parents, Hong Kong, January 29, 1860, HL-33A, HBS.
10. Heard, *An Account of His Life*, 115.
11. Heard, *Old China and New*, 25, 28; Heard, *An Account of His Life*, 115.
12. John Foot, "Micro-History of a House: Memory and Place in a Milanese Neighbourhood, 1890–2000," *Urban History* 34, no. 3 (2007): 435.
13. Melanie Backe-Hansen and David Olusoga, *A House Through Time* (Basingstoke, UK: Pan Macmillan, 2020), 5. See also Gillian Tindall, *Three Houses, Many Lives: The Story of a Cotswold Vicarage, a Surrey Boarding School and a London Home* (London: Vintage Books, 2013).
14. Backe-Hansen and Olusoga, *A House Through Time*, 1.
15. Ann Laura Stoler, "Rethinking Colonial Categories: European Communities and the Boundaries of Rule," *Comparative Studies in Society and History* 31, no. 1 (1989): 133.
16. Lisa Hellman, *This House Is Not a Home: European Everyday Life in Canton and Macao, 1730–1830* (Leiden: Brill, 2018), 105.
17. Prasannajit de Silva, "Representing Home Life Abroad: British Domestic Life in Early-Nineteenth-Century India," *Visual Culture in Britain* 12, no. 3 (2011): 315.
18. Peter James Marshall, "British Society in India Under the East India Company," *Modern Asian Studies* 31, no. 1 (1997): 101; Bickers, *Scramble for China*, 116.
19. Rajeshwar Mittapalli and Susmita Roye, "Introduction," in *The Male Empire Under the Female Gaze*, ed. Rajeshwar Mittapalli and Susmita Roye (Amherst, NY: Cambria Press, 2013), 4. See also Marilyn Francus, *Monstrous Motherhood: Eighteenth Century Culture and the Ideology of Domesticity* (Baltimore: Johns Hopkins University Press, 2012).
20. Jane Rendall, "The Condition of Women, Women's Writing and the Empire in Nineteenth-Century Britain," in *At Home with the Empire: Metropolitan Culture in the Imperial World*, ed. Catherine Hall and Sonya O. Rose (Cambridge: Cambridge University Press, 2006), 104.
21. De Silva, "Representing Home Life Abroad," 314.
22. Marshall, "British Society in India Under the East India Company," 101.
23. Francus, *Monstrous Motherhood*, 4. See also Leonore Davidoff and Catherine Hall, *Family Fortunes: Men and Women of the English Middle Class, 1780–1850* (Oxford: Routledge, 2002), 33.
24. Sara Mills, *Gender and Colonial Space* (Manchester: Manchester University Press, 2009), 35, 130. See also Claire Lowrie, *Masters and Servants: Cultures of Empire in the Tropics* (Manchester: Manchester University Press), 3.
25. Hellman, *This House Is Not a Home*, 113.
26. Jacques Downs, *The Golden Ghetto: The American Commercial Community at Canton and the Shaping of American China Policy, 1784–1844* (London: Associated University Press, 1997), 27.
27. Heard, *Old China and New*, 15.
28. Stoler, "Rethinking Colonial Categories," 136, 155.
29. For further reading on the connection between the India and Canton houses, see Michael Greenberg, *British Trade and the Opening of China 1800–42* (Cambridge: Cambridge University Press, 1951), and James Fichter, *So Great a Proffit: How the East Indies Trade Transformed Anglo-American Capitalism* (Cambridge, MA: Harvard University Press, 2010).

2. A HOUSE IS NOT A HOME

30. Downs, *The Golden Ghetto*, 27.
31. Johnathan A. Farris, "Thirteen Factories of Canton: An Architecture of Sino-Western Collaboration and Confrontation," *Building & Landscapes: Journal of the Vernacular Architecture Forum* 14 (2007): 79.
32. Jung-fang Tsai, *Hong Kong in Chinese History: Community and Social Unrest in the British Colony, 1842–1913* (New York: Columbia University Press, 1993), 44.
33. Heard, *Old China and New*, 28.
34. Contract between Tam Achoy (Tan Yacai 譚亞才), L. N. Hitchcock, & Augustine Heard Jr., Victoria, January 1856, Case 27, HBS.
35. Heard, *Old China and New*, 28.
36. Heard, *Old China and New*, 28.
37. Albert F. Heard to his parents, Hong Kong, February 12, 1857, HL-3, HBS.
38. Christopher Munn, *Anglo-China: Chinese People and British Rule in Hong Kong, 1841–1880* (London: Routledge, 2001), 104.
39. Suresh Chandra Ghosh, *The Social Condition of the British Community in Bengal, 1757–1800* (Leiden: E. J. Brill, 1970), 100–101.
40. Plan for house (unused), 1857, Case 30, HBS; Plan for house, undated, Case 30, HBS.
41. A. Heard & Co., rental agreement for 6, 3, & 10, Rua Dos Prazeres, Macao, 1867, Case 27, HBS; George F. Weller, rental agreement for 39 Praya Grande, Macao, 1873, Case 27, HBS.
42. Heard, *Old China and New*, 20.
43. Downs, *The Golden Ghetto*, 50.
44. "John" to Messrs. Augustine Heard & Co., Hong Kong, June 8, 1864, Case 30, HBS; Augustine Heard & Co. to "Mr Lewis," Hong Kong, November 3, 1865, Case 30, HBS.
45. Gustavus Tuckerman to Mr Whitney, Hong Kong, January 17, 1859, GT.
46. Farris, "Thirteen Factories of Canton," 72.
47. Gustavus Tuckerman to Tom, Hong Kong, January 11, 1858, GT.
48. George Heard to Augustine Heard Jr., Hong Kong, February 19, 1873, JL-2, HBS.
49. George Heard to Augustine Heard Jr., Hong Kong, March 5, 1873, JL-2, HBS.
50. John Bowring, as quoted in John Carroll, *A Concise History of Hong Kong* (New York: Rowman & Littlefield, 2007), 36.
51. Mills, *Gender and Colonial Space*, 107. See also Bickers, *Scramble for China*, 131.
52. Land Sale Agreement, Hong Kong, 1865, Case 27, HBS.
53. Carroll, *A Concise History of Hong Kong*, 36.
54. Albert F. Heard to Mary Heard, Hong Kong, July 17, 1874, HL-5, HBS.
55. Carroll, *A Concise History of Hong Kong*, 36. See also Harald Fischer-Tiné, "The Making of a 'Ruling Race': Defining and Defending Whiteness in Colonial India," in *Racism and the Modern World: Historical Perspectives on Cultural Transfer and Adaptation*, ed. Manfred Berg and Simon Wendt (New York: Berghahn Books, 2011), 213–35.
56. "1868 Topside Wages: Pokfulam," Petty Cash Ledger, Hong Kong, 1862–1869, vol. 71, Heard HBS; Stuart Braga, "Making Impressions: The Adaptation of a Portuguese Family to Hong Kong, 1750–1900" (PhD diss., Australian National University, 2012), 180; *London and China Telegraph*, February 18, 1860, 124.
57. Heard, *Old China and New*, 25.
58. John M. Carroll, *Edge of Empires: Chinese Elites and British Colonials in Hong Kong* (Cambridge, MA: Harvard University Press, 2005), 90. See also Irene Cheng,

2. A HOUSE IS NOT A HOME

Clara Ho Tung: A Hong Kong Lady, Her Family and Her Times (Hong Kong: Hong Kong University Press, 1976), and Henry J. Lethbridge, *Hong Kong: Stability and Change: A Collection of Essays* (Hong Kong: Oxford University Press, 1978).

59. Mills, *Gender and Colonial Space*, 113–14.
60. Ghosh, *The Social Condition of the British Community in Bengal*, 104.
61. Farris, "Thirteen Factories of Canton," 74.
62. Albert F. Heard to his parents, Hong Kong, June 11, 1859, HL-33A, HBS; Albert F. Heard to his parents, Shanghai, June 23, 1859, HL-33A, HBS; Albert F. Heard to Augustine Heard Sr., Hong Kong, January 14, 1860, HL-33A, HBS; Bickers, *The Scramble for China*, 117; Albert F. Heard to his parents, Shanghai, March 5, 1857, HL-3, HBS.
63. George Heard to Augustine Heard Jr., Hong Kong, February 19, 1873, JL-2, HBS.
64. Albert F. Heard to Mary Heard, Hong Kong, July 25, 1874, HL-5, HBS; Albert F. Heard, Unaddressed, Hong Kong, c.1859 HL-33A, HBS.
65. Jane Hunter, *Gospel of Gentility: American Women Missionaries in Turn-of-the-Century China* (New Haven, CT: Yale University Press, 1984), 128.
66. Gustavus Tuckerman to Mr Whitney, Hong Kong, January 17, 1859, GT.
67. Mills, *Gender and Colonial Space*, 114.
68. Hunter, William C., *The "Fan Kwae" at Canton: Before the Treaty Days, 1825–1844* (Shanghai: The Oriental Affairs, 1882), 31.
69. Jonathan Goldstein, "Philadelphia's Old China Trade and Early American Images of China," *Pennsylvania Legacies* 12, no. 1 (2012), 8. See also Margot Finn and Kate Smith, eds., *The East India Company at Home, 1757–1857* (London: UCL Press, 2018).
70. Stoler, "Rethinking Colonial Categories," 141.
71. Søren Mentz, "Cultural Interaction Between the British Diaspora in Madras and the Host Community, 1650–1790," in *Asian Port Cities 1600–1800: Local and Foreign Cultural Interactions*, ed. Masashi Haneda (Singapore: National University of Singapore Press, 2009), 164, 173.
72. Ghosh, *The Social Condition of the British Community in Bengal*, 127.
73. Downs, *The Golden Ghetto*, 36–37.
74. Augustine Heard Sr. to Albert F. Heard, Boston, June 17, 1863, HN-6-2, HBS; J. Heard, *An Account of His Life*, 164.
75. Gustavus Tuckerman to Mr. Whitney, Hong Kong, January 17, 1859, GT.
76. Augustine Heard Sr. to Albert F. Heard, Boston, May 10, 1864, HN-6-2, HBS.
77. Heard, *An Account of His Life*, 164.
78. Augustine Heard Jr. to Mr. Endicott, Hong Kong, August 13, 1875, GL-5-3, HBS.
79. Heard, *Old China and New*, 15.
80. Petty Cash Ledger, Hong Kong, 1869–1874, Vol. 72, HBS.
81. Mills, *Gender and Colonial Space*, 119.
82. Farris, "Thirteen Factories of Canton," 38.
83. Heard, *An Account of His Life*, 118–19; Heard, *Old China and New*, 15; Albert F. Heard to Mary Heard, Hong Kong, June 13, 1874, HL-5, HBS.
84. Downs, *The Golden Ghetto*, 39; Heard, *An Account of His Life*, 29; Heard, *Old China and New*, 15.
85. Memo of stores belonging to the house, Canton, 1845, Case 27, HBS.
86. Ghosh, *The Social Condition of the British Community in Bengal*, 125; Marshall, "British Society in India Under the East India Company," 94, 107.

2. A HOUSE IS NOT A HOME

87. Francis Wood, *No Dogs and Not Many Chinese: Treaty Port Life in China, 1843–1943* (London: John Murray, 1998), 126.
88. Albert F. Heard, Diary, December 13, 1854, Hong Kong, HP-2, HBS; George Heard to Augustine Heard Jr., Hong Kong, February 19, 1873, JL-2, HBS; George Heard to Augustine Heard Jr., Hong Kong, February 25, 1873, JL-2, HBS.
89. Heard, *An Account of His Life*, 40.
90. Caroline Rosenthal, "Drinks, Domesticity and the Forging of an American Identity in Susan Warner's *The Wide, Wide, World* (1850)," in *Drink in the Eighteenth and Nineteenth Centuries*, ed. Susanne Schmid and Barbara Schmidt-Haberkamp (London: Pickering and Chatto, 2014), 32; John Carter Wood, "Drinking, Fighting and Working-Class Sociability in Nineteenth-Century Britain," in Schmid and Schmidt-Haberkamp, *Drink in the Eighteenth and Nineteenth Centuries*, 72.
91. Augustine Heard Sr. to Albert F. Heard, Boston, February 8, 1864, HN-6-2, HBS.
92. Harald Fischer-Tiné, "'The Drinking Habits of Our Countrymen': European Alcohol Consumption and Colonial Power in British India," *Journal of Imperial and Commonwealth History* 40, no. 3 (2012): 385.
93. Albert F. Heard to Augustine Heard Jr., Hong Kong, January 7, 1875, HL-5, HBS.
94. Fischer-Tiné, "The Drinking Habits of Our Countrymen," 386.
95. George Heard to Augustine Heard Jr., Hong Kong, August 7, 1873, JL-2, HBS.
96. Albert F. Heard to Henry Livingston, Hong Kong, October 28, 1874, HL-5, HBS.
97. Albert F. Heard to Mary Heard, Hong Kong, October 5, 1874, HL-5, HBS.
98. Augustine Heard Sr. to Albert F. Heard, Boston, May 17, 1862, HN-6-2, HBS.
99. Augustine Heard Sr. to Albert F. Heard, Boston, October 24, 1861; Augustine Heard Sr. to Albert F. Heard, Boston, December 9, 1861; Augustine Heard Sr. to Albert F. Heard, Boston, August 2, 1864; Augustine Heard Sr. to Albert F. Heard, Boston, October 23, 1864, all HN-6-2, HBS.
100. Downs, *The Golden Ghetto*, 39.
101. Albert F. Heard to Mr & Mrs Livingston, Hong Kong, November 24, 1874, HL-5, HBS; George Heard to Augustine Heard Jr., Hong Kong, February 19, 1873, JL-2, HBS.
102. Ghosh, *The Social Condition of the British Community in Bengal*, 119.
103. Marshall, "British Society in India Under the East India Company," 102.
104. Ryan Johnson, "European Cloth and 'Tropical' Skin: Clothing Material and British Ideas of Health and Hygiene in Tropical Climates," *Bulletin of the History of Medicine* 83, no. 3 (2009): 531.
105. Margaret Maynard, *Fashioned from Penury: Dress as Cultural Practice in Colonial Australia* (Cambridge: Cambridge University Press, 1994), 100. See also Johnson, "European Cloth and 'Tropical' Skin," 558; Indrani Sen, "Memsahibs and Health in Colonial Medical Writings, c. 1840 to c. 1930," *South Asia Research* 30, no. 3 (2010): 263–64.
106. Albert F. Heard to his parents, Shanghai, June 23, 1859, HL-33A, HBS; Albert F. Heard to Mary Heard, Hong Kong, June 25, 1874, HL-5, HBS; Hunter, *Gospel of Gentility*, 138–40.
107. Helen Beal to Lizzie Beal, Shanghai, December 4, 1851, Ms N-1818, MHS; Henry Warden to Elizabeth Beal, Hong Kong, June 19, 1859, Ms N-49.55, MHS; Lucy Lord Howes Hooper, Hong Kong, Diaries, 1862–1909, August 31, 1866, Ms N-307, MHS.
108. Albert F. Heard to his parents, Canton, January 3, 1854, HL-1, HBS.

2. A HOUSE IS NOT A HOME

109. Downs, *The Golden Ghetto*, 36.
110. Ruth Bradford, Diary, May 9, 1862, in *"Maskee!" The Journal and Letters of Ruth Bradford, 1861–1872* (Hartford, CT: The Prospect Press, 1938), 83; Francis Blackwell Forbes to his sister, Hong Kong, August 6, 1858, Ms N-49, MHS; Heard, *An Account of His Life*, 127; Rebecca Kinsman to Nathaniel Kinsman, Macao, February 7, 1844, MSS-43, MHS.
111. Munn, *Anglo-China*, 64; additional inventory for "Office House," November 1, 1859, Case 27, HBS.
112. Henrique Caetano Victor de Figueiredo, #37892, Macanese Families; José Miguel Victor de Figueiredo, #22555, Macanese Families; Inácio Pires Pereira Jr., #14702, Macanese Families; Olímpio Augusto da Cruz, #11112, Macanese Families; Francisco António de Seabra, #17407, Macanese Families.
113. Li hetong ren He Gan, Wang Changie, 立合同人何乾, 王昌傑 (Contract for He Gan and Wang Changjie), Hong Kong, 1866, Case 9, HBS.
114. Heard, *An Account of His Life*, 33.
115. Kaori Abe, *Chinese Middlemen in Hong Kong's Colonial Economy, 1830–1890* (Abingdon, UK: Routledge, 2017), 59–66.
116. *Li Hetong Xie Yayu* 立合同謝亞玉 (Contract for Xie Yayu), Hong Kong, 1862, Case 9, HBS.
117. *Li danbao ren Ya Yang* 立擔保人亞楊 (Guarantee for Ya Yang), Hong Kong, 1860, Case 9, HBS; *He Gongsi ding qing Liang Yadian, Wen Yazhang* 喝公司訂請梁亞甸, 溫亞章 (Agreement with Augustine Heard & Co., to Engage Liang Yadian and Wen Yazhang), Hong Kong, 1860, Case 9, HBS; Memo, Agreement Between Augustine Heard & Co. and Akow, Hong Kong, June 7, 1860, Case 9, HBS.
118. See Radhika Mohanram, *Imperial White: Race, Diaspora, and the British Empire* (Minneapolis: University of Minnesota Press, 2007); Ann Laura Stoler, "Making Empire Respectable: The Politics of Race and Sexual Morality in 20th-Century Colonial Cultures," *American Ethnologist* 16, no. 4 (1989): 634–60.
119. Albert F. Heard to his parents, Hong Kong, February 23, 1860, HL-33A, HBS; George Heard, *Diary on Board the U.S.S. Hartford*, 1860, JP-2, HBS, 36–37; Albert F. Heard to Mary Heard, Hong Kong, September 1, 1874, HL-5, HBS; Albert F. Heard, Diary, April 23, 1855, Canton, HP-1, HBS; Heard, *An Account of His Life*, 127; George Heard to Augustine Heard Jr., Hong Kong, June 5, 1873, JL-2, HBS.
120. Carolyn Steedman, *Labours Lost: Domestic Service and the Making of Modern England* (Cambridge: Cambridge University Press, 2009), 16.
121. Lowrie, *Masters and Servants*, 2.
122. Stoler, "Rethinking Colonial Categories," 137–38. See also Noel Ignatiev, *How the Irish Became White* (New York: Routledge, 1995); Eileen P. Scully, *Bargaining with the State from Afar: American Citizenship in Treaty Port China, 1844–1942* (New York: Columbia University Press, 2001).
123. Kate Lowe and Eugene Mclaughlin, "'Caution! The Bread Is Poisoned': The Hong Kong Mass Poisoning of January 1857," *Journal of Imperial and Commonwealth History* 43, no. 2 (2015): 193. See also Norman Etherington, "Colonial Panics Big and Small in the British Empire," in *Anxieties, Fear and Panic in Colonial Settings: Empires on the Verge of a Nervous Breakdown*, ed. Harald Fischer-Tiné (London: Palgrave Macmillan, 2016), 202; Munn, *Anglo-China*, 264, 280.

2. A HOUSE IS NOT A HOME

124. Augustine Heard Jr., *The Poisoning in Hong Kong: An Episode of Life in China Forty Years Ago* (1894), GQ-2-1, HBS, 2, 8; Munn, *Anglo-China*, 208.
125. Heard, *Old China and New*, 32.
126. Bradford, Diary, May 15, 1862, 78; June 7, 1862, 83; June 21, 1862, 87; June 28, 1862, 89; June 9, 1862, 83.
127. Lowrie, *Masters and Servants*, 89.
128. Helen Beal to Thomas Beal, Shanghai, November 9, 1851, Ms N-1818, MHS.
129. Ruth Bradford to her father, Shanghai, January 7, 1871, Ms N-49.6, MHS.
130. Francis B. Forbes to his sister, Hong Kong, August 6, 1858, Ms N-49, MHS.
131. J. Heard, *An Account of His Life*, 118.
132. Munn, *Anglo-China*, 280.
133. Albert F. Heard to his parents, Hong Kong, May 13, 1859, HL-33A; Albert F. Heard to Augustine Heard Sr., Hong Kong, May 16, 1859, HL-33A, HBS; Albert F. Heard to his parents, Hong Kong, January 29, 1860, HL-33A, HBS; George Heard to Augustine Heard Jr., Hong Kong, February 19, 1873, JL-2, HBS.
134. George Heard to his parents, Hong Kong, May 18, 1859, JL-1, HBS; Albert F. Heard to Henry Livingston, Hong Kong, February 27, 1873, HL-49, HBS; John Heard to Leverett, Boston, March 7, 1893, FN-1-4, HBS; Heard, *An Account of His Life*, 124.
135. Albert F. Heard to his parents, Shanghai, June 23, 1859, HL-33A, HBS; George Heard to Albert F. Heard, Hong Kong, March 28, 1873, JL-2, HBS; George Heard to Augustine Heard Jr., Hong Kong, February 25, 1873, JL-2, HBS.
136. Heard, *An Account of His Life*, 124.
137. Francus, *Monstrous Motherhood*, 2.
138. Davidoff and Hall, *Family Fortunes*, 151.
139. Anne Summers, "British Women and Cultures of Internationalism, c. 1815–1914," in *Structures and Transformations in Modern British History*, ed. David Feldman and Jon Lawrence (Cambridge: Cambridge University Press, 2011), 187, 189.
140. Mills, *Gender and Colonial Space*, 32. See also Gayatri Chakravorty Spivak, "Can the Subaltern Speak?" in *Marxism and the Interpretation of Culture*, ed. Lawrence Grossberg and Cary Nelson (Urbana: University of Illinois Press, 1988), 296–97.
141. Mittapalli and Roye, "Introduction," 8–9.
142. Ellen Coolidge to "Mrs John M. Forbes," Macao, January 7, 1841, Ms N-2404, MHS; Rebecca Kinsman to Nathaniel Kinsman, Macao, January 27, 1844, MSS-43, PEM.
143. Rachel Tamar Van, "The 'Woman Pigeon': Gendered Bonds and Barriers in the Anglo-American Commercial Community in Canton and Macao, 1800–1849," *Pacific Historical Review* 83, no. 4 (2014): 567, 578, 580, 587.
144. Peter Parker to Maria Fay, December 23, 1842, as quoted in Van, "The 'Woman Pigeon,'" 587.
145. Heard, *Old China and New*, 43.
146. Albert F. Heard to Capron, Canton, January 5, 1854, HL-1, HBS; Albert F. Heard to his parents, Shanghai, June 23, 1859, HL-33A, HBS.
147. Albert F. Heard to Gray, Hong Kong, January 14, 1860, HL-33A, HBS; Heard, *Old China and New*, 15; George Heard to Augustine Heard Jr., Hong Kong, March 19, 1873, JL-2, HBS.
148. George Dixwell to John Heard, Hong Kong, December 10, 1871, FM-13-1, HBS.
149. Stoler, "Rethinking Colonial Categories," 154.

2. A HOUSE IS NOT A HOME

150. Marshall, "British Society in India Under the East India Company," 114. See also Emma Jinhua Teng, *Eurasian: Mixed Identities in the United States, China, and Hong Kong, 1842–1943* (Berkley: University of California Press, 2013).
151. John Heard to Charles Brown, September 26, 1844, as cited in Van, "The 'Woman Pigeon,'" 582.
152. Personal correspondence with Lam's descendants, May 30, 2022; Carl T. Smith, "Abandoned Into Prosperity: Women on the Fringe of Expatriate Society," in *Merchants' Daughters: Women, Commerce, and Regional Culture in South China*, ed. Helen F. Siu (Hong Kong: Hong Kong University Press, 2010), 134.
153. John Heard to Messrs. Augustine Heard & Co., Hong Kong, November 1, 1862, Case 28, HBS.
154. John Heard, Will, Hong Kong, 1862, Case 28, HBS.
155. Van, "The 'Woman Pigeon,'" 582.
156. Charles Sargent Dixwell, Massachusetts, United States, 1889, "United States Passport Applications, 1795–1925," FamilySearch, http://FamilySearch.org. See Thomas N. Layton, *The "Other" Dixwells: Commerce and Conscience in an American Family* (Germantown, PA: Society for Historical Archaeology, 2021), 483; Charles S. Dixwell and Harriet G. Arnold Williams, September 16, 1897, "Massachusetts Marriages, 1841–1915," FamilySearch.
157. George Heard to Augustine Heard Jr., Hong Kong, May 30, 1873, JL-2, HBS. Given the context of the letter, it is unclear which "Fearon" George Heard is referencing.
158. Albert F. Heard to Fred, Canton, January 15, 1854, JL-1, HBS; Albert F. Heard to Josh, Canton, January 5, 1854, JL-1, HBS.
159. Stoler, "Rethinking Colonial Categories," 141.
160. Lowrie, *Masters and Servants*, 105.
161. Robert Bickers, *China Bound: John Swire & Sons and Its World, 1816–1980* (London: Bloomsbury, 2020), 124.
162. Heard, *An Account of His Life*, 164; George Heard to Augustine Heard Jr., Hong Kong, February 19, 1873, JL-2, HBS; Albert F. Heard to John Heard, Hong Kong, June 10, 1873, HL-49, HBS; Albert F. Heard to Henry Livingston, Hong Kong, October 28, 1874, HL-5, HBS; Francis B. Forbes to Isabel Forbes, Hong Kong, April 10, 1874, Ms N-49, MHS.
163. George Heard to Albert F. Heard, Hong Kong, March 23, 1873, JL-2, HBS; George Heard to John Heard, Hong Kong, June 9, 1873, JL-2, HBS.
164. Rebecca Kinsman, to Nathaniel Kinsman, Macao, February 16, 1844; Rebecca Kinsman to Nathaniel Kinsman, Macao, February 29, 1844; Rebecca Kinsman to Nathaniel Kinsman, Macao, December 4, 1844; Rebecca Kinsman to Nathaniel Kinsman, Macao, November 28, 1844, all MSS-43, PEM.
165. See Annual Administration Reports for 1860 and 1870, in *Hong Kong Annual Administration Reports 1841–1941: vol. 1, 1841–1886*, ed. R. L. Jarman (London: Archive Edition, 1996), 265–67, 332–90.

3. LIVES LIVED IN PUBLIC

1. Elisa Tamarkin, *Anglophilia: Deference, Devotion, and Antebellum America* (Chicago: University of Chicago Press, 2008), 118.

3. LIVES LIVED IN PUBLIC

2. Martin Burke, *The Conundrum of Class: Public Discourse on the Social Order in America* (Chicago: University of Chicago Press, 1995), 22.
3. William A. Link, "Southerners Abroad: Europe and the Cultural Encounter, 1830–1895," in *The U.S. South and Europe: Transatlantic Relations in the Nineteenth and Twentieth Centuries*, ed. Cornelis A. van Minnen and Manfred Berg (Lexington: University of Kentucky Press, 2013), 18.
4. James Fichter, *So Great a Proffit: How the East Indies Trade Transformed Anglo-American Capitalism* (Cambridge, MA: Harvard University Press, 2010), 280; Nell Irvin Painter, "Thinking About the Languages of Money and Race: A Response to Michael O'Malley, 'Specie and Species,'" *American Historical Review* 99, no. 2 (1994): 402; Stephen Rice, *Minding the Machine: Languages of Class in Early Industrial America* (Berkeley: University of California Press, 2004), 5.
5. Jacques Downs, *The Golden Ghetto: The American Commercial Community at Canton and the Shaping of American China Policy, 1784–1844* (London: Associated University Press, 1997), 229.
6. Noam Maggor, *Brahmin Capitalism: Frontiers of Wealth and Populism in America's First Gilded Age* (Cambridge, MA: Harvard University Press, 2017), 10.
7. Paul Goodman, "Ethics and Enterprise: The Values of a Boston Elite, 1800–1860," *American Quarterly* 18, no. 3 (1996): 348; Ross McKibbin, *Class and Cultures: England 1918–1951* (Oxford: Oxford University Press, 1998), 3; Emma Goldsmith, "In Trade: Wealthy Business Families in Glasgow and Liverpool" (PhD diss., Northwestern University, 2017), 247.
8. Tamarkin, *Anglophilia*, 253–55; Edward L. Glaeser, "Reinventing Boston: 1630–2003," *Journal of Economic Geography* 5 (2005): 126.
9. Stephen Tuffnell, *Made in Britain: Nation and Emigration in Nineteenth-Century America* (Berkeley: University of California Press, 2020), 19.
10. Linda Colley, *Britons: Forging the Nation, 1707–1837* (New Haven, CT: Yale University Press, 2005), 365–68.
11. Peter Mandler, *The English National Character: The History of an Idea from Edmund Burke to Tony Blaire* (New Haven, CT: Yale University Press, 2006), 17.
12. Elizabeth Sinn, "Introduction," in *Meeting Place: Encounters Across Cultures in Hong Kong, 1841–1984*, ed. Elizabeth Sinn and Christopher Munn (Hong Kong: Hong Kong University Press, 2017), ix–x.
13. "Calling," *China Punch*, May 31, 1873.
14. Eadaoin Agnew, *Imperial Women Writers in Victorian India: Representing Colonial Life, 1850–1910* (Basingstoke, UK: Palgrave Macmillan, 2016), 171.
15. "Calling," *China Punch*, May 31, 1873.
16. Richard L. Bushman, *The Refinement of America: Persons, Houses, Cities* (New York: Knopf, 1992), 404.
17. Paul Goodman, "Ethics and Enterprise," 441–42.
18. Helen Beal to Thomas P. Beal, Shanghai, December 1850, Ms N-1818, MHS.
19. Ruth Bradford, Diary, May 2, 1862, in *"Maskee!" The Journal and Letters of Ruth Bradford, 1861–1872* (Hartford, CT: The Prospect Press, 1938), 75.
20. Bradford, Diary, August 12, 1862, 101; August 22, 1862, 104.
21. Bradford, Diary, April 20, 1862, 70.
22. Elizabeth Buettner, *Empire Families: Britons and Late Imperial India* (Oxford: Oxford University Press, 2004), 6; Harald Fischer-Tiné, " 'White Women

3. LIVES LIVED IN PUBLIC

Degrading Themselves to the Lowest Depths': European Networks of Prostitution and Colonial Anxieties in British India and Ceylon ca. 1880–1914," *Indian Economic and Social History Review* 40, no. 2 (2003): 166. See also Inderpal Grewal, *Home and Harem: Nation, Gender, Empire, and the Cultures of Travel* (Durham, NC: Duke University Press, 1996).

23. Phillipa Levine, "Introduction: Why Gender and Empire?" in *Gender and Empire*, ed. Phillipa Levine (Oxford: Oxford University Press, 2004), 10.
24. Sara Mills, *Gender and Colonial Space* (Manchester: Manchester University Press, 2009), 37.
25. "The Extravagant Woman," *China Mail*, May 16, 1861; "Tasteless Woman—Reprinted from the London Review," *China Mail*, May 16, 1861; "Women in Our Colonies," *China Mail*, November 27, 1862; "Household Life in America," *China Mail*, August 27, 1863; "Female Values," *China Mail*, January 19, 1865.
26. Albert F. Heard to Everett, Hong Kong, November 28, 1872, HL-48, HBS; *Hong Kong Annual Administration Reports, 1841–1941: vol 1, 1841–1886*, ed. R. L. Jarman (Hong Kong: Archive Editions, 1996), 265, 332.
27. Albert F. Heard to Mary Heard, Hong Kong, June 13, 1874, HL-5, HBS; Albert F. Heard to Mary Heard, Hong Kong, June 25, 1874, HL-5, HBS; Albert F. Heard to Jane Heard, Hong Kong, December 18, 1872, HL-48, HBS; Albert F. Heard to Henry Livingston, Hong Kong, February 11, 1873, HL-48, HBS.
28. See "A. Heard & Co., Letters Sent—1874–1875," HL-5, HBS. See also Thomas R. Warren, *Dust and Foam: Or, Three Oceans and Two Continents; Being Ten Years' Wanderings in the East and West Indies, China, Philippines, Australia, and Polynesia* (New York: C. Scribner & S. Low, 1859), 292.
29. Albert F. Heard to Jane Heard, Hong Kong, December 18, 1872, HL-48, HBS; Albert F. Heard to his brothers, Hong Kong, December 25, 1872, HL-48, HBS; Ruth Bradford to her father, Shanghai, January 7, 1871, Ms N-49.6, MHS; Helen Beal to "Lizzie," Shanghai, June 11, 1851, Ms N-1818, MHS; Helen Beal to Elizabeth Beal, Shanghai, March 9, 1851, Ms N-1818, MHS.
30. James M. Howe Jr., "George Rogers Hall, Lover of Plants," *Journal of the Arnold Arboretum* 4, no. 2 (1923): 91.
31. Hooper, December 28, 1866, Hong Kong, Diaries, Ms N-307, MHS.
32. Thomas H. Cox, " 'Money, Credit, and Strong Friends': Warren Delano II and the Importance of Social Networking in the Old China Trade," in *The Private Side of the Canton Trade, 1700–1840: Beyond the Companies*, ed. Paul A. Van Dyke and Susan E. Schopp (Hong Kong: Hong Kong University Press, 2018), 135.
33. George Dixwell to Augustine Heard Sr., Canton, November 17, 1844, EM-3-2, HBS; George Dixwell to Augustine Heard Sr., Canton, March 19, 1845, EM-3-2, HBS; John Heard, *An Account of His Life and the History of Augustine Heard & Co.*, 1891, FP-4, HBS, 51.
34. Robert Bennet Forbes to Rose Forbes, Canton, January 25, 1839, in *Letters from China: The Canton-Boston Correspondence of Robert Bennet Forbes, 1838–1840*, ed. Phyllis Forbes Kerr (Mystic, CT: Mystic Seaport Museum, 1996), 89.
35. Dwijendra Tripathi, *The Oxford History of Indian Business* (New Delhi: Oxford University Press, 2004), 83.
36. See Paula Hastings, " 'Our Glorious Anglo-Saxon Race Shall Ever Fill Earth's Highest Place': The Anglo-Saxon and the Construction of Identity in

3. LIVES LIVED IN PUBLIC

Late-Nineteenth-Century Canada," in *Canada and the British World: Culture, Migration, and Identity*, ed. Phillip Buckner and R. Douglas Francis (Vancouver: University of British Columbia Press, 2006), 93–107.
37. Benjamin Ball, *Rambles in Eastern Asia, Including China and Manila: During Several Years Residence* (Boston: James French & Company, 1855), 91.
38. May-bo Ching, "Chopsticks or Cutlery? How Canton Hong Merchants Entertained Foreign Guests in the Eighteenth and Nineteenth Centuries," in *Narratives of Free Trade: The Commercial Cultures of Early US-China Relations*, ed. Kendall Johnson (Hong Kong: Hong Kong University Press), 106.
39. Ching, "Chopsticks or Cutlery?" 112.
40. Elizabeth Beal to "Julia," Shanghai, June 10, 1870, Ms N-49.55, MHS.
41. Ball, *Rambles in East Asia*, 207.
42. John Murray Forbes to his father, Hong Kong, January 31, 1868, Ms N-156, MHS.
43. Elizabeth Beal to "Julia," Shanghai, March 25, 1870, Ms N-49.55, MHS; Helen Beal to Thomas Beal, Shanghai, April 1, 1852, Ms N-1818, MHS; Ruth Bradford to her father, Shanghai, October 23, 1871, Ms N-49.6, MHS; Albert F. Heard to John Heard, Hong Kong, June 10, 1873, HL-49, HBS.
44. Andrea Greenwood and Mark W. Harris, *An Introduction to the Unitarian and Universalist Traditions* (Cambridge: Cambridge University Press, 2011), 60.
45. Glaeser, *Reinventing Boston*, 125; Tuffnell, *Made in Britain*, 30.
46. Goodman, "Ethics and Enterprise," 446, 452.
47. Augustine Heard Sr. to John Heard, Canton, January 26, 1841, FM-1-1, HBS; Augustine Heard Sr. to John Heard, Boston, December 13, 1844, FM-1-1, HBS; Augustine Heard Sr. to Albert F. Heard, Boston, May 10, 1864, HN-6-2, HBS; Heard, *An Account of His Life*, 19.
48. Harald Fischer-Tiné, "'The Drinking Habits of Our Countrymen': European Alcohol Consumption and Colonial Power in British India," *Journal of Imperial and Commonwealth History* 40, no. 3 (2012): 386; James M. Volo and Dorothy Deneen Volo, *Family Life in 17th and 18th Century America* (Westport, CT: Greenwood Press, 2006), 17–18.
49. Jane Hunter, *The Gospel of Gentility: American Women Missionaries in Turn-of-the-Century China* (New Haven, CT: Yale University Press, 1984), 169.
50. Gregory Anderson, *Victorian Clerks* (Manchester: Manchester University Press, 1976), 41.
51. Helen Beal to Elizabeth Beal, Shanghai, May 25, 1851, Ms N-1818, MHS.
52. Albert F. Heard to Augustine Heard Jr., Hong Kong, April 25, 1873, HL-49, HBS.
53. "There Is a Giant in Hong Kong," *China Mail*, September 18, 1862; "To the Editor of 'China Mail,'" *China Mail*, September 24, 1862.
54. Tamarkin, *Anglophilia*, 255.
55. Elsie van Nederveen Meerkerk, "Introduction: Domestic Work in the Colonial Context: Race, Color, and Power in the Household," in *Towards a Global History of Domestic and Caregiving Workers*, ed. Dirk Hoerder, Elsie van Nederveen Meerkerk, and S. Neunsinger (Leiden: Brill, 2015), 246.
56. Christopher Munn, "Hong Kong, 1841–1870: All the Servants in Prison and Nobody to Take Care of the House," in *Masters, Servants and Magistrates in Britain and the Empire, 1562–1955*, ed. Douglas Hay and Paul Craven (Chapel Hill: University of North Carolina Press, 2004), 369–70.

3. LIVES LIVED IN PUBLIC

57. Claire Lowrie, *Masters and Servants: Cultures of Empire in the Tropics* (Manchester: Manchester University Press, 2016), 71–72.
58. Kristina Booker, *Menials: Domestic Service and the Cultural Transformation of British Society, 1650–1850* (Lewisburg, PA: Bucknell University Press, 2017), 3–5.
59. Munn, "Hong Kong, 1851–1870," 376; Lowrie, *Masters and Servants*, 2.
60. Martha Green, Hong Kong, Journal, December 1, 1863, Ms N-49.30, MHS.
61. Christopher Munn, *Anglo-China: Chinese People and British Rule in Hong Kong, 1841–1880* (London: Routledge, 2001), 339.
62. Green, Hong Kong, Journal, December 1, 1863.
63. Ball, *Rambles in East Asia*, 215; William M. Wood, *Fankwei: Or, the San Jacinto in the Seas of India, China, and Japan* (New York: Harper & Brothers, 1859), 267.
64. Jeffrey A. Auerbach, *Imperial Boredom: Monotony and the British Empire* (Oxford: Oxford University Press, 2018), 181.
65. Robert Bickers, *The Scramble for China: Foreign Devils in the Qing Empire, 1932–1914* (Sydney: Allen Lane, 2011), 162–63; John M. Carroll, *Edge of Empires: Chinese Elites and British Colonials in Hong Kong* (Cambridge, MA: Harvard University Press, 2005), 27; Bryna Goodman, "Improvisations on a Semi Colonial Theme: Or, How to Read a Celebration of Transnational Urban Community," *Journal of Asian Studies* 59, no. 4 (2000): 899.
66. Satoshi Mizutani, *The Meaning of White: Race, Class, and the "Domiciled Community" in British India, 1858–1930* (Oxford: Oxford Historical Monographs, 2011), 46–48.
67. "With Regard to the Praya," *China Mail*, July 17, 1862; Robert Fortune, *Three Years' Wanderings in the Northern Provinces of China, Including a Visit to the Tea, Silk, and Cotton Countries: With an Account of the Agriculture and Horticulture of the Chinese, New Plants, etc.* (London: John Murray, 1847), 17.
68. Stacilee Ford, *Troubling American Women: Narratives of Gender and Nation in Hong Kong* (Hong Kong: Hong Kong University Press, 2011), 53.
69. Eileen P. Scully, "Prostitution as Privilege: The 'American Girl' of Treaty-Port Shanghai, 1860–1937," *International History Review* 20, no. 4 (1998), 856–57.
70. Ian Haney Lopez, *White by Law: The Legal Construction of Race* (New York: New York University Press, 1996), 1.
71. See Harald Fischer-Tiné, ed., *Anxieties, Fear, and Panic in Colonial Settings: Empires on the Verge of a Nervous Breakdown* (Cham, Switzerland: Palgrave Macmillan, 2016).
72. Francis Wood, *No Dogs and Not Many Chinese: Treaty Port Life in China, 1843–1943* (London: John Murray, 1998), 120.
73. "Cricket," *China Mail*, January 23, 1862.
74. Bradford, Diary, July 3, 1862, 90; July 4, 1862, 90. See Coleman Hutchison, "Whistling 'Dixie' for the Union (Nation, Anthem, Revision)," *American Literary History* 19, no. 3 (2007): 604.
75. "The Fourth of July, reprinted from *The Times*," *China Mail*, September 4, 1862.
76. "The Fourth of July in Shanghai," *Hong Kong Daily Press*, July 10, 1873; "The Fourth of July at Canton," *China Mail*, July 6, 1877.
77. "The Fourth of July," *China Mail*, July 7, 1868.
78. "Hongkong, July 4th, 1876," *Hong Kong Daily Press*, July 4, 1873.

3. LIVES LIVED IN PUBLIC

79. W. Wetton & Co., Bill for services, Hong Kong, April 1870, Case 28, HBS; T. E. Hawkins, Veterinary Bill, Hong Kong, 1873, Case 4, HBS; James Murray Forbes, *Dogs and Horses*, 1921, Ms N-49.67, MHS.
80. Augustine Heard Sr., to Albert F. Heard, Boston, October 24, 1861, HN-6-2, HBS; Augustine Heard Sr., to Albert F. Heard, Boston, December 9, 1861, HN-6-2, HBS; Albert F. Heard to Henry Livingston, Hong Kong, November 24, 1874, HL-5, HBS; Albert F. Heard to Henry Livingston, Hong Kong, May 15, 1873, HL-49, HBS; Ruth Bradford to her brother, Hong Kong, December 6, 1870, Ms N-49.6, MHS.
81. Light Litterateur, "Two Weeks Before the Races," *China Mail*, February 12, 1863.
82. Vaudine England, *Kindred Spirits: A History of the Hong Kong Club* (Hong Kong: Hong Kong Club, 2016), 42.
83. Indira Ghose, "The Memsahib Myth: Englishwomen in Colonial India," in *Women & Others: Perspectives on Race, Gender, and Empire*, ed. Celia R. Daileader and Rhoda E. Johnson (Basingstoke, UK: Palgrave Macmillan, 2007), 114; Wood, *No Dogs and Not Many Chinese*, 120; Norman Edwards, *The Singapore House and Residential Life, 1819–1939* (Oxford: Oxford University Press, 1990), 102; Catherine Hall, *Civilising Subjects: Metropole and Colony in the English Imagination, 1830–1867* (Chicago: University of Chicago Press, 2002), 65.
84. Downs, *The Golden Ghetto*, 233.
85. Tamarkin, *Anglophilia*, 254.
86. George B. Kirsch, "The Fate of Cricket in the United States: Revisited," *Journal of Sport History* 43, no. 2 (2016): 171.
87. See John M. Forbes, Keechong Club Records, 1879–1888, Ms N-49.67, MHS. "Keechong" is a transliteration of Russell & Co.'s Chinese name.
88. Wai-kwan Chan, *The Making of Hong Kong Society: Three Studies of Class Formation in Early Hong Kong* (Oxford: Clarendon Press, 1991), 35.
89. *The Directory & Chronicle for China, Japan, & The Philippines* (Hong Kong: Daily Press, 1868), 133–35.
90. England, *Kindred Spirits*, 11.
91. Heard, *An Account of His Life*, 76.
92. James M. Forbes, Keechong Club Records, 1879–1888, Ms N-49.67, MHS.
93. "Happy Thoughts," *China Punch*, November 8, 1867; "More 'Scotland Yet,'" *China Punch*, December 9, 1867.
94. England, *Kindred Spirits*, 44.
95. "St. Andrew's Dinner," *China Mail*, December 15, 1864.
96. "Response from the Editor," *China Mail*, August 1, 1861.
97. Dominic Malcolm, *Globalizing Cricket: Englishness, Empire and Identity* (London: Bloomsbury Academic, 2013); Laurent Dubois, "Diffusion and Empire," *The Oxford Handbook of Sports History*, ed. Robert Edelman and Wayne Wilson (Oxford: Oxford University Press, 2017), 171–78; Ronojoy Sen, *Nation at Play: A History of Sport in India* (New York: Columbia University Press, 2015), 55.
98. "Annual Regatta," *China Mail*, November 3, 1864; Heard, *An Account of His Life*, 54; Canton Fahkee Boat Club, 1843–1847, Case 29, HBS.
99. "Victoria Regatta, 1873," *Hong Kong Daily Press*, December 6, 1873.
100. *Chronicle & Directory for China, Japan, the Philippines &c.* (Hong Kong: Daily Press Office, 1874), 133–35.

101. Austin Coates, *China Races* (Hong Kong: Hong Kong University Press, 1983), 67.
102. "Hong Kong Races," *China Mail*, February 20, 1862. See Downs, *The Golden Ghetto*, 53.
103. Albert F. Heard to Henry Livingston, Hong Kong, February 27, 1873, HL-49, HBS.
104. Alethea Appleby Moller to "Friend," February 11, 1873, Ms N-49.55, MHS.
105. Elizabeth Beal to "Julia," Shanghai, March 25, 1870, MHS; Elizabeth Beal to "Julia," Shanghai, January 23, 1871; Elizabeth Beal to "Julia," Shanghai, February 20, 1871, all Ms 49.55, MHS.
106. Dao Zi Huang, "'You May Go to Hong Kong for Me': British Views of a Chinese Colony" (PhD diss., University of Hong Kong, 2018), 143.
107. Coates, *China Races*, 70; "Sketches in China—Hong-Kong Races, 1858," *Illustrated London News*, May 15, 1858.
108. "Peep O' Day on the Hong Kong Races," *China Mail*, February 27, 1862.
109. Coates, *China Races*, 71.
110. "Peep O' Day on the Hong Kong Races."
111. Albert F. Heard to his parents, Hong Kong, February 23, 1860, HL-33, HBS.
112. Coates, *China Races*, 71.
113. Heard, *An Account of His Life*, 172.
114. Albert F. Heard to his parents, Hong Kong, February 23, 1860, HL-33A, HBS. In writing "Congalese," Heard likely meant Sinhalese.
115. Douglas Lorimer, "From Victorian Values to White Virtues: Assimilation and Exclusion in British Racial Discourse, c. 1870–1914," in *Rediscovering the British World*, ed. Phillip Buckner and R. Douglas Francis (Calgary: University of Calgary Press, 2005), 111.
116. Tamarkin, *Anglophilia*, xxviii.
117. Nell Irvine Painter, *The History of White People* (New York: Norton, 2010), 174–75.
118. Bluford Adams, "World Conquerors or a Dying People? Racial Theory, Regional Anxiety, and Brahmin Anglo-Saxonists," *Journal of the Gilded Age and Progressive Era* 8, no. 2 (2009): 192.
119. Painter, *The History of White People*, 201; Noel Ignatiev, *How the Irish Became White* (New York: Routledge, 1995), 186–87. For a necessary counterpoint, see Radhika Mohanram, *Imperial White: Race, Diaspora, and the British Empire* (Minneapolis: University of Minnesota Press, 2007), xvi.
120. Carroll Smith-Rosenberg, *This Violent Empire: The Birth of an American National Identity* (Chapel Hill: University of North Carolina Press, 2010), 33.
121. Stacey Robertson, "'On the Side of Righteousness': Women, the Church, and Abolition," in *Women, Dissent, and Anti-Slavery in Britain and America, 1790–1865*, ed. Elizabeth J. Clapp and Julie Roy Jeffrey (Oxford: Oxford University Press, 2011), 157.
122. Carl T. Smith, *Chinese Christians: Elites, Middlemen, and the Church in Hong Kong* (Oxford: Oxford University Press, 1985), 3.
123. Stuart Wolfendale, *Imperial to International: A History of St. John's Cathedral Hong Kong* (Hong Kong: Hong Kong University Press, 2013), 39.
124. Bradford, Diary, August 3, 1862, 99; David Cheung, *Christianity in China: The Making of the First Native Protestant Church* (Leiden: Brill, 2004), 284; Gerald Francis De Jong, *The Reformed Church in China, 1842–1951* (Grand Rapids, MI: Eerdmans, 1992), 54.

3. LIVES LIVED IN PUBLIC

125. Ruth Bradford to "Dinny," Hong Kong, December 6, 1870; Ira Crowell to Mr Bradford, Hong Kong, December 5, 1870, both Ms N-49.6, MHS.
126. Oliver Wendell Holmes, *Elsie Venner: A Romance of Destiny* (Boston: Houghton Mifflin, 1861), 412.
127. Helen Beal to Elizabeth Beal, Shanghai, May 14, 1842, Ms N-1818, MHS; Helen Beal to her parents, Shanghai, March 21, 1852, Ms N-1818, MHS; Bradford, Diary, June 1, 1862, 81.
128. Helen Beal to Thomas P. Beal, Shanghai, c. December 1850, Ms N-1818, MHS; Helen Beal to Thomas P. Beal, Shanghai, April 1, 1852, Ms N-1818, MHS; Elizabeth Beal to "Julia," Shanghai, March 25, 1870, Ms N-49.55, MHS; Hooper, December 28, 1866, Hong Kong, Diaries, Ms N-307, MHS; Helen Beal to Thomas Beal, Shanghai, April 1, 1852, Ms N-1818, MHS. See Tuffnell, *Made in Britain*, 75.
129. For an example, using French printers, of how to unpack historical humor, see Robert Darnton, *The Great Cat Massacre: and Other Episodes in French Cultural History* (New York: Basic Books, 1984), 6. See also Joan Judge, "Review: The Power of Print? Print Capitalism and News Media in Late Qing and Republican China," *Harvard Journal of Asiatic Studies* 66, no. 1 (2006): 233–54, which, focusing on texts produced by Chinese writers for Chinese readers at the turn of the twentieth century, reviews Barbara Mittler's *A Newspaper for China* and Christopher Reed's *Gutenberg in Shanghai*, drawing attention to methodological considerations for the study of print media; Christopher G. Rea, "'He'll Roast All Subjects That May Need the Roasting': Puck and Mr Punch in Nineteenth-Century China," in *Asian Punches: A Transcultural Affair*, ed. Hans Harder and Barbara Mittler (Heidelberg: Springer, 2013), 394.
130. "Introductory Edition," *China Punch*, April 24, 1867.
131. Francis B. Forbes to Isabel Forbes, Hong Kong, April 10, 1874, Ms N-49.77, MHS. Forbes is likely referring to the Hong Kong Attorney General John Bramston and his wife Eliza Isabella Russell.
132. *China Punch*, June 28, 1875.
133. "Exchange," *China Punch*, November 18, 1873.
134. "Notice," *China Punch*, February 1873.
135. *The China Directory* (Hong Kong: The China Mail Office, 1874), 189.
136. "A Song in #G," *China Punch*, May 25, 1874.
137. "Abstract," *China Punch*, June 11, 1867; "Hongkong, Canton, & Macao Steam Ferry Company," *China Punch*, May 2, 1874; "Hongkong, Canton, and Macao Steamboat Company Ltd.," *China Punch*, November 21, 1874.
138. "Our Uncle," *China Punch*, April 28, 1875.
139. William Henry Wills, "The Uncles of England," *Punch, or The London Charivari*, January–June 1845; W. H. Wills in M. H. Spielmann, *The History of "Punch"* (London: Cassell and Company Ltd., 1895), 283.
140. "To China Traders, Cordial Chinese, and Others," *China Punch*, June 28, 1875, as formatted in the paper.
141. Prescott Clarke and Frank H. H. King, *A Research Guide to China-Coast Newspapers, 1822–1911* (Cambridge, MA: Harvard University Press, 1965), 6. See also Yizheng Zou, "English Newspapers in British Colonial Hong Kong: The Case of the *South China Morning Post* (1903–1941)," *Critical Arts* 29, no. 1 (2015): 26–40.

3. LIVES LIVED IN PUBLIC

142. See "Punch's Essence of Parliament," *Punch, or The London Charivari*, April 6, 1867; "American Slangography," February 5, 1870; "American Outspeaking," December 24, 1870; "The Price of Peace," September 20, 1873.
143. See Stephen Tuffnell, "'The International Siamese Twins': The Iconography of Anglo-American Inter-Imperialism," in *Comic Empires: Imperialism in Cartoons, Caricature, and Satirical Art*, ed. Richard Scully and Andrekos Varnava (Manchester: Manchester University Press, 2019), 93, for how *Punch*-inspired illustrations in America articulated both Anglo-American imperial reciprocity and American Anglophobia.
144. "Abstract," *China Punch*, June 11, 1867.
145. "A 'Special' Donkey," *China Punch*, August 10, 1867.
146. Joseph Conforti, *Imagining New England: Explorations of Regional Identity from the Pilgrims to the Mid-Twentieth Century* (Chapel Hill: University of North Carolina Press, 2001), 124, 154.
147. "The Condensed Directory of Hwang-Kwang," *China Punch*, May 25, 1874.
148. Clarke, King, *A Research Guide to China-Coast Newspapers*, 6, 62.
149. "Editorial," *China Mail*, December 25, 1856.
150. "Emerson on English Character," *China Mail*, February 19, 1857; "Household Life in America," *China Mail*, August 27, 1863.
151. "The Fourth of July—From the Times," *China Mail*, September 4, 1862.
152. Chandrika Kaul, *Reporting the Raj: The British Press and India, c. 1880–1922* (Manchester: Manchester University Press, 2003), 8–9.
153. For similar eighteenth-century concerns, see Emma Rothschild, *The Inner Life of Empires: An Eighteenth-Century History* (Princeton, NJ: Princeton University Press, 2011), 177.
154. Helen Beal to Thomas P. Beal, Shanghai, December 1850, Ms N-1818, MHS.
155. Indrani Sen, *Gendered Transactions: The White Woman in Colonial India, c. 1820–1930* (Manchester: Manchester University Press, 2017), 9.
156. "Poem to Alexis," *China Punch*, March 22, 1873; Althea Appleby Moller to "Friend," Shanghai, March 11, 1873, Ms 49.55, MHS.
157. Francis B. Forbes to Isabel Forbes, Hong Kong, April 10, 1874, Ms N-49.77, MHS.
158. Sen, *Gendered Transactions*, 5.
159. Albert F. Heard to John Heard, Paris, 10 January 1880, HN-3-1, HBS.
160. Nancy F. Cott, "Divorce and the Changing Status of Women in Eighteenth-Century Massachusetts," *William and Mary Quarterly* 33, no. 4 (1976): 109, 114.
161. Robert B. Forbes, *Personal Reminiscences*, 2nd ed. (Boston: Little, Brown, and Company, 1882), 378. See also Thomas F. Waters, *Augustine Heard and His Friends* (Salem, MA: Newcomb & Gauss, 1916).

4. MISSED OPPORTUNITIES

1. "'Extract,' *China Mail*, July 5, 1871," in David H. Bailey to Bancroft Davis, Hong Kong, July 4, 1871, vol. 7, NARA.
2. "The Fourth of July—Reprinted from *The Times*," *China Mail*, September 4, 1862; "The Fourth of July," *China Mail*, July 7, 1868.
3. David H. Bailey to Bancroft Davis, Hong Kong, July 4, 1871, vol. 7, NARA.

4. MISSED OPPORTUNITIES

4. "Extract."
5. Geneva Arbitration Tribunal, *Papers Relating to the Treaty of Washington, vol. 4, Geneva Arbitration* (Washington, DC: U.S. Government Printing Office, 1872), 8.
6. Akira Iriye, *Global and Transnational History: The Past, Present, and Future* (Basingstoke, UK: Palgrave Macmillan, 2013), 11; Chris Bayly et al., "AHR Conversation: On Transnational History," *American Historical Review* 111, no. 5 (2006): 1446.
7. Ann Laura Stoler, *Duress: Imperial Durabilities in Our Time* (Durham, NC: Duke University Press, 2016), 198.
8. Bernard Attard and Andrew Dilley, "Finance, Empire and the British World," *Journal of Imperial and Commonwealth History* 41, no. 1 (2013): 6. See also Gary Magee and Andrew Thompson, *Empire and Globalisation: Networks of People, Goods and Capital in the British World, c. 1850–1914* (Cambridge: Cambridge University Press, 2010), 14; Dominic Sachsenmaier, "Global History and Critiques of Western Perspectives," *Comparative Education* 42, no. 3 (2006): 462.
9. See John S. Galbraith, *Reluctant Empire: British Policy on the South African Frontier, 1834–1854* (Berkeley: University of California Press, 1963), 21.
10. Song-chuan Chen, *Merchants of War and Peace: British Knowledge of China in the Making of the Opium War* (Hong Kong: Hong Kong University Press, 2017), 8.
11. Dael Norwood, "Trading in Liberty: The Politics of the American China Trade, c. 1784–1862" (PhD diss., Princeton University, 2012), 268, 269.
12. Chen, *Merchants of War and Peace*, 138–40; Gordan H. Chang, *Fateful Ties: A History of America's Preoccupation with China* (Cambridge, MA: Harvard University Press, 2015), 28.
13. Stoler, *Duress*, 186. See also Teemu Ruskola, "Canton Is Not Boston: The Invention of American Imperial Sovereignty," *American Quarterly* 57, no. 3 (2005): 861.
14. Michal Gobat, "'Our Indian Empire': The Transimperial Origins of U.S. Liberal Imperialism," in *Crossing Empires: Taking U.S. History Into Transimperial Terrain*, ed. Kristin L. Hoganson and Jay Sexton (Durham, NC: Duke University Press, 2020), 71–72. See also Anthony Hopkins, *American Empire: A Global History* (Princeton, NJ: Princeton University Press, 2018), 317–19.
15. Michael Hardt and Antonio Negri, *Empire* (Cambridge, MA: Harvard University Press, 2000), 170. While Hardt and Negri write about the postimperial project, their explanation on how the paradoxes of empire and democratic republicanism are reconciled is particularly useful to this study. For a critique of their argument, see Amy Kaplan, *The Anarchy of Empire in the Making of U.S. Culture* (Cambridge, MA: Harvard University Press, 2002), 15; Martin Shaw, "Post-Imperial and Quasi-Imperial: State and Empire in the Global Era," *Millennium: Journal of International Studies* 31, no. 2 (2002): 327–36; and Tarak Barkawi and Mark Laffey, "Retrieving the Imperial: Empire and International Relations," *Millennium: Journal of International Studies* 31, no. 2 (2002): 109–27.
16. Maartje Abbenhuis, *An Age of Neutrals: Great Power Politics, 1815–1914* (Cambridge: Cambridge University Press, 2014), 177.
17. Volker Barth and Roland Cvetkovski, "Introduction—Encounters of Empires: Methodological Approaches," in *Imperial Co-operation and Transfer, 1870–1930: Empires and Encounters*, ed. Volker Barth and Roland Cvetkovski (London: Bloomsbury, 2015), 11.

4. MISSED OPPORTUNITIES

18. Stephen Tuffnell, *Made in Britain: Nation and Emigration in Nineteenth-Century America* (Berkeley: University of California Press, 2020), 145. See also Paul A. Kramer, "Empires, Exceptions, and Anglo-Saxons: Race and Rule between the British and United States Empires, 1880–1910," *Journal of American History* 88, no. 4 (2002): 1340.
19. "*Huangshang chen zhi* 皇上陳之" (The Emperor's Statement), in *Chou ban yi wu shi mo* 籌辦夷務始末 (The Record of Organizing Barbarian Affairs), v. 64, c. 1842, 44a, ed. Wenqing 文慶 (Beijing: Gugong bowuyuan, 1930).
20. Mao Haijian, *The Qing Empire and the Opium War: The Collapse of the Heavenly Dynasty* (Cambridge: Cambridge University Press, 2016), 219.
21. Joint edict by Lin Zexu and Deng Tingzhen to Chinese merchants, c. 1840, FO 682, TNA; Qiying to Francis C. MacGregor, Canton, April 16, 1846, FO 682, TNA.
22. Chang Hsin-pao, *Commissioner Lin and the Opium War* (Cambridge, MA: Harvard University Press, 1964), 31; Mao, *The Qing Empire and the Opium War*, 227, 457.
23. Man-huong Lin, *China Upside Down: Currency, Society, and Ideologies, 1808–1856* (Cambridge, MA: Harvard University Press, 2006), 192.
24. Christopher Munn, *Anglo-China: Chinese People and British Rule in Hong Kong, 1841–1880* (London: Routledge, 2001), 66.
25. "Xiguo tong shang su yuan" 西國通商溯源 (The History of Foreign Intercourse with China), *Xia'er guanzhen* 遐邇貫珍 (Chinese Serial), October 1853; Jixi kai huang jian zhi xi guo yuanliu 極西開荒建治析國源流 (The Discovery of America and Independence of the United States), *Xia'er guanzhen* 遐邇貫珍, November 1853. The articles' English names, recorded as such in the paper's table of contents, notably differed from the Chinese translations, the former being "The source of commercial relations with Western nations," and the second "The establishment of rule over the uncultivated wastelands of the far west, and the source of their separation."
26. Xu Guoqi, *Chinese and Americans: A Shared History* (Cambridge, MA: Harvard University Press, 2014), 8.
27. Augustine Heard & Co., King & Co., Russell & Co., to Dr Peter Parker, Hong Kong, March 23, 1857, Case 31, HBS.
28. James Hevia, *English Lessons: The Pedagogy of Imperialism in Nineteenth-Century China* (Durham, NC: Duke University Press, 2012), 32.
29. Albert F. Heard, Diary, Ipswich, September 1, 1843, HP-1, HBS; Albert F. Heard, Diary, Shanghai, February 25, 1856, HP-1, HBS; Albert F. Heard to his parents, Canton, December 27, 1854, HL-2, HBS.
30. Albert F. Heard to parents, Canton, July 14, 1854, HL-1, HBS.
31. Robert Bickers, *The Scramble for China: Foreign Devils in the Qing Empire, 1832–1914* (London: Allen Lane, 2011), 144.
32. Thomas Waldron to Augustine Heard & Co., Hong Kong, May 3, 1844, EM-3-5, HBS.
33. Augustine Heard Jr., *The Poisoning in Hong Kong: An Episode of Life in China Forty Years Ago* (1894), GQ-2-1, HBS, 8, 12.
34. Qiying reply to no. 21, January 23, 1846, FO 682, TNA.
35. James Keenan to U.S. Assistant Secretary of State, Hong Kong, May 15, 1857, vol. 3, NARA.
36. James Keenan to Peter Parker, Hong Kong, May 11, 1857, vol. 3, NARA.

4. MISSED OPPORTUNITIES

37. Amelia Kay King, "James Keenan: United States Consul to Hong Kong" (MA thesis, North Texas State University, 1978), 84, 87.
38. Keenan to U.S. Assistant Secretary of State, Hong Kong, May 15, 1857.
39. Augustine Heard Sr. to Thomas Waldron, Canton, January 1844; Augustine Heard Sr. to Thomas Waldron, Canton, March 24, 1844; Augustine Heard Sr. to Thomas Waldron, Canton, April 13, 1844; Augustine Heard Sr. to Thomas Waldron, Canton, March 22, 1844, all EL-6-4, HBS.
40. Xu Yuebiao 徐曰彪, "Xianggang de shehui jiegou 香港的社會結構" (Hong Kong's Social Composition), *Shijiu Shiji de Xianggang* 十九世紀的香港 (Nineteenth-Century Hong Kong), ed. Yu Shengwu 余繩武, Liu Cunkuan 劉存寬, Zhu Bian 主編, (Beijing: Zhonghua Shuju 中華書侷, 1993), 361.
41. Albert F. Heard to Augustine Heard Sr., Hong Kong, May 16, 1859, HL-33A, HBS; George F. Heard to his parents, Hong Kong, May 18, 1859, JL-1, HBS.
42. Gillian Bickley, ed., *Through American Eyes: The Journals of George Washington (Farley) Heard* (Hong Kong: Proverse Hong Kong, 2017), 37.
43. Bickers, *The Scramble for China*, 173; Stephen Platt, *Autumn in the Heavenly Kingdom: China, the West, and the Epic Story of the Taiping Civil War* (New York: Vintage Books, 2012), 47; George Heard, "USS 'Powhatan,' off the Peiho, June 27, 1859," in *Through American Eyes*, 97–99.
44. Hunt, *The Making of a Special Relationship*, 83.
45. William M. Wood, *Fankwei: Or, the San Jacinto in the Seas of India, China, and Japan* (New York: Harper & Brothers, 1859), 423–24.
46. George Heard, *Diary on Board the U.S.S. Hartford*, 8 August 1860, Peiho, v. JP-2, HBS.
47. Jenny Huangfu Day, *Qing Travelers to the Far West: Diplomacy and the Information Order in Late Imperial China* (Cambridge: Cambridge University Press, 2018), 25.
48. Albert F. Heard to Augustine Heard Sr., Shanghai, November 18, 1860, EM-3-1, HBS.
49. Chang, *Fateful Ties*, 84, 91–92.
50. Hunt, *The Making of a Special Relationship*, 37; Munn, *Anglo-China*, 58.
51. Li Ding-yi 李定一. *Zhongmei waijiao shi vol. 1*, 中美外交史第一冊 (The History of Sino-American Diplomacy, vol. 1) (Taipei: Qingshui Publishing, 1960), 278. See also Yao Tingfang 姚廷芳, *Yapian Zhanzheng yu: Daoguang Huangdi, Lin Zexu, Qishan, Qiying* 鴉片戰爭與: 道光皇帝, 林則徐, 琦善耆英 (The Opium War and the Daoguang Emperor, Lin Zexu, Qishan, and Qiying) (Taipei: Sanmin shuju, 1970), 298.
52. James Buchanan, Treaty of Tientsin, Tianjin, 1858.
53. Knight Biggerstaff, "The Secret Correspondence of 1867–1868: Views of Leading Chinese Statesmen Regarding the Further Opening of China to Western Influence," *Journal of Modern History* 22, no. 2 (1950): 123. See also Walter LaFeber, *The New Empire: An Interpretation of American Expansion, 1860–1898* (Ithaca, NY: Cornell University Press, 1963), 30.
54. Eileen P. Scully, *Bargaining with the State from Afar: American Citizenship in Treaty Port China, 1844–1942* (New York: Columbia University Press, 2001), 47.
55. Albert F. Heard to Augustine Heard Sr., Shanghai, November 18, 1860, EM-3-1, HBS.
56. John Heard, "A Trading Trip up the Yangtsze," A. Heard & Co. Diaries, 1861–1863, FP-3, HBS, 50.
57. Benito J. Legarda Jr., *After the Galleons: Foreign Trade, Economic Change & Entrepreneurship in the Nineteenth-Century Philippines* (Manila: Ateneo de Manila University Press, 1999), 272.

4. MISSED OPPORTUNITIES

58. Hunt, *The Making of a Special Relationship*, 143–44.
59. See Jen Yu-wen, *The Taiping Revolutionary Movement* (New Haven, CT: Yale University Press, 1973); Kwang-ching Liu, *Anglo-American Steamship Rivalry in China, 1862–1874* (Cambridge, MA: Harvard University Press, 1962), 13, 38, 67; Platt, *Autumn in the Heavenly Kingdom*; Anne Reinhardt, *Navigating Semi-Colonialism: Shipping, Sovereignty, and Nation-Building in China, 1860–1937* (Cambridge, MA: Harvard East Asian Monographs, 2018). For more on the Taiping, see Thomas H. Reilly, *The Taiping Heavenly Kingdom: Rebellion and the Blasphemy of Empire* (Seattle: University of Washington Press, 2004); Jonathan D. Spence, *God's Chinese Son: The Taiping Heavenly Kingdom of Hong Xiuquan* (New York: Norton, 1996); Frederic Wakeman Jr., *The Fall of Imperial China* (New York: Free Press, 1975).
60. "A Report from the *North China Herald*," *North China Herald*, January 15, 1853; William T. Rowe, *Hankou: Conflict and Community in a Chinese City, 1796–1895* (Stanford, CA: Stanford University Press, 1989), 3, 36.
61. Yung Wing, *My Life in China and America* (New York: Henry Holt and Company, 1909), 123–36; "'A Report by R. J. Forrest,' *BPP*, 1862, C. 2976, 43–44," in *Western Reports on the Taiping: A Selection of Documents*, ed. Prescott Clarke and J. S. Gregory (London: Croom Helm 1982), 43.
62. "'A Report by Robert M. McLane, US Minister to China,' *U.S. Congressional Papers*, 35th Congress, 2nd Session, Senate Executive Document 22, vol. VII, pp. 50–55," in Clarke and Gregory, *Western Reports on the Taiping*, 131; Bickers, *The Scramble for China*, 136.
63. Kuai Shixun 蒯世勋, *Shanghai gong gong zu jie shi gao* 上海公共租界史稿 (A History of Shanghai's International Settlement) (Shanghai: Shanghai renmin chubanshe, 1980), 359; Michael Marme, "From Suzhou to Shanghai: A Tale of Two Systems," *Journal of Chinese History* 2, no. 1 (2018): 87–89; Jung-fang Tsai, *Hong Kong in Chinese History: Community and Social Unrest in the British Colony, 1842–1913* (New York: Columbia University Press, 1993), 22; Madeline Zelin, "The Structure of the Chinese Economy During the Qing Period: Some Thoughts on the 150th Anniversary of the Opium War," in *Perspectives on Modern China: Four Anniversaries*, ed. Kenneth Lieberthal et al. (Armonk, NY: M. E. Sharpe, 1991), 32.
64. Spence, *God's Chinese Son*, 303; Wakeman, *The Fall of Imperial China*, 156.
65. Bickers, *The Scramble for China*, 177.
66. "Decision of Mr. McLane About Tea Duties," Shanghai, November 23, 1854, L5-6, JMA.
67. Jen, *The Taiping Revolutionary Movement*, 147–49; "Local News," *China Mail*, November 8, 1863; Spence, *God's Chinese Son*, 310–11.
68. Legarda, *After the Galleons*, 296.
69. Platt, *Autumn in the Heavenly Kingdom*, 244.
70. Spence, *God's Chinese Son*, 308.
71. Heard, "A Trading Trip," 24–26.
72. Yung, *My Life in China and America*, 135–37.
73. Heard, "A Trading Trip," 28, 33.
74. Bickers, *The Scramble for China*, 122.
75. Chang, *Fateful Ties*, 62.
76. Jen, *The Taiping Revolutionary Movement*, 274–76.
77. Xu, *Chinese and Americans*, 27.

4. MISSED OPPORTUNITIES

78. Day, *Qing Travelers to the Far West*, 15; Xu, *Chinese and Americans*, 31; Wakeman, *The Fall of Imperial China*, 176.
79. Jen, *The Taiping Revolutionary Movement*, 450, 525; Platt, *Autumn in the Heavenly Kingdom*, 212.
80. Robert Bickers, "British Concessions and Chinese Cities, 1910s–1930s," in *New Narratives of Urban Space in Republican Chinese Cities: Emerging Social, Legal and Governance Orders*, ed. Billy K. L. So and Madeline Zelin (Leiden: Brill, 2013), 170; Heard, "A Trading Trip," 40–43, 45, 50.
81. Heard, "A Trading Trip," 47, 51.
82. Hunt, *The Making of a Special Relationship*, 169.
83. Stephen C. Lockwood, *Augustine Heard and Company, 1858–1862: American Merchants in China* (Cambridge, MA: Harvard East Asian Monographs, 1971), 74–75.
84. "Qinchai dachen xueshi huguang guanwen zou 欽差大臣學士湖廣官文奏" (Memorial by the Imperial Commissioner Guanwen of Huguang), in *Chou ban yi wu shi mo* 籌辦夷務始末 (The Record of Organizing Barbarian Affairs), v. 78, 1861, 3a–4b; *The China Directory for 1863* (Hong Kong: A. Shortrede & Co., 1863), 51.
85. Reinhardt, *Navigating Semi-Colonialism*, 29–30, 39.
86. Heard, "A Trading Trip," 90.
87. Liu, "Financing a Steam Navigation Company in China, 1861–1862," *Business History Review* 49, no. 2 (1954): 164, 166–67.
88. Liu, *Anglo-American Steamship Rivalry in China*, 15. See also Robert Bickers, *China Bound: John Swire & Sons and Its World, 1816–1980* (London: Bloomsbury, 2020), 62–63.
89. Heard, "A Trading Trip," 2.
90. Heard, "A Trading Trip," 88, 90, 101–7.
91. Thomas Schoonover, *Uncle Sam's War of 1898 and the Origins of Globalization* (Lexington: University of Kentucky Press, 2003), 39.
92. "From Our Overland Edition," *China Mail*, May 30, 1861.
93. "Naval," *New York Times*, July 24, 1863.
94. Archibald Duncan Blue, "The China Coast: A Study of British Shipping in Chinese Waters, 1842–1914" (PhD diss., University of Strathclyde, 1982), xxxvi.
95. George W. Heard to John Heard, Ipswich, July 8, 1862, HN-5-3, HBS.
96. John Heard to Augustine Heard Jr., Boston, 1864, GM-1-5, HBS.
97. Liu, *Anglo-American Steamship Rivalry in China*, 22–24; Liu, "Financing a Steam Navigation Company in China," 164.
98. "Ta-Kiang," *Dictionary of American Naval Fighting Ships*, Naval History and Heritage Command (Washington, DC: Naval Historical Center).
99. "Fahkee" and "Howquah," *Dictionary of American Naval Fighting Ships*.
100. Bickers, *The Scramble for China*, 179; "Naval News," *New York Times*, April 16, 1863; "Dai-Ching," "Fuchsia," and "Tulip," *Dictionary of American Naval Fighting Ships*.
101. Liu, "Financing a Steam Navigation Company in China," 167.
102. Peter J. Hugill, "The American Challenge to British Hegemony, 1861–1947," *Geographical Review* 99, no. 3 (2009): 408.
103. John Carroll, *A Concise History of Hong Kong* (New York: Rowman & Littlefield, 2007), 17; Chi-kong Lai, "The Qing State and Merchant Enterprise: The China Merchants' Company, 1872–1902," in *To Achieve Security and Wealth: The Qing*

4. MISSED OPPORTUNITIES

Imperial State and the Economy, 1644–1911, ed. Jane Kate Leonard and John R. Watt (Ithaca, NY: Cornell East Asia Series, 1992), 139–56; Reinhardt, *Navigating Semi-Colonialism*, 61–93.

104. "Local Intelligence," *New York Times*, March 18, 1866.
105. John Heard to Augustine Heard Jr., Boston, April 24, 1864, GM-1-5, HBS.
106. Augustine Heard & Co., Shanghai, to Augustine Heard & Co., Yokohama, May 13, 1868, JMA.
107. F. Blake to Augustine Heard & Co., Hiogo, May 10, 1868; July 31, 1868, JMA.
108. George Dixwell to John Heard, Hong Kong, June 5, 1871; October 8, 1871; October 19, 1871, FM-13-1, HBS.
109. Dael Norwood, *Trading Freedom: How Trade with China Defined Early America* (Chicago: University of Chicago Press, 2022), 160.
110. Bickers, *China Bound*, 62–66.
111. Horace Congar to William Seward, Hong Kong, May 26, 1862, vol. 5, NARA.
112. Blue, "The China Coast," 162; Accounting statistics in Norwood, *Trading Freedom*, 93, corroborate the steady post–Civil War decline in trade.
113. Horace Congar to William Seward, Hong Kong, February 15, 1862, vol. 5, NARA.
114. Blue, "The China Coast," 142; Robert B. Ekelund, John D. Jackson, and Mark Thornton, "The 'Unintended Consequences' of Confederate Trade Legislation," *Eastern Economic Journal* 30, no. 2 (2004): 188.
115. Bickers, *The Scramble for China*, 306. See also I. F. Clarke, *Voices Prophesying War, 1763–1984* (London: Panther, 1970).
116. Ann Laura Stoler, "Rethinking Colonial Categories: European Communities and the Boundaries of Rule," *Comparative Studies in Society and History* 31, no. 1 (1989): 137.
117. Robert Bickers, *Getting Stuck in for Shanghai, or Putting the Kibosh on the Kaiser from the Bund; The British at Shanghai and the Great War* (Sydney: Penguin Books, 2014), 50.
118. Bickers, *The Scramble for China*, 144; Wood, *Fankwei*, 427; Elizabeth Ann Farley to her sons, Ipswich, January 20, 1862, HN-5-3, HBS; Howard Jones, *Blue and Gray Diplomacy: A History of Union and Confederate Foreign Relations* (Chapel Hill: University of North Carolina Press, 2010), 600.
119. Kenneth Bourne, "British Preparations for War with the North, 1861–1862," *English Historical Review* 76, no. 301 (1961): 601; D. W. Brogan, "The Remote Revolution: A British View," *Proceedings of the American Philosophical Society* 106, no. 1 (1962), 3; Sven Beckert, "Emancipation and Empire: Reconstructing the Worldwide Web of Cotton Production in the Age of the American Civil War," *American Historical Review* 109, no. 5 (2004): 1417.
120. Ronald J. Zboray and Mary Saracino Zboray, "Cannonballs and Books: Reading and the Disruption of Social Ties on the New England Home Front," in *The War Was You and Me: Civilians in the American Civil War*, ed. Joan E. Cashin (Princeton, NJ: Princeton University Press, 2002), 244.
121. Elizabeth Ann Farley to her sons, Ipswich, January 20, 1862, HN-5-3, HBS; Elizabeth Ann Farley to her sons, Ipswich, February 3, 1862, HN-5-3, HBS; George W. Heard to John Heard, Ipswich, July 8, 1862, HN-5-3, HBS; Augustine Heard Sr. to Albert F. Heard, Boston, May 1862, HN-6-2, HBS.

4. MISSED OPPORTUNITIES

122. Thomas R. Kemp, "Community and War: The Civil War Experience of Two New Hampshire Towns," in *Toward a Social History of the American Civil War: Exploratory Essays*, ed. Maris A. Vinovskis (Cambridge: Cambridge University Press, 1990), 40.
123. Platt, *Autumn in the Heavenly Kingdom*, 262–63.
124. Horace Congar to William Seward, Hong Kong, February 15, 1862, vol. 5, NARA.
125. Albert F. Heard to Augustine Heard Jr., Hong Kong, February 14, 1860, HL-33A, HBS. See also Robert Erwin Johnson, *Far China Station: The U.S. Navy in Asian Waters, 1800–1898* (Annapolis, MD: Naval Institute Press, 1979), 108–13; Albert Heard to Gray, Hong Kong, February 13, 1860, HL-33A, HBS; American Merchants to C. K. Stribling & William Radford, Hong Kong, July 24, 1861, FM-17-1, HBS; C. K. Stribling to John Heard, the *Hartford*, July 10, 1861, FM-17-1, HBS; "Extract of a Letter from John Heard," Hong Kong, July 25, 1861, FM-17-1, HBS; Horace Congar to William Seward, Hong Kong, February 15, 1862, vol. 5, NARA; Horace Congar to William Seward, Hong Kong, May 26, 1862, vol. 5, NARA. See also Brainard Dyer, "Civil War Naval Activities in the Pacific: An Extract from the Autobiography of William B. Simmons," *Pacific Historical Review* 7, no. 3 (1938): 254–66.
126. "General News," *China Mail*, July 25, 1861.
127. "'Manifest Destiny' of Canada," *China Mail*, May 9, 1861; "From Our London Correspondent," *China Mail*, June 27, 1861; "Reprinted from Punch," *China Mail*, August 15, 1861.
128. George Athan Billias, *American Constitutionalism Heard Round the World* (New York: New York University Press, 2009), 203; Don H. Doyle, "Slavery or Independence: The Confederate Dilemma in Europe," in *The U.S. South and Europe: Transatlantic Relations in the Nineteenth and Twentieth Centuries*, ed. Cornelis A. van Minnen and Manfred Berg (Lexington: University Press of Kentucky, 2013), 109, 112.
129. "Supplement: The Causes of American Bitterness," *China Mail*, August 29, 1861.
130. "Supplement: English Opinions of America and the Americans," *China Mail*, August 24, 1861.
131. "Editorial on the *Trent* and the *San Jacinto*," *China Mail*, February 6, 1862.
132. "The Naval Position in the Event of War," *China Mail*, February 13, 1862.
133. "The Fourth of July," *North China Herald*, September 4, 1862; "Editorial on America," *China Mail*, November 27, 1862.
134. "British World" historians set a precedent for analyzing transforming identities across imperial contexts. See Rachel Bright and Andrew Dilly, "Historiographical Review: After the British World," *Historical Journal* 60, no. 2 (2017): 566; John Mackenzie, "Empires and States in Expansion and Contraction," *Britain and the World* 9, no. 1 (2016): 1; Tamson Pietsch, "Rethinking the British World," *Journal of British Studies* 52, no. 2 (2013): 456. See also Carroll Smith-Rosenberg, *This Violent Empire: The Birth of an American National Identity* (Chapel Hill: University of North Carolina Press, 2010), 33; Anthony Webster, "The Development of British Commercial and Political Networks in the Straits Settlements 1800–1868: The Rise of a Colonial and Regional Economic Identity," *Modern Asian Studies* 45, no. 4 (2011): 899–929.

4. MISSED OPPORTUNITIES

135. Augustine Heard Sr. to Albert F. Heard, Boston, May 17, 1862, HN-6-2, HBS; George Dixwell to John Heard, Shanghai, October 5, 1863, FM-13-1, HBS; James Murray Forbes to his father, Hong Kong, October 1863, Ms N-49, MHS.
136. "Supplement: Hong Kong," *China Mail*, August 29, 1861; "Supplement: Shipping Report," *China Mail*, September 12, 1861.
137. "Who Is 'Old Beeswax,'" *China Mail*, May 7, 1863.
138. "From Great Britain," *New York Times*, December 9, 1862.
139. Beckert, "Emancipation and Empire," 1416; "Diplomatic Correspondence," *New York Times*, December 14, 1862; "Limits of English Neutrality," *New York Times*, April 24, 1863.
140. "Affairs in England," *New York Times*, October 25, 1863.
141. Amity: Treaty of Washington, Washington, May 8, 1871.
142. Horace Congar to William Seward, Hong Kong, October 10, 1863; Horace Congar to William Seward, Hong Kong, October 26, 1863; Horace Congar to William Seward, Hong Kong, December 26, 1863, all vol. 5, NARA.
143. "Shipping Charters & Settlements," *China Mail*, December 3, 1863.
144. "Extracts from Our Foreign Files," *New York Times*, January 29, 1864; Blue, "The China Coast," 132, records a similar situation in Bangkok, 1863. Legarda, *After the Galleons*, 296–98, describes similar circumstances at Manila.
145. James M. Morris, "America's Stepchild," *Wilson Quarterly* 11, no. 3 (1987): 122.
146. "Shipping Charters & Settlements," *China Mail*, May 12, 1864; "Local Interests," *China Mail*, August 4, 1864.
147. Colonial Secretary's Office to Horace Congar, Hong Kong, March 5, 1864, vol. 5, NARA.
148. Horace Congar to W. S. Mercer, Hong Kong, March 8, 1864, vol. 5, NARA; Colonial Secretary's Office to Horace Congar, Hong Kong, March 9, 1864, vol. 5, NARA; Hercules Robinson to the Duke of Newcastle, Hong Kong, March 10, 1864, CO 129/97, TNA.
149. Isaac Jackson Allen to William Seward, Hong Kong, February 10, 1864, vol. 5, NARA; C. N. Goulding to Hamilton Fish, Hong Kong, February 10, 1870, vol. 7, NARA; David H. Bailey to Bancroft Davis, Hong Kong, April 25, 1871, vol. 7, NARA. For further reading on the "coolie" trade, see Chang, *Fateful Ties*, 75–77; Paul A. Kramer, "The Golden Gate and the Open Door: Civilization, Empire, and Exemption in the History of U.S. Chinese Exclusion, 1868–1910," in *China's Development from a Global Perspective*, ed. Maria Dolores Elizalde and Wang Jianlang (Cambridge: Cambridge Scholars Publishing, 2017), 196–219; Moon-ho Jung, "Outlawing 'Coolies': Race, Nation, and Empire in the Age of Emancipation," *American Quarterly* 57, no. 3 (2005): 677–901; Elizabeth Sinn, "In-between Place: A New Paradigm for Hong Kong Studies," in *Rethinking Hong Kong: New Paradigms, New Perspectives*, ed. Elizabeth Sinn, Siu-lun Wong, and Wing-hoi Chan (Hong Kong: Hong Kong University Centre of Asian Studies, 2009), 252–58; Tsai, *Hong Kong in Chinese History*, 23.
150. Nicolas Barreyre, "The Politics of Economic Crises: The Panic of 1873, the End of Reconstruction, and the Realignment of American Politics," *Journal of the Gilded Age and Progressive Era* 10, no. 4 (2011): 406–8.
151. Lockwood, *Augustine Heard and Company, 1858–1862*, 110–11.

152. George Heard to Albert F. Heard, Hong Kong, March 28, 1870; George Heard to Augustine Heard Jr., Hong Kong, February 19, 1873; George Heard to Albert F. Heard, Hong Kong, April 5, 1873, all JL-2, HBS.
153. Bryna Goodman, "Improvisations on a Semi Colonial Theme: Or, How to Read a Celebration of Transnational Urban Community," *Journal of Asian Studies* 59, no. 4 (2000): 893.
154. See Articles I, VI, and XII, Treaty of Washington, May 8, 1871; Hugill, "The American Challenge to British Hegemony," 409.
155. "Extract, China Mail, July 5, 1871," David Bailey to Bancroft Davis, July 1871, vol. 7, NARA; LaFeber, *The New Empire*, 34.
156. See Thomas M. Larkin, "Mapping Sino-Foreign Networks and Mobility in China," Digital Repository, 2022.
157. Lockwood, *Augustine Heard and Company*, 114–15.
158. Bickers, *China Bound*, 44–45.

5. FRIENDS NEAR AND FAR

1. John Heard, *An Account of His Life and the History of Augustine Heard & Co.* (1891), FP-4, HBS, 164.
2. George Heard to Albert F. Heard, Hong Kong, March 28, 1873, JL-2, HBS.
3. Augustine Heard Jr., *Old China and New* (1894), GQ-2-2, HBS, 36.
4. Vivian Kong, "Whiteness, Imperial Anxiety, and the 'Global 1930s': The White British League Debate in Hong Kong," *Journal of British Studies* 59, no. 2 (2020): 345.
5. John M. Carroll, *Edge of Empires: Chinese Elites and British Colonials in Hong Kong* (Cambridge, MA: Harvard University Press, 2005), 4–5.
6. Elizabeth Sinn, "In-Between Place: A New Paradigm for Hong Kong Studies," in *Rethinking Hong Kong: New Paradigms, New Perspectives*, ed. Elizabeth Sinn, Siu-lun Wong, and Wing-hoi Chan (Hong Kong: Hong Kong University Centre of Asian Studies, 2009), 250. See also Elizabeth Sinn and Christopher Munn, eds., *Meeting Place: Encounters Across Cultures in Hong Kong, 1841–1984* (Hong Kong: Hong Kong University Press, 2017).
7. Gregor Benton and Hong Liu, eds., *Dear China: Emigrant Letters and Remittances, 1820–1980* (Berkeley: University of California Press, 2018), 8, 49.
8. Heard, *An Account of His Life*, 76–81.
9. Elizabeth Ann Heard to her sons, Ipswich, April 29, 1862, HN-5-3, HBS.
10. See Tansen Sen, "The Intricacies of Premodern Asian Connections," *Journal of Asian Studies* 4, no. 69 (2010): 991–99; Amitav Acharya, "Asia Is Not One," *Journal of Asian Studies* 4, no. 69 (2010): 1001–13.
11. Leonard Blusse, *Visible Cities: Canton, Nagasaki, and Batavia and the Coming of the Americans* (Cambridge, MA: Harvard University Press, 2008), 10–11, 25.
12. Ng Chin-keong, *Trade and Society: The Amoy Network on the China Coast, 1683–1735* (Singapore: National University of Singapore Press, 2015), 4, 26, 173; Gary G. Hamilton, "The Organizational Foundations of Western and Chinese Commerce: A Historical and Comparative Analysis," in *Asian Business Networks*, ed. Gary G. Hamilton (Berlin: Walter de Gruyter, 1996), 52–53.

5. FRIENDS NEAR AND FAR

13. James M. Forbes, *Old Shipping Days in Boston*, n.d., Ms N-49.67, MHS.
14. John D. Wong, *Global Trade in the Nineteenth Century: The House of Houqua and the Canton System* (Cambridge: Cambridge University Press, 2016), 148.
15. Søren Mentz, "Cultural Interaction Between the British Diaspora in Madras and the Host Community, 1650–1790," in *Asian Port Cities 1600–1800: Local and Foreign Cultural Interactions*, ed. Masashi Haneda (Singapore: National University of Singapore Press, 2009), 165; Alain Le Pichon, *Aux origines de Hong Kong: Aspects de la civilisation commerciale à Canton—Le fonds de commerce de Jardine, Matheson & Co., 1827–1839* (Paris: L'Harmattan, 1998), 160.
16. Paul A. Kramer, "Empires, Exceptions, and Anglo-Saxons: Race and Rule Between the British and United States Empires, 1880–1910," *Journal of American History* 88, no. 4 (2002): 1318.
17. Jacques Downs, *The Golden Ghetto: The American Commercial Community at Canton and the Shaping of American China Policy, 1784–1844* (London: Associated University Press, 1997), 229; Albert F. Heard, Legal Statement, Biarritz, February 2, 1881, HN-3-1, HBS; Heard, *An Account of His Life*, 18, 162.
18. Downs, *The Golden Ghetto*, 155, 415.
19. Nearly identical relationships in Glasgow and Liverpool appear in Emma Goldsmith, "In Trade: Wealthy Business Families in Glasgow and Liverpool" (PhD diss., Northwestern University, 2017), 72.
20. For kinship ties in China, see Thomas H. Cox, "'Money, Credit, and Strong Friends': Warren Delano II and the Importance of Social Networking in the Old China Trade," in *The Private Side of the Canton Trade, 1700–1840: Beyond the Companies*, ed. Paul A. Van Dyke and Susan E. Schopp (Hong Kong: Hong Kong University Press, 2018), 132.
21. Tim Sturgis, *Rivalry in Canton: The Control of Russell & Co. 1838–1840 and the Founding of Augustine Heard & Co.* (London: The Warren Press, 2006), 80; Wong, *Global Trade in the Nineteenth Century*, 71.
22. Kessresung Khushalchand to Augustine Heard & Co., Bombay, April 9, 1846, EM-1-7, HBS; Stephen C. Lockwood, *Augustine Heard and Company, 1858–1862: American Merchants in China* (Cambridge, MA: Harvard East Asian Monographs, 1971), 27.
23. Heard, *Old China and New* (1892), GQ-2-2, MHS, 2–3; Augustine Heard Jr., *The Poisoning in Hong Kong: An Episode of Life in China Forty Years Ago* (1894), GQ-2-1, HBS, 1, 12; Heard, *An Account of His Life*, 27, 52, 115; Albert F. Heard to "Josh," Canton; Albert F. Heard to John Heard, Canton, both January 5, 1854, HL-1, HBS.
24. Albert F. Heard to his parents, Hong Kong, February 12, 1857, HL-3, HBS; Albert F. Heard to his parents, Shanghai, March 5, 1857, HL-3, HBS; Albert F. Heard to his parents, Hong Kong, May 13, 1859, HL33-A, HBS. See also Gillian Bickley, ed., *Through American Eyes: The Journals of George Washington (Farley) Heard* (Hong Kong: Proverse Hong Kong, 2017).
25. See graph A.
26. Queeny Pradhan, *Empire in the Hills: Simla, Darjeeling, Ootacamund, and Mount Abu, 1820–1920* (Oxford: Oxford University Press, 2017), xxiv; Claire Lowrie, *Masters and Servants: Cultures of Empire in the Tropics* (Manchester: Manchester University Press, 2016), 73; William C. Hunter, *The "Fan Kwae" at Canton: Before the Treaty Days, 1825–1844*, 1st ed. (Shanghai: The Oriental Affairs, 1882), 77; Ann Laura

5. FRIENDS NEAR AND FAR

Stoler, "Making Empire Respectable: The Politics of Race and Sexual Morality in 20th-Century Colonial Cultures," *American Ethnologist* 16, no. 4 (1989): 646; Augustine Heard Sr. to Albert F. Heard, Boston, October 24, 1861, HN-6-2, HBS.
27. Freda Harcourt, *Flagships of Imperialism: The P&O Company and Its Politics of Empire from Its Origins to 1867* (Manchester: Manchester University Press, 2006), 90.
28. Angela Woollacott, *Settler Society in the Australian Colonies: Self-Government and Imperial Culture* (Oxford: Oxford University Press, 2015), 13; Heard, *An Account of His Life*, 23, 82.
29. Elizabeth Buettner, *Empire Families: Britons and Late Imperial India* (Oxford: Oxford University Press, 2004), 17.
30. Tamson Pietsch, "Rethinking the British World," *Journal of British Studies* 52, no. 2 (2013): 448.
31. Sinn, "In-Between Place," 266.
32. Heard, *An Account of His Life*, 81, 86–99, 104; Albert F. Heard, Legal Statement, Biarritz, February 2, 1881, HN-3-1, HBS; Jane Heard to John Heard, Paris, June 29, 1865, FN-2-3, HBS; Albert F. Heard to John Heard, Paris, January 10, 1880, HN-3-1, HBS.
33. Matthew O. Jackson, *Social and Economic Networks* (Princeton, NJ: Princeton University Press, 2008), 36.
34. Jackson, *Social and Economic Networks*, 9.
35. A range of specific occupations of varying prestige have been deliberately reduced to "Merchant," "Official," and "Other" in order to reflect the preponderance of commercial ties in the Heard network, and the tendency to forge official ties. Titles given here do not suggest that all holders were of equal social standing.
36. Wai-kwan Chan, *The Making of Hong Kong Society: Three Studies of Class Formation in Early Hong Kong* (Oxford: Clarendon Press, 1991), 35; Carroll, *Edge of Empires*, 72, observes a similar social phenomenon among Hong Kong's Chinese merchants.
37. Gregory Anderson, *Victorian Clerks* (Manchester: Manchester University Press, 1976), 20.
38. See Papers on Augustine Heard & Co., MS JM/F25/33, JMA.
39. *Chronicle & Directory for China, Japan, & the Philippines* (Hong Kong: Daily Press, 1874), 190; *Chronicle & Directory for China, Japan, & the Philippines* (Hong Kong: Daily Press, 1875), 190–91.
40. Paul Goodman, "Ethics and Enterprise: The Values of a Boston Elite, 1800–1860," *American Quarterly* 18, no. 3 (1996): 441–42. See also Downs, *The Golden Ghetto*, 233.
41. John Heard to Augustine Heard & Co., Hong Kong, November 1, 1862, Case 28, HBS; George Heard to Augustine Heard Jr., Hong Kong, May 30, 1873, JL-2, HBS.
42. Rachel Tamar Van, "The 'Woman Pigeon': Gendered Bonds and Barriers in the Anglo-American Commercial Community in Canton and Macao, 1800–1849," *Pacific Historical Review* 83, no. 4 (2014): 581.
43. See Liz Stanley, "Letter-Writing and the Actual Course of Things: Doing the Business, Helping the World Go Round," in *The Palgrave Handbook of Auto/Biography*, ed. Anne Chappell and Julie M. Parsons (Basingstoke, UK: Palgrave Macmillan, 2020), 166–68, 172, for "notions of reciprocity."
44. Elizabeth Ann Heard to her sons, Boston, March and April 1862, HN-5-3, HBS; Albert F. Heard to Augustine Heard Jr., Hong Kong, February 14, 1860, HL-33A,

5. FRIENDS NEAR AND FAR

HBS; Albert F. Heard to his parents, Shanghai, June 11, 1859, HL-33A, HBS. See also Woollacott, *Settler Society in the Australian Colonies*, 12.

45. Buettner, *Empire Families*, 189.
46. Albert F. Heard, Diary, February 14, 1854, Canton, HP-2, HBS; Jane Heard to John Heard, Paris, June 29, 1865, FN-2-3, HBS.
47. Nicola J. Thomas, "Mary Curzon: 'American Queen of India,'" in *Colonial Lives Across the British Empire: Imperial Careering in the Long Nineteenth Century*, ed. David Lambert and Adam Lester (Cambridge: Cambridge University Press, 2010), 296.
48. Albert F. Heard to "Devil" (William Henry Gleason), Canton, January 4, 1854; Albert F. Heard to "Acken," Canton, January 5, 1854; Albert F. Heard to "Fred," Canton, January 5, 1854; Albert F. Heard to "Hu'e" (Henry Babcock), Canton, January 5, 1854; Albert F. Heard to "Andrew," Canton, January 5, 1854; Albert F. Heard to "Johnny," Canton, January 4, 1854, all HL-1, HBS.
49. "George A. Johnson, 15th Attorney General," State of California Department of Justice Office of the Attorney General, https://oag.ca.gov/history/15johnson. See also Willard B. Soper, Order of Skull & Bones (Membership List by Year), c. 1905, New Haven, Yale University, Medical Historical Library.
50. Downs, *The Golden Ghetto*, 254.
51. Elizabeth Ann Heard to Albert F. Heard, Boston, September 26, 1862, HN-5-3, HBS; Albert F. Heard to George Dixwell, Hong Kong, November 23, 1872, HL-48, HBS; Heard, *An Account of His Life*, 168; Thomas F. Waters, *Augustine Heard and His Friends* (Salem, MA: Newcomb & Gauss, 1916), 48–49.
52. Jane Lydon, *Imperial Emotions: The Politics of Empathy Across the British Empire* (Cambridge: Cambridge University Press, 2019), 144–45; Kathleen D. McCarthy, *American Creed: Philanthropy and the Rise of Civil Society, 1700–1865* (Chicago: University of Chicago Press, 2003), 202; John J. Pauly, "The Great Chicago Fire as a National Event," *American Quarterly* 36, no. 5 (1984): 675.
53. Heard, *An Account of His Life*, 161; See also: Elizabeth A. Harvey, "'Layered Networks': Imperial Philanthropy in Birmingham and Sydney, 1860–1914," *Journal of Imperial Commonwealth History* 41, no. 1 (2013): 128–29.
54. Downs, *The Golden Ghetto*, 322.
55. George Heard to Augustine Heard Jr., Hong Kong, June 5, 1873, JL-2, HBS.
56. James Murray Forbes, *Recollections and Events from the Threshold of Eighty-Five* (Boston, 1930), 23.
57. Forbes, *Recollections and Events*, 31; James Murray Forbes to his mother, Hong Kong, January 14, 1864, Ms N-49, P-55.
58. Robert Bennet Forbes to Rose Forbes, Canton, December 12, 1839, in *Letters from China: The Canton-Boston Correspondence of Robert Bennet Forbes, 1838–1840*, ed. Phyllis Forbes Kerr (Mystic, CT: Mystic Seaport Museum, 1996), 190; Robert Bennet Forbes to Rose Forbes, 28 June 1840, in *Letters from China*, 237; Robert Bennet Forbes, "Rambling Recollections Connected with China," in *Personal Reminiscences*, 2nd ed. (Boston: Little, Brown, and Company, 1882), 399.
59. Albert F. Heard to Mary Heard, Hong Kong, June 25, 1874, HL-5, HBS; James Murray Forbes to his father, Hong Kong, February 14, 1864, Ms 49, P-55; James Murray Forbes to his mother, Hong Kong, February 29, 1864, Hong Kong, Ms 49, P-55.

5. FRIENDS NEAR AND FAR

60. Kramer, "Empires, Exceptions, and Anglo-Saxons," 1330.
61. Carl Bridge and Kent Fedorowich, "Mapping the British World," *Journal of Imperial and Commonwealth History* 31, no. 2 (2010): 3; Carroll, *Edge of Empires*, 84.
62. See Chiara Betta, "From Orientals to Imagined Britons: Baghdadi Jews in Shanghai," *Modern Asian Studies* 37, no. 4 (2003): 1006. See also Elizabeth Buettner, "Problematic Spaces, Problematic Races: Defining 'Europeans' in Late Colonial India," *Women's History Review* 9, no. 2 (2000): 278; Margot Finn, "Family Formations: Anglo India and the Familial Proto-State," in *Structures and Transformations in Modern British History*, ed. David Feldman and Jon Lawrence (Cambridge: Cambridge University Press, 2011), 111–12; Peter James Marshall, "British Society in India Under the East India Company," *Modern Asian Studies* 31, no. 1 (1997): 107.
63. See *Morris's Directory for China, Japan, and the Phillipines* [sic] *&c.* (Hong Kong: Morris & Co., 1870), A1–A35.
64. *The Chronicle & Directory for China, Japan, & the Philippines* (Hong Kong: Daily Press, 1873), 185, 188.
65. *The Chronicle & Directory for China, Japan, and the Philippines* (Hong Kong: Daily Press, 1874), 190; George Heard to Mr Beard, Hong Kong, September 21, 1873, JL-2, HBS.
66. *The Chronicle & Directory for China, Japan, and the Philippines* (Hong Kong: Daily Press, 1875), 190–91.
67. Vaudine England, *Kindred Spirits: A History of the Hong Kong Club* (Hong Kong: Hong Kong Club, 2016), 11, 193.
68. "Naval Intelligence," *China Punch*, October 8, 1853.
69. A list of the Heard Compradors is provided in Yen-p'ing Hao, "The Rise and Fall of the Comprador," in *Chinese Business Enterprise*, ed. Rajeswary Ampalavanar Brown (London: Routledge, 1996), 2:281, 285.
70. Kaori Abe, *Chinese Middlemen in Hong Kong's Colonial Economy, 1830–1890* (Abingdon, UK: Routledge, 2017), 62–66.
71. Kaori Abe, "Intermediary Elites in the Treaty Port World: Tong Mow-chee and His Collaborators in Shanghai," *Journal of the Royal Asiatic Society* 3, no. 25 (2015): 471; Robert Bickers, *China Bound: John Swire & Sons and Its World, 1816–1980* (London: Bloomsbury, 2020), 135.
72. Bert Becker, "Western Firms and Their Chinese Compradors: The Case of the Jebsen and Chau Families," in Sinn and Munn *Meeting Place*, 125. See also Jungfang Tsai, *Hong Kong in Chinese History: Community and Social Unrest in the British Colony, 1842–1913* (New York: Columbia University Press, 1993), 66.
73. Henrique Caetano Victor de Figueiredo, #37892, Macanese Families; José Miguel Victor de Figueiredo, #22555, Macanese Families; Inácio Pires Pereira Jr., #14702, Macanese Families; Olímpio Augusto da Cruz, #11112, Macanese Families; Francisco António de Seabra, #17407, Macanese Families.
74. Catherine Chan, *The Macanese Diaspora in British Hong Kong: A Century of Transimperial Drifting* (Amsterdam: Amsterdam University Press, 2021), 20–23; Catherine Chan "Cosmopolitan Visions and Intellectual Passions: Macanese Publics in British Hong Kong," *Modern Asian Studies* 56, no. 1 (2022): 350.
75. Vincent Wai-kit Ho, "Duties and Limitations: The Role of United States Consuls in Macao, 1849–1869," in *Americans and Macao: Trade, Smuggling and Diplomacy*

on the South China Coast, ed. Paul A. Van Dyke (Hong Kong: Hong Kong University Press, 2012), 145.
76. Amelia Kay King, "James Keenan: United States Consul to Hong Kong" (MA thesis, North Texas State University, 1978), 25–26, 28.
77. *The Chronicle and Directory for China, Japan, & the Philippines* (Hong Kong: The Daily Press, 1865), 191; *The Chronicle and Directory for China, Japan, & the Phillippines* [sic] (Hong Kong: The Daily Press, 1864), 262; *The China Directory for 1862* (Hong Kong: Shortrede & Co., 1862), 45.
78. Heard, *An Account of His Life*, 124; *The China Directory for 1862*, 4, 28.
79. Albert F. Heard to Augustine Heard Sr., Hong Kong, February 24, 1860, HL-33A, HBS.
80. George Dixwell to John Heard, Hong Kong, September 21, 1872, FM-13-1, HBS; Heard, *An Account of His Life*, 124.
81. Albert F. Heard to "Macdonald," Hong Kong, February 11, 1873, HL-48, HBS; Albert F. Heard to Mr Mackin, Boston, July 25, 1875, HL-5, HBS.
82. Albert F. Heard to his parents, Hong Kong, May 13, 1859, HL-33A, HBS; Albert F. Heard to Augustine Heard Jr., Hong Kong, February 14, 1860, HL-33A, HBS; Albert F. Heard to his parents, Shanghai, June 23, 1859, HL-33A, HBS. See Heard, *An Account of His Life*, 147–53, for a detailed account of this voyage.
83. George Dixwell to John Heard, Shanghai, October 30, 1870, FM-13-1, HBS.
84. Heard, *An Account of His Life*, 169; Heard, *China Old and New*, 38–39; Robert W. Lovett, "The Heard Collection and Its Story," *The Business History Review* 35, no. 4 (1961): 570.
85. Harcourt, *Flagships of Imperialism*, 14; Chi-kong Lai, "The Qing State and Merchant Enterprise: The China Merchants' Company, 1872–1902," in *To Achieve Security and Wealth: The Qing Imperial State and the Economy, 1644–1911*, ed. Jane Kate Leonard and John R. Watt (Ithaca, NY: Cornell East Asia Series, 1992), 152; Lockwood, *Augustine Heard & Company, 1858–1862*, 117.
86. George Heard to Augustine Heard Jr., Hong Kong, May 30, 1873, HBS; John Heard, Will, Hong Kong, 1862, Case 28, HBS.
87. Van, "The 'Woman Pigeon,'" 582.
88. "Mrs. M. P. Heard," *South China Morning Post*, December 30, 1926.
89. *The Chronicle & Directory for China, Corea, Japan, the Philippines, Indo-China, Straits Settlement, Siam, Borneo, Malay States, &c* (Hong Kong: Daily Press Office, 1894), 219.
90. "The Fire Trucks," *North China Herald*, November 17, 1905; "Wedding," *North China Herald*, May 1, 1915.
91. "Jockey Leaving," *South China Morning Post*, April 12, 1935.
92. Peter Duus, "Zaikabō: Japanese Cotton Mills in China, 1895–1937," in *The Japanese Informal Empire*, ed. Peter Duus, Ramon H. Myers, and Mark R. Peattie (Princeton, NJ: Princeton University Press, 1989), 67.
93. "Obituary," *South China Morning Post*, April 16, 1913; "Mrs. M. P. Heard," *South China Morning Post*, December 30, 1926.
94. George Heard to Augustine Heard Jr., Hong Kong, May 30, 1873, JL-2, HBS.
95. Henry J. Lethbridge, "Condition of the European Working Class in Nineteenth Century Hong Kong," *Journal of the Hong Kong Branch of the Royal Asiatic Society* 15 (1975): 109.

6. WEALTH OR EXPERTISE

96. Carl T. Smith, "Protected Women in 19th-Century Hong Kong," in *Women and Chinese Patriarchy: Submission, Servitude and Escape*, ed. Maria Jaschok and Suzanne Miers (Hong Kong: Hong Kong University Press, 1994), 223.
97. Thomas N. Layton, *The "Other" Dixwells: Commerce and Conscience in an American Family* (Germantown, PA: Society for Historical Archaeology, 2021), 321–29.
98. Charles Sargent Dixwell, Massachusetts, United States, "United States Passport Applications, 1795–1925"; *S.S. Empress of Asia* Passenger Manifest, Vancouver, June 5, 1916; Fourteenth Census of the United States: 1920-Population, Department of Commerce—Bureau of the Census, all www.FamilySearch.com.
99. Catherine Ladds, "Eurasians in Treaty-Port China: Journeys Across Racial and Imperial Frontiers," in *Migrant Cross-Cultural Encounters in Asia and the Pacific*, ed. Jacqueline Leckie, Angela McCarthy, and Angela Wanhalla (Abingdon, UK: Routledge, 2017), 4.
100. Charles Sargent Dixwell, Massachusetts, United States, 1889, "United States Passport Applications, 1795–1925."
101. Finn, "Family Formations," 105.
102. Mary Wilkie, "Colonials, Marginals and Immigrants: Contributions to a Theory of Ethnic Stratification," *Comparative Studies in Society and History* 19, no. 1 (1977): 73.
103. Gustavus Farley Jr. to Augustine Heard Jr., Yokohama, December 20, 1875, in *Tea & Silk: The Letters of Gus Farley (1844–99)*, ed. Penelope West (n.p., 2020), 2:229.
104. Gustavus Farley Jr. to Albert Heard, Yokohama, November 25, 1876, in *Tea & Silk*, 2:239.
105. Marriage Announcement, *Boston Post*, March 27, 1880, in *Tea & Silk*, 11:253.
106. Katarine Cheney Farley to Mary Cheney, Yokohama, May 4, 1880, in *Tea & Silk*, 3:10.
107. Data pulled from the proof of concept for Thomas M. Larkin, "Mapping Sino-Foreign Networks and Mobility in China," University of Bristol, 2022.
108. Augustine Heard Jr. to "Harry," Hong Kong, December 20, 1876, and December 28, 1876; Augustine Heard Jr. to "Endicott," Hong Kong, August 13, 1875, all GL-5-3, HBS.
109. Frederick Cornes, New York, 1876, in *Tea & Silk*, 2:235.

6. WEALTH OR EXPERTISE

1. Albert F. Heard to Augustine Heard Jr., Hong Kong, January 7, 1875, HL-5, HBS; Albert F. Heard to James Fearon, Hong Kong, February 12, 1875, HL-5, HBS; Albert F. Heard to Mr Mackin, Boston, July 25, 1875, HL-5, HBS; Albert Heard, District Court of the United States for the District of Massachusetts, Boston, August 10, 1875, HQ-4-1.
2. Frederic Cople Jaher, "The Boston Brahmins in the Age of Industrial Capitalism," in *The Age of Industrialism in America: Essays in Social Structure and Cultural Values*, ed. Frederic Cople Jaher (New York: Free Press, 1968), 190–91.
3. Gregory Anderson, *Victorian Clerks* (Manchester: Manchester University Press, 1976), 129.

6. WEALTH OR EXPERTISE

4. John Heard, *An Account of His Life and the History of Augustine Heard & Co.* (1891), FP-4, HBS, 163–64.
5. Jaher, "The Boston Brahmins," 190.
6. Heard, *An Account of His Life*, 171; *Chronicle and Directory for China, Japan, & the Philippines* (Hong Kong: Daily Press Office, 1876), 144.
7. Copy of Agreement for Co-partnership of Heard & Co., for Albert F. Heard, October 30, 1876, EA-1-2, HBS.
8. Albert F. Heard to Jane Heard, Boston, July 30, 1875, HL-5, HBS.
9. John Heard to Augustine Heard Jr., Hong Kong, July 27, 1876, GM-1-5, HBS.
10. Heard, *An Account of His Life*, 169; Augustine Heard Jr., *Old China and New* (1894), GQ-2-2, HBS, 38–39; Robert W. Lovett, "The Heard Collection and Its Story," *Business History Review* 35, no. 4 (1961): 570.
11. Freda Harcourt, *Flagships of Imperialism: The P&O Company and Its Politics of Empire from Its Origins to 1867* (Manchester: Manchester University Press, 2006), 14; Chi-kong Lai, "The Qing State and Merchant Enterprise: The China Merchants' Company, 1872–1902," in *To Achieve Security and Wealth: The Qing Imperial State and the Economy, 1644–1911*, ed. Jane Kate Leonard and John R. Watt (Ithaca, NY: Cornell East Asia Series, 1992), 152; Stephen C. Lockwood, *Augustine Heard and Company, 1858–1862* (Cambridge, MA: Harvard University Press, 1971), 117.
12. Dael Norwood, *Trading Freedom: How Trade with China Defined Early America* (Chicago: University of Chicago Press, 2022), 160.
13. Augustine Heard Jr. to Albert F. Heard, New York, December 18, 1877; Augustine Heard Jr. to Albert F. Heard, Hong Kong, January 5, 1877; Augustine Heard Jr. to Albert F. Heard, Shanghai, March 14, 1877; Augustine Heard Jr. to Albert F. Heard, on board the *Alaska*, April 3, 1877; Augustine Heard Jr. to Albert F. Heard, Biarritz, September 22, 1877; Augustine Heard Jr. to Albert F. Heard, Paris, October 24, 1877, all HM-16-2, HBS.
14. Heard, *An Account of His Life*, 173.
15. John Heard to Augustine Heard Jr., Boston, May 17, 1878, FL-23, HBS; John Heard to Augustine Heard Jr., Ipswich, July 5, 1878, FL-23, HBS; Albert Heard to Parker, Boston, August 21, 1875, HL-5, HBS.
16. Notice regarding trusteeship of the Augustine Heard Estate, Hong Kong, December 23, 1878, FL-23, HBS; "Heard & Co.'s Failure," *Boston Daily Globe*, July 17, 1875.
17. Articles coming to 25 Tremont Row, Boston, 1875, FQ-3-1, HBS; John Heard Articles at Ipswich, Boston, 1875, FQ-3-1, HBS.
18. Memo of Contents, Sundry Cases, Belonging to Mrs. A. F. Heard, May 1872, HQ-3-2, HBS; Albert Heard to John Heard, 1873, HQ-3-2, HBS.
19. Purchase of shares for Livingston, Hong Kong, c. 1873, HQ-3-5.
20. Declaration between John Heard and William S. Dixter, Boston, April 12, 1872, FQ-3-1, HBS.
21. W. S. Russell, George Putnam Jr., Legal draft of Alice L. Heard's assets, Boston, August 18, 1875, FQ-3-2, HBS.
22. Erik Ringmar, *Liberal Barbarism: The European Destruction of the Palace of the Emperor of China* (New York: Palgrave Macmillan, 2013), 154.
23. Christine Howald and Léa Saint-Raymond, "Tracking Dispersal: Auction Sales from Yuanmingyuan Loot in Paris in the 1860s," *Journal for Art Market Studies* 2, no. 2 (2018): 3–4.

6. WEALTH OR EXPERTISE

24. Howald and Saint-Raymond, "Tracking Dispersal," 6. See also James L. Hevia, *English Lessons: The Pedagogy of Imperialism in Nineteenth-Century China* (Durham, NC: Duke University Press, 2003), 76–80; Tiffany Jenkins, *Keeping Their Marbles: How the Treasures of the Past Ended up in Museums—and Why They Should Stay There* (Oxford: Oxford University Press, 2016), 148.
25. Christopher Reed, *Bachelor Japanists: Japanese Aesthetics and Western Masculinities* (New York: Columbia University Press, 2017), 120; Noam Maggor, *Brahmin Capitalists: Frontiers of Wealth and Populism in America's First Gilded Age* (Cambridge, MA: Harvard University Press, 2017), 10.
26. "Old Heard House at Ipswich," *Boston Daily Globe*, December 19, 1909.
27. Kristin L. Hoganson, *Consumers' Imperium: The Global Production of American Domesticity, 1865–1920* (Chapel Hill: University of North Carolina Press, 2007), 19–20. See also Stephanie Barczewski, *Country Houses and the British Empire, 1700–1930* (Manchester: Manchester University Press, 2014), 177; Carl L. Crossman, *The Decorative Arts of the China Trade* (Woodbridge, UK: Antique Collectors' Club, 1991), 19; Mona Domosh, *American Commodities in an Age of Empire* (New York: Routledge, 2006), 5–6.
28. Joanna Cohen, *Luxurious Citizens: The Politics of Consumption in Nineteenth-Century America* (Philadelphia: University of Pennsylvania Press, 2017), 11–12. See also Thomas J. McCormick, *China Market: America's Quest for Informal Empire, 1893–1901* (Chicago: Quadrangle Books, 1967).
29. Barczewski, *Country Houses and the British Empire*, 176, 181; Helen Clifford, "Chinese Wallpaper: From Canton to Country House," in *The East India Company at Home, 1757–1857*, ed. Margot Finn and Katie Smith (London: UCL Press, 2018), 40; Jonathan Goldstein, "Philadelphia's Old China Trade and Early American Images of China," *Pennsylvania Legacies* 12, no. 1 (2012): 9.
30. Albert F. Heard, Inventory of Cases at Boston and Ipswich, 1872, HL-5, HBS.
31. John Heard to Albert Heard, Boston, January 8, 1879, FL-23, HBS.
32. Heard, *An Account of His Life*, 173.
33. Memo of John Heard's Personal Estate, Boston, c.1875, FQ-3-1, HBS.
34. John Heard Jr. to Albert Heard, Bonn, October 16, 1875, HN-6-4, HBS.
35. Lovett, "The Heard Collection and Its Story," 571.
36. Albert F. Heard to Jane Heard, Boston, July 30, 1875, HL-5, HBS.
37. Augustine Heard Jr. to Albert F. Heard, Biarritz, September 22, 1877, HM-16-2, HBS; Augustine Heard Jr. to Albert F. Heard, Biarritz, June 7, 1878, HM-16-2, HBS; Augustine Heard Jr. to Albert F. Heard, New York, May 4, 1880, HM-16-3, HBS; Frederic Cople Jaher, "Nineteenth-Century Elites in Boston and New York," *Journal of Social History* 6, no. 1 (1972): 49.
38. Sven Beckert, *The Monied Metropolis: New York City and the Consolidation of the American Bourgeoisie, 1850–1896* (Cambridge: Cambridge University Press, 2001), 238.
39. Beckert, *Monied Metropolis*, 155. For more on racial divisions in New York and Boston Society, see Hidetaka Hirota, *Expelling the Poor: Atlantic Seaboard States and the Nineteenth-Century Origins of American Immigration Policy* (Oxford: Oxford University Press, 2017), 205–9; John Kuo Wei Tchen, *New York Before Chinatown: Orientalism and the Shaping of American Culture, 1776–1882* (Baltimore: Johns Hopkins University Press, 1999), 225, 259.

6. WEALTH OR EXPERTISE

40. Augustine Heard Jr. to Albert F. Heard, New York, March 5, 1885; Augustine Heard Jr. to Albert F. Heard, New York, March 13, 1885; Augustine Heard Jr. to Albert F. Heard, New York, March 19, 1885; Augustine Heard Jr. to Albert F. Heard, New York, March 24, 1885; Augustine Heard Jr. to Albert F. Heard, New York, April 1, 1886, all HM-17-2, HBS.
41. Albert F. Heard to Augustine Heard Jr., Boston, July 24, 1875; Albert F. Heard to Jane Heard, Boston, July 30, 1875, both HL-5, HBS.
42. Woodsworth to Albert F. Heard, Chicopee, July 26, 1877, HQ-2-3, HBS. See Margarita Marinova, *Transnational Russian-American Travel Writing* (New York: Routledge, 2011), 92–93, for more on Russian and American perceptions of each other and the intellectual and material exchanges between the two countries in the late nineteenth century.
43. Albert Heard to John Heard, Paris, January 10, 1880, HN-3-1, HBS; John Heard to Mary Heard, Ipswich, June 18, 1878, FL-23, HBS; Mary Heard to John Heard, June 15, 1878, FN-2-9, HBS; John Heard to Albert Heard, Ipswich, June 20, 1878; Albert Heard, Legal Statement, Biarritz, France, February 2, 1881, HN-3-1, HBS; Mary Heard, Will, 1879, HQ-3-2, HBS.
44. Simon Sebag Montefiore, *The Romanovs, 1613–1918* (New York: Vintage Books, 2016), 462.
45. John Heard to Augustine Heard Jr., Ipswich, November 15, 1878, FL-23, HBS.
46. Woodsworth to Albert F. Heard, Chicopee, October 11, 1877, HQ-2-3, HBS; Albert F. Heard, Legal Statement, Biarritz, February 2, 1881, HN-3-1, HBS. See Nancy L. Green, *The Other Americans in Paris: Businessmen, Countesses, Wayward Youth, 1880–1941* (Chicago: University of Chicago Press, 2014), 16–21, for a detailed description of the elite American community in Paris.
47. Albert F. Heard to John Ward, Paris, November 28, 1877, HL-52, HBS; Albert F. Heard to John Heard, St. Petersburg, July 2, 1878, HL-52, HBS; Eugene de Zelenkoff to Albert F. Heard, St. Petersburg, March 14, 1879, HQ-2-3, HBS.
48. Julian Pauncefote to Albert F. Heard, London, June 30, 1879, HQ-2-3, HBS; Albert F. Heard to Julian Pauncefote, Paris, July 28, 1879, HL-53, HBS (the names referred to are vague—Rawson was likely Thomas Samuel Rawson, F. A. Campbell was likely Sir Frederick Alexander Campbell, and Admiral Hamilton is possibly Sir Richard Vesey Hamilton); White to Albert F. Heard, Hamburg, August 2, 1879, HQ-2-5, HBS.
49. Albert F. Heard to Admiral Lassofska, St. Petersburg, December 7, 1877, HL-52, HBS. Schilling is likely Nikolai von Schilling. See Nikolai von Schilling, *Nikolai Baron Schilling: Memoirs of an Ancient Mariner; Naval Officer of the Tsar, Exploration in the Tartar Sound, 1854–1856*, trans. Peter Girard (Moscow, 1892), 44.
50. Albert F. Heard to John Heard, St. Petersburg, June 25, 1878, HL-52, HBS; Albert F. Heard to Woodsworth, Paris, April 18, 1878, HQ-2-5, HBS; DeWitt Clinton Farrington to Albert F. Heard, Lowell, MA, March 6, 1879, HQ-2-3, HBS; Augustine Heard Jr. to Albert F. Heard, New York, April 18, 1878, HM-16-2, HBS; DeWitt Clinton Farrington to Albert F. Heard, Lowell, MA, May 13, 1879, HQ-2-3, HBS.
51. Albert F. Heard, Legal Statement, Biarritz, February 2, 1881, HN-3-1, HBS; Albert Heard to Livingston, Paris, July 26, 1879, HL-53, HBS; Albert F. Heard to John Heard, Paris, April 10, 1881, HN-3-1, HBS.

6. WEALTH OR EXPERTISE

52. Jacques Downs, *The Golden Ghetto: The American Commercial Community at Canton and the Shaping of American China Policy, 1874–1844* (New York: Associated Press, 1997), 229.
53. Downs, *The Golden Ghetto*, 335.
54. Thomas Franklin Waters, "Augustine Heard and His Friends," *Publications of the Ipswich Historical Society*, XII (Salem, MA: Newcomb & Gauss, 1916), 20, 30.
55. Waters, "Augustine Heard and His Friends," 34; Clippings of Augustine Heard Sr. Obituaries, 1868, FN-1-3, HBS.
56. Heard, *An Account of His Life*, 19. See also Robert Bennet Forbes, "Chapter VII, Addenda," in *Personal Reminiscences*, 2nd ed. (Boston: Little, Brown, and Company, 1882), 399; Jaher, "The Boston Brahmins," 228.
57. Clippings of Augustine Heard Sr. Obituaries, 1868, FN-1-3, HBS.
58. Heard, *An Account of His Life*, 162.
59. Cost of Furniture &c. at No. 3 Park Street, Boston, 1863–1864, FG-2, HBS.
60. Shanghai Effects c. 1880s, Papers of Francis Blackwell Forbes, Ms N-49, MHS.
61. James Fichter, *So Great a Proffit: How the East Indies Trade Transformed Anglo-American Capitalism* (Cambridge, MA: Harvard University Press, 2010), 280.
62. Joseph Coolidge to Algernon Coolidge Jr., Edinburgh, October 1, 1869; Joseph Coolidge to Algernon Coolidge Jr., Rome, May 2, 1869; Ellen Randolph Coolidge to Susan B. Coolidge, January 31, 1869; Ellen Randolph Coolidge to Susan B. Coolidge, Aix-les-Bains, July 16, 1869; Ellen Randolph Coolidge to Susan B. Coolidge, Pau, February 19, 1868, all Coolidge-Lowell Family Papers, Ms N-2404, MHS.
63. Joseph Coolidge to Algernon Coolidge Jr., Paris, August 27, 1869; Joseph Coolidge to Mary Coolidge, Great Malvern, September 3, 1868; Joseph Coolidge to Algernon Coolidge Jr., Edinburgh, October 1, 1869, all Ms N-2404, MHS.
64. Green, *The Other Americans in Paris*, 17, 40.
65. Ellen Randolph Coolidge to Susan B. Coolidge, Paris, March 30, 1870; Ellen Randolph Coolidge to Susan B. Coolidge, Les Artichauts, September 20, 1866; Ellen Randolph Coolidge to Susan B. Coolidge, Paris, March 30, 1870, all Ms N-2404, MHS.
66. Ellen Randolph Coolidge to Susan B. Coolidge, Les Artichauts, September 20, 1866, Ms N-2404, MHS.
67. Algernon Coolidge to Ellen Randolph Coolidge, Boston, October 30, 1866; Algernon Coolidge to Ellen Randolph Coolidge, Boston, August 24, 1868, Coolidge-Lowell Family Papers, Box 1, Folder 2, both Ms N-2404, MHS.
68. James M. Forbes, Keechong Club Records, 1879–1888, Ms N-49.67, MHS; James Murray Forbes, *Recollections and Events from the Threshold of Eighty-Five* (Boston, 1930), 37.
69. Henry Steele Commager, "The Century, 1887–1906," in *The Century, 1847–1946*, ed. Rodman Gilder et al. (New York: The Century Association, 1947), 56, 60; Kenneth T. Jackson et al., *The Encyclopedia of New York City* (New Haven, CT: Yale University Press, 2010), 226.
70. Commager, "The Century, 1887–1906," 62, 67.
71. Augustine Heard Jr. to the Century Association, New York, April 20, 1885, GL-5-3, HBS.
72. "The Saturday Club," Boston, December 26, 1885, Record Book Vol. 2, Ms N-857, MHS.

6. WEALTH OR EXPERTISE

73. See Leslie Butler, *Critical Americans: Victorian Intellectuals and Transatlantic Liberal Reform* (Chapel Hill: University of North Carolina Press, 2007), 130.
74. Record Book, Vol. 1, 1875–1887, Saturday Club, Boston Ms N-857, MHS; "Roll of Members of the Saturday Club," Boston, 1886, Ms N-857, MHS.
75. W. W. Goodwin, Notice, Boston, December 29, 1900, Record Book Vol. 2, Ms N-857, MHS.
76. Downs, *The Golden Ghetto*, 155.
77. Minutes of the First Meeting of the Keechong Club, November 25, 1879, Ms N-49.67, MHS.
78. Waters, "Augustine Heard and His Friends," 46.
79. Minutes of the Second Meeting of the Keechong Club, 1880, Ms N-49.67, MHS.
80. Minutes of the First Meeting of the Keechong Club.
81. Forbes, *Recollections and Events*, 23.
82. John Heard to brothers, Ipswich, August 5, 1873; John Heard to Augustine Heard Jr., Boston, April 15, 1873; John Heard to Albert Heard, Boston, June 19, 1873, all FL-18, HBS.
83. John Heard to J. S. Deblin, Boston, April 7, 1875; John Heard to Skipper Harman, Boston, April 4, 1875; John Heard to the Secretary of the Beverly Yacht Club, Boston, April 19, 1875; John Heard to H. B. Jackson, Boston, April 19, 1875, all FL-18, HBS.
84. Heard, *An Account of His Life*, 166–67.
85. John Heard to J. P. Gordan, Boston, April 19, 1875; John Heard to J. F. Tuckerman, Boston, April 19, 1875; John Heard to S. K. Lollard, Boston, April 19, 1875; John Heard to the Senators of the Somerset Club, Boston, April 19, 1875, all FL-18, HBS.
86. "R. B. Forbes Dead," *Boston Daily Globe*, November 24, 1889.
87. Augustine Heard Jr. to Alice Heard, Washington, November 1, 1895, FN-2-10, HBS.
88. Memo, John Heard Personal Estate, Boston, 1875, FQ-3-1, HBS.
89. John Heard to Augustine Heard Jr., Ipswich, October 20, 1878; John Heard to Augustine Heard Jr., Ipswich, November 5, 1878, both FL-23, HBS.
90. Heard, *An Account of His Life*, 162, 174–75, 178.
91. Shaun O'Connell, *Boston: Voices and Visions* (Amherst: University of Massachusetts Press, 2010), 87.
92. Stephen Kendrick and Paul Kendrick, *Sarah's Long Walk: The Free Blacks of Boston and How Their Struggle for Equality Changed America* (Boston: Beacon Press, 2004), 21–24.
93. Moying Li-Marcus, *Beacon Hill: The Life and Times of a Neighborhood* (Boston: Northeastern University Press, 2019), 23, 26, 38–39.
94. O'Connell, *Boston*, 134–35.
95. Reed, *Bachelor Japanists*, 122–23; Albert F. Heard, Diary, November 23, 1884, and February 20, 1885, Boston, HP-7, HBS.
96. O'Connell, *Boston*, 138.
97. Albert F. Heard, Diary, November 1, November 8–21, and November 23, 1884, Boston, HP-7, HBS; Elsie Heard to John Heard, Boston, March 18, 1890, FN-6-2, HBS. Based on proximity, it is reasonable to assume Albert Heard attended the Somerset Club.
98. Elsie Heard to John Heard, Boston, March 18, 1890; Elsie Heard to John Heard, Boston, March 20, 1890, both FN-6-2, HBS.

6. WEALTH OR EXPERTISE

99. "Art and Artists," *Boston Daily Globe*, March 1, 1908.
100. Augustine Heard Jr. to Albert F. Heard, New York, May 28, 1885; Augustine Heard Jr. to Albert F. Heard, New York, October 20, 1885, both HM-17-2, HBS.
101. Helen Maxima Heard to John Heard, Seoul, November 1, 1892, FN-2-8, HBS.
102. Helen Maxima Heard to John Heard, Shanghai, July 24, 1892; Helen Maxima Heard to John Heard, Seoul, November 1, 1892, both FN-2-8, HBS.
103. Helen Maxima Heard to John Heard, Seoul, April 13, 1893; Helen Maxima Heard to John Heard, Indian Ocean, May 19, 1893, both FN-2-8, HBS.
104. Norwood, *Trading Freedom*, 96, 130.
105. Augustine Heard Jr. to Albert F. Heard, New York, March 5, 1885, HM-17-2, HBS.
106. Augustine Heard Jr. to Albert F. Heard, New York, March 19, 1889; Augustine Heard Jr. to Albert F. Heard, New York, March 30, 1889; Augustine Heard Jr. to Albert F. Heard, Bar Harbor, September 11, 1889, all HM-17-3, HBS.
107. Henry E. Mattox, *Twilight of Amateur Diplomacy: The American Foreign Service and Its Senior Officers in the 1890s* (Kent, OH: Kent State University Press, 1989), 20, 43, 145.
108. Francis M. Bacon to John Heard, New York, January 29, 1853, FN-1-4, HBS; "Francis McNeil Bacon Dead," *New York Times*, September 22, 1912.
109. David M. Pletcher, *Diplomacy of Involvement: American Economic Expansion Across the Pacific, 1784–1900* (Columbia: University of Missouri Press, 2001), 206. Although Pletcher provides details upon Rockhill's expertise in East Asian matters, there is a chronological gap in his narrative between 1890–1894, the period when Augustine Heard Jr. was active in Seoul.
110. Francis M. Bacon to John Heard, New York, April 19, 1893; John Heard to Leverett Saltonstall, Boston, March 7, 1893; Francis M. Bacon to John Heard, New York, April 19, 1893, all FN-1-4, HBS; Charles Warren, *History of the Harvard Law School and of Early Legal Conditions in America* (New York: Lewis Publishing Co., 1908), 1:329.
111. Francis M. Bacon to John Heard, New York, April 19, 1893, FN-1-4, HBS; "Centurions, 1847–1946," 371, 380; Francis M. Bacon to John Heard, New York, April 21, 1893, FN-1-4, HBS.
112. Augustine Heard Jr. to John Heard, New York, April 15, 1885, FN-2-4, HBS; Augustine Heard Jr., "France and Indo-China," *The Century Illustrated Monthly Magazine* 32 (1886): 416–20.
113. Augustine Heard Jr. to John Heard, St Louis, January 24, 1894, FN-2-4, HBS; Augustine Heard Jr. to John Heard, Washington, DC, November 1, 1894, FN-2-10, HBS; Augustine Heard Jr. to John Heard, St Louis, January 27, 1894, FN-2-4, HBS. See James Harrison Wilson, *China: Travels and Investigations in the "Middle Kingdom," A Study of Its Civilization and Possibilities with a Glance at Japan* (New York: D. Appleton & Company, 1894).
114. Augustine Heard Jr. to Albert F. Heard, Bar Harbor, September 19, 1889, HM-17-3, HBS.
115. Heard, *Old China and New*, 45–46.
116. Mattox, *Twilight of Amateur Diplomacy*, 33.
117. Heard, *An Account of His Life*, 181. See Albert F. Heard, *The Russian Church and Russian Dissent: Comprising Orthodoxy, Dissent, and Erratic Sects* (New York: Harper & Brothers, 1887).

6. WEALTH OR EXPERTISE

118. Albert F. Heard, Diary, March 7–31, 1885, and March 24–31, 1885, Boston, HP-7, HBS.
119. Albert F. Heard, Diary, March 31–April 1, 1885, April 5–15, 1885, Washington and Boston, HP-7, HBS; War Department, Circular, June 27, 1887, Washington City, HQ-1-3, HBS; Heard, *An Account of His Life*, 181.
120. Albert F. Heard, Diary, October 4, 1888, New Haven, HP-8, HBS.
121. Albert F. Heard, Diary, November 17, 1888, and January 18–19, 1889, Washington, DC, HP-8, HBS.
122. Albert F. Heard, Diary, January 28–February 1, 1889, Washington, DC, HP-8, HBS.
123. Heard, *The Russian Church and Russian Dissent*, iv.
124. Albert F. Heard, Diary, February 11–14, 1889, Boston and New York, HP-8, HBS; Heard, *An Account of His Life*, 181; War Department, Circular, February 1, 1889, Washington City, HQ-1-3, HBS.
125. Albert F. Heard to John Heard, Washington, February 28, 1890, FN-2-6, HBS; Elsie Heard to John Heard, Boston, March 18, 1890, FN-2-6, HBS; Samuel Endicott Peabody to John Heard, Boston, April 1, 1890, FN-2-7, HBS; George W. Baldwin to John Heard, Boston, August 24, 1890, FN-2-7, HBS; H. S. W. Bartlett to Alice Heard, Cambridge, MA, March 28, 1890, FN-2-7, HBS; John Heard Jr. to John Heard, York Harbor, ME, September 4, 1890, FN-2-8, HBS; Augustine Heard Jr. to Alice Heard, York Harbor, ME, September 29, 1895, FN-2-10, HBS.

CONCLUSION

1. John Heard, *An Account of His Life and the History of Augustine Heard & Co.* (1891), FP-4, HBS, 183.
2. Linda Anderson, *Autobiography* (Abingdon, UK: Routledge, 2001), 42, notes the ambiguity of memory within memoirs and autobiographies. See also Mary Jo Maynes, *Taking the Hard Road: Life Course in French and German Workers' Autobiographies* (Chapel Hill: University of North Carolina Press, 1995), 202.
3. John M. Carroll, *Canton Days: British Life and Death in China* (Lanham, MD: Rowman & Littlefield, 2020), 11. Carroll argues the point well, writing, "if scholars have often presented the colonized 'other' as an 'undifferentiated, unknowable category,' they have also frequently portrayed colonists and other Westerners in homogenous terms."
4. Elizabeth Sinn, "In-between Place: A New Paradigm for Hong Kong Studies," in *Rethinking Hong Kong: New Paradigms, New Perspectives*, ed. Elizabeth Sinn, Siulun Wong, and Wing-hoi Chan (Hong Kong: Hong Kong University Centre of Asian Studies, 2009), 251; John M. Carroll, "The Canton System: Conflict and Accommodation in the Contact Zone," *Journal of the Hong Kong Branch of the Royal Asiatic Society* 50 (2010): 52; John M. Carroll, "Colonial Hong Kong as a Cultural-Historical Place," *Modern Asian Studies* 40, no. 2 (2006): 519. See also Elizabeth Sinn and Christopher Munn, eds., *Meeting Place: Encounters Across Cultures in Hong Kong, 1841–1984* (Hong Kong: Hong Kong University Press, 2017).
5. Dale Tomich, "The Order of Historical Time: The Longue Durée, and Micro-History," in *The Longue Durée and World-Systems Analysis*, ed. Richard E. Lee (Albany: State University of New York Press, 2012), 29.

CONCLUSION

6. See Catherine Chan, *The Macanese Diaspora in British Hong Kong: A Century of Transimperial Drifting* (Amsterdam: Amsterdam University Press, 2021); Catherine Ladds, "Eurasians in Treaty-Port China: Journeys Across Racial and Imperial Frontiers," in *Migrant Cross-Cultural Encounters in Asia and the Pacific*, ed. Jacqueline Leckie, Angela McCarthy, and Angela Wanhalla (Abingdon, UK: Routledge, 2017), 19–35; Vicky Lee, "The Code of Silence Across the Hong Kong Eurasian Community," in Sinn and Munn, *Meeting Place*, 41–63; Eileen P. Scully, "Prostitution as Privilege: The 'American Girl' of Treaty-Port Shanghai, 1860–1937," *International History Review* 20, no. 4 (1998): 855–83; Emma Jinhua Teng, *Eurasian: Mixed Identities in the United States, China, and Hong Kong, 1842–1943* (Berkeley: University of California Press, 2013); Don J. Wyatt, *The Blacks of Premodern China* (Philadelphia: University of Pennsylvania Press, 2010), 58.

BIBLIOGRAPHY

PRIMARY SOURCES

Archival sources

BAKER LIBRARY SPECIAL COLLECTIONS, HARVARD BUSINESS SCHOOL, CAMBRIDGE, MA

FP-4. John Heard, *An Account of His Life and the History of Augustine Heard & Co.* (1891).
GQ-2-1. Augustine Heard Jr. *The Poisoning in Hong Kong: An Episode of Life in China Forty Years Ago* (1894).
GQ-2-2. Augustine Heard Jr., *Old China and New* (1894).
Mss:1414. Portrait Photograph Collection. Baker Library Historical Collections Department.
Mss:766 1754–1898. Heard Family Business Records.
Mss:766 1847–1898 T896.Gustavus Tuckerman, Jr. Papers.

HISTORICAL PHOTOGRAPHS OF CHINA (HTTPS://WWW.HPCBRISTOL.NET)

VH, Vacher-Hilditch Collection. Bath: Bath Royal Literary and Scientific Institution.

CAMBRIDGE UNIVERSITY LIBRARY, CAMBRIDGE

GBR/0012/MS JM. Jardine Matheson Archive.

BIBLIOGRAPHY

THE NATIONAL ARCHIVES OF THE UNITED KINGDOM, KEW

CO 129 War and Colonial Department and Colonial Office: Hong Kong, Original Correspondence.
CO 700 Colonial Office and predecessors: Maps and Plans: Series I.
FO 17 Foreign Office: Political and Other Departments: General Correspondence before 1906, China.
FO 682 Foreign Office: Chinese Secretary's Office, Various Embassies and Consulates, China: General Correspondence.
FO 925 Foreign Office: Library: Maps and Plans.

MASSACHUSETTS HISTORICAL SOCIETY, BOSTON

Ms 272, Boston Views Album.
Ms N-49, Forbes family papers, 1732–1931.
Ms N-49.55, Warden family papers, 1747–1940.
Ms N-49.6, Crowell family papers, 1869–1976.
Ms N-49.67, James Murray Forbes papers, 1868–1957. Includes Forbes, *Old Shipping Days in Boston*, undated.
Ms N-156, John Murray Forbes letters [copies], 1863–1869.
Ms N-307, Lucy Lord Howes Hooper diaries, 1862–1999; bulk: 1862–1909.
Ms N-857, Saturday Club Records.
Ms N-1818, Beal family papers, 1802–1931; bulk: 1843–1862.
Ms N-2404, Coolidge-Lowell Family Papers.
Photos-XL.

PHILLIPS LIBRARY, PEABODY ESSEX MUSEUM, SALEM, MA

MSS-43. Nathaniel Kinsman Papers, 1784–1882.

U.S. NATIONAL ARCHIVES

RG: 59. Despatches from the U.S. Consuls in Hong Kong, 1844–1906. General Records of the Department of State.

Published primary sources

OFFICIAL REPORTS

Geneva Arbitration Tribunal. *Papers Relating to the Treaty of Washington, vol. 4, Geneva Arbitration*. Washington, DC: U.S. Government Printing Office, 1872.
Historical and Statistical Abstract of the Colony of Hong Kong. Hong Kong: Noronha & Co., 1911.

BIBLIOGRAPHY

Jarman, R. L., ed. *Hong Kong Annual Administration Reports 1841-1941: Vol. 1, 1841-1886*. London: Archive Edition, 1996.
Wenqing 文慶, ed. *Chou ban yi wu shi mo* 籌辦夷務始末 (The Record of Organizing Barbarian Affairs). Beijing: Gu gong bo wu yuan, 1930.

TREATIES

Treaty of Wanghia: Treaty of Peace, Amity, and Commerce Between the United States of America and the Chinese Empire. Wangxia, 1844.

CONTEMPORARY GUIDEBOOKS AND DIRECTORIES

An Anglochinese Calendar for the Year 1845, Corresponding to the Year of the Chinese Cycle Era 4482, or the 42d Year of the 75th Cycle of Sixty; Being the 25th Year of the Reign of Ta'ukwa'ng. Victoria, Hong Kong: The Chinese Repository, 1845.
Bridgman, Elijah Cole, and Samuel Wells Williams. *The Chinese Repository, Vol. 11*. Canton, 1842.
The China Directory. Hong Kong: China Mail Office, 1874.
The China Directory for 1863. Hong Kong: A. Shortrede & Co., 1863.
The China Directory for 1862. Hong Kong: A. Shortrede & Co., 1862.
Chronicle & Directory for China, Corea, Japan, the Philippines, Indo-China, Straits Settlement, Siam, Borneo, Malay States, &c. Hong Kong: Daily Press Office, 1894.
Chronicle & Directory for China, Japan, & the Phillippines [sic]. Hong Kong: Daily Press, 1864.
Chronicle & Directory for China, Japan, & the Philippines. Hong Kong: Daily Press, 1865.
Chronicle & Directory for China, Japan, & the Philippines. Hong Kong: Daily Press, 1868.
Chronicle & Directory for China, Japan, & the Philippines. Hong Kong: Daily Press, 1873.
Chronicle & Directory for China, Japan, & the Philippines. Hong Kong: Daily Press, 1874.
Chronicle & Directory for China, Japan, & the Philippines. Hong Kong: Daily Press, 1875.
Morris's Directory for China, Japan, and the Phillipines [sic] &c. Hong Kong: Morris & Co., 1870.

BOOKS AND ARTICLES

Allan, Nathan. *An Essay on the Opium Trade Including a Sketch of its History, Extent, Effects, Etc., as Carried on in India and China*. Boston: John P. Jewett & Co., 1850.
Ball, Benjamin. *Rambles in Eastern Asia, Including China and Manila: During Several Years Residence*. Boston: James French & Company, 1855.
Bradford, Ruth. *"Maskee!" The Journal and Letters of Ruth Bradford, 1861-1872*. Hartford, CT: Prospect Press, 1983.
Clarke, Prescott, and J. S. Gregory, eds. *Western Reports on the Taiping: A Selection of Documents*. London: Croom Helm, 1982.
Emerson, Ralph Waldo. *English Traits*. Boston: Phillips, Sampson & Company, 1856.

Forbes, James M. *Recollections and Events from the Threshold of Eighty-Five.* Boston, 1930.

Forbes, Robert Bennet. "Rambling Recollections Connected with China." In *Personal Reminiscences*, 2nd ed., 333–412. Boston: Little, Brown, and Company, 1882.

Forbes, Robert Bennet. *Letters from China: The Canton-Boston Correspondence of Robert Bennet Forbes, 1838–1840.* Edited by Phyllis Forbes Kerr. Mystic: Mystic Seaport Museum Inc., 1996.

Fortune, Robert. *Three Years' Wanderings in the Northern Provinces of China, Including a visit to the Tea, Silk, and Cotton Countries; With an Account of the Agriculture and Horticulture of the Chinese, New Plants, etc.* London: John Murray, 1847.

Heard, Albert. *The Russian Church and Russian Dissent: Comprising Orthodoxy, Dissent, and Erratic Sects.* New York: Harper & Brothers, 1887.

Heard, Augustine, Jr. "France and Indo-China." *The Century Illustrated Monthly Magazine* 32 (1886): 416–20.

Hillard, Katharine, ed. *My Mother's Journal: A Young Lady's Diary of Five Years Spent in Manila, Macao, and the Cape of Good Hope, From 1829–1834.* Boston: Geo. H. Ellis Co., 1900.

Holmes, Oliver Wendell. *Elsie Venner: A Romance of Destiny.* Boston: Houghton Mifflin, 1861.

Hunter, William C. *The "Fan Kwae" at Canton: Before the Treaty Days, 1825–1844.* Shanghai: The Oriental Affairs, 1882.

Knox, Thomas W. *John, or Our Chinese Relations: A Study of our Emigration and Commercial Intercourse with the Celestial Empire.* New York: Harper & Brothers, 1879.

Palmer, Aaron Haight. *Letter to the Hon. John M. Clayton, Secretary of State, Enclosing a Paper, Geographical, Political, Commercial, on the Independent Oriental Nations; and Containing a Plan for Opening, Extending, and Protecting American Commerce in the East &c.* Washington, DC: Gideon & Company 1849.

Phillips, James Duncan, ed. *The Canton Letters, 1839–1841, of William Henry Low.* Salem, MA: Essex Institute, 1948.

Schilling, Nikolai von. *Nikolai Baron Schilling: Memoirs of an Ancient mariner; Naval Officer of the Tsar, Exploration in the Tartar Sound, 1854–1856.* Trans. Peter Girard. Moscow, 1892.

Warren, Thomas R. *Dust and Foam: Or, Three Oceans and Two Continents; Being Ten Years' Wanderings in the East and West Indies, China, Philippines, Australia, and Polynesia.* New York: C. Scribner & S. Low, 1859.

Wei Yuan 魏源. *Haiguo Tuzhi* 海國圖志 (Illustrated Treatise on the Maritime Kingdoms), 1844.

West, Penelope, ed. *Tea & Silk: The Letters of Gus Farley (1844–99), vol. II.* Unpublished.

———. *Tea & Silk: The Letters of Gus Farley (1844–99), vol. III.* Unpublished.

Wilson, James Harrison. *China: Travels and Investigations in the "Middle Kingdom": A Study of Its Civilization and Possibilities with a Glance at Japan.* New York: D. Appleton & Company, 1894.

Wood, William M. *Fankwei: Or, the San Jacinto in the Seas of India, China, and Japan.* New York: Harper & Brothers, 1859.

Xu Jiyu 徐繼畬. *Ying huan zhi lüe* 瀛環志略 (A Short Account of the Maritime Circuit), 1849.

Yung Wing. *My Life in China and America*. New York: Henry Holt and Company, 1909.

SECONDARY SOURCES

Abe, Kaori. *Chinese Middlemen in Hong Kong's Colonial Economy, 1830–1890*. Abingdon, UK: Routledge, 2018.
Abe, Kaori. "Intermediary Elites in the Treaty Port World: Tong Mow-chee and his Collaborators in Shanghai." *Journal of the Royal Asiatic Society* 3, no. 25 (2015): 461–80.
Abbenhuis, Maartje. *An Age of Neutrals: Great Power Politics, 1815–1914*. Cambridge: Cambridge University Press, 2014.
Acharya, Amitav. "Asia Is Not One." *Journal of Asian Studies* 4, no. 69 (2010): 1001–13.
Adams, Bluford. "World Conquerors or a Dying People? Racial Theory, Regional Anxiety, and the Brahmin Anglo-Saxonists." *Journal of the Gilded Age and Progressive Era* 8, no. 2 (2009): 189–215.
Adelman, Jeremy. "What Is Global History Now?" *Aeon Essays*, March 2, 2017. https://aeon.co/essays/is-global-history-still-possible-or-has-it-had-its-moment.
Agnew, Eadaoin. *Imperial Women Writers in Victorian India: Representing Colonial Life, 1850–1910*. Basingstoke: Palgrave Macmillan, 2016.
Ahuja, Ravi. "Mobility and Containment: The Voyages of South Asian Seamen, c. 1900–1960." In *Coolies, Capital and Colonialism: Studies in Indian Labour History*, ed. Rana P. Behal and Marcel van der Linden, 111–41. Cambridge: International Review of Social History, 2006.
Anderson, Gregory. *Victorian Clerks*. Manchester: Manchester University Press, 1976.
Anderson, Linda. *Autobiography*. Abingdon, UK: Routledge, 2001.
Arkush, R. David, and Leo O. Lee. "Exotic America." In *Land Without Ghosts: Chinese Impressions of America from the Mid-Nineteenth Century to the Present*, ed. R. David Arkush and Leo O. Lee, 15–18. Berkeley: University of California Press, 1989.
Attard, Bernard, and Andrew Dilley. "Finance, Empire and the British World." *Journal of Imperial and Commonwealth History* 41, no. 1 (2013): 1–10.
Auerbach, Jeffrey A. *Imperial Boredom: Monotony and the British Empire*. Oxford: Oxford University Press, 2018.
Backe-Hansen, Melanie, and David Olusoga. *A House Through Time*. Basingstoke, UK: Pan Macmillan, 2020.
Barczewski, Stephanie. *Country Houses and the British Empire, 1700–1930*. Manchester: Manchester University Press, 2014.
Barkawi, Tarak, and Mark Laffey. "Retrieving the Imperial: Empire and International Relations." *Millennium: Journal of International Studies* 3, no. 2 (2002): 109–27.
Barreyre, Nicholas. "The Politics of Economic Crisis: The Panic of 1873, the End of Reconstruction, and the Realignment of American Politics." *Journal of the Gilded Age and Progressive Era* 10, no. 4 (2011): 403–23.
Barth, Volker and Cvetkovski, Roland. "Introduction—Encounters of Empires: Methodological Approaches." In *Imperial Co-operation and Transfer, 1870–1930: Empires and Encounters*, ed. Volker Barth and Roland Cvetkovski, 3–34. London: Bloomsbury, 2015.

Bayly, Chris, et al. "AHR Conversation: On Transnational History." *American Historical Review* 111, no. 5 (2006): 1441–64.
Becker, Bert. "Western Firms and Their Chinese Compradors: The Case of the Jebsen and Chao Families." In *Meeting Place: Encounters Across Cultures in Hong Kong, 1841–1984*, ed. Elizabeth Sinn and Christopher Munn, 107–30. Hong Kong: Hong Kong University Press, 2017.
Beckert, Sven. "Emancipation and Empire: Reconstructing the Worldwide Web of Cotton Production in the Age of the American Civil War." *American Historical Review* 109, no. 5 (2004): 1405–38.
Beckert, Sven. *The Monied Metropolis: New York City and the Consolidation of the American Bourgeoisie, 1850–1896*. Cambridge: Cambridge University Press, 2001.
Bell, David. "This Is What Happens When Historians Overuse the Idea of the Network." *New Republic*, October 25, 2013. https://newrepublic.com/article/114709/world-connecting-reviewed-historians-overuse-network-metaphor.
Benton, Gregor, and Hong Liu, eds. *Dear China: Emigrant Letters and Remittances, 1820–1980*. Berkeley: University of California Press, 2018.
Betta, Chiara. "From Orientals to Imagined Britons: Baghdadi Jews in Shanghai." *Modern Asian Studies* 37, no. 4 (2003): 999–1023.
Bickers, Robert. "British Concessions and Chinese Cities, 1910s–1930s." In *New Narratives of Urban Space in Republican Chinese Cities: Emerging Social, Legal and Governance Orders*, ed. Billy K. L. So and Madeline Zelin, 157–96. Leiden: Brill, 2013.
———. "The *Challenger*: Hugh Hamilton Lindsay and the Rise of British Asia, 1832–1865." *Transactions of the Royal Historical Society* 22 (2012): 141–69.
———. *China Bound: John Swire & Sons and Its World, 1816–1980*. London: Bloomsbury, 2020.
———. *Empire Made Me: An Englishman Adrift in Shanghai*. London: Allen Lane, 2003.
———. *Getting Stuck in for Shanghai, or Putting the Kibosh on the Kaiser from the Bund: The British at Shanghai and the Great War*. Sydney: Penguin Books, 2014.
———. *The Scramble for China: Foreign Devils in the Qing Empire, 1832–1914*. London: Allen Lane, 2011.
Bickley, Gillian, ed. *Through American Eyes: The Journals of George Washington (Farley) Heard*. Hong Kong: Proverse Hong Kong, 2017.
Biggerstaff, Knight. "The Secret Correspondence of 1867–1868: Views of Leading Chinese Statesmen Regarding the Further Opening of China to Western Influence." *Journal of Modern History* 22, no. 2 (1950): 122–36.
Billias, George Athan. *American Constitutionalism Heard Round the World, 1776–1989*. New York: New York University Press, 2009.
Blue, Archibald Duncan. "The China Coast: A Study of British Shipping in Shipping in Chinese Waters, 1842–1914." PhD diss., University of Strathclyde, 1982.
Blue, Gregory. "Opium for China: The British Connection." In *Opium Regimes: China, Britain, and Japan, 1839–1952*, ed. Timothy Brook and Bob Tadashi Wakabayashi, 31–54. Berkeley: University of California Press, 2000.
Blussé, Leonard. *Visible Cities: Canton, Nagasaki, and Batavia and the Coming of the Americans*. Cambridge, MA: Harvard University Press, 2008.
Booker, Kristina. *Menials: Domestic Service and the Cultural Transformation of British Society, 1650–1850*. Lewisburg, PA: Bucknell University Press, 2017.

BIBLIOGRAPHY

Bourne, Kenneth. "British Preparations for War with the North, 1861–1862." *English Historical Review* 76, no. 301 (1961): 600–632.
Braga, Stuart. "Making Impressions: The Adaptation of a Portuguese Family to Hong Kong, 1750–1900." PhD diss., Australian National University, 2012.
Bridge, Carl, and Kent Fedorowich. "Mapping the British World." *Journal of Imperial and Commonwealth History* 31, no. 2 (2010): 1–15.
Brogan, D. W. "The Remote Revolution: A British View." *Proceedings of the American Philosophical Society* 106, no. 1 (1962): 1–9.
Buckner, Phillip, and R. Douglas Francis, eds. *Rediscovering the British World*. Calgary: University of Calgary Press, 2010.
Buettner, Elizabeth. *Empire Families: Britons and Late Imperial India*. Oxford: Oxford University Press, 2004.
———. "Problematic Spaces, Problematic Races: Defining 'Europeans' in Late Colonial India." *Women's Historical Review* 9, no. 2 (2000): 277–98.
Burke, Martin J. *The Conundrum of Class: Public Discourse on the Social Order in America*. Chicago: University of Chicago Press, 1995.
Burton, Antoinette. "Archive Stories: Gender in the Making of Imperial and Colonial Histories." In *Gender and Empire*, ed. Philippa Levine, 281–94. Oxford: Oxford University Press, 2004.
Bushman, Richard L. *The Refinement of America: Persons, Houses, Cities*. New York: Knopf, 1992.
Butler, Leslie. *Critical Americans: Victorian Intellectuals and Transatlantic Liberal Reform*. Chapel Hill: University of North Carolina Press, 2007.
Byrne, Bridget. "The Crisis of Identity? Englishness, Britishness, and Whiteness." In *Empire and After: Englishness and Post-Colonial Perspectives*, ed. Graham Macphee and Prem Poddar, 139–58. New York: Berghahn Books, 2007.
Carroll, John M. *Canton Days: British Life and Death in China*. Lanham, MD: Rowman & Littlefield, 2020.
———. "The Canton System: Conflict and Accommodation in the Contact Zone." *Journal of the Hong Kong Branch of the Royal Asiatic Society* 50 (2010): 51–66.
———. "Colonial Hong Kong as a Cultural-Historical Place." *Modern Asian Studies* 40, no. 2 (2006): 517–43.
———. *A Concise History of Hong Kong*. New York: Rowman & Littlefield, 2007.
———. *Edge of Empires: Chinese Elites and British Colonials in Hong Kong*. Cambridge, MA: Harvard University Press, 2005.
Chan, Catherine. "Cosmopolitan Visions and Intellectual Passions: Macanese Publics in British Hong Kong." *Modern Asian Studies* 56, no. 1 (2022): 350–77.
———. *The Macanese Diaspora in British Hong Kong: A Century of Transimperial Drifting*. Amsterdam: Amsterdam University Press, 2021.
Chan, Wai Kwan. *The Making of Hong Kong Society: Three Studies of Class Formation in Early Hong Kong*. Oxford: Clarendon Press, 1991.
Chang, Gordon H. *Fateful Ties: A History of America's Preoccupation with China*. Cambridge, MA: Harvard University Press, 2015.
Chang, Hsin-pao. *Commissioner Lin and the Opium War*. Cambridge, MA: Harvard University Press, 1964.
Chen, Song-chuan. *Merchants of War and Peace: British Knowledge of China in the Making of the Opium War*. Hong Kong: Hong Kong University Press, 2017.

Chen Zu'en. *Xunfang Dongyangren: Jindai Shanghai de Riben Juliumin* 尋訪東洋人：近代上海的日本居留民 (Looking for Orientals: Japanese Residents in Modern Shanghai). Shanghai: Shanghai Academy of Social Sciences, 2007.

Cheng, Irene. *Clara Ho Tung: A Hong Kong Lady, Her Family and Her Times*. Hong Kong: Hong Kong University Press, 1976.

Cheung, David. *Christianity in China: The Making of the First Native Protestant Church*. Leiden: Brill, 2004.

Ching, May-bo. "Chopsticks or Cutlery? How Canton Hong Merchants Entertained Foreign Guests in the Eighteenth and Nineteenth Centuries." In *Narratives of Free Trade: The Commercial Cultures of Early US–China Relations*, ed. Kendall Johnson, 99–116. Hong Kong: Hong Kong University Press, 2011.

Clarke, I. F. *Voices Prophesying War, 1763–1984*. London: Panther, 1970.

Clarke, Prescott, and Frank H. H. King. *A Research Guide to China-Coast Newspapers, 1822–1911*. Cambridge, MA: Harvard University Press, 1965.

Clifford, Helen. "Chinese Wallpaper: From Canton to Country House." In *The East India Company at Home, 1757–1857*, ed. Margot Finn and Katie Smith, 39–67. London: UCL Press, 2018.

Coates, Austin. *China Races*. Hong Kong: Hong Kong University Press, 1983.

Cohen, Joanna. *Luxurious Citizens: The Politics of Consumption in Nineteenth-Century America*. Philadelphia: University of Pennsylvania Press, 2017.

Colley, Linda. *Britons: Forging the Nation, 1707–1837*. New Haven, CT: Yale University Press, 2005.

Commager, Henry Steele. "The Century, 1887–1906." In *The Century, 1847–1946*, ed. Rodman Gilder et al., 54–79. New York: The Century Association, 1947.

Conforti, Joseph. *Imagining New England: Explorations of Regional Identity from the Pilgrims to the Mid-Twentieth Century*. Chapel Hill: University of North Carolina Press, 2001.

Cott, Nancy F. "Divorce and the Changing Status of Women in Eighteenth-Century Massachusetts." *William and Mary Quarterly* 33, no. 4 (1976): 586–614.

Cox, Thomas H. " 'Money, Credit, and Strong Friends': Warren Delano II and the Importance of Social Networking in the Old China Trade." In *The Private Side of the Canton Trade, 1700–1840: Beyond the Companies*, ed. Paul A. Van Dyke and Susan E. Schopp, 132–47. Hong Kong: Hong Kong University Press, 2018.

Crossman, Carl L. *The Decorative Arts of the China Trade*. Woodbridge, UK: Antique Collectors' Club, 1991.

Darnton, Robert. *The Great Cat Massacre and Other Episodes in French Cultural History*. New York: Basic Books, 1984.

Davidoff, Leonore, and Catherine Hall. *Family Fortunes: Men and Women of the English Middle Class, 1780–1850*. Oxford: Routledge, 2002.

Day, Jenny Huangfu. *Qing Travelers to the Far West: Diplomacy and the Information Order in Late Imperial China*. Cambridge: Cambridge University Press, 2018.

De Jong, Gerald Francis. *The Reformed Church in China, 1842–1951*. Grand Rapids, MI: Eerdmans, 1992.

de Silva, Prasannajit. "Representing Home Life Abroad: British Domestic Life in Early-Nineteenth-Century India." *Visual Culture in Britain* 12, no. 3 (2011): 313–31.

Derks, Hans. *History of the Opium Problem: The Assault on the East, ca. 1600–1950*. Leiden: Brill, 2012.

BIBLIOGRAPHY

Dikötter, Frank. *The Discourse of Race in Modern China*. London: Hurst & Company, 1992.
Domosh, Mona. *American Commodities in an Age of Empire*. New York: Routledge, 2006.
Downs, Jacques M. *The Golden Ghetto: The American Commercial Community at Canton and the Shaping of American China Policy, 1784–1844*. London: Associated University Press, 1997.
Doyle, Don H. "Slavery or Independence: The Confederate Dilemma in Europe." In *The U.S. South and Europe: Transatlantic Relations in the Nineteenth and Twentieth Centuries*, ed. Cornelis A. van Minnen and Manfred Berg, 105–24. Lexington: University Press of Kentucky, 2013.
Drayton, Richard, and David Motadel. "Discussion: The Futures of Global History." *Journal of Global History* 13, no. 1 (2018): 1–21.
Dubois, Laurent. "Diffusion and Empire." In *The Oxford Handbook of Sports History*, ed. Robert Edelman and Wayne Wilson, 171–78. Oxford: Oxford University Press, 2017.
Duus, Peter. "Zaikabō: Japanese Cotton Mills in China, 1895–1937." In *The Japanese Informal Empire*, ed. Peter Duus, Ramon H. Myers, and Mark R. Peattie, 65–100. Princeton, NJ: Princeton University Press, 1989.
Dyer, Brainard. "Civil War Naval Activities in the Pacific: An Extract from the Autobiography of William B. Simmons." *Pacific Historical Review* 7, no. 3 (1938): 254–66.
Edwards, Norman. *The Singapore House and Residential Life, 1819–1939*. Oxford: Oxford University Press, 1990.
Ekelund, Robert B., John D. Jackson, and Mark Thornton. "The 'Unintended Consequences' of Confederate Trade Legislation." *Eastern Economic Journal* 30, no. 2 (2004): 187–205.
Ellsworth, E. W. "Introduction to the Journal: Journal of Occurrences at Canton During the Cessation of Trade at Canton, 1839." *Journal of the Hong Kong Branch of the Royal Asiatic Society* 4 (1964): 9–36.
England, Vaudine. *Kindred Spirits: A History of the Hong Kong Club*. Hong Kong: Hong Kong Club, 2016.
———. "Zindel's Rosary Hill—Hong Kong's Forgotten War." *Journal of the Royal Asiatic Society Hong Kong Branch* 57 (2017): 36–66.
Etherington, Norman. "Colonial Panics Big and Small in the British Empire." In *Anxieties, Fear and Panic in Colonial Settings: Empires on the Verge of a Nervous Breakdown*, ed. Harald Fischer-Tiné, 201–44. London: Palgrave Macmillan, 2016.
Fairbank, John K. *Trade and Diplomacy on the China Coast: The Opening of the Treaty Ports, 1842–1854*. Stanford, CA: Stanford University Press, 1964.
Farris, Johnathan A. *Enclave to Urbanity: Canton, Foreigners, and Architecture from the Late Eighteenth to the Early Twentieth Centuries*. Hong Kong: Hong Kong University Press, 2016.
———. "Thirteen Factories of Canton: An Architecture of Sino-Western Collaboration and Confrontation." *Building & Landscapes: Journal of Vernacular Architecture Forum* 14 (2007): 66–83.
Fichter, James R. *So Great a Proffit: How the East Indies Trade Transformed Anglo-American Capitalism*. Cambridge, MA: Harvard University Press, 2010.

Finn, Margot. "Family Formations: Anglo India and the Familial Proto-State." In *Structures and Transformations in Modern British History*, ed. David Feldman and Jon Lawrence, 100–117. Cambridge: Cambridge University Press, 2011.

Finn, Margot, and Kate Smith, eds. *The East India Company at Home, 1757–1857*. London: UCL Press, 2018.

Fischer-Tiné, Harald. "'The Drinking Habits of Our Countrymen': European Alcohol Consumption and Colonial Power in British India." *Journal of Imperial and Commonwealth History* 40, no. 3 (2012): 383–408.

———. "The Making of a 'Ruling Race': Defining and Defending Whiteness in Colonial India." In *Racism in the Modern World: Historical Perspectives on Cultural Transfer and Adaptation*, ed. Manfred Berg and Simon Wendt, 213–35. New York: Berghahn, 2011.

———. "'White Women Degrading Themselves to the Lowest Depths': European Networks of Prostitution and Colonial Anxieties in British India and Ceylon, ca. 1880–1914." *Indian Economic and Social History Review* 40, no. 2 (2003): 163–90.

Fischer-Tiné, Harald, ed. *Anxieties, Fear, and Panic in Colonial Settings: Empires on the Verge of a Nervous Breakdown*. Cham, Switzerland: Palgrave Macmillan, 2016.

Foot, John. "Micro-History of a House: Memory and Place in a Milanese Neighbourhood, 1890–2000." *Urban History* 34, no. 3 (2007): 431–52.

Ford, Stacilee. *Troubling American Women: Narratives of Gender and Nation in Hong Kong*. Hong Kong: Hong Kong University Press, 2011.

Francus, Marilyn. *Monstrous Motherhood: Eighteenth Century Culture and the Ideology of Domesticity*. Baltimore: John Hopkins University Press, 2012.

Galbraith, John S. *Reluctant Empire: British Policy on the South African Frontier, 1834–1854*. Berkeley: University of California Press, 1963.

Ghose, Indira. "The Memsahib Myth: Englishwomen in Colonial India." In *Women & Others: Perspectives on Race, Gender, and Empire*, ed. Celia R. Daileader and Rhoda E. Johnson, 107–28. Basingstoke, UK: Palgrave Macmillan, 2007.

Ghosh, Suresh Chandra. *The Social Condition of the British Community in Bengal, 1757–1800*. Leiden: E. J. Brill, 1970.

Ginzburg, Carlo. "Microhistory: Two or Three Things That I Know About It." In *Theoretical Discussions of Biography: Approaches from History, Microhistory, and Life Writing*, ed. Hans Renders and Binne de Haan, 39–168. Leiden: Brill, 2014.

Glaeser, Edward L. "Reinventing Boston: 1630–2003." *Journal of Economic Geography* 5 (2005): 119–53.

Gobat, Michael. "'Our Indian Empire': The Transimperial Origins of U.S. Liberal Imperialism." In *Crossing Empires: Taking U.S. History into Transimperial Terrain*, ed. Kristin L. Hoganson and Jay Sexton, 69–92. Durham, NC: Duke University Press, 2020.

Goldsmith, Emma. "In Trade: Wealthy Business Families in Glasgow and Liverpool." PhD diss., Northwestern University, 2017.

Goldstein, Johnathan. "Nathan Dunn (1782–1844) as Anti-Opium Trader and Sino-Western Cultural Intermediary." In *The Private Side of the Canton Trade, 1700–1840: Beyond the Companies*, ed. Paul A. Van Dyke and Susan E. Schopp, 95–114. Hong Kong: Hong Kong University Press, 2018.

Goldstein, Jonathan. "Philadelphia's Old China Trade and Early American Images of China." *Pennsylvania Legacies* 12, no. 1 (2012): 6–11.

BIBLIOGRAPHY

Goodman, Bryna. "Improvisations on a Semi Colonial Theme: Or, How to Read a Celebration of Transnational Urban Community." *Journal of Asian Studies* 59, no. 4 (2000): 889–926.

Goodman, Paul. "Ethics and Enterprise: The Values of a Boston Elite, 1800–1860." *American Quarterly* 18, no. 3 (1966): 437–51.

Government of Hong Kong, Government Records Service. Carl Smith Collection. Government of Hong Kong Special Administrative Region, 2018. https://search.grs.gov.hk/en/searchcarladv.xhtml.

Grace, Richard J. *Opium and Empire: The Lives and Careers of William Jardine and James Matheson*. Montreal: McGill-Queen's University Press, 2014.

Green, Nancy L. *The Other Americans in Paris: Businessmen, Countesses, Wayward Youth, 1880–1941*. Chicago: University of Chicago Press, 2014.

Greenberg, Michael. *British Trade and the Opening of China 1800–42*. Cambridge: Cambridge University Press, 1951.

Greenwood, Andrea, and Mark W. Harris. *An Introduction to Unitarian and Universalist Traditions*. Cambridge: Cambridge University Press, 2011.

Grewal, Inderpal. *Home and Harem: Nation, Gender, Empire, and the Cultures of Travel*. Durham, NC: Duke University Press, 1996.

Hall, Catherine. *Civilising Subjects: Metropole and Colony in the English Imagination, 1830–1867*. Chicago: University of Chicago Press, 2002.

Hamilton, Gary G. "The Organizational Foundations of Western and Chinese Commerce: A Historical Comparative Analysis." In *Asian Business Networks*, ed. Gary G. Hamilton, 43–58. Berlin: Walter de Gruyter, 1996.

Hao, Yen-p'ing. "The Rise and Fall of the Comprador." In *Chinese Business Enterprise*, ed. Rajeswary Amplavanar Brown, 2:275–94. London: Routledge, 1996.

Harcourt, Freda. *Flagships of Imperialism: The P&O Company and Its Politics of Empire from Its Origins to 1867*. Manchester: Manchester University Press, 2006.

Hardt, Michael, and Antonio Negri. *Empire*. Cambridge, MA: Harvard University Press, 2000.

Harvey, Elizabeth A. " 'Layered Networks': Imperial Philanthropy in Birmingham and Sydney, 1860–1914." *Journal of Imperial and Commonwealth History* 41, no. 1 (2013): 120–42.

Hastings, Paula. " 'Our Glorious Anglo-Saxon Race Shall Ever Fill Earth's Highest Place': The Anglo Saxon and the Construction of Identity in Late-Nineteenth-Century Canada." In *Canada and the British World: Culture, Migration, and Identity*, ed. Phillip Buckner and R. Douglas Francis, 93–107. Vancouver: University of British Columbia Press, 2006.

He, Sebing. "Russell and Company and the Imperialism of Anglo-American Free Trade." In *Narratives of Free Trade: The Commercial Cultures of Early US-China Relations*, ed. Kendall Johnson, 83–98. Hong Kong: Hong Kong University Press, 2011.

Hellman, Lisa. *This House Is Not a Home: European Everyday Life in Canton and Macao, 1730–1830*. Leiden: Brill, 2018.

Hevia, James. *English Lessons: The Pedagogy of Imperialism in Nineteenth-Century China*. Durham, NC: Duke University Press, 2003.

——. *The Imperial Security State: British Colonial Knowledge and Empire-Building in Asia*. Cambridge: Cambridge University Press, 2012.

Hirota, Hidetaka. *Expelling the Poor: Atlantic Seaboard States and the Nineteenth-Century Origins of American Immigration Policy.* Oxford: Oxford University Press, 2017.

Ho, Vincent Wai-kit. "Duties and Limitations: The Role of United States Consuls in Macao, 1849-1869." In *Americans and Macao: Trade, Smuggling and Diplomacy on the South China Coast,* ed. Paul A. Van Dyke, 143-52. Hong Kong: Hong Kong University Press, 2012.

Hoganson, Kristin L. *Consumers' Imperium: The Global Production of American Domesticity, 1865-1920.* Chapel Hill: University of North Carolina Press, 2007.

Hopkins, Anthony. *American Empire: A Global History.* Princeton, NJ: Princeton University Press, 2018.

Howald, Christine, and Léa Saint-Raymond. "Tracking Dispersal: Auction Sales from Yuanmingyuan Loot in Paris in the 1860s." *Journal for Art Market Studies* 2, no. 2 (2018): 1-23.

Howe, James M., Jr. "George Rogers Hall, Lover of Plants." *Journal of the Arnold Arboretum* 4, no. 2 (1923): 92-98.

Huang, Dao Zi. " 'You May Go to Hong Kong for Me': British Views of a Chinese Colony." PhD diss., University of Hong Kong, 2018.

Hugill, Peter J. "The American Challenge to British Hegemony, 1861-1947." *Geographical Review* 99, no. 3 (2009): 403-25.

Hunt, Michael H. *The Making of a Special Relationship: The United States and China to 1914.* New York: Columbia University Press, 1983.

Hunter, Jane. *The Gospel of Gentility: American Women Missionaries in Turn-of-the-Century China.* New Haven, CT: Yale University Press, 1984.

Hutchison, Coleman. "Whistling 'Dixie' for the Union (Nation, Anthem, Revision)." *American Literary History* 19, no. 3 (2007): 603-28.

Ignatiev, Noel. *How the Irish Became White.* New York: Routledge, 1995.

Immerwahr, Daniel, *How to Hide an Empire: A Short History of the Greater United States.* New York: Vintage Books, 2020.

Iriye, Akira. *Global and Transnational History: The Past, Present, and Future.* Basingstoke, UK: Palgrave Macmillan, 2013.

Israel, Jerry. *Progressivism and the Open Door: America and China, 1905-1921.* Pittsburgh, PA: University of Pittsburgh Press, 1971.

Jackson, Kenneth T., et al. *The Encyclopedia of New York City.* New Haven, CT: Yale University Press, 2010.

Jackson, Matthew O. *Social and Economic Networks.* Princeton, NJ: Princeton University Press, 2008.

Jaher, Frederic Cople. "The Boston Brahmins in the Age of Industrial Capitalism." In *The Age of Industrialism in America: Essays in Social Structure and Cultural Values,* ed. Frederic Cople Jaher, 188-262. New York: Free Press, 1968.

———. "Nineteenth-Century Elites in Boston and New York." *Journal of Social History* 6, no. 1 (1972): 32-77.

Jen, Yu-wen. *The Taiping Revolutionary Movement.* New Haven, CT: Yale University Press, 1973.

Jenkins, Tiffany. *Keeping Their Marbles: How the Treasures of the Past Ended up in Museums—and Why They Should Stay There.* Oxford: Oxford University Press, 2016.

Johnson, Robert Erwin. *Far China Station: The U.S. Navy in Asian Waters, 1800–1898*. Annapolis, MD: Naval Institute Press, 1979.
Johnson, Ryan. "European Cloth and 'Tropical' Skin: Clothing Material and British Ideas of Health and Hygiene in Tropical Climates." *Bulletin of the History of Medicine* 8, no. 3 (2009): 530–60.
Jones, Howard. *Blue and Gray Diplomacy: A History of Union and Confederate Foreign Relations*. Chapel Hill: University of North Carolina Press, 2010.
Judge, Joan. "Review: The Power of Print? Print Capitalism and News Media in Late Qing and Republican China." *Harvard Journal of Asiatic Studies* 66, no. 1 (2006): 233–54.
Jung, Moon-ho. "Outlawing 'Coolies': Race, Nation, and Empire in the Age of Emancipation." *American Quarterly* 57, no. 3 (2005): 677–901.
Kaplan, Amy. *The Anarchy of Empire in the Making of U.S. Culture*. Cambridge, MA: Harvard University Press, 2002.
Kaul, Chandrika. *Reporting the Raj: The British Press and India, c. 1880–1922*. Manchester: Manchester University Press, 2003.
Kemp, Thomas R. "Community and War: The Civil War Experience of Two New Hampshire Towns." In *Toward a Social History of the American Civil War: Exploratory Essays*, ed. Maris A Vinovskis, 31–77. Cambridge: Cambridge University Press, 1990.
Kendrick, Stephen, and Paul Kendrick. *Sarah's Long Walk: The Free Blacks of Boston and How Their Struggle for Equality Changed America*. Boston: Beacon Press, 2004.
Kessler, Marlene, Kristen Lee, and Daniel Menning, eds. *The European Canton Trade 1723: Competition and Cooperation*. Oldenburg, Germany: De Gruyter, 2016.
Killingray, David. "'A Good West Indian, a Good African, and, in Short, a Good Britisher': Black and British in a Colour-Conscious Empire, 1760–1950." *Journal of Imperial and Commonwealth History* 36, no. 3 (2008): 363–81.
King, Amelia Kay. "James Keenan: United States Consul to Hong Kong." MA thesis, North Texas State University, 1978.
Kirsch, George B. "The Fate of Cricket in the United States: Revisited." *Journal of Sport History* 43, no. 2 (2016): 168–91.
Kong, Vivian. *Multiracial Britishness: Global Networks in Hong Kong, 1910–45*. Cambridge: Cambridge University Press, 2023.
———. "Multiracial Britons: Britishness, Diasporas, and Cosmopolitanism in Interwar Hong Kong." PhD diss., University of Bristol, 2019.
———. "Whiteness, Imperial Anxiety, and the 'Global 1930s': The White British League Debate in Hong Kong." *Journal of British Studies* 59, no. 2 (2020): 343–71.
Kramer, Paul A. "The Golden Gate and the Open Door: Civilization, Empire, and Exemption in the History of U.S. Chinese Exclusion, 1868–1910." In *China's Development from a Global Perspective*, ed. Maria Dolores Elizalde and Wang Jianlang, 196–219. Cambridge: Cambridge Scholars Publishing, 2017.
Kramer, Paul A. "Empires, Exceptions, and Anglo-Saxons: Race and Rule Between the British and United States Empires, 1880–1910." *Journal of American History* 88, no. 4 (2002): 1315–53.
Kuai Shixun 蒯世勋. *Shanghai gonggong zujie shigao* 上海公共租界史稿 (A History of Shanghai's International Settlement). Shanghai: Shanghai renmin chubanshe, 1980.

Ladds, Catherine. "Eurasians in Treaty-Port China: Journeys Across Racial and Imperial Frontiers." In *Migrant Cross-Cultural Encounters in Asia and the Pacific*, ed. Jacqueline Leckie et al., 19–35. Abingdon, UK: Routledge, 2016.

———. "Imperial Ambitions: Russians, Britons, and the Politics of Nationality in the Chinese Customs Service, 1890–1937." In *Russia and Its Northeast Asian Neighbors: China, Japan, and Korea, 1858–1945*, ed. Kimitaka Matsuzato, 33–48. Lanham, MD: Lexington Books, 2016.

Lai Chi-kong. "The Qing State and Merchant Enterprise: The China Merchants' Company, 1872–1902." In *The Achieve Security and Wealth: The Qing Imperial State and Economy, 1644–1911*, ed. Jane Kate Leonard and John R. Watt, 139–56. Ithaca, NY: Cornell University Press, 1992.

Larkin, Thomas M. Mapping Sino-Foreign Networks and Mobility in China. 2022. https://doi.org/10.5523/bris.vdbur8omw21y262ylgaikiind.

Layton, Thomas N. *The "Other" Dixwells: Commerce and Conscience in an American Family*. Germantown, PA: Society for Historical Archaeology, 2021.

Lazich, Michael. "Placing China in Its 'Proper Rank Among the Nations': The Society for the Diffusion of Useful Knowledge in China and the First Systematic Account of the United States in Chinese." *Journal of World History* 22, no. 3 (2011): 527–52.

Le Pichon, Alain. *Aux origines de Hong Kong: Aspects de la civilisation commerciale à Canton—Le fonds de commerce de Jardine, Matheson & Co., 1827–1839*. Paris: L'Harmattan, 1998.

Lee, Vicky. "The Code of Silence Across the Hong Kong Eurasian Community." In *Meeting Place: Encounters Across Cultures in Hong Kong, 1841–1984*, ed. Elizabeth Sinn and Christopher Munn, 41–63. Hong Kong: Hong Kong University Press, 2017.

Legarda, Benito J., Jr. *After the Galleons: Foreign Trade, Economic Change & Entrepreneurship in the Nineteenth-Century Philippines*. Manila: Ateneo de Manila University Press, 1999.

Leonard, Jane Kate. *Wei Yuan and China's Rediscovery of the Maritime World*. Cambridge, MA: Council on East Asian Studies, Harvard University, 1984.

Lethbridge, Henry J. "Condition of the European Working Class in Nineteenth Century Hong Kong." *Journal of the Hong Kong Branch of the Royal Asiatic Society* 15 (1975): 88–112.

———. *Hong Kong: Stability and Change: A Collection of Essays*. Hong Kong: Oxford University Press, 1978.

Levine, Phillipa. "Introduction: Why Gender and Empire?" In *Gender and Empire*, ed. Phillipa Levine, 1–13. Oxford: Oxford University Press, 2004.

Li Ding-yi 李定一. *Zhongmei waijiao shi vol. 1* 中美外交史第一冊 (The History of Sino-American Diplomacy, vol. 1). Taipei: Qingshui Publishing, 1960.

Li-Marcus, Moying. *Beacon Hill: The Life and Times of a Neighborhood*. Boston: Northeastern University Press, 2019.

Lin, Man-huong. *China Upside Down: Currency, Society, and Ideologies, 1808–1856*. Cambridge, MA: Harvard University Press, 2006.

Link, William A. "Southerners Abroad: Europe and the Cultural Encounter, 1830–1895." In *The U.S. South and Europe: Transatlantic Relations in the Nineteenth and Twentieth Centuries*, ed. Cornelis A. van Minnen and Manfred Berg, 15–29. Lexington: University of Kentucky Press, 2013.

BIBLIOGRAPHY

Liu, Jianhui 劉建輝. "Birth of an East Asian Information Network." Trans. Joshua A. Fogel. *Sino-Japanese Studies* 16 (2009): 61–78.
Liu, Kwang-ching. *Anglo-American Steamship Rivalry in China, 1862–74*. Cambridge, MA: Harvard University Press, 1962.
Liu, Xincheng. "The Global View of History in China." *Journal of World History* 23, no. 3 (2012): 61–78.
Lockwood, Stephen C. *Augustine Heard & Company, 1858–1862: American Merchants in China*. Cambridge, MA: Harvard East Asian Monographs, 1971.
Lopez, Ian Haney. *White by Law: The Legal Construction of Race*. New York: New York University Press, 1996.
Lorimer, Douglas. "From Victorian Values to White Virtues: Assimilation and Exclusion in British Racial Discourse, c. 1870–1914." In *Rediscovering the British World*, ed. Phillip Buckner and R. Douglas Francis, 109–34. Calgary: University of Calgary Press, 2005.
Lovett, Robert W. "The Heard Collection and Its Story." *Business History Review* 35, no. 4 (1961): 567–73.
Lowe, Kate, and Eugene McLaughlin. " 'Caution! The Bread Is Poisoned': The Hong Kong Mass Poisoning of January 1857." *Journal of Imperial and Commonwealth History* 43, no. 2 (2015): 189–209.
Lowrie, Claire. *Masters and Servants: Cultures of Empire in the Tropics*. Manchester: Manchester University Press, 2016.
Lydon, Jane. *Imperial Emotions: The Politics of Empathy Across the British Empire*. Cambridge: Cambridge University Press, 2019.
Macanese Families. https://www.macanesefamilies.com.
Mackenzie, John. "Empires and States in Expansion and Contraction." *Britain and the World* 9, no. 1 (2016): 1–9.
Magee, Gary B., and Andrew S. Thompson. *Empire and Globalisation: Networks of People, Goods and Capital in the British World, c. 1850–1914*. Cambridge: Cambridge University Press, 2010.
Maggor, Noam. *Brahmin Capitalism: Frontiers of Wealth and Populism in America's First Gilded Age*. Cambridge, MA: Harvard University Press, 2017.
Malcolm, Dominic. *Globalizing Cricket: Englishness, Empire and Identity*. London: Bloomsbury Academic, 2013.
Mandler, Peter. *The English National Character: The History of an Idea from Edmund Burke to Tony Blair*. New Haven, CT: Yale University Press, 2006.
Mao, Haijian. *The Qing Empire and the Opium War: The Collapse of the Heavenly Dynasty*. Trans. Joseph Lawson, Craig Smith, and Peter Lavelle. Cambridge: Cambridge University Press, 2016.
Marinova, Margarita. *Transnational Russian-American Travel Writing*. New York: Routledge, 2011.
Marme, Michael. "From Suzhou to Shanghai: A Tale of Two Systems." *Journal of Chinese History* 2, no. 1 (2018): 79–107.
Marshall, Peter James. "British Society in India under the East India Company." *Modern Asian Studies* 31, no. 1 (1997), 89–108.
Mattox, Henry E. *Twilight of Amateur Diplomacy: The American Foreign Service and its Senior Officers in the 1890s*. Kent, OH: Kent State University Press, 1989.

Maynard, Margaret. *Fashioned from Penury: Dress as Cultural Practice in Colonial Australia*. Cambridge: Cambridge University Press, 1994.

Maynes, Mary Jo. *Taking the Hard Road: Life Course in French and German Workers' Autobiographies*. Chapel Hill: University of North Carolina Press, 1995.

McCarthy, Kathleen D. *American Creed: Philanthropy and the Rise of Civil Society, 1700–1865*. Chicago: University of Chicago Press, 2003.

McCormick, Thomas J. *China Market: America's Quest for Informal Empire, 1893–1901*. Chicago: Quadrangle Books, 1967.

McKibbin, Ross. *Class and Cultures: England 1918–1951*. Oxford: Oxford University Press, 1998.

Mentz, Søren. "Cultural Interaction Between the British Diaspora in Madras and the Host Community, 1650–1790." In *Asian Port Cities 1600–1800: Local and Foreign Cultural Interactions*, ed. Masashi Haneda, 162–74. Singapore: National University of Singapore Press, 2009.

Mills, Sara. *Gender and Colonial Space*. Manchester: Manchester University Press, 2009.

Mittapalli, Rajeshwar, and Susmita Roye. "Introduction." In *The Male Empire Under the Female Gaze: The British Raj and the Memsahib*, ed. Susmita Roye and Rajeshwar Mittapalli, 1–28. Amherst, NY: Cambria Press, 2013.

Mizutani, Satoshi. *The Meaning of White: Race, Class, and the "Domiciled Community" in British India, 1858–1930*. Oxford: Oxford Historical Manuscripts, 2011.

Mohanram, Radhika. *Imperial White: Race, Diaspora, and the British Empire*. Minneapolis: University of Minnesota Press, 2007.

Montefiore, Simon Sebag. *The Romanovs, 1613–1918*. New York: Vintage Books, 2016.

Morris, James M. "America's Stepchild." *Wilson Quarterly* 11, no. 3 (1987): 112–27.

Mosca, Matthew. *From Frontier Policy to Foreign Policy: The Question of India and the Transformation of Geopolitics in Qing China*. Stanford, CA: Stanford University Press, 2013.

Munn, Christopher. *Anglo-China: Chinese People and British Rule in Hong Kong, 1841–1880*. London: Routledge, 2001.

———. "Hong Kong, 1841–1870: All the Servants in Prison and Nobody to Take Care of the House." In *Masters, Servants and Magistrates in Britain and the Empire, 1562–1955*, ed. Douglas Hay and Paul Craven, 365–401. Chapel Hill: University of North Carolina Press, 2004.

Naval History and Heritage Command. Dictionary of American Naval Fighting Ships. Washington, DC: Naval Historical Center. https://www.history.navy.mil/research/histories/ship-histories/danfs.html.

Ng Chin-keong. *Trade and Society: The Amoy Network on the China Coast, 1683–1735*. Singapore: National University of Singapore Press, 2015.

Norwood, Dael. *Trading Freedom: How Trade with China Defined Early America*. Chicago: University of Chicago Press, 2022.

———. "Trading in Liberty: The Politics of the American China Trade, c. 1784–1862." PhD diss., Princeton University, 2012.

O'Connell, Shaun. *Boston: Voices and Visions*. Amherst: University of Massachusetts Press, 2010.

Painter, Nell Irvin. *The History of White People*. New York: Norton, 2010.

———. "Thinking About the Languages of Money and Race: A Response to Michael O'Malley, 'Specie and Species.'" *American Historical Review* 99, no. 2 (1994): 396–404.

Pauly, John J. "The Great Chicago Fire as a National Event." *American Quarterly* 36, no. 5 (1984): 668–83.

Pietsch, Tamson. "Rethinking the British World." *Journal of British Studies* 52, no. 2 (2013): 441–63.

Platt, Stephen. *Autumn in the Heavenly Kingdom: China, the West, and the Epic Story of the Taiping Civil War*. New York: Vintage Books, 2012.

———. *Imperial Twilight: The Opium War and the End of China's Last Golden Age*. London: Atlantic Books, 2018.

Pletcher, David M. *Diplomacy of Involvement: American Economic Expansion Across the Pacific, 1784–1900*. Columbia: University of Missouri Press, 2001.

Polachek, James M. *The Inner Opium War*. Cambridge, MA: Harvard East Asian Monographs, 1992.

Pradhan, Queeny. *Empire in the Hills: Simla, Darjeeling, Ootacamund, and Mount Abu, 1820–1920*. Oxford: Oxford University Press, 2017.

Rea, Christopher G. " 'He'll Roast All Subjects That May Need the Roasting': Puck and Mr. Punch in Nineteenth-Century China." In *Asian Punches: A Transcultural Affair*, ed. Hans Harder and Barbara Mittler, 389–442. Heidelberg: Springer, 2013.

Reed, Christopher. *Bachelor Japanists: Japanese Aesthetics and Western Masculinities*. New York: Columbia University Press, 2017.

Reilly, Thomas H. *The Taiping Heavenly Kingdom: Rebellion and the Blasphemy of Empire*. Seattle: University of Washington Press, 2004.

Reinhardt, Anne. *Navigating Semi-Colonialism: Shipping, Sovereignty, and Nation-Building in China, 1860–1937*. Cambridge, MA: Harvard East Asian Monographs, 2018.

Rendall, Jane. "The Condition of Women, Women's Writing and the Empire in Nineteenth-Century Britain." In *At Home with the Empire: Metropolitan Culture in the Imperial World*, ed. Catherine Hall and Sonya O. Rose, 101–21. Cambridge: Cambridge University Press, 2006.

Rice, Stephen. *Minding the Machine: Languages of Class in Early Industrial America* Berkeley: University of California Press, 2004.

Ringmar, Erik. *Liberal Barbarism: The European Destruction of the Palace of the Emperor of China*. New York: Palgrave Macmillan, 2013.

Robertson, Stacey. " 'On the Side of Righteousness': Women, the Church, and Abolition." In *Women, Dissent, and Anti-Slavery in Britain and America, 1790–1865*, ed. Elizabeth J. Clapp and Julie Roy Jeffrey, 155–74. Oxford: Oxford University Press, 2011.

Rosenthal, Caroline. "Drinks, Domesticity and the Forging of an American Identity in Susan Warner's *The Wide, Wide, World*, (1850)." In *Drink in the Eighteenth and Nineteenth Centuries*, ed. Susanne Schmid and Barbara Schmidt-Haberkamp, 23–24. London: Pickering and Chatto, 2014.

Rothschild, Emma. *The Inner Life of Empires: An Eighteenth-Century History*. Princeton, NJ: Princeton University Press, 2011.

Rowe, William T. *Hankou: Conflict and Community in a Chinese City, 1796–1895*. Stanford, CA: Stanford University Press, 1989.

Ruskola, Teemu. "Canton Is Not Boston: The Invention of American Imperial Sovereignty." *American Quarterly* 57, no. 3 (2005): 859–84.

Sachsenmaier, Dominic. "Global History and Critiques of Western Perspectives." *Comparative Education* 42, no. 3 (2006): 451–70.

Said, Edward. *Orientalism*. London: Routledge & Kegan Paul, 1978.

Schoonover, Thomas. *Uncle Sam's War of 1898 and the Origins of Globalization*. Lexington: University of Kentucky Press, 2003.

Scully, Eileen P. *Bargaining with the State from Afar: American Citizenship in Treaty Port China, 1844–1942*. New York: Columbia University Press, 2001.

———. "Prostitution as Privilege: The 'American Girl' of Treaty-Port Shanghai, 1860–1937." *International History Review* 20, no. 4 (1998): 855–83.

———. "Taking the Low Road to Sino-American Relations: 'Open Door' Expansionists and the Two China Markets." *Journal of American History* 82, no. 1 (1995): 62–83.

Sen, Indrani. *Gendered Transactions: The White Woman in Colonial India, c. 1820–1930*. Manchester: Manchester University Press, 2017.

———. "Memsahibs and Health in Colonial Medical Writings, c. 1840 to c. 1930." *South Asia Research* 30, no. 3 (2010): 253–74.

Sen, Ronojoy. *Nation at Play: A History of Sport in India*. New York: Columbia University Press, 2015.

Sen, Tansen. "The Intricacies of Premodern Asian Connections." *Journal of Asian Studies* 4, no. 69 (2010): 991–99.

Shaw, Martin. "Post-Imperial and Quasi-Imperial: State and Empire in the Global Era." *Millennium: Journal of International Studies* 31, no. 2 (2002): 327–36.

Sinn, Elizabeth. "In-Between Place: A New Paradigm for Hong Kong Studies." In *Rethinking Hong Kong: New Paradigms, New Perspectives*, ed. Elizabeth Sinn, Siu-lun Wong, and Wing-hoi Chan, 245–304. Hong Kong: Hong Kong University Centre of Asian Studies, 2009.

———. "Introduction." In *Meeting Place: Encounters Across Cultures in Hong Kong, 1841–1984*, ed. Elizabeth Sinn and Christopher Munn, ix–xx. Hong Kong: Hong Kong University Press, 2017.

Smith, Carl T. "Abandoned Into Prosperity: Women on the Fringe of Expatriate Society." In *Merchants' Daughters: Women, Commerce, and Regional Culture in South China*, ed. Helen F. Siu, 129–41. Hong Kong: Hong Kong University Press, 2010.

———. *Chinese Christians: Elites, Middlemen, and the Church in Hong Kong*. Oxford: Oxford University Press, 1985.

———. "Protected Women in 19th-Century Hong Kong." In *Women and Chinese Patriarchy: Submission, Servitude and Escape*, ed. Maria Jaschok and Suzanne Miers, 221–37. Hong Kong: Hong Kong University Press, 1994.

Smith-Rosenberg, Carroll. *This Violent Empire: The Birth of an American National Identity*. Chapel Hill: University of North Carolina Press, 2010.

Soper, Willard B. Order of Skull & Bones [Membership list by year], c. 1905. New Haven, CT: Yale University, Medical Historical Library.

Spence, Jonathan D. *God's Chinese Son: The Taiping Heavenly Kingdom of Hong Xiuquan*. New York: Norton, 1996.

Spielmann, M. H. *The History of "Punch."* London: Cassell and Company Ltd., 1895.

BIBLIOGRAPHY

Spivak, Gayatri Chakravorty. "Can the Subaltern Speak?" In *Marxism and the Interpretation of Culture*, ed. Lawrence Grossberg and Cary Nelson, 267–310. Urbana: University of Illinois Press, 1988.

Stanley, Liz. "Letter-Writing and the Actual Course of Things: Doing the Business, Helping the World Go Round." In *The Palgrave Handbook of Auto/Biography*, ed. Anne Chappell and Julie M. Parsons, 165–84. Basingstoke, UK: Palgrave Macmillan, 2020.

State of California, Office of the Attorney General. History of the Office of the Attorney General. State of California Department of Justice, 2020. https://oag.ca.gov/history.

Steedman, Carolyn. *Labours Lost: Domestic Service and the Making of Modern England*. Cambridge: Cambridge University Press, 2009.

Stein, Sarah Abrevaya. *Extraterritorial Dreams: European Citizenship, Sephardi Jews, and the Ottoman Twentieth Century*. Chicago: University of Chicago Press, 2016.

Stelle, Charles C. "American Trade in Opium to China, 1821–39." *Pacific Historical Review* 10, no. 1 (1941): 430–31.

Stoler, Ann Laura. *Duress: Imperial Durabilities in Our Times*. Durham, NC: Duke University Press, 2016.

———. "Making Empire Respectable: The Politics of Race and Sexual Morality in 20th-Century Colonial Cultures." *American Ethnologist* 16, no. 4 (1989): 634–60.

———. "Rethinking Colonial Categories: European Communities and the Boundaries of Rule." *Comparative Studies in Society and History* 31, no. 1 (1989): 134–61.

Sturgis, Tim. *Rivalry in Canton: The Control of Russell & Co. 1838–1840 and the Founding of Augustine Heard & Co*. London: Warren Press, 2006.

Summers, Anne. "British Women and Cultures of Internationalism, c. 1815–1914." In *Structures and Transformations in Modern British History*, ed. David Feldman and Jon Lawrence, 187–209. Cambridge: Cambridge University Press, 2011.

Tamarkin, Elisa. *Anglophilia: Deference, Devotion, and Antebellum America*. Chicago: University of Chicago Press, 2008.

Tchen, John Kuo Wei. *New York Before Chinatown: Orientalism and the Shaping of American Culture, 1776–1882*. Baltimore: Johns Hopkins University Press, 1999.

Teng, Emma Jinhua. *Eurasian: Mixed Identities in the United States, China, and Hong Kong, 1842–1943*. Berkley: University of California Press, 2013.

Thomas, Nicola J. "Mary Curzon: 'American Queen of India.'" In *Colonial Lives Across the British Empire: Imperial Careering in the Long Nineteenth Century*, ed. David Lambert and Adam Lester, 285–308. Cambridge: Cambridge University Press, 2010.

Tindall, Gillian. *Three Houses, Many Lives: The Story of a Cotswold Vicarage, a Surrey Boarding School and a London Home*. London: Vintage, 2013.

Tomich, Dale. "The Order of Historical Time: The Longue Durée, and Micro-History." In *The Longue Durée and World-Systems Analysis*, ed. Richard E. Lee, 9–34. Albany: State University of New York Press, 2012.

Tripathi, Dwijendra. *The Oxford History of Indian Business*. New Delhi: Oxford University Press, 2004.

Tsai, Jung-fang. *Hong Kong in Chinese History: Community and Social Unrest in the British Colony, 1842–1913*. New York: Columbia University Press, 1993.

Tuffnell, Stephen. " 'The International Siamese Twins': The Iconography of Anglo-American Inter-Imperialism." In *Comic Empires: Imperialism in Cartoons, Caricature, and Satirical Art*, ed. Richard Scully and Andrekos Varnava, 92–133. Manchester: Manchester University Press, 2019.

——. *Made in Britain: Nation and Emigration in Nineteenth-Century America*. Berkeley: University of California Press, 2020.

Van, Rachel Tamar. "The 'Woman Pigeon': Gendered Bonds and Barriers in the Anglo-American Commercial Community in Canton and Macao, 1800–1849." *Pacific Historical Review* 83, no. 4 (2014): 561–91.

Van Dyke, Paul A. *Americans and Macao: Trade, Smuggling, and Diplomacy on the South China Coast*. Hong Kong: Hong Kong University Press, 2012.

——. *Canton Trade: Life and Enterprise on the China Coast, 1700–1845*. Hong Kong: Hong Kong University Press, 2005.

——. "Smuggling Networks of the Pearl River Delta Before 1842: Implications for Macao and the American China Trade." *Journal of the Hong Kong Branch of the Royal Asiatic Society* 50 (2010): 67–97.

van Nederveen Meerkerk, Elsie. "Introduction: Domestic Work in the Colonial Context: Race, Color, and Power in the Household." In *Towards a Global History of Domestic and Caregiving Workers*, ed. Dirk Hoerder, Elsie van Nederveen Meerkerk, and S. Neunsinger, 243–54. Leiden: Brill, 2015.

van Rossum, Matthias. "The Dutch East India Company in Asia, 1595–1811." In *A Global History of Convicts and Penal Colonies*, ed. Clare Anderson, 157–82. London: Bloomsbury Academic, 2018.

Volo, Dorothy Deneen, and James M. Volo. *Family Life in 17th and 18th Century America*. Westport, CT: Greenwood Press, 2006.

von Oppen, Achim, and Silke Strickrodt. "Introductions: Biographies Between Spheres of Empire." *Journal of Imperial and Commonwealth History* 44, no. 5 (2016): 717–29.

Wakeman, Frederick Jr. *The Fall of Imperial China*. New York: Free Press, 1975.

Warren, Charles. *History of the Harvard Law School and of Early Legal Conditions in America*, vol. 1. New York: Lewis Publishing Co., 1908.

Waters, Thomas F. "Augustine Heard and His Friends." *Publications of the Ipswich Historical Society, XXI*. Salem: Newcomb & Gauss, 1916.

Webster, Anthony. "The Development of British Commercial and Political Networks in the Straits Settlements 1800–1868: The Rise of Colonial and Economic Identity?" *Modern Asian Studies* 45, no. 4 (2011): 899–929.

Wolfendale, Stuart. *Imperial to International: A History of St. John's Cathedral Hong Kong*. Hong Kong: Hong Kong University Press, 2013.

Wong, John D. *Global Trade in the Nineteenth Century: The House of Houqua and the Canton System*. Cambridge: Cambridge University Press, 2016.

Wong, J. Y. *Deadly Dreams: Opium, Imperialism, and the Arrow War (1856–1860) in China*. Cambridge: Cambridge University Press, 1998.

Wood, Francis. *No Dogs and Not Many Chinese: Treaty Port Life in China, 1843–1943*. London: John Murray, 1998.

Wood, James Carter. "Drinking, Fighting, and Working-Class Sociability in Nineteenth-Century Britain." In *Drink in the Eighteenth and Nineteenth Centuries*, ed. Susanne Schmid and Barbara Schmidt-Haberkamp, 71–80. London: Pickering and Chatto, 2014.

Woollacott, Angela. *Settler Society in the Australian Colonies: Self-Government and Imperial Culture*. Oxford: Oxford University Press, 2015.

Wyatt, Don J. *The Blacks of Premodern China*. Philadelphia: University of Pennsylvania Press, 2010.

Xu, Guoqi. *Chinese and Americans: A Shared History*. Cambridge, MA: Harvard University Press, 2014.

Xu Yuebiao 徐曰彪. "Xianggang de shehui jiegou 香港的社會結構 (Hong Kong's Social Composition)." In *Shijiu Shiji de Xianggang* 十九世紀的香港 (Nineteenth-Century Hong Kong), ed. Yu Shengwu 余繩武, Liu Cunkuan 劉存寬, and Zhu Bian 主編, 337–426. Beijing: Zhonghua Shuju, 1993.

Xue, Zhang. "Imperial Maps of Xinjiang and Their Readers in Qing China, 1660–1860." *Journal of Chinese History* 4, no. 1 (2020): 111–33.

Yao Tingfang 姚廷芳. *Yapian Zhanzheng yu: Daoguang Huangdi, Lin Zexu, Qishan, Qiying,* 鴉片戰爭與: 道光皇帝, 林則徐, 琦善, 耆英 (The Opium War and: the Daoguang Emperor, Lin Zexu, Qishan, and Qiying). Taipei: Sanmin shuju, 1970.

Zelin, Madeline. "The Structure of the Chinese Economy During the Qing Period: Some Thoughts on the 150th Anniversary of the Opium War." In *Perspectives on Modern China: Four Anniversaries*, ed. Kenneth Lieberthal et al., 31–67. Armonk, NY: M. E. Sharpe, 1991.

Zou, Yizheng. "English Newspapers in British Colonial Hong Kong: The Case of the South China Morning Post (1903–1941)." *Critical Arts* 29, no. 1 (2015): 26–40.

INDEX

Page numbers in italics indicate figures.

Agassiz, Alex, 202
Agassiz, Louis, 202
Alabama (ship), 121, 139, 143–44, 146–47, 222
Alaska (ship), 189–90
alcohol/drinking, 64, 67–69, 94
Alexandrovich, Alexei, 76, 104, 176, 184–85, 195–96
alienation, 17, 30, 85, 91, 125
ambivalence, 11, 13, 23, 82, 91
Americanness, 8–9, 221
Amoy/Xiamen (廈門), xxi, 5, 7, 74, 88–89, 98–99, 108–9
Anglican church, 108
Anglo-American, 9, 95, 108, 114, 173, 183–85, 190; conflicts, 33, 121, 139–46; cooperation, 37, 42–43, 49, 125, 128; identity and, 219; rivalries, 133
Anglo-French, 53, 58, 126, 191
Anglo-Indian, 57, 65–66, 173
Anglo-Saxon(s), 3–4, 93, 103, 108, 147, 173, 218; heritage, 9, 84, 107, 115; whiteness of, 117
Antelope (steamer), 137

"Anui" (daughter of Augustine Heard Jr. and "Apook"), xvii, 79, 168, 179–80
Apook (protected woman of Augustine Heard Jr.), xvii, 79
architecture of merchant houses, 17, *59*, 59–60, 65–66, 82
Armstrong, James, 128
Arrow incident. *See* Second Opium War
art/curios, Chinese, 64–65, 191–93, 198, 215
assimilation/assimilative spaces, 56, 85, 97, 101, 107, 147, 173, 185, 221
Atlantic Monthly (periodical), 64
Augustine Heard & Co., xx, *162*, 215, 219–20; Baring Brothers & Co and, 155, 161; in Canton, 2–4, 7, 22, 31, 58, 67, 153–54; *China Punch* on, 119; Joseph Coolidge, 37, 40; failure of, 6, 19–20, 67, 81, 183–85; finances of, 66–67, 145, 148, 149, 178; First Opium War and, 23–24, 41–42, 45; founding of, 2, 7, 16–17, 113–14, 153, 172, 183, 197; in Hong Kong, 4–5, 7, 58, 59–71, *61*, *62*, 149–55, *162*, 162–63, 165; Jardine

INDEX

Augustine Heard & Co. (*continued*)
    Matheson & Co. and, 23–24, 49, 166;
    kinship networks and, 2, 166–68, *167*,
    168, 183; in Macao, 25, 60, *60*, 76, 181;
    opium trade by, 45–48; Portugal
    and, 165; Russell & Co. and, 153, 166,
    172–73, 187, 203; in Shanghai, *7*, 76,
    154, 161, 165; *Suwonada*, 137. *See also*
    bankruptcy of Augustine Heard & Co.
Aurora (schooner), 22
autobiographies/memoirs, 132–33, 272n2;
    of John Heard, 214–15, 217

Babcock, Henry, 171, 212
Back Bay, Boston, xxi, 204–6, *206*, *208*
Bacon, Francis McNeil, 210–11
Bacon & Co., 210
Bailey, David, 120
Baldwin, George W., 214
banking/banking systems, 178, 189
bankruptcy, 130–31, 199, 207, 210–11, 215
bankruptcy of Augustine Heard & Co.,
    xvii–xix, *7*, 161, 177, 181–82, 186–94,
    217–18; financial mismanagement
    leading to, 2, 66–67, 145, 148, 149, 178;
    satire about, 110–11
Baptists, 108
Bar Harbor, Maine, 204–5
Baring Brothers & Co, 155, 161, 190, 210
Bayard, Thomas, 212–13
Bayonne, France, 193, 196
Beacon Hill, Boston, xxi, 187, 199, 205–6,
    206, *208*
Beal, Helen, xx, 71, 74–75, 81, 91–95, 104,
    109–10, 116
Beart, Ed, 111
Bengal Club (Calcutta), 102, 150
Biarritz, France, 188, 190, 193, 195–96
bilingualism, 201
black market, 132, 191–92
Black people, 107, 205–6, 223, 248n114
Blaine, James, 194
Bombay, India, 40, 45–46, 153–55
Bonaparte, Lucien, 199
Bonham, George, 133
Boston, Massachusetts, 155, 184, 199–200,
    221–22; Albert Heard in, 194–96,
    205–7, 212–14; John Heard in, 188, 191,
    204–6, 215–16; Augustine Heard Sr.
    in, 197; racial barriers in, 205–6;
    Sturgis in, 209–10. *See also specific
    neighborhoods/areas*
Boston Brahmins, the, xx–xxi, 94, 172,
    187–88, 197–203, 216; in class
    hierarchy, 85; prejudice of, 205–6
Boston Common, xxi, 187, 203,
    205–6, *208*
Boston Concern (community), xxi,
    28–29, *29*, 153, 172–73, 196, 202–3
Bowring, John, 52
Bradford, Ruth, xviii, 74–75, 88, 91–92,
    94, 99–100, 108–9
Brandt, August von, 209
Bridgman, Elijah Coleman, 36
Britain/British people, 120–21, 164–65,
    195, 199; firms, 13, 17, 31, 39–40, 47, 134,
    166; identity, 13, 85; merchants, 13, 21,
    25, 27, 37, 42, 46–49, 51, 92, 174;
    Opium Wars and, 122–24; Qing and,
    12–14, 122–28; Second Opium War
    and, 52–53; U.S. Civil War and,
    140–46. *See also* Sino-British
    relations
Britain/British colonialism, 8–20, 55, 57,
    84, 118, 125–26, 151, 218–20, 222–23;
    assimilation/assimilative spaces in,
    56, 85, 97, 101, 107, 147, 173, 185, 221;
    calling culture, 86–87, 92, 95–96, 118;
    elites, 97, 101, 109, 118, 173–74. *See also*
    Hong Kong
Brother Jonathan (pseudonym for New
    Englanders), xxi, 40, 72
Burlingame, Anson, 133
Busch, Frederick, 127
Butterfield, Swire & Co, 72, 145, 190

Calcutta, India, xx, 45, 102, 150, 153–54
calling culture, British, 86–87, 92,
    95–96, 118
Campbell, Kenneth W., 179
Canada, 141–42
Canton/Guangzhou (廣州), xxi, 21,
    53–54, 92, 172, 189–90; American
    women, 10, 25; Augustine Heard & Co.

INDEX

in, 2–4, 7, 22, 31, 58, 67, 153–54; Joseph Coolidge in, 22–23, 28–38, 32, 124; George Dixwell, 124; gender in, 77–78; Albert Heard in, 78, 80, 125, 154, 171; John Heard in, 25, 31, 79, 153–54, 161, 169, 176; as "masculine," 56–57; Second Opium War in, 126. *See also* Thirteen Factories

Canton Press, 22, 32–33, 37, 49, 230n40
Canton Register, 31–34, 32, 37, 49
Canton System, 10, 24–28, 26, 51
capitalism, 10
caricatures, 100, 104, 106, 111, 112
Centennial Exposition (1876), 189–90
Century Association, 201, 207, 210–11, 215–16
Century Illustrated Monthly Magazine, 211
Cercal, Baron do, 173
Chapeaux, Albert Leon, 179
Chefoo/Yantai (煙台), 209
Cheney, Katharine, 181
Chih-Kiang/Tulip, USS, 137
China. *See specific topics*
China (Wilson), 211
China Mail, 95, 99–104, 106–7, 110, 115, 119, 120, 135, 142
"China Old and New" (talk), 211–12
China Punch (publication), 86–89, 100–104, 105, 110–11, 113–15, 119, 174
Chinese community, 16, 59, 73, 104, 126
Chinese merchants, 21, 31, 48, 124, 152
Chinese Repository, The (1841), 8
Chinnery, George, 65
Choate, Josiah, 211
Chongyao (Yang Haoguan 央浩官), 153
Christianity, 108–9
Civil War: Japanese, 138; Taiping, 19, 121, 131–32, 139, 146–47; U.S., 99, 122, 130–31, 133, 138–48, 222
class (social), xxii, 54–55, 68, 77, 84, 165; lower, 74, 80, 106, 166; mercantile, 1, 18–20, 115, 165, 166, 169, 261n35; middle, 68, 175; upper, 14, 18, 27, 85, 101, 109, 192
Cleveland, Grover, 201
coal mining, 190

colonialism/colonial, 173, 184, 211; culture, 55, 65, 85–86, 95–98, 110; domestic spaces/households under, 54–60, 65–74, 86–89; elites, 68, 98, 116, 119, 219; etiquette, 86–88, 100, 114, 116; hierarchies, 4, 11, 18, 65–66, 98, 166; in Hong Kong, 123–24, 145–46, 170, 218–23. *See also* Britain/British colonialism
communalism, 27, 54, 57, 71, 93
company/merchant houses, 54, 58–71
competency, 94, 150, 186–88, 196–209
compradors, Chinese, xxi, 54, 152, 169–70, 174–75, 184; in social hierarchies, 72–73
Concise Account of the United States of America (Bridgman), 36
Confederacy, U.S., 13, 99, 136–37, 142–44
Congalese people, 107, 248n114
Congar, Horace, 139, 141
Consoo House (gongsuo 公所), xxi
consuls: British, 52, 132; U.S., xix, 34, 53, 92, 120, 121, 125–26, 127, 139, 177, 216
consumerism, 192
"contact zones," 12, 150–51, 220, 222–23
Convention of Peking, 130
Coolidge, Algernon, 200
Coolidge, Ellen W. (née Randolph), xviii, 81, 94, 199–200
Coolidge, Jefferson, 189
Coolidge, Joseph, xviii–xx, 16–17, 153, 172–73, 197, 199, 202; Augustine Heard & Co. and, 37, 40; in Canton, 22–23, 28–38, 32, 124; First Opium War and, 48–51
"Coolie" trade, 189–90
cooperation, Anglo-American, 37, 42–43, 49, 125, 128
correspondence by letters, 15, 59, 122, 140–41, 148, 171–72, 181; addressing gender/women, 79–81; health in, 68–70; race in, 73
Cortes (steamer), 135
cotton, 179, 197, 234n108
Coxon, Atwell, 100
Coxon, Louisa, 100
Crowell, Ira, xviii, 92

Crowell, Ruth (née Bradford), xviii, 109
Cruz, Olímpio Augusto da, 72, 175
Cunningham, Jim, 172
curfew, 59
curios/art, Chinese, 64–65, 191–93, 198, 215
Curtis, Dan, 04
Cushing, Caleb, 34, 123

Dacotah (steamer), 141
Dai-Ching (steamer), 137
Davis, Bancroft, 120
Davis, Jefferson, 143
deaths, 25, 135, 200, 202; of Albert Heard, 214; of George Heard, 174, 186; of Mary Heard (née Livingston), 196; of Richard Howard Heard, 179; of Augustine Heard Sr., 187, 197
dehumanization, 75
Delano, "Dora," xix
Delano, Warren, 22
democratic republicanism, 123, 251n15
demurrage, xxii, 45–46, 234n108
Deng Tingzhen (鄧廷楨), 45
Dent, John, 174
Dent & Co., 13, 53, 132, 134
Department of State, U.S., 126, 145
Dexter, Gordon, 189
dinner parties/dining culture, 27, 46–47, 67–68, 89, 92–96, 102
diplomatic/consular postings, 126–27, 175–76, 182–83, 188, 210, 212–16, 220
diplomatic policies/diplomacy, 177, 188, 210; U.S., 18–19, 42, 53, 122–29, 133
divorce, 117, 188, 194–96
Dixter, William, 191
Dixwell, Charles, xix, 79, 180
Dixwell, George B., xix–xx, 16–27, 48–51, 64, 143, 153, 161, *162*, 180; in Macao, 23–24, 38–47
Dixwell, John James, xix, 40
domestic hierarchies, 61–62, 65–66, 71–75, 82
domesticity. *See* houses/homes in Hong Kong

East Asian theater, 143–44
Eastern Yacht Club, 203

East India Company, 13, 27, 57, 65–66
East India Squadron, U.S., 128, 134
Economist (publication), 142
elites/elite society, 213–14; American, 93–95, 101, 109, 131, 165, 171–73, 200, 221; Anglo-Americans, 183–84; British, 97, 101, 109, 118, 173–74; Canton system, 27; colonial, 68, 98, 116, 119, 219; Hong Kong, 18, 117, 163, 166, 172–75; kinship ties in, 28–29, 29, 85, 88, 153, 185; merchant, 27, 102, 127, 170, 183, 185, 187–88; New England, 84–85, 187–88, 192–93, 196–207, 215–16, 223; Shanghai, 209; white, 18, 63, 66, 218. *See also specific groups/clubs*
Elliot, Charles William, 21–22, 31, 33, 48, 50, 202
Emerson, Ralph Waldo, 84–85, 115, 119, 202
Empire (Hardt, Negri), 251n15
Empress of China (ship), 1
Endicott, William Crowninshield, 194, 201–2
England, 1, 120, 154–55, 161, 223
"entente cordiale," 120, 146–48
etiquette, 86–88, 100, 114, 116
Eurasians, 12, 179–82, 184
Europe, 154–55, 161, 182–83, 199–200, 212. *See also specific countries*
Everett, Percival Lowell, xix, 178, 189
E-wo Hong (Yihe Hang 怡和行), xx, 153
exoticism, 191–92
"expertise," trade, 129, 170, 182, 184, 212–16
extraimperial communities, 8, 11, 16

Fahkee (steamer), 137
Fah Kee Yacht Club, xxii, 103
failure of Augustine Heard & Co., 6, 19–20, 67, 81, 183–85
family ties. *See* kinship networks
Farley, Eunice, xvii, 81
Farley, Gustavus, xvii, 180
Farrington, DeWitt Clinton, 196
fashion/dress, 70–71, 106

INDEX

Fast Crab/Kuai xie (快蟹, opium smuggling vessel), xxii, 45
Fearon, Low & Co., 181–82, 211
feminine/femininity, 55–57, 77, 81
Figueiredo, Henrique Caetano Victor de, 72, 175, 189
Figueiredo, José Miguel Victor de, 72, 175
finances of Augustine Heard & Co., 66–67, 145, 148, 149, 178
Fire Dart (steamer), 130, 133, 135–36
firms. *See specific topics*
First Opium War, xxi, 4, 13, 22, 28, 30–31, 120–21, 153; Augustine Heard & Co. and, 23–24, 41–42, 45; rivalries and, 34–37, 40, 48–51; The Thirteen Factories impacted by, 24–28, 33–35
Flambeau (steamer), 137
Fong Ah-ming, 52
Forbes, Francis (Frank) Blackwell, xix, 75, 81, 110, 117, 198
Forbes, James Murray, xix, 47, 99, 143, 172, 202–3
Forbes, John Malcolm, 202
Forbes, John Murray, xix, 209
Forbes, Paul Siemen, xix, 30, 202
Forbes, Robert Bennet, xix, 65, 92–93, 153, 172–73, 199, 202, 209; First Opium War and, 38–40; Houqua and, 30–31
Forbes, Sarah Hathaway, 202
Forbes, Thomas T., 30
Forbes, William Howell, xix, 110, 174, 190, 195
foreign commerce, xxi, 42, 125, 130, 178, 182, 189
founding of Augustine Heard & Co., 2, 7, 16–17, 113–14, 153, 172, 183, 197
France, 35, 169, 187, 199; Bayonne, 193, 196; Biarritz, 188, 190, 193, 195–96; John Heard in, 150; Augustine Heard Jr. in, 207. *See also* Paris, France
Fraser, Farley & Co., 180–81
Fraser, Jack, 180–81
Freemasonry, 97, 103, 163
free trade, 146, 221
Fuzhou (福州, port city), xxii, 4, 73, 148, 154, 217–18

Gemmel & Co., 31
gender, 10–11, 90–91, 117, 185, 187–88, 191–92, 215; in Amoy, 88–89; in domestic spaces, 55–57, 77–80, 86–87; femininity and, 55–57, 77, 81; masculinity and, 55–57, 80–83, 223
General Chamber of Commerce, Hong Kong, 103, 163, 174
Geneva, Switzerland, 154–55
Germany, 150, 155
Gibb, Hugh B., 174
Gibb, Livingston &Co., 166, *167*, 174
Gilder, Richard Watson, 211
Gleason, William Henry, 171
global recession, 178
Godkin, Edwin Lawrence, 211
Godown (warehouses), xxii
Gong/Yixin (奕欣, prince), 134–35
gossip, 110–11, *112*, 113–17
government, U.S., 42, 121–23, 126, 137–38, 175, 177
Gray, Russell, 211
Great Fire, Boston, 171, 206
Green, Martha, 96
Griswold, John, 189
guilt, 48, 189

haijin/maritime ban (海禁), 151
Hall, George, 91–92
Hankow (Hankou 漢口), xxii, 5, *7*, 130–31, 134–35, 176
Harris, Townsend, 177
Hartford (publication), 141
Hartt, John, 79
Harvey, Frederick, 132
Havana, Cuba, 153
health, 63, 68–70, 209; of Albert Heard, 214; of George Heard, 186; of Mary Heard (née Livingston), 81, 196
Heard, Albert Farley, xvii–xviii, 1, *5*, *158*, *162*, 179, 182–83, 187, 203, 216; bankruptcy of, 186, 191, 207; in Boston, 194–96, 205–7, 212–14; in Canton, 78, 80, 125, 154, 171; on diplomatic relationships, 170; divorce of, 117, 194–96; financial mismanagement by, 2, 70, 95, 149;

INDEX

Heard, Albert Farley (*continued*)
  Mary Heard, (née Livingston) and, 90, 117; Augustine Heard Jr. and, 207, 212; in Hong Kong, 62–65, 67–69, 73, 90–91, 141, 161, 215; leaving China, 188–90, 209; in Paris, 201; political pursuits of, 116, 194, 210–14; private assets/estate of, 192–93, 215; reputation of, 207, 214; Russia and, 176–77, 194–96, 215; in Shanghai, 130, 176; in Skull & Bones society, 171
Heard, Alice (née Leeds), xvii, 81, 187, 191–92, 198; at Hotel Oxford, 204–5
Heard, Augustine, Jr., xvii, 4, 153, 157, 182, 187–88, 193–94; autobiographical memoir of, 214–15; in the Century Association, 201, 207; "China Old and New" talk by, 211–12; in Hong Kong, 17, 54, 58, 60, 64, 68, 189–90; in Korea, 207–12; leaving China, 60–61; old China trade and, 169
Heard, Augustine, Sr., xvii–xix, 2, 66–67, 70, 127, 186; death o f, 187, 197; on the opium trade, 45–46; reputation of, 113–14, 117, 153, 172, 197
Heard, Daniel, 25
Heard, Elizabeth Ann (née Farley), xvii, 140–41, 171
Heard, Elsie, 207, 214
Heard, George Farley, xviii, 6, 124, 154, 159, 162, 195, 204, 242n157; alcohol consumed by, 68–69; death of, 174, 186; on finances of Augustine Heard & Co., 145, 149; on Hong Kong, 62–65, 73, 78, 153, 174, 186; in Hong Kong Club, 101–2; in Hong Kong Yacht Club, 174; satire/jokes by, 110–11; Ward and, 76, 127, 169–70, 177, 184–85
Heard, George Washington, xvii–xviii, 135–36, 138, 170
Heard, Helen Maxima, 208–9
Heard, Jane (née deConinck), xviii, 91, 194
Heard, John, xviii, 3, 37, 156, 187–88, 195, 210–11; autobiographical memoir of, 214–15, 217; in Boston, 188, 191, 204–6, 215–16; in Caton, 25, 31, 79, 153–54, 161, 169, 176; financial mismanagement and, 66–67, 129; *Fire Dart* belonging to, 130; on First Opium War, 41; in Hankou, 134; in Hong Kong, 64–65, 150, 169, 189–90, 207, 217, 219; at Hotel Oxford, 204–5; leaving China, 79, 154, 183; old China trade and, 169; philanthropy of, 171–72; private assets of, 197–99, 215; racialization by, 75; resignation from private clubs of, 203–4; on Second Opium War, 52–53
Heard, Mary (née Livingston), xviii, 62–63, 69–70, 80–81, 188, 190–91; divorce of, 117, 194–96; Albert Heard and, 90–91, 117
Heard, Richard Howard, xviii, 79, 178–80
"Heard & Co.," 6, 114, 181, 188–89
Helland, George, 173
hierarchies, 12, 80, 85, 117–19, 152, 219; colonial, 4, 11, 18, 65–66, 98, 166; domestic, 61–62, 65–66, 71–75, 82; racial, 9, 13–14, 74, 82, 107–8, 218
Hiogo (Hyōgo), Japan, 154
"Hoh-yan-ki" (Cantonese man), 189–90
Holmes, Oliver Wendell, Jr., 202
Holmes, Oliver Wendell, Sr., 85, 202
homophily, 164–65, 173
Hong Kong, xvii–xviii, 130, 216; American women/wives in, 57, 71, 81, 86–94, 104; Augustine Heard & Co. in, 4–5, 7, 58, 59–71, 61, 62, 149–55, 162, 162–63, 165; calling culture in, 86–87, 91–92, 95–96, 118; Chinese community in, 16, 59, 73, 104, 126; colonialism in, 123–24, 145–46, 170, 218–23; as a "contact zone," 12, 150–51, 220, 222–23; demographics, 8, 56–57, 81–82, 90, 152, 217–23, 225n7; dinner parties/dining culture in, 27, 46–47, 67–68, 89, 92–96, 102; elites, 18, 117, 163, 166, 172–75; foreign community in, 217–18; free trade in, 221; Albert Heard in, 62–65, 67–69, 73, 90–91, 141, 161, 215; George Heard in, 62–65, 73, 78, 153, 174, 186; John Heard in,

INDEX

64–65, 150, 169, 189–90, 207, 217, 219; Augustine Heard Jr. in, 17, 54, 58, 60, 64, 68, 189–90; as an "in-between place," 183, 220; networks in, 169–78; satire/media in, 110–11, *112*, 113–19; Taipingshan, xxiii, 58, 60, 98. *See also* houses/homes, merchant; public spaces, Hong Kong

Hong Kong Bay, 38–39, 51

Hong Kong Club, 101–3, 163, 201, 204

Hong Kong Sailor's Home, 166, 174, 204

Hong Kong Yacht Club, 97, 111, *112*, 163, 166, 174

Hooper, Lucy, 71, 92

horses/horse riding, 63–64, 72, 99–101, *100*, 103–5, 118

hosting culture, 27, 46–47, 67–68, 89, 92–96, 102

Hotel Oxford (Boston), 204–5, *205*, 207

Houqua (Wu Bingjian, 伍秉鑑), xx, 21, 30–31, 37, 46, 152–53

houses/homes, merchant, 54–83, *59*, *60*, *61*, *62*; American households in, 18, 55–56, 95–96; architecture of, 17, *59*, 59–60, 65–66, 82; colonial, 54–60, 65–74, 86–89; hierarchies in, 61–62, 65–66, 71–75, 82; as private spaces, 55–56, 63, 67, 71–83, 87, 221; as public spaces, 86–97

Howes, Benjamin P., 92

Howquah (steamer), 137

Humane Society, Massachusetts, 203

Hunter, William C., 79

Hu Ts'ai-shun, 79, 180

identity/identities, 129, 180, 217; American, 55, 147–48, 219; British, 13, 85; colonialism and, 150; Hong Kong, 150; imperial context and, 219–21, 258n134; national, 9, 14, 17, 171–72, 192, 216, 218; political, 34, 115, 147; racial, 13–14, 171–72, 178

illegitimate children, 178–82, 184; "Anui" as, xvii, 79, 168, 179–80

illiteracy, 211

Illustrated London News, 104, *106*

imperialism, 12–13, 55, 98, 123, 151; British, 84, 120–21, 219–20; identities and, 219–21, 258n134; transimperialism as, 11, 23–24, 123, 219–20; US, 192, 209

"in-between place," Hong Kong as, 183, 220

indemnification, 31–32, *32*, 124, 143–44

India, 55–56, 58–60, 63–64, 68, 144; Bombay, 40, 45–46, 153–55; Calcutta, xx, 45, 102, 150, 153–54

infantilization, 75, 96

interracial relationships, 79, 82, 170, 175, 178–80

interwar period (1842–56), 24

intraregional context, 16, 18–20, 121, 130, 146–48

Ipswich Cotton Mill, 197

Ipswich Public Library, 171, 197

Italy, 150, 155, 199

Japan, 65, 76, 151, 163, 177, 189, 192, 198; Augustine Heard & Co. in, 154; Civil War, 138; Yokohama, 5, *7*, 154, 180–81

Jardine, David, 31, 92–93

Jardine, William, 27

Jardine Matheson & Co., 13, 31, 39–40, 53, 153, *167*, 170, 190, 234n108; Augustine Heard & Co. and, 23–24, 49, 166; Richard Howard Heard at, 178–79; opium trade and, 45–48

Jefferson, Thomas, xviii, 28

Jejeebbhoy, Jamsetji, 46, 153

John Bull (caricatured personification of England), xxii

Johnson, George A., 171

junk (Chinese sailing vessel), xxii, 45, 52

Karberg, Peter, 173

Keechong Club, 102, 202, 204, 216

Keenan, James, 53, 126–28

Kemp, James, 102

Kennedy, Thomas, 52

Keswick, William, 174, 190

Khushalchand, Kessresung, 153

Kiangse (steamer), 135

Kiang-Soo/Fuchsia, USS, 137

INDEX

kinship networks, 19, 25, 92, 101, 116, 150, 152, 169, 171–72; Augustine Heard & Co. and, 2, 166–68, *167*, *168*, 183; Boston Concern, 28–29, *29*; elites in, 28–29, *29*, 85, 88, 153, 185; English, 167; Mok Sze Yeung, 174–75; nationality and, 164
Kinsman, Nathaniel, xx, 40
Kinsman, Rebecca (née Chase), xx, 94
Kip, Leonard W., 108–9
Kiukiang/Jiujiang (九江), xxii, 5, 133, 148, 154
Knickerbocker Club (New York), xxii, 102, 200–201
Korea, 188, 211; Augustine Heard Jr. in, 207–12; Seoul, 208–10, 271n109

labor, Chinese, 16, 27, 71, 189–90
Lam Kew-fong, 79
Lapraik, Douglas, 64
lascar (sailors or militiamen), xxii, 104, 106
Legge, James, 124
leisure, 101, 187
Lessovski, Stepan, 196
Li Hongzhang (李鴻章), 133
Lindsay, Hugh Hamilton, 37
Lindsay & Co., 134
Linstead, Theophilus G., 190
Lintin/Nei lingding (內伶仃), xxii, 22, 25, 39, 43–45
Lin Zexu (林則徐), 21, 35–36, 39, 45, 122
London, England, 154–55, 161
Longfellow, Henry Wadsworth, 202
looting/pillaging, 191–92
lorcha (sailing vessel), xxii
Loring, William J., 68
Low, A. A., 202
Low, Edward, 182, 210–11
Low, Harriet, 25, 77–78
Low, William, 41
Lowell, James Russell, 85
Lowell Gun Company, 194–96
lower-class, 74, 80, *106*, 166

Macao/Macanese, xviii, xx, 12, 153–54, 173, 175–76, 185, 223; Augustine Heard & Co. in, 25, 60, *60*, 76, 181; George B. Dixwell in, 23–24, 38–47; as "feminine," 56–57; First Opium War and, 38–39; "protected women" in, 79; shroffs, 152
macrohistory, 16, 222
Magniac Smith, 27
Maine, 204–5
Manila, 72, 189
"Manila men" (foreign watchmen), 58–59, 104, 106
Marcy, William L., 126
Marshall, Humphrey, 133
masculine/masculinity, 55–57, 80–83, 223
Massachusetts, 183, 220; Ipswich, xvii–xviii, 140–41, 170–71, 190–93, 197, 207, 215. *See also* Boston, Massachusetts
Massachusetts State House, xxi, 187, *198*
Matheson, Alexander, 39, 46–47, 92
McLane, Robert, 133
media, 110–11, *112*, 113–17. *See also specific publications*
memory/memories, 72n2, 113, 211
memsahib (white or upper-class women), xxii, 77
mercantile class, 1, 18–20, 115, *165*, 166, 169, 261n35. *See also specific topics*
Mercantile Club, 74, 149
merchants. *See specific topics*
microhistory, 9–10, 20, 24, 54, 219–20
middle-class, 68, 175
missionaries, 10, 27, 36, 65, 108–9, 124, 126, 209, 211
Mok Sze Yeung (Mo Shiyang 莫仕揚), xix, 72, 174–75
Mok Tso Chun (Mo Zaoquan 莫藻泉), xix, 72
Moller, Alethea, 116
Morrison, Robert, 27, 36
Morss, William Howard, 22
Mouqua (Lu Wenjin, 盧文錦), 21
Murray, Hugh, 36
Murray, James Mason, 140
Murray Barracks, Hong Kong, 58, 60–61

INDEX

Nanjing, 130–34
Nanyang/south sea (南洋) trade, 151–52
national identity, 9, 14, 17, 192, 216, 218
nationality, 164, *164*, 169
nepotism, 28–29
"neutrality," U.S., 22, 120–21, 123, 126, 129, 133, 140, 146, 148; First Opium War and, 34–35, 38, 50–51
New England elites, 84–85, 187–88, 192–93, 196–207, 215–16, 223
New York, 136, 155, 188–89, 193–94, 200–201; Augustine Heard Jr. in, 207
New York Times, 143
Ng Ahip (Wu Ye 吳葉), 72
nonwhite people/communities, 72, 97–98, *106*, 107–8, 173
North China Herald (publication), 131
Norwood, Dael, 42
Nye, Gideon, Jr., 174, 202–3

O'Brien, Richard, 186
occupations/titles, *165*, 165–66, 261n35. *See also specific occupations*
"Officials" (occupational title), *165*, 165–66, *167*, 261n35
old China trade, 1–2, 10, 57, 66, 93, 166, 169, 183, 220; John Heard in, 161; Thirteen Factories in, 77
Olyphant & Company, 22, 41
opium trade, xxii, 17, 21, *44*, 46, 48–51, 127, 130, 153, 219, 234n108; smuggling and, 40–45, 47, 124, 128, 146–47
Opium Wars, 17–18, 93, 219; Second (Arrow War), 52–53, 74–75, 114–15, 121–22, 125–28, 140, 146; Sino-British relations and, 24–25, 38–48, 52–53, 122–29. *See also* First Opium War
Ordinance No. 2, Hong Kong, 59
Orne, Charles, 172
"Other" (occupational title), *165*, 165–66, 261n35
"other/otherness" (social status), 16, 96, 98, 110, 118, 272n3

Panic of 1873, 145, 189
parasitic relationships, 13, 22–23, 34, 49

Paris, France, 154–55, 161, 190, 195–96, 201; Ellen Coolidge on, 199–200
Parker, Charles Edward, 189
Parker, Francis ("Frank"), 61–62, 71, 189
Parker, Peter, 78, 126
Parkes, Harry, 52
Pauncefote, Julian, 195
Peabody, Samuel Endicott, 214
Pearl River Delta, xxii, 41, *43*, 43–45, 47, 50, 60
Peiho/White River/Hai River, xxii, 127, 129
Pembroke (steamer), 135
Pereira, Inácio Pires, Jr., 72, 175
performativity, 17, 34, 55, 86–88, 117–19, 146
Perkins, Thomas, 28
Perkins and Co, 30
philanthropy, 170–72, 174
Philippines, 72, 151, 154, 189
Pierce, Franklin, 133
pirates/piracy, 3, 52, 92, 144–45
Plover (ship), 127–28
Pok Fu Lam, Hong Kong, 63–64
political identity, 34, 115, 147
port cities, Chinese, 19, 152
Portugal/Portuguese, 38, 165, 169, 175
post–Civil War, 138, 187, 256n112
P&O steamers, 155
postimperialism/postimperial project, 251n15
private assets/estate, 190–95, 197–203, 215
private clubs, 101–3, 167, 200–204, 207. *See also specific clubs*
private spaces, 54–56, 63, 67, 71–83, 87, 221
prostitutes, 80, 98
protected women, 178, 182, 185; Apook as, xvii, 79, 167
Protestantism, 9, 85, 94, 100
public spaces, Hong Kong, 65, *90*, 98–104, *105*, 106–10, *110*, 118–19, 221; homes as, 17–18, 75–77, 86–97
punkah (cloth fan), xxiii, 67, 70, 72
Purcell, Mary, 178–79
Purcell Heard, Augustine John "Johnny," 179

INDEX

Qin Chai/"Imperial Envoy" (欽差), xxiii
Qing Empire, 1, 53, 129, 131–34, 137, 146–48, 217, 219–20; British colonialism and, 12–14, 122–28; First Opium War and, 34–40; gender and, 77–78; haijin/maritime ban (海禁), 151
Qishan (琦善), 35
Quincy, Josiah, 211

race/racism, 8, 104, 106, 137, 175, 205, 209; class and, 85–86, 97–98, 107, 119; in domestic spaces, 54–55, 57–59, 61–66, 71–80, 95–96; hierarchies, 9, 13–14, 74, 107–8, 218; identities and, 13–14, 171–72, 178; interracial relationships and, 79, 82, 170, 175, 178–80
racialization, 3–4, 74–75, 80, 104
Radford, William, 141
railroads, transcontinental, 209
Randolph, Ellen Wayles, 28
Rawson (merchant), 195, 268n48
Ray, W. W., 190
Reed, William Bradford, 127, 129–30
religion, 110, 117–18; Anglican church, 108; Baptists, 108; Christianity, 108–9; missionaries and, 10, 27, 36, 65, 108–9, 124, 126, 209, 211; Protestantism, 9, 85, 94, 100
Reminiscences (Forbes, Robert Bennet), 30–31, 172–73
remittances, 170
reputation(s), 38, 50, 98, 100–101, 107, 110, 190; of Augustine Heard & Co., 67; of Albert Heard, 207, 214; of Augustine Heard Sr., 113–14, 117, 153, 172, 197
respectability, 14, 86, 89, 97
retrenchment, 67, 130–31, 203, 215
Revolutionary War, U.S., 114
rituals, 18, 66–67, 86–88, 99, 103, 107–8
rivalries, 11, 13, 17, 35, 85, 93, 120–21, 133; firm, 166, 172–73; First Opium War and, 34–37, 40, 48–51; opium trade, 47; transimperial, 23–24
Roberts, Joseph, 37
Rockhill, William, 210
Rowett, Richard, 111
Russell, William, 191

Russell & Co., xviii–xx, 28–30, 41–42, 137–39, 145, *167*, 198, 211, 223; Augustine Heard & Co. and, 153, 166, 172–73, 187, 203; Keechong Club and, 102, 202
Russia, 153, 188; Albert Heard and, 176–77, 194–96, 215
Russian Church and Russian Dissent, The (Heard, Albert), 212

Saginaw, USS, 134, 141
sahib ("owner" in Arabic), xxiii, 62, 77
Sailor's Snug Harbor, 203–2004
"Sai Louey" (John Heard's protected woman), xvii, 79, 167
Saltonstall, Leverett, II, 211–12
San Francisco, California, 154, 181
San Jacinto, USS, 140
Sassoon, Solomon David, 174
satire, 86–89, *112*, 116–18; in *China Punch*, 86–89, 100–104, *105*, 110–11, 113–15, 119, 174
Saturday Club (Boston), 201–2
Scrambling Dragon/Pa long (爬龍). *See* Fast Crab (opium smuggling vessel)
Seabra, Francisco António de, 72, 175
Second Opium War (or "*Arrow* War"), 5, 52–54, 60, 74–75, 114–15, 121, 125–28, 140, 146
segregation, 12, 63–64, 96
semicolonial spaces, 12, 20, 63, 223
Seoul, Korea, 208–10, 271n109
servants, 32, 32–33, 56, 62–66, 71–75, 81–83, 89, 95–96
Seward, George, 127
Seward, William, 133, 139, 143, 177
Shamian (沙面), 54
Shanghai, China, 1, *44*, 132, 143, 155, 177–79, 189–90, 198; Augustine Heard & Co. in, *7*, 76, 154, 161, 165; Helen Beal in, 74–75, 109; British colonizers in, 55; domestic spaces in, *59*, 59–60, 63; Albert Heard in, 130, 176; Helen Heard in, 209
Shanghai Steam Navigation Company, 135
Shantung (steamer), 138

INDEX

Shaw, Robert Gould, 28
shroff (Western firm employees), xxiii, 46, 133, 148, 152
Silva, U.S. da, 173
Sino-American relations, 9–10, 18–20, 24, 30, 37, 120–21, 210, 220; old China trade and, 1–2; Qing and, 35; U.S. Civil War and, 139–48; U.S. diplomacy and, 122–29; Yangzhi and, 129–39
Sino-British relations, 37, 120–21; conflict in, 3, 24, 34, 48, 50, 52–53, 146; Opium Wars and, 24–25, 38–48, 52–53, 122–29; U.S. Civil War and, 139–48; Yangzi and, 129–39
Sino-foreign relations/trade, 9, 17–18, 51, 53–54, 74–75, 122–22, 128, 218
Skull & Bones Society, Yale, 171, 213
Slidell, John, 140
smuggling, opium, 43–45, 47, 124, 128, 146–47
social capital, 77, 82, 92, 97, 101, 106–7, 118, 177, 214
social networks/networking, 25, 75–77, 106–7, 116, 150, 164, 184; calling culture and, 87–88
Somerset Club, Boston, 101–2, 200–201, 203–5, 270n97
Sonnō Jōi movement, 138
sovereignty, Chinese, 9, 17, 42
Spanish dollars, 230n40
Spectator (publication), 142
sporting culture, 101–3
steamers/steamships, 135–39, *136*, *137*. See also *specific ships*
stereotypes, 77, 96, 104
St. Louis Mercantile Association, 211
St. Petersburg, Russia, 153, 195–96
Stribling, Cornelius, 76, 134, 141
Sturgis, Russell, xx, 150, 155, 161, 209–10
Suez canal, 154–55
supercargo (cargo ship employee), xxiii, 25, 47, 197
Susquehanna (steamer), 133
Suwonada (steamer), 137–38
Swett, Susan, 192–93, 199–200

Swett, William, 199–200
Swire, John Samuel, 139
Switzerland, 154–55, 199
symbiotic relationships, 13, 23, 175

Taiping Civil War, 19, 121, 131–32, 139, 146–47
Taipingshan (Hong Kong neighborhood), xxiii, 58, 60, 98
Ta-Kiang (steamer), 137
Taku Forts/Dagu Forts, xxiii
Tam Achoy (Tan Yacai 譚亞才), 58
Tattnall, Josiah, 75–76, 128–29, 142
technology, 146; steamship, 87, 135; telegraphy as, 140, 149, 155, 186; transcontinental railroads as, 209
telegraphy, 140, 149, 155, 186
temporality/impermanence of merchant life, 57, 60–66, 69–71, 154
Thirteen Factories, The (shi san hang/十三行), Canton, xxiii, 1, 26, 57, 92, 126, 153–54, 183; Joseph Coolidge and, 31; First Opium War impacting, 24–28, 33–35; foreign women barred from, 77–78; razing of, 17, 53–54
Thwing & Perkins, 153
Tientsin/Tianjin (天津), xxiii, 5, 154
Tonnochy, Malcolm Straun, 173
trade/traders. See *specific topics*
transcontinental railroads, 209
transience, 57, 65, 71, 82, 117, 175
transimperialism, 11, 23–24, 123, 219–20
translations, Chinese, 252n5
transnational/global networks, 150–55, 155–60, 161–69, *162*, *163*, *164*, *165*, *167*, *168*, 170, 184–85. See also kinship networks
transnational politics, 121, 140, 143, 148
transshipping, 39–40, 48
Treaties of Tianjin, 121, 127
Treaty of Nanking, 42
Treaty of Tientsin (1858), xxiii, 129–31, 154, 177
Treaty of Wanghia, 34, 42, 123, 129–30
Treaty of Washington, 120–21, 146

INDEX

treaty ports, 2–3, 151, 163, 166, 169, 190, 218; Amoy as, xxi, 5, *7*, 74, 88–89, 98–99, 108–9; Anglo-American conflicts impacting, 121; domestic spaces in, 56; Fuzhou as, xxii, 4, 73, 148, 154, 217–18; Hankow, xxii, 5, *7*, 130–31, 134–35, 176; Japanese, 177; in transnational networks, 130
Tremont Row, Boston, 191–92, 197, *198*, 205
Trent affair, 139–42, 144–45, 147
Tsarskoye Selo, xxiii, 196
Tuckerman, Gustavus, xx, 61–62, 65

"Uncles of England, The" (Wills), 113
Union army, U.S., 136–38, 140–41, 143
Union Club (New York), 200–201
Unitarianism, 109
United States (U.S.), 1, 170, 180–81, 190, 199; American identity, 55, 147–48, 219; Americanness, 8–9, 221; Civil War, 99, 122, 130–31, 133, 138–48, 222; class system in, 84–85; Confederacy, 13, 99, 136–37, 142–44; consuls, xix, 34, 53, 92, 120, 121, 125–26, 127, 139, 177, 216; Department of State, 126, 145; diplomacy, 18–19, 42, 53, 122–29, 133; as distinct from Britain/British people, 27, 34–42, 48–51, 84–86, 117–19; East India Squadron, 128, 134; elites, 93–95, 101, 109, 131, 165, 171–73, 200, 221; government, 42, 121–23, 126, 137–38, 175, 177; independence, 84–85; national identity of, 192; Qing and, 122–25; Union army, 136–38, 140–41, 143; War Department, 210, 213–14. *See also* Anglo-Americans; Sino-American relations; women/wives, American; *specific states*
United States merchants, 57, 84–86, 122–29, 170, 172, 175, 186, 261n35; American households in Hong Kong of, 18, 55–56, 95–96; First Opium War and, 34–42; satire about, 110–11, *112*, 113–17; Yangzi trade/access by, 134–35. *See also* "neutrality," U.S.
upper class, 14, 18, 27, 85, 101, 109, 192
U.S. *See* United States

Venus (steamer), 138
Victoria Regatta, 103, 174
Vietnam, 154
Virginia, 190, 200

Wade, Thomas Francis, 190
Waldron, Thomas, 125, 177
Ward, John, 127, 154, 169–70, 177, 184–85, 194–95; in Hong Kong, 75–76; Qing authorities and, 137
Warden, Elizabeth (née Beal), xx, 93–94
Warden, Henry H., xx, 177, 202
War Department, U.S., 210, 213–14
War of Independence, U.S., 1
Washington, DC, 188, 212–14
Wednesday Evening Club, 203–4
Wei Yuan (魏源), 36, 124
Weller, George, 60
Wetmore & Company, 40
Whampoa Island/Huangpu (黃埔), xxiii, 22, 25–26, 39–40, 43–44, 48
white elites, 18, 63, 66, 218
whiteness, 11, 13–14, 93, 97–98, 117
white people, 14, 56, 84, 141, 173, 179–80, 184
white women, 55, 77–78, 80, 87, 90, *90*
Whitney, Asa, 209
Whitney, William Collins, 212
Whittall, James, 190
Wilcocks, Benjamin, 79
Williams, C. D., xix, 130
Wills, William Henry, 113
Wilson, James Harrison, 211
women/wives, 74, *105*, 117; horses/riding, 99–100, *100*; respectability and, 88–89; white, 55, 77–78, 80, 87, 90, *90*. *See also* protected women
women/wives, American, 82; in Canton, 10, 25; in Hong Kong, 57, 71, 81, 86–94, 104
Wood, William, 128

Xia'erguanzhen (遐邇貫珍) (serial), 124–25
Xu Jiyu (徐繼畬), 36

INDEX

Yang Run 楊閏, 58
Yangzi river trade/access, 5–6, 122, 129–39, 147, 154, 181; Russell & Co., 145, 203, 211
Yeh Mingchen (Ye Mingchen 葉名琛), 52
Yilibu (伊里布), 124
Ying huanzhi lüe 瀛環志略 (Xu), 36

Yokohama, Japan, 5, 7, 154, 180–81
Yuanmingyuan (圓明園), 191–92
Yung Wing, 132–33

Zelenkoff, Eugene de, 195
Zeng Guofan (曾國藩), 133
Zimmern, Adolf, 173

GPSR Authorized Representative: Easy Access System Europe, Mustamäe tee
50, 10621 Tallinn, Estonia, gpsr.requests@easproject.com